CHRONIC
FATIGUE
SYNDROME

ALSO BY JESSE A. STOFF, CHARLES PELLEGRINO

Darwin's Universe (1st and 2nd editions) (Pellegrino, Stoff)
Friendly Fire (in preparation) (Stoff, Rossman)
Time Gate (Pellegrino)
Chariots for Apollo (Pellegrino, Stoff)
Her Name, Titanic (Pellegrino)
Unearthing Atlantis (Pellegrino)
Fatal Frontier (Pellegrino, Powell, Asimov)
Flying to Valhalla (Pellegrino; fiction)

CHRONIC FATIGUE SYNDROME

REVISED EDITION

Jesse A. Stoff, M.D.

Charles R. Pellegrino, Ph.D.

HarperPerennial

A Division of HarperCollins*Publishers*

HarperCollins books may be purchased for educational, business, or sales promotional use. For information, please call or write: Special Markets Department, HarperCollins Publishers, Inc., 10 East 53rd Street, New York, NY 10022. Telephone: (212) 207-7528; Fax: (212) 207-7222.

First HarperPerennial Edition published 1990
Second HarperPerennial Edition published 1992

Designed by Irv Perkins Associates

Library of Congress Cataloging-in-Publication Data

Stoff, Jesse A.
Chronic fatigue syndrome / Jesse A. Stoff, Charles R. Pellegrino.
—Rev. ed., 2nd HarperPerennial ed.
    p.   cm.
  Includes bibliographical references (p.   ) and index.
  ISBN 0-06-092260-5 (pbk.)
  1. Chronic fatigue syndrome.   I. Pellegrino, Charles R.
II. Title.
RB150.F37S76   1990b
616.9'25—dc20   91-50504

98 99 RRD 20 19 18 17

For Colleen, Laurel (a.k.a. Snookerpuss),
and Gloria (a.k.a. Merove)

CONTENTS

FOREWORD TO
THE REVISED EDITION

We live in an age of revelation where personal insights and new levels of self-awareness are becoming commonplace, accepted and encouraged. As human beings, we travel our own path of personal growth and evolution. Over time our physical body changes and so too does our perspective on ourselves and the world around us. If these changes keep pace with each other, then one will grow old graciously and with wisdom, but if the processes are not in synch, then a state of imbalance (disease) occurs.

For many, the awakening of one's own consciousness in the absence of a spiritual framework to hold and understand it, allows new awarenesses to unfold in places where they do not belong, which are then interpreted as discomforts. If this awakening of consciousness is perceived only through a materialistic understanding of man, one might conclude, as Norman Cousins did, that we have become "a nation of hypochondriacs." On the other hand, when the unexpected appearance of consciousness and consequent perception of a physical symptom/chronic disease is viewed from a spiritual perspective, it provides an opportunity for personal growth and development, a realigning of one's own personal process of evolution.

The mind/body continuum cannot be arbitrarily separated and studied. Much is known about the physical manifestations of disease. More is becoming known about the nature of the mind and its effects upon the body. In this book, we will endeavor to describe a framework for understanding both, and how to foster their realignment in the context of helping people with chronic fatigue syndrome find their own creative path in life, and thus to heal.

"Chronic fatigue syndrome" is an umbrella description of a

collection of rather dramatic, but largely subjective, symptoms. The underlying cause or specific diagnosis must be sought through careful, thorough investigation.

In our experience, it occurs in people who suffer from overwhelming levels of stress over a prolonged period of time. Simply speaking, stress occurs when the body expends energy faster than it can be regenerated, and stress can occur for any one of a thousand different reasons. On a cellular level, it doesn't matter what the stressor is. The result is that there is a net deficiency of "energy" and physiological dysfunction soon follows. There is a progressive weakening of the immune system and with the weakened immune system comes the opportunity for a chronic viral infection to become established or to reactivate from a state of latency.

Thus, to work with someone with chronic fatigue syndrome is to work with a being in need, a being in crisis. The crisis can extend over many levels: physical, emotional, cognitive, and higher. To truly help someone onto a healing path requires a comprehensive, integrated, multidimensional team-treatment strategy that can hold all of the nuances of these imbalances. Furthermore, the physician must help the patient to create the framework of understanding for himself so that his full individual potential can blossom and manifest itself in the principles of love and freedom.

JESSE A. STOFF, CHARLES PELLEGRINO
Great Barrington, MA

PREFACE

"A rose by any other name . . ."

Relatively recently in the annals of modern medicine the mischief of a virus or viruses has been recognized at work in a syndrome marked by debilitating fatigue, among other symptoms. When this viral "flower" blooms, it creates a thorny health-care problem. The syndrome goes by many names—chronic fatigue syndrome, chronic mononucleosis, neuromyasthenia, the "yuppie plague," "Raggedy Ann" syndrome, HBLV disease—but is most commonly referred to as chronic Epstein-Barr virus (CEBV) disease, for the virus first linked to this complex multisystem dysfunction. As a "newcomer" to the medical scene, it is still grossly underdiagnosed, even by good, caring physicians.

While there may be several strains, or related herpes class or B-cell viruses that can trigger this syndrome, the mechanism and progress of the infection are quite clear and are typified by the workings of the Epstein-Barr virus, whose course we follow throughout this book. With the tools outlined here, you will be able to change the course of the disease if you have it or help protect yourself and your loved ones from getting it.

ACKNOWLEDGMENTS

The poet Carl Sandburg once said, "nothing happens unless first a dream." Therefore, we would first like to thank Vinnie Viola and Larry Clarke for sharing in the dream of a comprehensive holistic health-care facility where the entirety of the treatments described within this book can fully manifest to offer hope and care to those who suffer or desire a higher quality of life.

Ideas and books do not simply materialize out of thin air. In the case of this book, we were fortunate to have a lot of love and support guiding us until all was right. We would like to thank the following people for their help, comments, and support in our literary endeavor: Bears Kaufman, Donna Astion, Amanda New-man, Victoria Pryor, Sarah Bingham, Neil Orenstein, Jeff Ross-man, Diane Rossman, Jim L., Katherine Soskin, Elyse Goodwin, and the nurses of the North Troy Trauma Center of Leonard Hospital. For his untiring research assistance, we would like to thank Ira Rogoff, R.N. Furthermore, we would like to thank the following people whose help we very much appreciated: Gloria Tam, THE Don Peterson, Steve Schoep, Glen Marcus, Ed Bishop, Isaac Asimov (the natural resource), Walter Lord, Robert Ballard, Barbara and Dennis Harris, Mrs. Dobie, Agnes Saunders, Ed McGunnigle, Joshua Stoff, Iris Regn (who had her own subtle impact on this book), and Jandis of Oceanside.

As a very special note of love and thanks, we wish to thank Sheldon and Lorraine Stoff and John and Jane Pellegrino, for with-out their love and support, and disbelief in test scores, none of this would have been possible.

ACKNOWLEDGMENTS

*I never had friends again like I had when
I was twelve years old. Jesus. Who does?*

—STEPHEN KING,
Stand By Me

1

IN THE BEGINNING

Poems are made by fools like me,
but only God can make a tree.

—Joyce Kilmer

There is every reason to suppose, Joyce Kilmer
aside, that no man, given his free choice,
would try to make a tree anyway.

—Isaac Asimov

4,294,965,298 B.C.
Monday
About Lunchtime

The Earth was practically new, a mere three hundred million years old, give or take a few tens of millions of years. Much of the planet was still steaming from the heat of accretion and from the decay of short-lived radioactive elements injected into the solar system almost at the moment of Earth's formation.

From continent-spanning nets of wrinkles and ruptures emerged outflows of basaltic lava wide enough to accommodate the Red Sea. There was steam and dust and radioactivity in the air, and torrential rains. No splashes of green challenged the forces of erosion. Almost as quickly as it formed, the bare bedrock was hewn down into gravel and powder. Where the seas—actually little more

1

than oversized lakes—met land, the beaches were glittering black bands of volcanic sand.

This was the protocell era, from which simple organic molecules emerged as the phenomena we call life. In seas that were only then accumulating from the exhalations and regurgitations of a very young Earth, little bags of protein had already self-assembled into clumps of microspheres and long hollow tubes with tantalizing septaelike divisions. They looked like colonies of living cells, but they were nothing more than the equilibrium of forms naturally assumed by random collections of amino acids. Their seemingly multicellular arrangement was no different from the behavior of fresh-blown soap bubbles, which form spontaneously into such familiar, stable shapes as hollow globes and hemispherical doublets. Organic microstructures obey the same physical laws and also seek stability. Multicellularity was there at the beginning, on Day One, and was dictated by nothing more exotic than basic physics.

As for what formed the microstructures in the first place, that was no cause for astonishment, either. You can cook up the very same structures in your own kitchen in about twenty hours. Simply take any combination of substances containing carbon, hydrogen, oxygen, and nitrogen, and apply any form of energy—electricity, heat, shock waves—then shake the resulting mixture of protein building blocks vigorously, and you will come up with little bags and tubes of protein: protocells. They are not life (though some of them will scavenge more protein, grow, and divide), and they were not life 4.3 billion years ago, but they were getting close to it.

The truly astonishing thing was that stray bits of crystalline RNA and DNA, riding on the winds and currents, occasionally found their way into protocells. Some would eventually take control of the protocells, and a day would come when protocell descendants—creatures that were then only latent on Earth—would ripple with energy-releasing and -capturing molecules that conducted symphonies written on DNA and performed by protein. Other knots of nucleic acid would form viruses and try to rewrite the score, threatening to throw the entire symphony into chaos.

This is the story of one aberrant bit of nucleic acid, the Epstein-Barr virus, and its impact on one protocell descendant: *Homo sapiens,* a.k.a. Man—specifically one Charles Pellegrino.

EXCERPT FROM THE DIARIES OF CHARLES R. PELLEGRINO
JULY 20, 1985
VIRAL CAPSID ANTIGEN TITER 2560

"Epstein-Barr virus," my physician friend with the sheets of blood test results said as we stepped into my office, which is also my laboratory, which is also my bedroom. Just three words: "Epstein-Barr virus."

"What exactly does that mean?" I asked.

"Well, are you interested in fascinating diseases?"

"Yeah. Sort of."

"Well, Charlie, you've got one!"

One of my titers is 2560. Of all the diagnostic tests available to my friend Jesse, the *titer* has been the most telling. It works something like this. In testing for an antibody to a specific virus, an anti-antibody is used. If the anti-antibody reacts with a sample of my blood, then the antibody to the virus is present and I have, at the very least, been exposed to the virus. To find out how serious the exposure has become, the blood serum is diluted (primarily with saline solution, or "sea water," which is what blood is mostly made of). The specific antibody tested by the viral anti-antibody is intended (by my body) to attack the outer, spherical shell of an invader (the virus) possessing only seventy genes and so small that two thousand of them could be strung side by side across the width of an eyelash. The serum to be tested is diluted to one part serum in ten parts of saline, then one in twenty, one in forty, and so on. At some point the serum becomes so dilute that viral antibodies are no longer detectable. A person who has had mononucleosis, one of the more common manifestations of the Epstein-Barr virus, might produce a viral capsid antigen titer of 20, or even 40. When the titer goes well beyond one part blood serum to 80 parts saline and viral antibodies are still detectable, the physician begins to suspect that he is dealing with a major league infection. When tests for antibodies to other portions of the virus's anatomy are similarly "off the scales," and when serum iron levels are half what they ought to be, copper levels are 25 percent above normal values, and additional blood results indicate a state of inflammation throughout the entire body, the physician knows that the activity and the sheer population density of virus particles in the patient have reached the panic range—especially when people at the blood testing laboratory call from across the continent to tell him he's sent them one of the highest titers on record. "Just out of curiosity," they want to know, "what condition is the patient in?"

For starters—just for starters—I have developed an unusual form of arthritis. The vertebrae of my spine have fused from the base of my neck all the way down. Now my neck is fusing and I cannot get into my car without banging my head. My immune system seems to be confused by the virus. It's attacking my bones and collagen (connective tissue). The very antibody-producing cells that are supposed to defend me against the invaders are not merely losing the war—they've joined the other side!

And there is anemia—anemia so overmastering that there have been days when I could stay awake only four hours. Several weeks ago I almost fell asleep during an interview with a *Newsday* reporter about the antimatter rockets Jim Powell and I have been designing at Brookhaven National Laboratory. I barely remember the interview; yet, as near as I can tell, it reads well, perhaps because even when I am full of virus, the last part of my brain to shut off is the one that deals with rockets and space. Yes, the interview reads well, but I caught myself dozing off at the wheel three times during the drive home from the lab. Twice I was well on my way off the road.

Rockets and space . . . about a year ago NASA administrator James Beggs and Grumman Aerospace president George Skurla were talking about sending a few scientist-authors aloft on the space shuttle to describe the view in accurate yet understandable terms—to turn geology, astronomy, and engineering into poetry. Mine was one of the names that came up. Anyone who has read my books understands that few people love technology and exploration as much as I do. When I began getting sick, I was afraid that the arthritis might keep me back. Though it never stopped me from scuba diving or canoeing or biking, I worried about passing NASA's physical exams. That's the least of my worries today. It's gone beyond arthritis. Now there are muscle aches and spasms, and pain that is always there, and tiredness, and something like superflu. I used to be afraid that, if I was lucky enough to pass through NASA's selection process all the way to the physicals, they might turn me down there. Now I'm afraid that if they told me tomorrow I could climb aboard *Challenger* or *Atlantis,* I just wouldn't feel up to it. I don't have the energy. And the pain makes it impossible to get a good night's sleep . . . and the lack of sleep, I know, further lowers my resistance . . . allows the virus to come on again stronger . . . brings on more pain . . . less able to sleep . . . more tired . . . weakens my immune system . . . worsens the infection.

Just three words: Epstein-Barr virus.

My body has become a DNA battlefield. It would be fascinating if it were not so painful: the genetic code at war with itself.

EXCERPT FROM DR. JESSE A. STOFF'S NOTES ON THE CONDITION OF
DR. CHARLES PELLEGRINO, EPSTEIN-BARR VIRUS (EBV) PATIENT
JULY 20, 1985

Subjective: The fatigue, arthralgias, and ability to concentrate are apparently worsening. He reports weakening of his will and lapsing into periods of depression.

Objective: His blood tests show a virulent chronic-active-EBV infection with severe inflammatory changes. Varieties of antiinflammatory drugs have been tried which have only irritated his stomach. Fortunately, his professional goals are still intact and seem to be motivating him.

Analysis: Having considered and rejected gamma-globulin shots and antidepressants, I see no support in sight for his disintegrating metabolism and immune system. His body is solidifying almost in front of my eyes with the ravages of arthritis. The prognosis for him to continue his professional activities is growing dim.

Plan: Having researched various protocols to stabilize and strengthen his immune system utilizing natural medicines, I believe this is the best choice for treatment. I will present this option to him and hope to institute it immediately. Nothing else is working or available.

Charles Pellegrino comments: Dr. Jesse Stoff has had the good fortune to study at New York Medical College where, as part of his curriculum, he was introduced to the medicinal uses of herbs and nutritional supplements. Another stroke of luck was his 1982 acceptance (after he completed an M.D. in traditional medicine in the United States) into a fellowship program in London, where he could further study the natural medicines that had by then become an integral part of Great Britain's national health system.

Working at the outpatient clinic of the Royal London Homeopathic Hospital, he saw patients referred there with fatigue and chronic pain caused by the Coxsackie virus. There he learned how to help Coxsackie sufferers through the use of homeopathic remedies—medicines derived primarily from herbs and minerals and administered in very small, nontoxic doses—and often witnessed miraculous improvements in the patients' conditions.

He thought a great deal about his experiences at the hospital as he examined me in the summer of 1985. During preceding months he'd prescribed what should have been the right supplements and remedies, along with a diet that, more often than not, proved effective in the control of arthritis. But my condition continued to deteriorate. The traditional antiinflammatory drugs from the arthritis clinic, too, were failing. Indeed, they seemed to be doing more harm than good by taxing the liver and stripping the stomach. Even if the antiinflammatories did work, essentially all they could do was mask the pain—which is to say that they got nowhere near targeting the cause of the pain. By July 20, 1985, we understood that the anemia and the pain were aggravated by my blood being full of Epstein-Barr virus. And even supposing traditional medicine could conjure up some magical drug to seek and destroy the virus, it still wouldn't eliminate the source of the infection. The infection was the result of a weakness or defect in my body. More to the point, some portion of my immune system had gone off the rails. Jesse suggested that the bets could be stacked slightly in my favor by removing most fats, sugar, red meats, alkaloids (found in tea, potatoes, tomatoes, eggplant), and dairy products from my diet, thereby avoiding unnecessary insults to the liver and other centers of immunity. Conversely, such things as iron-rich vegetables might provide some of the ammunition I needed.

The only real route to fighting the symptoms was to somehow put the immune system back on the right track, which might then topple the virus, alleviating the symptoms. The orthodox, back-to-front remedies, such as caffeine to keep me awake and painkillers to mask the pain were little more than firebreaks, akin to chopping down portions of a forest to prevent it from getting burned. One had to treat the core of the problem. One had to work with the health of the entire organism—in this case, one Charlie Pellegrino. That's the essence of holistic-natural medicine.

Jesse Stoff explains: Holistic medicine is an approach to health care that addresses the entirety of the individual affected and his or her life circumstances. If we look at someone in a holistic, nonjudgmental way, we can observe four levels of functioning.

First, and most obviously, we can touch, see, and hear the *physical body*. This is a very important aspect of human health because it is on this level that the immunologic-viral war is ultimately fought. It is also the level that is most accessible to testing, that lets us most easily monitor the raging battle.

Viral titers closely approximate the level of functioning of the physical body during the battle. It is at this physical level that nutritional supplements and medicinal herbs act to reinforce the ailing defenses of the body. Unlike drugs, which are given for their own intrinsic effect (i.e., an antibiotic is given specifically to kill a bacterium and does nothing to help—and in fact may hinder—the body's own defenses), natural medicines act in harmony with the body to strengthen the immune system and bring equilibrium to the metabolism. For example, the medicinal herb *Echinacea*, when prepared and administered correctly, has a powerful effect in stimulating the macrophages—the garbage collectors of the immune system (see chapter 3 for more on them).

The physical body and its biochemistry have further importance in that it is here that the other levels of human functioning become visible.

Less visible, but no less important, is the *doing-will* function of a person. Doing-will is what provides the oomph to get out of bed in the morning. Owing to the tremendous drain on the body's energy-will reserves by the immune system as it battles the virus, a sinister feeling of lethargy creeps in. A correlation between such lethargy and abnormalities in liver function blood tests is often clearly seen. The overwhelming fatigue destroys the victim's stamina and with it the energy to work and to lead a normal life. Some victims—the special victims, like Charlie—are able to maintain enough of their motivating goals to overcome the erosion of the will.

Emotion is the next level of human function. Many chronic diseases have a component of depression associated with them. Chronic fatigue syndrome (CFS) is no exception; accompanying depression often proves to be the rule. As a result of the immunologic turmoil caused by the virus(es), the body will often produce antibodies against its own thyroid gland. This results in a slowing of the metabolism and a sense of doom and depression that threatens to engulf the victim in a shroud of hopelessness, moodiness, and irritability—feelings that are often directed toward those most loved.

Finally, we come to the paramount level of human function, that of *cognitive activity*. Here the processes of memory and the ability to concentrate and think linearly are often compromised. The Epstein-Barr virus can attack the brain and in doing so will impair the cognitive functions.

Thus, we can see the potential for this virus to wreak havoc on the four levels of human functioning, or "members." The *physical body* tending to disintegrate in a sea of inflammation, the *doing-will* activity paralyzed and wanting, the *emotions* overshadowed by despair, and the *cognitive functions* threatened to the point that the victim loses the ability to express his or her individuality.

CFS is a sinister and powerful foe, yet with a commitment by patient and physician to a comprehensive and holistic approach, it can be successfully fought off and its symptoms completely reversed. By addressing and supporting the four members of human functioning, a victim may not only overcome the present challenge to his or her health but can gain new and useful insights that may lead to a more fulfilled and happier life in the future. This coordinated approach includes a nutritional regime along with specific techniques and exercises to bolster the will, lighten the moods, and sharpen the mind, as outlined in chapters 7 through 9.

And if in a worst case scenario—CFS—the effectiveness of these methods can be demonstrated, couldn't they be modified to prevent disease in and improve the quality of life of those not affected?

Might they have a coherent and powerful effect on strengthening and enriching the lives of all?

"It sounds like magic to me," Charlie said. "But I don't have an awful lot of choices, do I? This is supposed to be one hundred percent untreatable. If I hadn't grown up with you I'd be tempted to call you mad. But you've been right about too many other things. So, what the hell? I guess it's that time—guinea pig time."

The response was dramatic. Within two weeks Charlie was awake sixteen hours a day, every day. In July, extrapolating the rate of his declining health, he'd looked ahead and seen that he'd soon be unable to work at all. Instead, in December he was sailing on an expedition with famed explorer Robert Ballard, working the 2:00–6:00 A.M. shift with the robot that found the *Titanic*. None of his fellow scientists or crew noticed anything different about Charlie Pellegrino except a stiffness in his back. By November 1986, his viral capsid antigen titer had declined from 2560 to 160, and he had begun to regain mobility in his neck and lower back. The progress of his arthritis had not merely been arrested, it had actually begun to reverse itself. No one expected that result.

I have since applied the same holistic approach to more than fifteen hundred other CFS patients, with rewarding results.

Is Charlie cured? No, at least not yet; no one has yet found a way to eliminate the Epstein-Bar virus from the body. But in Charlie the virus is in remission, perhaps forever. With its remission his symptoms have subsided, and no one would guess—as he continues to explore the ocean's deepest reaches, as he designs new machines for the conquest of space, as he hurries from one part of the world to another, and organizes symposia and writes four books simultaneously—that his joints were once fusing so rapidly that physicians advised him that he might soon have to decide whether to spend the rest of his (shortened) life frozen in a sitting or a reclining position.

And you'd never know, to see him today, that there was a time within recent memory when he could work only a four-hour day.

THE WORST GOSSIPS IN THE WORLD

Viruses can be viewed as wandering collections of genes. They are not merely carriers of mononucleosis, chronic Epstein–Barr syndrome, and random death. They are compulsive communicators. From the very beginning, from Day One, they have migrated from protocell to protocell, and finally from organism to organism, passing on snatches of genetic information. Sometimes they peel away a string of DNA from you or me and carry it away into the air. Viruses pass from humans to cats to seagulls and whales, with the result that the chromosomes of certain cats bear genes that can be found in the DNA of monkeys and baboons, and appear also in a particular virus. From kittens to fireflies to weeds, into the sea and back again, the viruses wander without aim, snipping off a piece of heredity here, depositing it there, exchanging the code of life like bits of gossip passed over a backyard fence.

Watching a cauliflower mosaic virus transfer firefly genes to a tobacco plant, and then seeing the plant acquire the glow-in-the-dark characteristics of the firefly, one wonders how much of our evolutionary history derives from "something in the air."

Millions of years ago, it seems viruses spirited away the normal genes that regulate the rapid-fire growth of embryonic cells and are permanently shut off later in life. Carrying these displaced pieces of genome in tow, the viruses dropped them off from time to time in human chromosomes, where they traveled down with sperm and egg to the first cell of the newborn. Researchers have uncovered dozens of these stray genes—called oncogenes—that appear to trigger runaway cell growth when they are switched on. The cells become expanding spheres of flesh—colonies from which highways soon branch.

Centuries ago, Hippocrates opened a cadaver and discovered such colonies. The highways radiating from them looked to him like crab claws, and he named the condition after the Greek word for crab—which came into the twentieth century as "cancer."

Viruses needn't splice genes in the wrong place to throw an orderly biology into a chaos of cancer cells (somewhat as if you were to randomly splice snippets of a Ramones concert onto a recording of Beethoven's Ninth, or vice versa). Viruses can incite cancer right on the spot, all by themselves. Scientists learned this from David, "the boy in the plastic bubble." David suffered from a rare genetic defect that left him powerless to produce antibodies. Outside of the ultrasterile environment of his specially constructed bubble, he was doomed by the air we breathe. In an attempt to provide him with the natural defenses most of us take for granted, a bone marrow transplant was attempted in 1983. But blood cells in his sister's marrow contained minute traces of the Epstein-Barr virus, as does the blood and marrow of almost anyone who has lived past the age of thirty, we now know. Within days, David's blood was roiling with the most extreme Epstein-Barr activity in the history of medical experience. One week later, the first cancer cells appeared in his lymph glands. They formed tumors in almost no time at all. Within four months he was dead.

The Epstein-Barr virus, once thought to be harmless, has since been associated with an immune cell cancer (Burkitt's lymphoma) that usually is found in children. The virus is also known to play a leading role in a deadly and horribly disfiguring cancer that strikes the noses and throats of some fifty thousand people a year.

MIT biologist Nancy Hopkins comments, "Cancer arises from a number of insults to the DNA. Viruses are one insult. They start the ball rolling."

Treating the cancer-triggering virus may prevent it from making the insult, meaning that we might fight cancer before cancer cells actually exist. In studying the virus, we enter a world more fascinating than science fiction. Picture an organism so strange that many evolutionary biologists have trouble accepting it as "alive." The Epstein-Barr virus cannot even reproduce itself unless you insert it into a living cell. Once inside, it hijacks the cell's chemical machinery, adding its own genes to the genes of the infected cell, so that the protein and nucleic acid producing factories of the cell treat the viral DNA as if it belongs there. Copy after copy of new viral DNA accumulates in the cytoplasm (the clear, watery fluid within the cell), to become packaged with ever-growing supplies of viral proteins. The population of virus particles doubles, and doubles again. And the center of infection is in certain white blood cells called B cells, the very cells that are supposed to make the antibodies to kill the virus.

Once the Epstein-Barr virus enters the body, whether it triggers full-fledged mononucleosis or merely a sore throat (the soreness is the outcry from nerves bundled around cells torn open and leaking new virus particles), it lingers forever. In most cases it remains hidden in the B cells. Only those virus particles remaining latent inside the B cells, those particles that have ceased reproduction, shut off most of their genes, and made themselves "invisible" are able to survive the initial assault by the immune system. But every so often a B cell will transform into a virus factory, expelling new virus particles into the blood. More often than not, the particles will attract immediate attention—by the immune system's formation of antibodies—to themselves and be destroyed. A day, a week, or a month later, another B cell will swell and spew virus particles. It is as if the viruses are testing the water.

Sometimes they win. Sometimes a little piece of the host's immune system shuts down—the very piece that recognizes the virus or produces a specific antibody against some portion of it, such as the honeycomb-shaped viral capsule. The virus has then passed successfully through a kind of natural selection filter, and finds itself immune to immunity.

Since 1984, researchers have been discovering connections between Epstein-Barr virus and various chronic and relapsing symptoms. In a study published in the January 1985 issue of the *Annals of Internal Medicine,* some eighteen clinical features of EBV are outlined, including prolonged and debilitating fatigue (the most common symptom), intermittent low-grade fever, sudden onset of multiple allergies, chronic sore throat, swollen glands, difficulty in concentrating, arthritic symptoms, migraines, and psychological disturbances (particularly depression, which may derive from experiencing the other symptoms). Cases are now being diagnosed in numbers dwarfing the AIDS (acquired immune deficiency syndrome) epidemic, including clusters in Nevada, Hollywood, and Manhattan. It's beginning to look as if we are in the midst of a spreading plague; but perhaps it only looks that way. Possibly, large numbers of cases are now being identified primarily because the condition was never recognized before. Until 1984 people simply suffered from constant and inexplicable fatigue along with some combination of the other symptoms of chronic fatigue syndrome, or they developed lymphatic cancer or nasal pharyngeal cancer or yeast infections or one of several varieties of neurological complications (including a chronic pain syndrome, such as reflex sympathetic dystrophy). All of these symptoms are but the footprint of CFS. The disease itself saps physical, mental, emotional, and immunologic strength. It may be progressive and unrelenting, and the ultimate scope of the problem is still unknown.

The news is not all bad, however. The following chapters present guidelines that will enable patients and physicians to identify the syndrome and, once it is identified, provide a safe and effective therapeutic strategy that will strengthen the victim's immune system to the point where the virus goes into remission and stays in remission—perhaps permanently.

There are three possible responses to a viral assault on the body. Initially, the immune system responds homeostatically: it tries to correct the imbalance (for example, with increased numbers of white blood cells) and then return everything to the status quo. This approach works well for most threats. However, in the susceptible individual an episode of CFS proves to be so overwhelming to the homeostatic mechanisms of the immune system that outside help is needed; hence, the other two possible responses. The first way in which help can be given from outside the body is through drugs. Drugs are hyperpurified, "dead" substances that act directly and specifically on the disease process itself, rather than by strengthening the body's natural defenses against disease. There are no drugs presently known to be effective against EBV or most of its partners in crime.

There is, nevertheless, another possible response—the holistic one. We can stimulate the immune system to a heightened level of competence that will not merely beat back the virus but will leave the body more resistant to disease in general. In other words, the body itself is enlisted as an active participant in its own defense. The holistic approach utilizes therapeutic agents including diet, exercise, vitamin supplements, and prescription natural remedies (homeopathic medicines). It also requires the patient to assume a measure of responsibility for his or her own recovery. The relationship between the patient and the physician thus becomes a partnership in an approach that ultimately makes the science of medicine more humanly relevant.

2

WHAT LITTLE EBVS ARE MADE OF

The way we look to a distant constellation that's dying
in a corner of the sky—
These are the days of miracle and wonder,
And don't cry, baby, don't cry,
Don't cry.
Medicine is magical and magical is art
And the boy in the bubble
And the baby with the baboon heart.

—PAUL SIMON

EXCERPT FROM THE DIARIES OF CHARLES R. PELLEGRINO
SEPTEMBER 9, 1987
VIRAL CAPSID ANTIGEN TITER 160

I had the good fortune of growing up with Jesse Stoff. If you'd gone out to Riverhead, Long Island, some fifteen years ago, you would have seen two teenagers sitting on a log fence and arguing about carbonaceous meteorites—with meteorites in hand. I guess by most teenagers' standards even thinking about such things, much less spending a summer talking about them, must have qualified us as "nerds." There were a lot of nerds wandering around Riverhead in those days. Some of us have become life-long friends.

In any case, based on those meteorites, Jesse and I eventually drew models suggesting that underground streams once existed inside asteroids, and that actual oceans might now exist inside certain icy moons of Jupiter, Saturn, and Neptune—even inside Pluto and Charon. We began publishing joint articles on the subject, and in 1980, University of Hawaii astrobiologist Clair Folsome became interested in some of the things Jesse and I had been saying. He told us it was time Jesse and I got around to writing a book, and he offered us his publisher. So, as I traveled to New Zealand to investigate the dinosaur extinction puzzle, and as Jesse went to London to study holistic medicine—and as muscle spasms began to rake my back—we wrote our first book together, literally from the antipodes of the Earth.

If you read between the lines of my preface to that first book, you will see that I was bemoaning Jesse's departure from evolutionary biology into medicine. I felt as if we had begun to go our separate ways. And therein lies a rare and personal irony. What I did not know was that I was already showing symptoms of chronic active EBV, and that Jesse was walking off into the very branch of medical study that, five years later, would halt and even reverse my body's descent into chaos—with only months to spare.

It's almost enough to make one believe that a kind of fate governs our lives. Now it's strange to think that, in the summer of 1985, there were days when I could stay awake only four hours—and strangest of all to think that I once regretted my friend's growing interest in medicine.

"Are you interested in fascinating diseases?" Jesse had said. "Well, you've got one!"

Under an electron microscope, the Epstein-Barr virus looks more like a collection of machine-made parts than a creation of carbon chemistry. Proteins have been shaped into hollow tubes, hexagons, and equilateral triangles. The virus's genetic code is enclosed in a doughnut-shaped core. Its genome consists of 170 kilobase pairs. For those familiar with computers, this would be comparable to 170 K of memory, or slightly less than the amount of information programmed into most of today's arcade computer games.

Virtually everyone is eventually infected with EBV. It comes to life the moment it makes contact with the skin cells lining the mouth and throat. From there it spreads to the B cells in the blood, *what activates EBV* {

which circulate through the body, churning out virus-attacking antibodies. Most people beat back the virus with no ill effects; but once infected, they are infected for life. Even in its dormant phase, the EBV genome becomes a permanent fixture in the genome of the B cells, dividing with them into succeeding generations, and waiting patiently for the ever-watchful immune system to be weakened by other diseases, old age, overwhelming stress, or by such unnatural influences as alcohol, cocaine, and marijuana abuse for a chance to reemerge.

From its outpost in the mouth, EBV spreads among children via shared lollipops and other less-than-sanitary eating habits, and among adults by kissing and shared dining utensils. According to some estimates, nearly 100 percent of the population is infected by age thirty.

The incidence of a constellation of EBV-type symptoms that simply refuse to go away exhibits the pattern of a rising epidemic. Between 1984 and 1987, the number of patients appearing in doctors' offices with the same devastating symptoms doubled, then doubled again, and has been doing so since the condition was first noticed in 1977. The pattern of increase is hauntingly similar to the AIDS outbreak.

"It's probably not the traditional EBV," theorizes Dr. Anthony Komaroff, chief of internal medicine at Peter Bent Brigham and Women's Hospital in Boston. "It could be a new mutant strain of EBV or it could be a whole new virus that somehow reawakens old EBV dormant in the patient's system. In fact, there is a suspect: human B-lymphotropic virus (HBLV, now known as human herpes virus 6), first identified in late 1986. Like EBV and chicken pox, it is in the herpes family of viruses, and it invades B cells, just as EBV does. HBLV could be making people sick all by itself and, in the process, reawakening dormant EBV."

I remember being diagnosed as having mononucleosis during my freshman year in college. It was no big deal. A little tiredness. Some aches in the legs. It spread from clique to clique. We jokingly called it the "kissing sickness." But what made it come back years later, and with such terrific force? It's fascinating to think about, when I look back from a vantage point of recovered health.

I mentioned in the preceding pages that one of my most painful experiences with EBV was a surge of arthritis. I had the arthritis before the virus bloomed out of control in my blood; it is now known that an EBV bloom will aggravate a preexisting chronic condition, such as arthritis.

And here's the fascinating part: the form of arthritis I suffered from has been diagnosed as ankylosing spondylitis, characterized by a hardening of the ligaments and tendons that bind the vertebrae together. There is apparently nothing new about this condition; I've seen dinosaur spines that exhibit the same characteristics. (Poor *Ornithomius,* did he do as I once did in New Zealand—find an active volcano and settle into a hot mud pool for relief?) There is a genetic marker for this disease, and my white blood cells do indeed carry the marker. Until recently, no one had any idea how this genetic trait was expressed, or why many people who carried the ankylosing spondylitis gene complex never developed the disease.

Now it begins to look as if the coevolution of viruses and humans may be responsible. The genetic marker, known as the HLA-B27 haplotype, contains six consecutive amino acids identical to a sequence in a protein of the *Klebsiella pneumoniae* bacterium. Somewhere among the countless million forebears whose blood runs in my veins, something truly remarkable happened. A virus must have snipped off and carried away a little string of DNA belonging to a *K. pneumoniae* bacterium. This is one thing viruses are very good at: stealing away bits of heredity and redepositing it where it does not belong. Viruses are the worst gossips in the world. Through them, every living thing on this planet is shedding little snippets of DNA, much as a cat sheds hair. With such grace did a virus enter one of my ancestors, carrying a stolen *K. pneumoniae* genome in tow. It turned my ancestor's body into a virus factory, making replicas of itself and of its new-found *K. pneumoniae* genome, too. Before the infection passed, one of the replicants chanced upon a nucleus that was destined to become a sperm or egg and there deposited the bacterial gene, tagging it to the DNA of the yet unborn. Once so tagged, the change could be passed on indefinitely.

The world seems to tilt irrationally as I look at my hand, as the concept of "the stranger within" shifts from symbol and myth to a dawning reality, as I realize that my DNA is not entirely my own, that I am not fully "human." How many years have passed since an ancestral chromosome was transformed into something part human, part bacterium? A thousand? A million? I will probably never know. What I do know is that I came down with *K. pneumoniae* symptoms during the winter of 1976, and by May arthritis was gnawing at the base of my spine.

Once exposed to *K. pneumoniae,* my immune system began producing antibodies against it. In very short order, the bacterium was hunted out of existence. But there remained my bacterial genome, which had, probably from the time of my birth, been manufacturing a bacterial protein in my ligaments and tendons. Apparently my immune system no longer knew the difference between me and the invading bacterium. It mistook my own sequence of amino acids from the HLA-B27 region for a foreign antigen and mounted an assault on the part of me that was not truly me. It began as a slow erosion of the connective tissue in my spine and deteriorated from that point to a general feeling of achiness, inflammation, fever, and fatigue. In time, as my immune system became more and more confused, the Epstein-Barr virus—the most commonplace of all viruses known to reside in human blood—reawakened. As EBV further weakened my body, further confused my immune defenses, a sort of kindling temperature was reached, a flash point at which EBV quickened to the tempo of ankylosing spondylitis. The resulting surge of inflammation weakened me still further, made my blood even more hospitable to EBV. The whole process became cyclic and self-sustaining, like a snake connected head to tail.

A CHEMISTRY LESSON

The study of viruses is more fascinating than most science fiction. Left on its own, completely out of contact with living creatures, the Epstein-Barr virus is inanimate, as silent and lifeless as a mineral—which, perhaps, it is. Close up, the hexagons and triangles that comprise its shell look like clusters of crystals. But they are very strange crystals. They are chains of hydrocarbons, and they have been seeded by DNA.

Cyril Ponnamperuma, director of the Laboratory for Chemical Evolution at the University of Maryland, warns:

> The division of matter into living and nonliving is perhaps an artificial one, convenient for distinguishing such extreme cases as a man and a stone but quite inappropriate when describing other cases such as a virus particle. Indeed, the crystallization of a virus by Wendell Stanley in the 1960s brought about the need for revising our definition of "life" and "living." Pirie has compared our use of the terms *living* and *nonliving* to the words *acid* and *base* as used in chemistry. While sodium hydroxide is distinctly alkaline [i.e., base] sulfuric acid is a powerful acid. But in between these two extremes is a whole variation in strength. The chemist has overcome the confusion arising from these rigid categories by inventing the nomenclature of "hydrogen ion concentration" [pH]. In this way, all the observed phenomena can be described in terms of one quantity. We may have to invent a similar quantity to avoid any vagueness that might arise in applying the term "life" to borderline cases such as the virus.

Once it is brought into contact with human B cells, EBV comes "alive." The outer shell (or capsid) of the virus is shaped like a geodesic sphere and is composed of hollow, proteinaceous hexagons called capsomeres. The capsomeres are arranged into hexagonal arrays, giving the surface of the geodesic sphere a honeycombed appearance. The Epstein-Barr virus is unimaginably minute. Because the virus is actually smaller than the wavelengths of light, it lives in a world without color; everything is black and white. And yet it displays extraordinary detail, geometrically complex and perfect, like a Herkimer diamond. That it is dangerous only adds spice to its beauty. Its capsomeres fit receptors on the membrane of the B cell, fusing with them as if the B cell were a loading dock built for its exclusive use. Once inside the host B cell, EBV sheds its capsomeres and eventually grabs control of the cell's DNA, reprogramming it to make copies of the virus with a speed and sophistication even Xerox would envy. (Alternatively, the viral

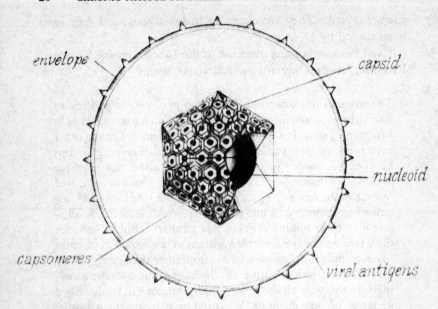

envelope   *capsid*

nucleoid

capsomeres   *viral antigens*

DNA can persist in a dormant state, awaiting the division and replication of the host cell, which will duplicate the EBV genes, too.) As hordes of new virus particles emerge from the cell nucleus into the cytoplasm, they begin to pile up against the inner surface of the cell membrane, through which they are eventually extruded. In this process, the newly formed viral capsids are coated with a protective envelope manufactured from stolen pieces of cell membrane. The break-out of new virus particles—indeed, the mere synthesis of such components as the viral capsid antigen (or viral capsid protein)—kills the B cell.

Combating the virus is part of what makes EBV sufferers—or even common cold sufferers—feel sick. The fatigue, fever, and achiness are not a result of a few infected cells dying. You feel awful because your body is mass producing antibodies and/or secreting mucus at an abnormally rapid pace. Persistent infection shifts the body into maximum overdrive, triggering such complications as chronic inflammation.

No, the virus does not always harm you directly. Sometimes it is subtle and severe. Sometimes it deceives your own body into wearing itself down.

A HISTORY LESSON

Virus, the ancient enemy.

During the course of its evolution, the Epstein-Barr virus has established a nearly perfect parasitic relationship with humans. An imperfect parasite, such as the more recently evolved AIDS virus, is too new to the game and kills its host. No competent viral strategist would dream of a 100 percent kill rate. Were a strain of AIDS to emerge that could spread more easily (and, given a reservoir of millions infected with this most rapidly mutating of all known viruses, that is not entirely out of the question), and assuming no viable treatment, humanity might disappear in a single generation, utterly and without decendants. So too would the AIDS virus.

A perfect parasite, such as the Epstein-Barr virus, ensures the survival of both parasite and host. In most cases, EBV knows when to stop. The host generally survives infection, and infectious virus particles are thereafter released periodically into the saliva, facilitating its spread to every new generation of uninfected hosts.

During the Stone Age, and the Wood Age before it, introduction to EBV probably took place when a person was very young, which is what happens in many undeveloped parts of the world today where sanitation is often primitive. When EBV strikes young children, only rarely does it cause significant illness. No one understands why this age-based selectivity occurs.

With the improved hygiene standards of developed countries, first contact with EBV is usually put off until adolescence—but then at a price. In adolescence and early adulthood EBV infection is often expressed as mononucleosis. In the United States and Japan, between 35 and 80 percent of the freshmen entering college test positive to EBV antibodies. Ten to 15 percent of those uninfected will contract the virus during freshman year, another 10 to 15 percent during sophomore year, a like percentage during junior year, and so on and so on until, by the age thirty, at least 97 percent will test positive. Sixty percent of these belatedly infected individuals will become ill, often with great detriment to their academic and professional careers.

Interest in this viral syndrome dates back to 1889, when Dr. E. Pfeiffer described what he called a "glandular fever," which included a variety of disorders closely resembling acute EBV disease. To this day in the medical literature, the syndrome is occasionally referred to as Pfeiffer's disease. Since the 1920s, it has been known as infectious mononucleosis, so named because of an associated lymphocyte (white blood cell) with a peculiar morphology. The disease is also characterized by a marked increase in white blood cells and in many respects exhibits properties of a "self-limiting leukemia." In leukemia, the overproduction of cells in the bone marrow (where B lymphocytes originate) and thymus (where T lymphocytes are manufactured) mushrooms out of control. However, patients with mononucleosis generally recover, and the abnormal proliferation of white blood cells eventually subsides.

In a tissue culture, normal healthy B cells are unable to grow and multiply. As a rule, they die off about three weeks after being transferred to a petri dish. By contrast, "sick" B cells—those infected with EBV—blossom into ever-expanding colonies. They will grow for years in a petri dish, like tumor cells, and for similar reasons. The sick, "immortalized" cells simply don't know when to stop growing. In people with infectious mononucleosis, one B cell in five thousand is transformed into an abnormal lymphocyte capable of growing indefinitely in culture. In healthy individuals with dormant EBV infections, only one lymphocyte in ten million is transformed. EBV's participation in the genesis of cancers seems clear, for the proliferation of immortalized mutant cells is cancer, by sheer definition.

In 1958 Dr. Denis Burkitt of Makerere University in Uganda discovered an unusual lymphoma (a cancer of the immune system). It seemed to strike initially in the head and neck. In one patient, the malignant growth doubled in size every two days, distorting the face until it resembled a mass of balloons with eyes. It metastasized rapidly—and lethally—to other parts of the body.

By 1964 the condition bore the name Burkitt's lymphoma. That was the year M. Anthony Epstein, B. G. Achong, and Y. M. Barr of London's Middlesex Hospital began studying Burkitt's lymphoma cells under an electron microscope. Within the cells they found virus particles, which they named (as you've probably guessed by this point) Epstein-Barr virus. We now know that it belongs to the herpes family of viruses, characterized by a double strand of DNA and an ability to lie in wait—forever—in those it infects. The family includes the genital herpes virus, the chicken pox virus, and cytomegalovirus (also known as CMV).

In 1983 four members of one California family—two cousins, a daughter of one of the cousins, and a sister-in-law of the second—learned they had contracted the rarely encountered Burkitt's lymphoma. The facts surrounding the case are compelling, yet difficult to interpret. The four had been visited a year earlier by a South African aunt who was touring the United States. They recalled that the aunt had suffered from a sore throat, fatigue, and other EBV-like symptoms. Blood tests showed that at least one of the four victims had experienced a recent EBV infection (one died before her blood could be tested). Genetic origins of the cancer can be ruled out because not all of the victims are blood relatives.

Dr. Joseph Pagano of the University of North Carolina feels that "EBV and/or some other virus is a more likely explanation [for the cancer cluster] than any other. Is it possible, then, that we are looking at a contagious cancer? Can that be true?"

Examination of African populations has shown that EBV antibodies are present in the blood of all children suffering from Burkitt's lymphoma; they are also in the blood of nearly all healthy African children under age four. The difference is in the antibody titers. In those children expressing lymphoma (approximately one case in ten thousand children per year) the titers for the viral capsid antigen (and for other viral proteins) are well over 80, at least ten times higher than the titers of healthy children. Clearly, the lymphoma children are responding abnormally to the virus and, as Epstein and Barr found, Burkitt's lymphoma in Africa is strongly associated with the virus that bears their names. But is association enough to conclude cause and effect?

Ninety-two percent of critically ill patients with certain lymphomas are now known to exhibit abnormally high EBV antibody titers. Their bodies have actually become virus-replicating machines. As in the case of one Charlie Pellegrino's experience of ankylosing spondylitis, a two-way feedback effect may be at work: the lymphoma weakens the body, allowing the virus to flourish, and the virus in turn weakens and confuses the immune system, allowing both lymphoma and virus to proliferate. In some patients, the virus may provide one of several insults that initiates the lymphoma. In others, the disease may arise from nonviral insults, and dissolution of the immune system simply makes life more comfortable for the virus. A point to keep in mind—an ironic point—is that the standard chemotherapy, meant to treat the lymphoma, actually weakens the immune system and makes the patient more susceptible to blooms of the virus believed to initiate the very lymphoma being treated. This explains, perhaps, why EBV-associated lymphomas are notoriously resistant to chemotherapy.

Epidemiological studies have indicated that Burkitt's lymphoma has a peculiar geographic distribution. The disease spreads across a broad band of equatorial Africa, occurring only in areas with elevations under 1,800 meters (6,000 feet), a great amount of annual rainfall (more than 60 centimeters), and a minimum average temperature of 16°C (60°F). These are areas where malaria-carrying mosquitoes thrive. As already noted, cancer usually results from a series of insults to the DNA and immune system. EBV is one insult. In the epidemiology of Burkitt's lymphoma, the malaria parasite (far more complex than a virus or a bacterium, this mosquito-transmitted organism is a protozoan, a cousin of the amoebae and paramecia so popular in high school biology classes) could be another powerful insult, for the parasite raises havoc with the liver and other centers of immunity and, like ankylosing spondylitis, may lay a foundation for the flourishing of EBV.★

★Treatments for malaria vary around the world. We know an aerospace engineer who contracted the disease in India. There the standard treatment was to give the patient small doses of arsenic. In time the human body develops a tolerance for arsenic; the malaria parasite does not. As the dose of arsenic is gradually increased, the parasites die off. Of course, the poison does make the patient ill; our friend became so weak that he could do little more than sit in his yard sipping tea and reading. One day, when his blood arsenic content was at its peak, he felt a mosquito land on his arm. Instinctively he moved to swat it with his book, but a thought stopped him. Instead, he sat and watched quietly as the insect sank its

In 1972, an experiment was begun that would eventually probe and prove the impact of the Epstein-Barr virus on human immune function and propel it to the number-one candidacy for a virus involved in human cancers. The experiment would have great significance to one scientist-turned-laboratory rat, Charles Pellegrino, and to the EBV patients who would ultimately follow him into recovery. But the experiment also raised questions about what we believe is the increasing dehumanization of scientific inquiry.

According to reports in the popular press, a boy named David was born without a functioning immune system (a hereditary sex-linked condition known as severe combined immune deficiency syndrome, or SCIDS, a defect that can turn a common cold, or even the putrefactive bacteria of decay, into a fatal disease). A report in *Time* proclaimed that "David owed his survival to doctors who had anticipated the condition before his birth because an older brother had died (while still an infant) of immunodeficiency."*

---

proboscis into his skin. In seconds it was sucking up warm blood. It paused abruptly, then seemed to shudder. Its legs stretched out, stiffened in the awkward attitude of sudden death. The engineer smiled. "Gotcha!"

*What the world never did see on television or read in the magazines, was that David's life had been planned for, even before he was conceived, by medical professionals. And herein lies the human dilemma. David's parents wanted to have a child, but his father carried the SCIDS gene and the chances of expressing the disease were 50 percent if the child was male. The parents were encouraged to conceive and carry the child to term—encouraged by doctors who proclaimed from highest authority that even if the child was born with the disease, knowledge about genetics and immunity was doubling every two years and a cure would be found within two years. The statement about the rate of technological progress was true, but this was no basis for predicting that a cure would be found within the period of the next doubling, any more than such predictions can be made for curing the AIDS plague, which, at this writing, continues to bring calamity to the world.

Thus did David become a laboratory rat. But he was no volunteer, and he happened to be human.

"The question," wrote Reverend Raymond J. Lawrence in the *Journal of the American Medical Association,* "is on what moral basis can the community permit such a momentous decision to be made and implemented. Did a handful of physicians and scientists have the moral right to create the kind of laboratory life that David was to endure?"

Reverend Lawrence was the director of Clinical Pastoral Education at St.

Amniocentesis confirmed that the fetus was male, and therefore stood a 50–50 chance of being born with SCIDS. The first module of a sterile enclosure was quietly prepared. David was delivered by cesarean section to prevent bacterial and viral contamination by passage through the vagina. He was transferred directly from the womb into a sterile bubble. Tests soon confirmed that he did indeed have the SCID syndrome.

By age six, David had become the only boy in the world never to have been sick, even for a day, even for an hour, even with the slightest hint of a sniffle or an upset stomach. He'd never smelled his own sweat, for the bacteria that produced body odor did not exist in the bubble. All food delivered to him (through air locks) had been sterilized thoroughly. Children's books, clothing, crayons, and the air he breathed—all of it had to be rendered germfree.

One of David's attending physicians noted that he was growing into a handsome and intelligent boy, with a tested IQ of 126—approaching genius. "He has tested the hypothesis that skin-to-skin contact and ventral clinging are essential to an infant's normal development," observed the doctor, "and he has found that hypothesis wanting. He has defied the better-to-be-dead-than-isolated crowd by regarding his bubble as his home and protecting it, rather than trying to 'escape' from it. Moreover, he has answered the sympathetic little old ladies, who would make him out to be an

---

Luke's Children's Hospital and in time would come to know David personally. He would also have contact with the medical team that cared for the boy. "Profound and disturbing ethical and humanitarian issues have been raised by David's life," he says. "From the beginning, I was personally troubled by what appeared to be neglect of the potential emotional, psychological, and spiritual— that is to say human—implications of continued life in the plastic bubble. I developed some impressions as a result of my personal contact with David. I felt concern about his imprisonment and its potential consequences, as well as a not very scientific feeling that perhaps the project should never have been begun in the first place."

But there were few alternatives once the boy had been conceived. The only other choices were to prevent his birth or let him die once born. So they opted for life and carried on with the project. David's life became a dramatic and historic first: he would live twelve years in a sterile plastic cocoon, never feeling the touch of his mother's hand. And when at last the outside world did touch him, he would from that moment be doomed.

object of pity, by laughing (loudly) in their faces."

David "escaped" the bubble only once, in 1978, by aid of a spacesuit designed and built by NASA scientists. He was able to explore the world beyond the hospital halls, to hold a garden hose and water the grass, while all around him the press crowded. Such limited freedom was possible only until he began to outgrow the suit. He then returned to his series of sterile modules and lived there much as a space traveler might live while bound for the stars. Eventually he began to fancy himself as just that: an alien among humans, whose spaceship happened to be contained within the walls of a hospital, on a world whose air was poisonous to him. His impression of the world was quite unlike that of anyone else who had ever lived. He found it hard to believe that the buildings he saw from his window actually had another side to them—that there were other doors and windows hidden from view. When he first stepped onto a front lawn in his spacesuit, he believed that he could walk to the back of the building directly by crossing the street in front of it. This was half true. David knew that he would reach the back by walking completely around the world, but he had never before had an opportunity to feel—to truly feel—the distances of the outside. He did not know how big a mile was. Only the responses of African pygmies can furnish criteria for how David saw lawns and streets and houses. Brought out of the dense forests for the first time, pygmies, too, could not immediately comprehend the vast distances of the outside, and thought that men standing near the horizon must indeed be very small.

Had David been cured, his exploration of the world would have become a fantastic adventure. For a time, the things we take for granted—the feel of a leaf in the palm of one's hand—would have been as astonishing as those first steps on the moon were to the astronauts. His exploration of Earth could have taught us much about ourselves, but what, we will never know.

He began life without any T cells and with B cells unable to produce antibodies. By age six, T cells had suddenly developed and his B cells had begun producing small amounts of antibodies. It began to seem possible that before science had learned enough to cure him, he might outgrow his disease.

This turned out to be wishful thinking. By age twelve, David's

B cells were still producing only faintly detectable antibodies, and his T cells were nonfunctional. Most of today's AIDS victims are better equipped to fend off disease. His only hope of being able to live on the outside was a transplant of bone marrow from a genetically compatible sibling. If the transplant took (that is, if defender cells produced by the newly introduced bone marrow did not recognize David's body as foreign and attack it), a rapidly growing source of antibody-producing white cells could provide a defensive barrier against viruses and bacteria. David had a fifteen-year-old sister whose cell type did not match his, but a new washing procedure made it possible to prevent the transplanted marrow from making antibodies against its new home. On October 21, 1983, 45 grams (1.6 ounces) of his sister's bone marrow were washed and injected intravenously. David assisted physicians from inside his bubble, placing the needle in his own arm. The feared antibody attack did not occur, but his sister's B cells carried with them the Epstein-Barr virus (as do the B cells of most healthy adolescents). As her cells divided, some of them spewed EBV, and the virus took control of David's own B cells, which were totally defenseless against the assault. He soon developed recurrent flulike symptoms. Three months later persistent fever, diarrhea, and vomiting made it necessary to examine and treat him outside the bubble.

On February 7, 1984, David crawled through the air lock and felt, for the first time, the touch of his mother's hand unprotected by a glove. Later, she ran a comb through his hair. It had been his wish to walk barefoot on the grass; soon he was too sick to consider such things. During the two weeks that followed he developed ulcers in his digestive tract. Fluid accumulated in his lungs and around his heart. David's B cells were multiplying rapidly—too rapidly. They were abnormally large, and they piled up in his intestines, lungs, and spleen. His body was a chaos of Epstein-Barr disease and B cell lymphoma. On February 22, 1984, breathing became so difficult that a decision was made to put him on mechanical respiration.

"Here we have all these tubes and all these tests," David told his doctor, "and nothing is working. And I'm getting tired. Why don't we just pull all these tubes and let me go home?"

"I'm going to breathe for you," the doctor said. "And in order to do that I'm going to give you something that is going to make you very sleepy."

David winked at him. And then he went home.

In David's lymph nodes, in his arms, in his feet—wherever blood was sampled—the evidence was plain. For twelve years his system had been completely germfree, and now the Epstein-Barr virus was everywhere. It was the only virus that seemed to be present, so all the damage—the ulcerated stomach and intestines, the swollen liver and spleen, the tumors—must have been wrought by EBV.

But that was impossible, or so it seemed. EBV was supposed to be a relatively harmless infection, little more than a kissing sickness, barely worse than a common cold. It couldn't have caused cancer. Couldn't have.

It was difficult to believe, but there it was.

Jesse Stoff comments: We now know that David's death was as extraordinary as his life. Introduced into a healthy but defenseless body, the Epstein-Barr virus flourished. In that same year, the virus was also flourishing in Charlie Pellegrino's blood, and he, too, was on the verge of becoming one of the most severe and best-documented cases of EBV disease. But the damage to Charlie's body had required years of viral assault and, as sick as he would become during the coming months, his experience was nothing compared to the unwinnable war that was waged in David's bloodstream. In David's case, a scenario that normally takes years, if not decades, was compressed into the space of a few short weeks. And that taught us something.

For a start, we have seen that even "relatively harmless" viruses can be more important than anyone has hitherto suspected. We have seen demonstrated, as if by time-lapse photography, the path of destruction that runaway EBV disease is likely to follow—right on up to the very first undisputed observation of a viral trigger for cancer.

Fortunately, the majority of people with EBV, even those suffering from chronic EBV disease (also known as recurrent mononucleosis, recurrent sleeping sickness, or chronic fatigue syndrome), do not develop cancer as a result of their infection. The symptoms they do develop depend largely on the length of time infected and the progress of infection.

Most encounters with EBV result in flulike symptoms, including sore throat, nasal congestion, low-grade fever, and swollen glands in the neck. In young children the infection may appear to be just another cold, and is generally of no greater significance (except that the virus remains latent in the B cells). In teenagers the virus tends to penetrate deeper before being neutralized by the immune system. The typical "mono" syndrome may last six to eight weeks, sometimes accompanied by the sudden onset of multiple allergies. This deeper infection triggers enlargement of the lymph nodes in the axilla (arm pits), groin, and neck. The spleen may also swell, functioning as a sort of halfway house for shell-shocked white blood cells seeking refuge from the battle. This swelling may cause a dull ache where the spleen lies, under the lower ribs on the left side. This in itself is no major cause for concern, but on rare occasions a blow to the abdomen or a hard sneeze may rupture a swollen spleen and create a life-threatening situation.

The liver, too, can become infected. Mononucleosis usually produces a mild hepatitis (inflammation of the liver). This swelling is often felt as a dull ache under the lower right side of the rib cage, and is manifested in the blood as an increase in the abundance of liver enzymes.

If the initial acute infection is delayed until adulthood (as is often the case in wealthy, industrialized nations), the patient is in for a difficult battle. First encounters in the twenties are characterized by an exacerbation of all of the above symptoms. The throat is not merely sore, it seems to burn with a roaring hellfire, making speech extremely difficult. Swollen glands may become softball-sized balloons, making swallowing and even breathing a chore. Fevers of 103–104°F (39.5–40°C), accompanied alternately by sweats and chills, are not uncommon. The hepatitis symptoms are also more extreme, leading to marked abdominal pain, nausea, vomiting, digestive imbalances, and a feeling of extreme exhaustion ("as if someone has pulled the plug"). Even lifting one's head off the pillow takes on a new definition of work. And add to this throbbing headaches and a blurring of visual and mental capabilities.

Still, in most cases the immune system eventually rallies (in fact, the hepatitis and swollen glands are the outcry of an extreme immune response), and the virus goes into remission. Unfortunately, this is not always so. Some victims cannot completely overcome the infection. Their immune systems can only control it intermittently. This is known as chronic active EBV disease (CEBV), and it afflicts 5 percent of those who develop mononucleosis. In such cases symptoms can last for years or even a lifetime if nothing is done to help the overwhelmed immune system.

If the infection persists long enough and penetrates deep enough, the immune system may ultimately turn against the patient. Antinuclear antibodies (assigned to attack your own DNA) and even lupus can appear. In essence, the body actually begins to eat itself in midstride.

Chronic active EBV patients sometimes experience peripheral nerve pain, numbness, seizures, paralysis, and even encephalitis (a swelling of the brain that can cause blindness, deafness, and death). Much of this damage is produced by the body's own antibody-producing cells, not by the virus itself. As antibodies attack the thyroid, the metabolism slows and falters still further. Antibodies against muscle protein can cause myositis (muscle inflammation), while antibodies against nerve tissue can further exacerbate viral infection as well as cripple.

Even in such extreme cases, complete recovery is possible—and more. Within such chaos lies the opportunity to take a far more constructive approach to life than one possessed prior to the onset of illness. But like most such opportunities, it may come disguised as a lot of hard work.

FROM THE DIARIES OF CHARLES R. PELLEGRINO
SEPTEMBER 22, 1987

When I look back upon it now, my illness seems a most unlikely blessing. It's strange, but I am actually thankful that it happened.

I was stripped of my health in the summer of 1985. The virus had put a terrible look on my face. The deterioration seemed to be progressing with mathematical certainty toward an end only two years away. I'd decided that I would fight as long as I could; but if and when I saw a point at which recovery was impossible and all that stretched ahead of me was a three-month downhill slide, I would end it early and peacefully, before somebody decided to put all those tubes in and tried to breathe for me. That option gave me comfort. It gave me a measure of control, however little.

Stripped of my health, I'd come to a place where I had nothing. Absolutely nothing. And perhaps that gave me more than I'd ever have had otherwise. In that cold, empty place, I finally learned the value of all things.

It is something I would wish on my best friend: to be terribly ill young, and then to recover. Sometimes a dose of ill health can be good for you.

Epstein-Barr virus has shuffled my priorities and made them come up all new. Oh, I still let little things bother me from time to time, but the important things are that I can run, or look at a tree, or marvel over the Manhattan skyline, or feel the warmth of Gloria's hand. Somehow it renews you, to emerge from a place where you could see no farther than two years of life in constant pain, to crawl out of the pit into a place where forty, fifty, sixty years of reasonably good health suddenly stretch out ahead of you. The future is filled with infinite possibilities.

And I find myself feeling strangely and increasingly responsible for the planet's future.

One of the builders of *Apollo* once told me that he'd known all the astronauts before they went to the moon, and that when they returned, without exception, their personalities were a little different; they seemed more pensive. Commenting on this, astronaut Edgar Mitchell described exactly how I feel today, even though he was talking about coming back from the moon, not from EBV. "It's what I prefer to call instant global consciousness," says Mitchell. "Each of us has come back from the moon with a feeling that we were no longer American citizens; we became planetary citizens. We don't like the way things are, and we want to improve it."

I wish David could have come out of his bubble and discovered the world. I think he would have emerged a planetary citizen. And I think he would have done well. Instead, he taught us about EBV, and the fact that he focused attention on the right virus at the right time is partly the reason I am alive today.

Thank you, David, wherever you are.

3

GETTING TO KNOW YOUR LIVER

The liver of Charles Pellegrino
Can be ruined by excess of vino.
—Or a virus or two
—May bore its way through
With results quite destructive. Yes, we know.

—Isaac Asimov

The liver is one of the primary targets of EBV, CMV, and some of the other viruses associated with CFS. Indeed, most people suffering from acute EBV disease (mononucleosis) or chronic EBV disease (CEBV) develop a subacute hepatitis. The liver is also one of the major powerhouses of the body and, when it is badly infected, disruption of both the metabolism and the immune system results, followed by fatigue, a main hallmark of CEBV disease, and depression. Thus, it is essential that the liver be treated.

But in order to understand and treat the liver, it is necessary to take a closer look at the frontline of immune defense: the blood. Since you began reading this chapter your body has created some four million new immune cells and hundreds of thousands of antibody molecules. Most are now coursing through your bloodstream. Such massive production may seem overzealous until you consider that, even if you are perfectly healthy, thousands of different viruses may be present in your blood, only about 10 percent of which have been identified.

The immune system exerts its control by virtue of circulating components capable of acting at sites far removed from their points of origin. The complexity of this system rivals that of the nervous system, and in fact the similarities between the two are quite real. It is no accident of nature that the thymus gland, the bone marrow, and the lymph nodes—all major centers of immunity—are bundled in ropes of nerve. The brain is known to transmit both electrical and chemical signals along nerves to stimulate and amplify immune responses to infection. As the signals stream out from the brain, they often pass warnings from the immune centers flying in the opposite direction. The immune system is not merely a tool manipulated by the brain; it is a sensory organ as well, transmitting chemical messages about bacteria, fungi, viruses, bits of dead tissue, and cancer cells, which seem to arise every day in everybody and must be disposed of. The wonder of it is that such organization is possible, as only a few distinct cell types, whose members are widely scattered throughout the body, are used.

Most immune cells originate in bone marrow, a soft, spongy material located at the centers of all major bones.

Under a microscope, the most easily identifiable of all the immune cells is the _macrophage_. Its nucleus (the part of the cell where DNA, the substance that directs all protein production, is contained) looks like a dark, horseshoe-shaped blob and occupies much of the space inside the cell. The cell itself is usually quite large when compared against other cells of the immune system. If you have ever played the Pac Man arcade game, you will have a good idea of what the macrophage does: it scavenges.

The macrophages develop from stem cells in the bone marrow and in their infancy are called _monocytes_. Monocytes become macrophages when they are released into the blood and migrate into tissues. They then mature into large, amoebalike eating machines. Local accumulations of macrophages in the body from a sort of network called the reticuloendothelial system (RES). Such accumulations are most prominent in the walls of the intestines, and in the nervous system, spleen, lungs, and connective tissue. The greatest concentration of RES is in the liver, where the macrophages are known as _Kupffer cells_ and play an active and important role in helping the liver clear viruses from the blood. Kupffer cells

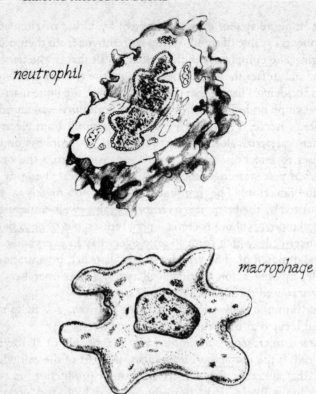

The cast of characters of your immune system all trace their roots to a highly versatile "stem cell" that resides in the bone marrow. It differentiates and matures into one of two types of early white blood cells (progenitor cells). These cells then mature into a cell of either the myeloid *series, which includes cells that are important for the allergic and inflammatory response, or into the* lymphoid *series, which is basically responsible for the immunologic response.*

comprise about 10 percent of the liver's total mass. Macrophages also accumulate in tissues that are injured or inflamed, such as arthritic joints. There they seek out infectious agents or irritants. Like the amoeba, the macrophage pushes out lobes or tentacles and surrounds the offending agent (or prey), bringing it into itself. Deep within the cell, enzymes are released. The prey is dismantled; its nutrients absorbed. After dining on a bacterium or fungus, or on a large clump of viruses tied together by antibodies (the macrophage is incapable of "seeing" individual virus particles and handles only those packaged into large clumps by other cells), the macrophage can "study" it, then transmit chemical alarms that resemble partial clones of the invasive agent. Other cells of the immune system pick up the "clones" and direct antibody production against any originals that might still be wandering about.

The level of organization in immune cells is astonishing when you stop to consider that they look and behave like free-living amoebae. Indeed, Lynn Margulis, a biologist specializing in primordial organisms at Yale University, has suggested that our white blood cells might not be entirely ours if we trace their evolutionary history back far enough. Small cells might simply have entered our forebears and stayed aboard to produce something new. If Margulis is right, we were colonized by strangers who, some billion years later, just happen to be working in our best interest.*

*Or is it the other way around? Perhaps we are here merely to serve the macrophages' interests by providing a warm place to live, dead cells and cancers to eat, and by attracting bacteria and fungi and viruses to add variety to their diet—even packaging them for easy consumption.

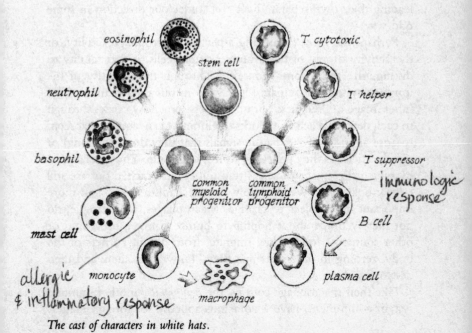

The cast of characters in white hats.

Such get-togethers seem to occur all the time. Termites, for example, are unable to digest cellulose and lignin, which make up the structural girders that give trees their woody texture and allow them to stand upright, on their own. The girders *can* be digested by certain amoebalike microbes to whom most of the termites' digestive system has been turned over. Without them the insects would starve to death. If an amoeboid becoming part of an insect does not sound very dramatic, then consider that one amoeboid species *(Mixotricha paradoxa)* living in a termite moves about on rows of undulating flagella that are actually bacteria harnessed to the surface of the cell (bacteria to which the flagella lining the cells in your throat bear a striking and possibly ancestral resemblance). Even more remarkable is the fact that the actual fermentation of cellulose is carried out, not by the amoeboid, but by several types of bacteria living inside *Mixotricha paradoxa*—a commune of once independent and unrelated organisms now organized within a single protozoan, which is itself part of a still larger organization.

The human body seems to be similarly built. Our macrophages and lymphocytes are like little animals crawling around inside of us, leading their own separate lives, yet under our direction in some odd way.

Perhaps the most fascinating aspect of macrophage activity, or the activity of any of the immune system cells, is their ability to distinguish "self" from "nonself." Through the integrity of the immune system we remain separate from our environment. This inner image of "self-ness" or uniqueness somehow carries through to each defensive cell as it works to eliminate cancer cells that seem to arise almost daily (radiating signals that they do not belong) or virus particles as they penetrate from the outside. The mechanisms by which this image of self is transmitted and carried out are still largely unknown. We do know the mechanisms exist, and more important, are subject to change. Macrophages, for example, do not merely mope about hoping to bump against a bacterium or other source of food. They migrate, from distant corners of the body, zeroing in on targets that they "know" are alien, and then destroying them.

Like their macrophage cousins, the neutrophils, another immune system component, have a voracious appetite for foreign matter.

But they do not congregate in the spleen and liver as do macrophages. They tend to remain in the blood, where they are far more numerous than macrophages. Their role in immune response, however, is not as important as that of macrophages. Their principal food source is viral antigen (protein)/antibody complexes. Their major role, then, is to get rid of virus particles that have been attacked by antibodies. Like macrophages, neutrophils seem to migrate purposefully to trouble spots, particularly sites of antigen production. When they destroy foreign antigens, they also exude biochemicals into the blood, which trigger local inflammation and summon other defensive cells to action (a prolonged neutrophil-induced inflammation can become arthritis).

Eosinophils are also amoeboid and tend to show up at sites of allergic reactions and parasitic infection. They are known to secrete histaminase and other enzymes and appear to protect self tissues from other immune elements, such as inflammatory chemicals released by neutrophils. They also have the ability to devour whatever originally caused the allergic reaction.

The surface of the _basophil_ cell is coated with special antibodies called IgE. The antibodies are actually receptors, and indeed they do stick out like millions of tiny antennae. If a foreign antigen bumps against the cell, and one of the cell's antennae happens to be an antibody against that antigen, the virus to which the antigen belongs will become bound to the antenna much like a key fitted into a lock. This triggers a myriad of reactions within the basophil, including the release of such allergic mediators as histamine, which cause the blood vessels to dilate, quickening the rate at which blood courses through them and allowing neutrophils and eosinophils to get to the trouble spot very rapidly, there to seek out other copies of the antigen that set off the alarm. The intensity of the response is directly proportional to the number of basophils encountering the same antigen.

The _mast cell_ is almost identical to the basophil except that it is located in the tissues and does not circulate in the blood. Mast cells are stationed wherever infectious agents from the outside are most likely to enter the body, particularly the linings of the respiratory and digestive tracts.

What each of these cells has in common is a "personal," one-on-

one relationship with the foreign element it is attacking.

There is yet another amoeboid element in the immune system: the B and T lymphocytes. These are a family of cells that conspire together primarily to produce antibodies.

Both B and T cells are produced in bone marrow, possibly from a common precursor. T cells are so called because an essential stage in their development takes place in the thymus gland. The thymus is perched behind the breast bone, above the heart. After migrating from the bone marrow to the thymus, T cells undergo differentiation as they seep down from the thymus' outer cortex toward its core. The differentiation or "training" process is apparently quite strenuous, for more than half of the T cells will die and be absorbed by other amoeboids before they can reenter the circulatory system. As the cells differentiate, new proteins can be detected on their surfaces. These are designated by the numbers one through eleven and correspond to the specialized function of any given, mature T cell. It is from these numbered proteins that such names as "T-4 lymphocyte"—which seems so mysterious in press reports about AIDS—are derived.

The T cells have many tasks, including the recognition of hundreds of millions of different antigens that may appear in the body. These must be continually sought out and destroyed to keep the blood clean. At any given moment, the thymus is preparing tens of millions of T cells. Although only a few of these cells may recognize any single antigen (say, the capsid antigen of a herpes class virus), the collective scouting force is so vast and diversified that almost every possible type of antigen will be recognized.

The grand master of all T cells is called the *helper T cell*, or *T-4 lymphocyte* (so designated because its surface is laced with protein no. 4). The T-4 lymphocyte carries no antibody weaponry. It directs other T cells (hence its name, "helper" T cell). According to the latest available evidence, T-4 works like this: A macrophage, having dined on, say, a *Klebsiella pneumoniae* bacterium, secretes a substance called *interleukin-1 (IL-1)*, which excites the T-4 cell. IL-1 also feeds back to the brain, which responds by raising the body's temperature, which further stimulates the immune system. Meanwhile, the excited T-4 cell releases lymphokine *interleukin-2* (IL-2), which stimulates other T cells to grow and divide, and also stimulates the *T-8 lymphocyte* (named after protein no. 8, but more popularly known as the *"killer" cell*). The T-8 cell dissolves a target's cell wall and then moves on, leaving the foreigner to "bleed to death." Without a cell wall, components within the cell become separated from each other and pass into the bloodstream. Potential targets may include an invading bacterium, the cells of transplanted organs, or the body's own cells if they are cancerous or virus-infected. In addition to activating the T-8 cells, T-4 cells secrete a protein messenger that causes B cells to stop reproducing and switch over to the antibody production mode.

Once stimulated by the T-4 cell, thousands of B cells will start making one kind of antibody, tailor-made for a specific target. Other B cells may transform into what are called *memory cells*. Their job is to forever keep a sort of antibody blueprint in wide circulation. If the offending organism should reappear, antibodies will not be far behind.

The antibodies themselves come in many different "flavors," able to match the flavors of antigens on the surfaces of cells and viruses. They melt holes in the cells. They simply bind to the viruses, producing antigen-antibody complexes large enough for neutrophils and macrophages to home in on.

As all of these things are happening, the excited T-4 lymphocyte also produces a substance called *interferon,* which regulates the extent and speed with which all of the above activities proceed. Interferons (yes, these come in different flavors, too) are produced by a variety of other cells in response to the presence of a virus. The T-4 flavor simply keeps the process rolling.* Other flavors keep macrophages at the site of infection, where they will clean up debris, including packages of antigen-antibody complexes. Interferons further stimulate B cell antibody production, enhance T-8 killer activity, and greatly slow growth of the body's own cells in the infected area (to limit the number of new host cells available for infection and also to impede the formation of tumors).

It all seems unbelievably complex, yet there is a wonderful

---

*Zinc supplements support this aspect of the immune system; 25 milligrams of an amino-chelated zinc supplement once a day is usually sufficient to maintain good health.

feeling of simplicity underlying the whole scheme. Nature has pulled miracles from a disarmingly small bag of tricks: a few variations on an amoeboid theme—and the result is new cells that communicate with each other in extraordinarily precise ways by sending out little chemical warning beacons. Macrophage here . . . have located infection . . . working on it . . . secrete IL-1 . . . wake up, T-4 . . . T-4 here . . . working on it . . . secrete IL-2 . . . wake up, T-8. Let the immune process go too far and in most cases the T-8 cells, made uncomfortable by an excess of certain biochemicals in their surroundings, will chime in with alarm bells of their own, expressed as secretions that suppress the activity of T-4 and B cells.

Yes, there *is* a simplicity to the whole scheme, and beauty, too, when we pause to consider that a thousand million years ago, when the brightest things on the planet were probably worms, simple creatures engulfed a whole lot of still simpler, amoeboid ones that have stayed on inside them, fusing with them, exchanging metabolic products and even DNA, yet remaining relatively unchanged ever since. Some of the amoeboids must have been parasites at first, but that kind of activity might have resulted in the eventual death of both amoeboid and host. Instead, those amoeboids that, by sheer chance, found themselves able to live inside the host—and by happy circumstance also preferred to eat incoming competitors rather than the flesh of the host—emerged suddenly into a world where a new way of living offered multiple advantages and, as such, became self-reinforcing. Look at the veins in your left hand, and think for a few seconds about the macrophages down there: cells that might originally have been nonself, yet now are orchestrated to defend self from nonself.

The orchestration of the immune system and its tendency to destroy is tied, in part, to the liver, a hive of B cell and macrophage activity. Viruses bound by B-cell–generated antigen-antibody complexes are adrift in the blood. Though rendered impotent by cages of antibodies, the dictates of human physiology are such that the only good virus is a dead virus (arguments about whether viruses are technically living or dead aside). The immune complexes are cleared from the body as blood flows through the liver's RES network (which, you may recall, is packed with macrophages,

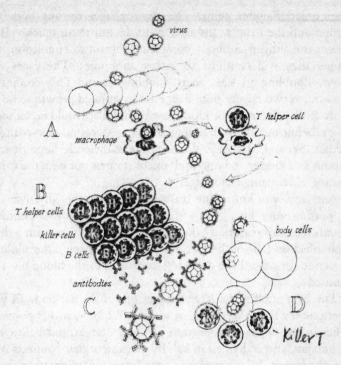

The Heat of the Battle

A) The *virons* penetrate the outer defenses of the body and attack the cells and tissues of the body. Some of the virons are trapped and consumed by the *macrophages*, which generate a code or message from their viral lunch and secrete *interleukin-1*, activating the *helper T cells* and alerting them to the invasion.

B) Once activated, the helper T cells begin to multiply, resulting in the release of *interleukin-2*, which in turn stimulates the production of still more helper T cells and also *killer T cells*. As their numbers increase, they release a substance called *B cell growth factor*, which stimulates the production of B cells and their differentiation into plasma cells—antibody factories (i.e., IgG, IgA, IgM, IgD, IgE).

C) The antibodies bind to the virons and create large complexes that are easy prey for the macrophages, which can recognize the virus in this form and destroy it.

D) The body cells that have been infested with the virons are attacked by the killer T cells, which sacrifice these cells, hopefully before they can be turned into virus factories.

here called Kupffer cells). The macrophages devour both the viruses and their cages, and they must devour them quickly. The longer the antigen-antibody complexes remain in circulation, the longer they will continue to gather antibodies. The cages will grow, doubling in size, then doubling again. This continued growth has two effects, both bad. First, continued growth removes more antibodies from the blood, antibodies that would better serve us by being out there, building new cages around free-roaming viruses. Second, if a cage should grow sufficiently large, it may deposit in a kidney and find itself unable to pass out with the urine, causing a permanent blockage.

And now you know one reason for having a healthy liver. By supporting your liver, you are in fact supporting your immune system. For this reason, if you happen to be suffering from a deep viral infection (any of the CFS viruses will do nicely), the addition of alcohol or other liver-shocking substances to the blood must be avoided.

The liver itself is the largest organ (gland) in the body (if you overlook the skin). Weighing in at about 1.2 kilograms (3 pounds), it lies in the upper right portion of the abdomen, just below the diaphragm, and is divided in half by a ligament that connects it to the diaphragm. It is shaped into four lobes and, allowed to sit on a table, would spread out, something like a large jellyfish removed from water. The liver is quite soft, containing very little connective tissue, and in fact is only 4 percent less fluid than blood. It manages to hold its shape only by virtue of a thin capsule that completely surrounds it.

Playing a role in virtually every aspect of the body's growth and maintenance, the liver is the only organ with a dual blood supply. A large blood vessel called the *portal vein* carries blood that has already passed through the capillary beds of the digestive tract. This blood is rich in nutrients but relatively poor in oxygen. A second vessel, called the *hepatic artery,* pipes in fresh, well-oxygenated blood. The liver is tunneled through and through with canals, ducts, and vessels, allowing it easy access to pumped-in nutrients and rapid discharge of bile and other toxic products.

The first thing you'll notice, if ever you find yourself looking at ultrathin slices of liver under a microscope, is that the canals form hexagonal patterns reminiscent of a honeycomb or of the arrangement of capsomeres on the geodesic sphere of the Epstein-Barr virus. Hexagons appear repeatedly in nature, in objects as diverse as the interlocking plates of a turtle's shell, the vascular structures of a tree, the facets of an insect's eye, or the organic molecules within a segment of DNA. The shape has become universal because, unlike circles, hexagons can be packed shoulder to shoulder to fill a space completely, without leaving wasteful holes between them. Unlike squares, they are structurally stable, resistant to external pressure, and not easily broken (especially when arranged in arrays). They maximize the area within their confines, permitting each facet of an insect's eye to collect the greatest amount of light, or each canal within the liver to transport the greatest volume of blood, with a minimum of building materials (protein) required. As with that first symbiosis between a Precambrian amoeboid and a wormlike host, nature tends to preserve optimal solutions to common problems and, if a single solution (such as a hexagonal array) can solve more than one problem, it will be fostered—very quickly and very widely. We should not be surprised, therefore, to find hexagons in our liver or in any other living thing.

In addition to being laced through with hexagons, the liver is the warmest and perhaps the most biochemically active organ in the body. It has an uncanny ability to regenerate itself and will grow back almost as good as new even if three quarters of it is cut out and tossed away (as can happen to you if you walk into the wrong bar on the wrong side of Eighty-fourth Street and say the wrong thing to the wrong people).

This regenerative ability was recognized thousands of years ago by the Greeks. According to mythology, the minor god Prometheus (whose statue adorns Rockefeller Center in New York City) stole fire from the sun god, Apollo, and brought it to humankind. For this Zeus had him chained to a rock and every day sent an eagle to peck out his liver, which grew back to its full size every night. Once freed, Prometheus brought to people the art of healing. (It's no accident that the words *liver* and *life* bear a common linguistic root.)

There are many things that can injure or inflame the liver, and the CFS viruses are right up there in the top ten. The inflammation is itself a source of the fatigue often associated with mononucleosis and CFS. Liver-based fatigue produces a terrible sense of lifelessness and a loss of will. With the sapping of the will comes impairment of the ability for forethought. Exhaustion can become so overmastering that getting out of bed to begin the day requires monumental effort, let alone planning ahead for next week.

With a troubled liver, even the intestines can go awry. *Bile* is a bitter substance that is manufactured in the liver from old red blood cells. The bile is piped through canals and ducts into the gallbladder, a sort of holding tank. The passage of food from the stomach into the small intestine stimulates the gallbladder to excrete bile, which in turn stimulates the rest of the digestive system. Thus a waste product, instead of being pushed out through the kidneys, is actually recycled to assist in the breakdown and absorption of nutrients.

If bile is not correctly produced and released, food will be only partly digested and absorbed. Interestingly, individuals who are active by nature or characterized by anger tend to have correspondingly increased production and flow of bile. Napoleon, the choleric little general who chose the domination of Europe as his goal in life, is said to have had such a powerful digestive system that several attempts to poison him failed.

If we compare the production of bile by the liver with the building up of *anabolic metabolism* (whereby more complex substances are synthesized from simpler ones), we glean an important insight. All systems, organs, and metabolic processes have highs and lows in their cycles called *circadian rhythms.* Some cycles are very rapid (brain waves). Others are very slow (the twenty-eight-day menstrual cycle). Somewhere in between, you will find cycles involving bile production and the anabolic process of *glycogenesis* (the building in the liver of a long-chain molecule—mostly carbon and hydrogen and therefore called a carbohydrate—from smaller molecules).

In most of us, glycogenesis is on the upswing and bile production on the downslide in late afternoon. The peaks and troughs cross paths at about 3:00 P.M., reversing direction in the evening and then recrossing at about 3:00 A.M. Your body is tuned to glycogenesis and liver repair during the hours of darkness. This is a time of increased blood flow through the liver and increased activity in liver-centered components of the immune system. The cycle is followed whether you happen to be awake or sleeping.

You can help your liver (and if you are suffering from CFS, you have sufficient motivation to help in any way you can) by trying to go to sleep as close as possible to 9:00 P.M. This will maximize the healing time for the liver by not diverting energy (that is, nutrients) and blood to other regions, in particular the muscles. We also advise against afternoon naps, for these will interfere with sleeping at night.

In spite of the almost constant state of tiredness that is the most prominent symptom of CFS, victims often have great difficulty falling asleep and staying asleep. Owing to CFS-associated liver problems, patients have a very sensitive digestive system. They are disturbed when bile production increases (after midnight) and tend to wake up near 3:00 A.M. There is an opportunity here to (pardon the cliché) kill two birds with one stone. About an hour before going to bed—around 8:00 P.M.—take 500 milligrams of calcium. (Calcium lactate is a particularly gentle and easily absorbed form.) The calcium does two things. First, it actually tends to inhibit reproduction of the Epstein-Barr virus. Second, it facilitates the balance of neurotransmitters, making sleep easier. (Mother knew what she was doing when she gave you a glass of warm milk at bedtime.)

We also recommend supplementing your diet with a 400 milligram dose of amino-chelated magnesium (magnesium orotate), best taken first thing in the morning. The magnesium will keep the calcium in balance, help prevent the formation of kidney stones,

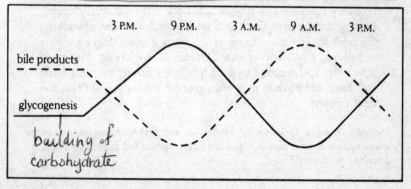

stimulate the gallbladder to release bile, and crank up your digestive system for the new day (this also has a detoxifying effect on the liver).*

The liver plays a leading role in the metabolism of three principal building blocks of the body: fat, carbohydrate, and protein. It also metabolizes and stores several vitamins (organic substances essential, in small quantities, in maintaining normal cell functioning and health). One of the more important vitamins, from our CFS perspective, is vitamin A, a fat-soluble substance essential to hormone metabolism and to the synthesis of certain proteins that augment the immune system. People suffering from Epstein-Barr disease are usually deficient in vitamin A, probably because the body uses up larger than normal amounts of it in the process of combating deep viral infections. Thus, CFS patients need more vitamin A in their diets than normal.

FROM THE DIARIES OF CHARLES R. PELLEGRINO
SEPTEMBER 28, 1987

I've become used to a diet rich in vegetables and fish. In fact, I've actually come to like it—though I am allowed that occasional steak or ice cream. About twice a year I succumb to "Big Mac attacks." And when I do eat steak, or pig out on a chocolate ice cream soda, I enjoy it much more than I used to. Even when I was at my weakest, such things were not strictly forbidden. I just ate them much less often, and savored them during the occasional splurge. Now that my illness has been tamed, I find myself still following the more sensible eating habits I developed during my recovery (there was a time when I ate red meat every night). During the therapy, the habits were simply a means of stacking the odds slightly more in my favor. Now it is no longer a matter of fighting EBV. It is strictly a matter of my having developed new tastes and wanting to do what little I can to keep my heart and liver and arteries in working order into the middle of the next century.

*Specific strategies to lessen the burden on the liver and support its various interactions with your metabolism, including a vitamin and mineral protocol, are described in chapter 7.

4

CANDIDA AND CANCER AND STREP—OH MY!: CHRONIC LONG-TERM COMPLICATIONS OF CFS

I could stay awake only two hours a day. If Charlie Pellegrino's four hours are any measure, then I had it twice as bad as he did. But I couldn't let this thing—this Epstein-Barr virus—kill me. I had all those books to write. And I beat it. I beat it! Now I'm back, you bastards!

—HARLAN ELLISON

It's a fascinating thing, when you come right down to it: the body at war with itself.

—CHARLES PELLEGRINO

PROVOCATION

Many of the viruses associated with CFS can, and often do, cause a transient immunodeficiency, characterized by a depleted B-cell population and bankrupted levels of immunoglobulins. The immune system will rise to the occasion by increasing the populations of certain T-cell types. The consequences of this sort of viral bloom, now frequently called chronic fatigue immune dysfunction syndrome,* differs markedly from an acquired immune deficiency syndrome (AIDS), in that AIDS is caused by the human immunodeficiency T-cell invading virus (HIV), which shifts the identity of its antigens so rapidly that the immune system cannot possibly keep up, and eventually wears down beyond recovery. In a case of CFS, we do not have to deal with a constantly shifting virus, though we may be working with an overtaxed immune system.

The immune systems of most CFS patients, given a little pampering (including the identification and removal of existing stressors or, at least, the avoidance of new ones), can be summoned to regroup, counterattack, and put the offending virus (or viruses) into remission or exile. If the patient is particularly stressed, and thus vulnerable, the deficiency may linger. What might have begun as, for example, an acute Epstein-Barr virus infection (mono), can become chronic active EBV disease. In this case the immune system can continue to disintegrate, leaving the patient susceptible to bacterial infection, particularly strep. Typically, this will cause recurrent bouts of tonsillitis and chronic sore throats. While strep itself is pathogenic (it can cause primary infection in most people), further deterioration of the immune system throws open the doors to opportunistic infections (those resulting from organisms that ordinarily do not cause primary disease). The main offenders in this group are yeasts, particularly *Candida albicans*. The *Candida* problems often cited in medical literature and popular books (for example, *The Yeast Connection* by Dr. William G. Crook, Vintage Books, 1987) are often the result of an underlying condition of CFS.

*For some reason, we Americans have a nasty habit of taking simple, easily understandable conditions and situations, then adding syllables until we drown all meaning in obscurity. Some say the habit began with the name of a condition known during World War I as "shell shock" (very straightforward). By World War II, shell shock had evolved into "battle fatigue," and by Vietnam, it achieved its most incomprehensible name, "post traumatic stress syndrome." With "plane crashes" now registered as "involuntary disassemblies of aircraft," with "civilian casualties" of war now reduced to "collateral damage," and the *"Challenger* explosion" to "the in-flight anomaly of STS-51L," does it really surprise anyone that a condition originally known as "Raggedy Ann syndrome" has become "chronic fatigue immune dysfunction syndrome," or that by the time it is through gathering syllables, merely attempting to pronounce its name may be all that is needed to bring on a case of chronic fatigue?

Hence, antifungal therapy aimed specifically at the yeast infection is, in many cases, a mere firebreak. You may temporarily remove the yeast infection, but you might have failed to deal with why the patient got the yeast infection in the first place, and thus it will return. The penultimate complication of prolonged active EBV is the production of random mitotic (cell division) processes, also known as cancer.

PENETRATION

EBV is a highly specialized parasite. It seems to strike humans exclusively, and its focus is the antibody-producing B cells of the immune system. It is as if the very cells with the task of destroying viruses actually entice the Epstein-Barr virus inside. As B cells carrying the viral genome begin manufacturing virus particles, the T lymphocytes try to stem the rising tide of nonself by secreting alphainterferon and suppressing the B-cell hosts. This is at best a questionable tactic, for it effectively weakens an already damaged immune system.

Sustained and deepening infection results in hyperproduction of T lymphocytes by the thymus, which in turn results in the release of many immature and atypical cells. In the latter case, the nucleus grows larger than normal and appears as a monocytoid (monocyte-like or resembling an immature macrophage), thus giving the name *mononucleosis* to the syndrome.

[margin handwriting: why mono is called mono]

The most benign of the secondary infections associated with CEBV is strep throat. The *Streptococcus* bacterium can establish an infection without the presence of EBV and is highly contagious. If strep throat occurs as a new layer of infection thrown on top of a chronic EBV infection, the usual symptoms of pus-covered tonsils and sore throat are amplified. In rare cases, an amplified strep infection can spread through the blood and lymphatic system to form abscesses in joints and internal organs. But as this is not likely to occur, the infection can, in most cases, be dealt with. Caution must be exercised in applying antibiotics, however, as they can actually have a suppressive effect on the immune system.

The fever that accompanies infection is in fact good for you (up to about 103°F, in any case). As noted in chapter 3, macrophages dining on foreign irritants secrete a substance called IL-1, which signals the brain to raise the body temperature, which further stimulates the immune system. This process should not be suppressed with antipyretic (fever-reducing) medicines, such as aspirin or Tylenol. If one has an acute infection (of strep, EBV, or anything else) unaccompanied by a fever, raising the body temperature from outside—by sitting in bathwater heated to 39.5°C (101–102°F) for 20 to 30 minutes, for example—can have a mild stimulatory effect on the immune response. If the strep infection is not completely pushed out, then a low-level chronic infection (called a carrier state), similar to chronic EBV disease, can occur. This represents a stalemate between the bacteria and the immune system.

CONTAMINATION

Under normal conditions, we can eat yeasts, inhale mold spores, and remain in perfectly good health. If, however, because of viral infection or some other stressful influence, the immune system is not hitting on all cylinders, one can become overly sensitive to yeasts (including the frothy yellow fungus used to make bread rise) or even be infected by them. Since *Candida albicans,* a common yeast species, is found living inside and outside the bodies of healthy people, the line between what is normal and what qualifies as infection is unclear.

Obviously, if you have yeast coating your tongue or if your blood is filled with it, if you are experiencing severe athlete's foot and irritating jock itch, you have crossed over the line to infection. However, yeasts can be subtle. Since *Candida* may be a "normal" inhabitant in healthy people, blood tests indicating its antibody titer are of little diagnostic value because they provide no element of perspective. Thus one needs a high index of suspicion and a broad spectrum of blood and stool tests to determine whether a patient is infected with yeast.

One likely candidate is a patient with an underlying viral infection. Another is a patient who has, for whatever reasons, been on cortisone or other immunosuppressive drugs, or one who has recently been subjected to broad-spectrum antibiotics (which first have a mild immunosuppressive effect and then, by killing many friendly bacteria lining the intestine, leave large surfaces open for yeasts—which are unaffected by antibiotics—to colonize). The research and case studies carefully documented by Dr. Crook in *The Yeast Connection* suggest that once the yeast fungus becomes established, it can trigger a self-reinforcing cycle. Yeast biochemicals can have a toxic, suppressive effect on the immune system even without an underlying dose of antibiotics or chronic virus. This, in turn, allows the yeast to flourish.

The diagnosis of a yeast problem is best determined by clinical evidence (symptoms). Since yeasts can suppress immune function, they may act as amplifiers of any underlying CFS symptoms, including fatigue, swollen glands, and sore throats. Specific yeast symptoms include obvious yeast infections of the mouth, groin, and feet. Other problems include significant digestive disorders, ranging from foul-smelling gas to bloating and abdominal pain.

Another important diagnostic tool if yeast infection is suspected is the patient's response to an antiyeast protocol; the simplest approach is a yeast-free diet (see chapter 7) combined with Nystatin. (Nystatin was first discovered by the New York State Department of Health Laboratories in Albany. Hence the name, NY-State-in.) This antifungal agent was isolated from a mold that was reportedly collected on a farm in Virginia. Initial and subsequent tests have shown Nystatin to be remarkably nontoxic, so there is minimal risk involved in taking it. Any adverse reaction is likely the result of too many yeasts dying too fast and putting a temporary toxic load on the body. By adhering to a yeast-free diet for a week prior to administration of Nystatin, the swelling and itching normally associated with yeast toxins can almost always be avoided. Nystatin powder, the prescription medicine made by the Lederle Pharmaceutical Company, is particularly pure and free of additives, as opposed to the liquid or tablet form. One generally begins by taking one-quarter of a teaspoon once per day, just to be on the safe side and to make sure the Nystatin is well tolerated. (The usual dose is a quarter of a teaspoon in a glass of water or fresh vegetable juice, four times a day.)

In some CFS cases, treating the secondary yeast infection removes enough stress from the immune system so that it is able to regroup and knock back the chronic viral infection. This is not normally the case, however, and a more specific program is usually required to deal with the primary virus infection.

Another common secondary CFS problem (and also a secondary yeast problem) is allergies. When everything is working properly, the immune system sends out antibodies to lock horns with potentially harmful intruders and put them out of action. During a chronic virus attack on the B cells, when everything is definitely not working properly, the eroded and confused immune system begins sending out antibodies against every possible irritant—even against such not-so-harmful intruders as pollen, even against self tissue. (Autoimmune syndromes commonly arise or, if already present, accelerate.) New and often unneeded legions of antibodies emerge in a frantic, desperate attempt to kill the virus and protect the body. Unfortunately, in this effort allergies against both environmental and food substances can develop literally overnight. Pollen, tobacco smoke, perfumes, detergents, diesel fumes, insecticides, shellfish, and milk can suddenly trigger swelling and nausea. The immune system goes after these substances as if they were viral antigens, even though a pollen grain or a molecule of floor cleaner is as inert as a fleck of stone and need not be caged and immobilized; the beleaguered body does not know any better and cages them anyway. The caged particles just stick there, as the body sends legion after legion of antibodies and white blood cells after them, like the Roman legions sent by the mad emperor Gaius (Caligula) to beat back the tide with their swords. But the tide can neither die nor give way to even the most sustained attack, and the nonviral intruders are caged and caged and caged. The tissues around them become swollen and red, as biochemical alarm bells sound chaotically, causing histamine vasoconstriction, neutrophil inflammations, and uneasy murmurs of interferon. There is coughing and sneezing, waves of mucus production, swollen itching eyes, shivering, and vomiting. Any or all of these symptoms will persist until the crabmeat or ragweed pollen or soap naturally flushes away. And because the immune system will remember them as irritants, the process will be repeated the next time the offending substances are ingested or inhaled, with the result that relatively harmless particles and the tissues that surround them pay the price that the offending virus should be paying, but to no avail.

In its last-ditch effort to knock out everything perceived as a threat, the immune system spreads itself thin and ultimately winds up weaker. In time the system may collapse completely, failing to respond to any provocation. This late CFS phase is known as *anergy*. The condition is revealed by skin scratch tests, using molds and other substances that most people have antibodies to. The anergic patient shows no skin reaction at all to these substances. The condition probably results from too many alarms, as the body's own tissues are injured and consumed by the very cells meant to protect them.

Such is the path of many CFS-causing viruses through the immune system: from initial confusion to hysteria to outright civil disorder, until at last the whole body is left defenseless.

EVOCATION

Even as you read, skin cells are dying and flaking away onto the page. Indeed, dead skin is the major constituent of dust in your home. At night, uncountable tens of thousands of microscopic, insectlike creatures share your bed with you, all of them uniquely adapted to feeding upon dead skin.* Every week your entire skin surface is shed and replaced. And that's not all. During the course of every meal, the entire lining of your mouth is washed down your throat and digested. Farther down the line, the intestines too are shedding cells. Roughly speaking, we lose about a soup bowl full of cells every day. And these must be replaced.

Your skin, your bone marrow, and other centers of cell growth continually make up for the loss. This amounts to millions—*billions*—of new cells. With so many throws of the dice, even without chemical and viral insults to the DNA, there must be at least a few misprints, mutants, and renegades. If you're looking for trouble, these are the local distributors. Nonself born of self, they are the basis of the ultimate identity crisis—cancer—and must be destroyed. And almost every day the body does destroy them. A cell

*We know of one invertebrate zoologist who considered submitting these creatures as dependents on his IRS tax form, but the thought of jail deterred him.

that ignores the group, marches to the beat of its own drummer, and threatens to establish an independent colony of endlessly self-replicating cells cannot be tolerated. If individualists are permitted to fulfill their own destiny, the colonies they establish will become tumors. Normal, healthy immune surveillance systems (natural killer cells [NK]) eliminate free-thinking cells as soon as they appear.* In the figurative sense, the body operates like a Communist dictatorship.

Many of the CFS-causing viruses not only weaken the surveillance system that guards against deviant cells, but are themselves oncogenic, meaning that under the right circumstances, they can create deviants and can cause several different varieties of cancer.

For years, epidemiologists have recognized a connection between the Epstein–Barr virus and a cancer that occurs in the pharynx and the back of the nose. Known as *nasopharyngeal carcinoma,* the condition is widespread in parts of China where EBV is normally contracted by very young children, almost without incident, and then remains latent throughout life. For some reason, cancer cells laced with virus particles sometimes appear spontaneously in later life, and nasopharyngeal cancer has begun to take the form of a growing epidemic in China.

Outside the human body researchers have been unable to incite normal human epithelial cells (skin cells) from the nasal passages and pharynx to become cancerous with application of the Epstein–Barr virus alone. As in the dual roles of malaria and EBV in Burkitt's lymphoma, some cofactor appears to be involved. The virus can harm you more efficiently with the collusion of a second or third destructive force.

In 1987, David Tomei and his colleagues at Ohio State University followed up on a study linking the geographic distribution of nasopharyngeal cancer with that of two families of phorbol ester–producing plants commonly used as herbal folk remedies in China. Phorbol esters from the plants were able to transform normal epithelial cells into cancer cells after the skin cells were exposed to

---

*It has often been noted that people with CFS will have abnormally low levels of NK cells.

EBV. Plant-derived esters alone lacked the power to transform cells; they required the presence of EBV.

Tomei notes:

> These results are compatible with current theories about the nature of carcinogenicity, in which an initiator (such as EBV) is thought to be potentiated by a "promoter" (such as phorbol ester). Unfortunately, the Chinese make hot tea from these ester-producing plants, and they spray the extract onto sore throats. So what you have is a folk remedy that has all the elements of tumor promotion in humans: spraying hot extracts of phorbol ester plants onto chronically inflamed tissue in an area where nearly everybody has Epstein-Barr virus.

throat cancer in China

Another means of EBV-associated tumor production has come to light. Organ transplantation has evolved from a highly experimental procedure to a commonplace one. Ordinarily, a healthy immune system will reject, in paranoid fashion, a transplanted heart or kidney despite the best intentions of the surgeon. The routine solution is to confuse the immune system, to make it unhealthy with powerful immunosuppressive drugs, and thus prevent an invasion force of white cells and antibodies from entering the transplanted organ. If the patient who receives the transplant has EBV in his blood (as people normally do) or if the transplanted tissue contains EBV (as in the case of David, the boy in the bubble), then taming the immune system with cortisone, prednisone, or other immunosuppressants will also prevent white cells and antibodies from subduing the virus. If EBV reactivates and flourishes without restraint, normal B cells can be transformed into "immortalized" B cells, and immortalized B cells may develop into B-cell lymphoma—which differs from Hodgkins' disease and other lymphomas in having a strong predilection for the central nervous system.

The list of CFS virus-associated cancers is growing. A casual relationship between the Epstein-Barr virus and a primary intracerebral lymphoma (an immune system cancer of the brain) is now suspected. EBV is also implicated in salivary gland cancers and thymic carcinoma (a particularly deadly cancer of the thymus gland). Researchers are presently looking at EBV-infected cells in more common cancers, such as those of the breast and colon, where it begins to look as if EBV may act as a copromoter. (Or does it just weaken the immune system enough to allow the cancer to take root?)

Epstein-Barr virus is not merely the bearer of "kissing sickness." Assisted by secondary viral insults, bacteria, fungi, protozoa, and environmental toxins, EBV may have a penetrating effect extending decades beyond the moment of first contact. With one out of every three Americans at risk of developing cancer in their lifetimes, the significance of EBV (and who knows how many other common viruses?) may be far greater than we have been led to believe.

5

FOOTPRINTS: THE DIAGNOSTIC DILEMMA

What rough beast, its hour come round at last, slouches towards Bethlehem to be born?

—WILLIAM BUTLER YEATS

It seems that diseases are getting harder to diagnose, or is it perhaps a reflection of the reluctance of the American medical system to face and acknowledge illnesses that, as of yet, can't be "conventionally" treated?

A decade ago, there was controversy and disinformation about a peculiar little virus with an insatiable appetite for T-4 lymphocytes. Only when the body bags started to mount and one or two Hollywood legends began to succumb did the lay press virtually force the medical establishment to come clean about what was really going on.

Depending on your perspective, people with CFS are either in a better or worse situation. Better, because the viruses associated with it don't usually have a lethal effect. Worse, because without aggressive diagnostic evaluations to clearly elucidate the affiliated immunologic and metabolic abnormalities, the symptoms and sufferers are often discounted as something akin to hysteria or malin-gering—thus creating the unneeded stress of disbelief from family members and work associates, compounded by the fact that most people with CFS don't "look" *that* sick.

Since the proclamation of the CFS criteria by the Centers for Disease Control in 1988 and the launching of controlled studies, including diagnostic protocols, in 1990, the medical profession had at least begun to formally and publicly acknowledge the existence and scope of the problem. As students of medical history, we believe that the illnesses of the future will be even more difficult to diagnose. They will further challenge our beliefs and understanding of how human physiology works and how pathology evolves. We believe that our understanding of the mind/body continuum will play a more crucial role in comprehending and conquering disease, even by the end of this century.

Currently, CFS ranks among the greatest diagnostic dilemmas of our time. You can't take a simple, routine throat culture, get it to grow in a petri dish, and look at it under the microscope. There is no animal model to match the cacophony of subjective symptoms that arise (animal-based research is a mainstay of our current medi-cal paradigm), thus adding to the perplexity. Presently, modern medicine does not proceed on clinical observation and experience alone but relies almost exclusively on objective laboratory data. Where CFS is concerned, it's hard to see the beast. Given the limitations of our present medical technology, we can only follow its footprints.

SOME NOTES OF A VIRUS WATCHER

Jesse Stoff comments: This chapter is intended primarily for the physician, although those of you who are either afflicted with this fascinating disease or just interested in learning more about it, will certainly be able to follow the discussion. (Physicians, please excuse the explanations of basic terms, which have been included for lay readers.) The rest of you are free to skip to chapter 6.

The principles and criteria for making and supporting a CFS diagnosis are based upon my clinical research with over sixteen hundred patients who had or have this disease. My results by and large reflect what other leading researchers have reported, but they differ in being tempered by a great deal more clinical experience than the limited number of patients (usually twenty-five or less) reported in previous studies. Making the diagnosis requires a high degree of skepticism. One must rule out other conditions (for example, lyme disease and leukemia) that might have some features in common with CFS.

I remember the process I went through in medical school during my physical diagnosis course. I spent many hours talking with patients, dutifully and uncritically recording all of their symptoms, hoping that some pattern or disease picture would jump out at me—a pattern that I could happily point out to my preceptor. Well, diagnosing CFS is very much the same process. It takes time to sort out and rule out all the other possibilities and to really understand what is going on. Diagnosing CFS is like using the Jones criteria to diagnose rheumatic fever: it's the constellation of signs and symptoms that counts, not just any one symptom or test.

It may be a matter of habit and personal preference, but I always start, after the initial introduction, by asking the patient, "What shall we discuss today?" I assume nothing, and give the patient an opportunity to tell me why he or she just traveled a thousand miles to attend our five-day CFS program. I don't lead and often don't say a thing; I just sit and quietly record the multitude of symptoms that the patient has to report. Then I often ask, "Anything else?" to be sure that nothing has been left out. Then I take it from the top:

- When did it all begin?
- Was anything special going on at the time, such as a job change, accident, other family illness, or divorce?
- Did you ever have these symptoms before, and if so, what was the diagnosis?

With a clearer picture of the beginning and course of the present illness, I ask about the patient's past medical history. In considering CFS, a history of mono, hepatitis, or a bad, long-lived "flu," of acute onset, may be revealing, especially if the person has never been well since. Family history of mono, CFS, or hepatitis may give me a clue in terms of close repetitive exposure. A family history of other infectious diseases, multiple allergies, anergy, asthma, and certain cancers may reveal some underlying immunological predisposition.

The patient's social history, including diet, is tremendously important. If one's diet or habits include taking various poisons into the body (alcohol, tobacco, recreational drugs, and the like), then one is clearly working with a weakened system since all of these factors are stressors. Current medications, or medications in the past, may also be significant (for example, prolonged and multiple antibiotic use, steroids, birth control pills, chemotherapy—each of which can have a suppressive effect on the immune system).

Having gathered this preliminary information, I go through a review of symptoms with the patient, looking for things he or she might have forgotten to tell me.

Since our topic of discussion is CFS, important things to look for are recurrent sore throats and/or swollen glands, frequent colds or other infections (including fungi and yeasts), and various hormonal imbalances (including thyroid, adrenal, pituitary, and ovarian dysfunction). I ask women about their periods. Are they regular? Are there any cramps or clots? Is there any swelling of their hands or ankles before, during, and/or after menstruation, or any abdominal bloating? Do they have marked irritability or depression before or during their periods? Do any specific symptoms occur with their periods, for example, headaches and indigestion? Have these symptoms occurred or changed since becoming ill? There is nothing particularly alarming or abnormal about any or all of these symptoms. There are many reasons why they can occur, but as I have said, it's the overall picture that's important. CFS patients commonly suffer from *hypoglycemia* (low blood sugar level). Many of the above-mentioned symptoms are indicative of hypoglycemia, a condition often most pronounced around the time of a woman's period. While hints of hypoglycemia alone do not necessarily point to CFS, if they occur alongside chronic sore throats, anemia, inflamed liver, and chronic fatigue, one might begin to suspect that blood tests, particularly for EBV, CMV, antibody titers, are called for.

Many of the viral agents associated with CFS have a profound effect on the liver (see chapter 7), causing inflammation and dysfunction. The liver has a very important role in regulating blood sugar levels. It works in concert with the pancreas, which manufactures and releases insulin in response to a rise in blood sugar. The insulin then brings down the sugar level. As the blood sugar drops, it's the pancreas's job to make glycogen, a substance that triggers the breakdown of the complex carbohydrate glycogen (manufactured by and stored in the liver) into glucose or blood sugar. The glucose then streams out into the blood, raising the sugar level again.   *hypoglycemia*

If a person's blood sugar is unstable, tending toward hypoglycemia, then there is a physiologic dysfunction of the liver—which is evident, to one degree or another, in almost all CFS patients. Symptoms of hypoglycemia include a significant loss of stamina one to one-and-a-half hours after meals, a craving for sugar or caffeine, sudden episodes of dizziness, lightheadedness and/or sweating, a rapid onset of fatigue in the midafternoon, and blurring of vision, often associated with a headache.

I find that CFS-associated symptoms are temporally related. They may all have appeared within a very short time, or more commonly, new ones will appear without the old ones disappearing.

Having reviewed the various systems and somatic symptoms, I then investigate the various functional levels for imbalances. These levels are very sensitive to psychological pressures and must be addressed as part of the overall therapeutic strategy.

To begin with, I ask patients about their overall level of energy. Is it stable or does it vary or cycle? In women, it often cycles in relation to their periods, with an energy drop commonly (for those with CEBV or CMV) occurring a few days before the period and lasting through it. It is important to know about the patient's stamina and how well he or she can maintain it, because any chronic disease that involves the respiratory tract and immune system, as does CFS, is going to lead to a marked decrease in stamina.

I've noticed a rather curious phenomenon that I find to be exaggerated in cases of CFS. To explain it, I'd like to characterize the patient's subjective experience of stamina (or energy) as either push or flow. What I mean by this is that many CFS sufferers find themselves having to expend a lot of effort to, say, push themselves out of bed and off to work, or to push themselves to a meeting, and so find themselves always feeling fatigued. However, at times when they are engaged in painting or playing the piano or in some hobby—something they consider to be fun, something they do with *enthusiasm*—the energy just seems to flow. Their stamina isn't necessarily any greater, but they are no longer pushing and they rarely seem to be conscious of making an effort. Doing something for fun with enthusiasm, daily, is healing. So go for it, but not to the point of exhaustion.

I've noticed something else, concerning exercise. When I mention exercise to CFS patients, the initial response (in more severe cases) is that they couldn't even think about it. However, if they enjoy a certain sport or, say, dancing, and I ask them about it, they will often respond in a positive way. Not only can many people with CFS play a favorite sport or dance, often for prolonged periods of time, but they actually feel better in some way after doing it. If the patient isn't severely ill, and if he or she is engaged in some physical activity, even quite strenuous activity, that he or she truly enjoys and does with enthusiasm, there often follows a short-term improvement, including decreased muscle and nerve pain and a general feeling of well-being again. (Just don't go to the point of exhaustion.)

In advanced cases, I'm lucky if the patient doesn't fall asleep in the office, but there are many patients in whom I have observed this phenomenon. Charlie Pellegrino is one of them.

Even when Charlie was so ill and dog-tired that he would go to his room shortly after lunch and sometimes sleep through a beautiful summer afternoon, he always seemed to have a purpose for every day. There were always projects: design studies for spacecraft, books to be written. Even at his sickest, he seemed to be tripping over new ideas every time he crawled out of bed. Charlie is one of those people who just pours out creation. I think it's what kept him going even against his most severe adversary.

I remember one fine afternoon in July 1985, when the illness was at its peak and we coaxed Charlie to the beach. Actually, he didn't take much coaxing. He wanted to build a sand castle. *Really* wanted to.

Sounds silly, doesn't it? First, let me explain what a sand castle is to Charlie. Sand *city* is more appropriate. On this particular July afternoon, Charlie began by digging a deep hole as the tide went out. I'm not into sand castles, but when I noticed, after about two or three hours, a large crowd of people gathered where Charlie had dug his hole, I went down to have a look. He must have transported hundreds of pounds of sand. The city stood all around him, looking like something out of *Lord of the Rings*. There were walls and ramparts, exquisitely sculptured. The buildings were tall and hollow, with bridges and archways connecting them. Some of the arches were so delicate that it seemed impossible that they could be holding their own against the force of gravity—yet there they were.

I was somewhat unprepared for the miracle before me—and I'm not talking about the sand castle, I'm talking about Charlie. I'd recently seen him so tired that his words slurred in the afternoon, and he was forever in danger of falling asleep somewhere on the Long Island Expressway between Brookhaven National Laboratory and Rockville Centre. I'd seen him barely able to lift a hand above the level of his shoulders, so bad was the pain. Yet his muscles now moved huge volumes of wet sand. No longer stiff, his hands raced agilely over the building he was creating. He worked as if in a trance. I don't think he noticed me standing there. I believe he scarcely noticed the crowd.

A few hours later, the sun was setting, the tide was turning back and the crowds had gone home for supper. Charlie finished, climbed out of the city, and stood up with not the slightest sign of pain. He seemed to be fully at peace with himself, and he breathed more freely.

We stood there for a long time, looking down at his creation. It was an unusual-looking thing. I knew it had been shaped by a human hand, yet somehow it didn't look that way. Overall, its construction had curiously biological overtones, as if it had grown there, rather than being built. In the center of the city was a deep pit. Two spiral staircases ran down to the bottom, where the water table was creeping up with the rising tide. In time, the walls of the pit began to slide down into the wash. Cracks appeared at the edges of the pit. Buildings plunged in, stirring up waves and further eroding the walls, causing more cracks to form.

"That's the way things come apart," Charlie explained, as he looked out across the crumbling city. "The center doesn't hold."

I suspect he was talking about the surge of Epstein-Barr virus inside of him as well, though I'll never know if he was aware of the parallel at the time.

As we drove home, Charlie seemed to be in particularly good spirits. We talked and laughed late into the night, and he did not appear fatigued at all. In the morning, however, the stiffness was back.

Instances of "flow" energy, such as Charlie experienced while building his sand city, appear in almost all patients, no matter how ill they are or what they are ill with. After questioning them about such instances and encouraging them to continue them, I move on to questions about memory. In the majority of CFS patients, I find a deficit in the function of short-term (recent) memory. Even if they are still working, at least part time, I find that their decreased ability to engage their short-term memory is very disturbing to them, and is often a major factor limiting their capacity to work.

Many people with CFS tell me that they are either always chilly or that they are generally more sensitive to the cold than they were before they got sick. In these people, I often find abnormalities in the adrenal and/or thyroid function tests. I'm sure this also accounts for the drop in energy level.

At this point in the interview, I usually ask about functional somatic abnormalities of the digestive, respiratory, and cardiovascular systems (that is, indigestion, gas, bloating, shortness of breath, wheezing, palpitations, etc.). As the liver becomes more and more inflamed, the patient's digestion often becomes irregular. I find it fairly common to hear complaints of abdominal pains one or two hours after eating, constipation, and funny tastes in the mouth. It's as if the whole digestive tract become slightly paralyzed, so that instead of being digested completely, food passes relatively intact through the system. Bacteria and yeasts can then act on it, producing gas and bloating. The heart and lungs also seem to be irritated by CFS-related viruses. Many of these organisms can cause a pneumonitis (inflammation of the lungs), pleuritis (inflammation of the lining of lungs), and pericarditis (inflammation of the membrane around the heart, as was seen in David's case). A less severe manifestation is difficulty in taking a deep breath or somewhat irregular breathing, symptoms patients often tell me about. Palpitations are likely to occur, and if they happen in response to a stressful event, they tend to continue for several hours beyond it.

I have mentioned that impairment of the ability to concentrate and think clearly often accompanies CFS. Because of, for example, the Epstein-Barr and Coxsackie viruses' predilection for nervous tissue, these symptoms are often the most disturbing, especially to patients who are professionals—a group who tend not to suffer in silence and are, therefore, CFS's most visible sufferers. (Their outcry has caused CFS to be erroneously dubbed "the Yuppie plague.") Patients have likened this aspect of the disease to a fog descending upon them, followed by a confusion of fleeting thoughts, none of them quite close enough to grasp and comprehend.

The emotional realm is often equally confused. Emotional lability (instability) tending toward depression is the most frequently described symptom in this area. Frustration and irritability, too, are common, and these are typically directed against those the victim feels most comfortable with—friends and family—rather than toward the world in general.

As we have seen in chapter 3, as the liver becomes more deeply involved, the sleep/wake cycle can be disturbed. Difficulties in falling asleep and staying asleep are common. Generally, sleep is much lighter than normal, often with lots of vivid dreaming in color. Curiously, patients with significant memory and concentration problems can often recall their dreams in astonishing detail.

This brings us to an important yet tricky part of the patient's history: self-image. Information on this is vital in order to formulate a specific approach to visualization therapy (more on this in chapter 10), which may prove very helpful. However, obtaining the information is tricky because you can't simply ask questions about self-image without the patient consciously coloring the response in some way. The information is about him or her in the most fundamental sense: *What kind of person are you and what do you really think of yourself?* I'll get to some specifics of diagnosing this in a moment, but first I want to say something about how to approach the patient.

To get this information in a meaningful way you need a focused, clear, calm, receptive mind. When you approach the patient it must be with an attitude of acceptance and love. You must accept people as they are, realizing that they are doing the best they can. Do not bring judgments, conditions, or expectations with you, but rather a respect for the inherent value of any human being. This will help you to approach the patient with a positive state of mind, so necessary in conveying a sense of hope, which is crucial in helping the patient to heal.

To enable you experience and develop this kind of openness or receptivity, let me describe a little exercise that I found to be quite helpful. I spent five minutes on this exercise, morning and night, for six months. I simply held an acorn in my hand, and for two or three minutes I examined it and dredged up every analytical fact that I could know about it. What color is it? How big? How much does it weigh? How is it shaped? What is its probable molecular composition? Did the carbon within actually come from the heart of a dying star? And so on. Then for two or three minutes I just allowed myself to be open to the awe, wonder, beauty, mystery, and power of life that it held within. I held in my hand a little parcel of DNA. If I planted it, it would reproduce itself with amazing rapidity throughout the structure of a tree. Charlie had told me that all the ropes of DNA contained in that tree, if laid end to end, would reach to the sun and back over three hundred times, yet they would occupy a total volume no bigger than an ice cube. It was quite a challenge, but very rewarding, to look at an acorn with a fresh eye every day. It renews your appreciation for the miracle of life on this planet. Try it!

Moving from the acorn to my patients, I look for several specific pieces of information that will be helpful in constructing a visualization therapy or in recommending a type of psychotherapy. The first two are general impressions about creativity and freedom. How creative are the patient's thought processes? When describing a pain, does the person point to a spot and say that it hurts, or does the patient say that every time a piece of bread is eaten, it is followed by a seething hell in the stomach that overflows like a volcano, releasing clouds of acid? The patient's description will probably be somewhere between these two extremes, but you get the idea. When I refer to the second piece of information—freedom—I am speaking about trying to get a sense of the extent to which this person can overcome momentary impulses and instincts. Acting on instinct and impulse is great in the jungle and is important in ensuring survival. However, in the workaday world of civilization, if one lives by sudden impulses, one often gets caught up in the details of the moment and loses perspective on life. Without perspective you can't see past the trees to the other side of the forest, which makes it difficult to set goals and thus find meaning to your life. Instead, things tend to disintegrate into a chaotic, stressful hustle and bustle, and one may become lost in the process. This is quite important to note, because in working with people with chronic diseases I do not merely intervene medically to reduce, suppress, or relieve symptoms. I also (and primarily) want to aid the patient in manifesting his or her maximum potential through personal growth and development. There is thus a humanistic goal to therapy. Through visualization techniques and psychotherapy, I try to guide the patient in mastering his life and himself. Not only does this have a powerful effect on the healing process, but the patient will emerge from the illness much healthier on all levels—mental, emotional, and physical—then he or she was before the illness.

Since CFS can affect all levels of human function, it presents a special opportunity for its victims, through the healing process, to actually re-create themselves and their lives. Illness becomes an opportunity to change. It is a challenge to cultivate one's fullest expression of love, creativity, and freedom from instincts and impulses. It is a chance to achieve harmony among our faculties of thinking, feeling, and the manifestation of the will, and thus to create an inner sense of balance and happiness. In designing a therapy for a disease, one designs a method for healthy living. If this method is maintained even after recovery, as evidence of the fact that previously unhealthful or unproductive activities have been changed, then the disease was not in vain, and the patient has had an opportunity to learn from illness. I think that if all physicians and patients realized this about disease and worked accordingly, there would be fewer relapses.

The remaining five pieces of information that I look for during the interview process, give me further insight into the person before me and provide clues as to where he or she may be stuck. Again, these are all points that, in order to achieve an accurate assessment, you have to discover intuitively and cannot ask about directly. Instead, you must pay close attention to the *quality* of the responses you receive to the matters you inquire about.

Point 1: Positive self-expectancy. By this I mean, does the patient have hope and optimism and does he live with gusto and enthusiasm? Or does he feel hopeless, lost and uncaring about his future, let alone his health?

2 -Point 2: Positive self-image. Where does she see herself heading, and how? Does she see herself as overcoming this illness and going ahead with life, or does she see herself as stuck, frustrated and with no way out?

3 - Point 3: Sense of positive self-control. Does this person take responsibility and act decisively, or does he always look for other people and external circumstances to blame? Placing blame on others and the environment bleeds away the impetus and motivation to change.

4 - Point 4: Positive self-esteem. Does this person project self-confidence and does she seem to have a sense of self-worth? Or does the patient seem to fear her own shadow?

5 - Point 5: Positive self-awareness. Empathy, openness and honesty are key characteristics to look for here.

These qualities are perhaps the most crucial elements of a patient's history. If patients are full of anger or guilt or hate, and not interested in looking at themselves to find out why, then there is little a physician can do. Negative mind-sets are powerful and are perhaps more destructive to one's health than smoking, alcohol, or drug abuse (any or all of which may be symptoms of self-hate).

First, we must encounter the individual, then we can address the disease. Taking a history and getting a sense of the person is the first step in formulating a diagnosis. Next comes a physical exam.

I don't intend to review physical examinations, but I do want to mention some of the findings that you may come across when CFS is suspected. Starting with the vital signs, the blood pressure will often average five to ten points lower than before the person became ill. Frequently the pulse will be faster and thinner. The temperature will usually average on the lower side of normal: 36–36.5°C (97.5–98°F), unless the patient is in the midst of a cyclic exacerbation, during which time a low-grade fever—37.5–38.5°C (99.5–101°F)—and an elevated pulse rate are common. Respiration is often slightly faster (14–16 breaths/minute), but is usually much shallower than before the patient got sick and may also have become somewhat irregular.

Working our way from head to toe, dark circles and bags under the eyes seem to underscore the fatigue the patient expresses. In the throat, tiny pinpoint hemorrhages testify to the war that rages there. The tonsils and the neck lymph nodes swell as more and more white blood cell legions are sent into battle.

All of the above are common findings during an acute exacerbation of CFS. As we work our way further down the body, the findings become less consistent. The lungs are generally clear unless the patient has pneumonitis—which fortunately is not very common. I have, however, seen three patients with an EBV pneumonitis that for all the world looked like a lymphoma on the chest X ray (which shows a patchy infiltrate with huge, swollen mediastinal lymph nodes). In these cases, an unproductive cough, accompanied by diffuse chest pain on deep inspiration, accompanied the pneumonitis. The heart is less likely to be directly affected, but, as mentioned earlier, a slightly higher than normal heart rate is common and, rarely, a pericarditis may occur.

The liver and spleen may swell and become tender. Diffuse bloating and mild abdominal tenderness are often found during all phases of CFS. Other common signs are diffuse myalgias and arthralgias (muscle and bone pain), which tend to be migratory. Even very mild exercise can trigger the pains and often they appear without any obvious provocation. There may be some swelling of the affected joints and trigger points (fibromyalgia) often occur.

During the more quiescent periods of the illness, the symptoms will not be quite so pronounced, but the patient does, in general, experience some combination of them.

With the exception of debilitating fatigue, no symptom shows up in 100 percent of CFS cases. In a case where no other symptoms are described and no other signs of illness are found in the physical exam (which would be highly unusual), the physician would then consider what other illnesses could manifest themselves primarily in fatigue. What follows is a list of some conditions to think about (and rule out) if CFS is not indicated and no other direction is gleaned from the history and physical:

    I. PSYCHOLOGIC
       A. Anxiety
       B. Depression
       C. Hypochondriasis
       D. Overwhelming psychoemotional stress
   II. ENDOCRINE—METABOLIC
       A. Hypothyroidism
       B. Diabetes mellitis
       C. Apathetic hyperthyroidism of the elderly
       D. Pituitary insufficiency
       E. Hyperparathyroidism or hypercalcemia
       F. Addison's disease
       G. Chronic renal failure
       H. Hepatocellular failure
  III. PHARMACOLOGIC
       A. Sleeping pills
       B. Antihypertensives
       C. Tranquilizers
       D. Antidepressants
       E. Alcoholism
       F. Illicit drug abuse
  IV. INFECTIOUS
       A. Subacute bacterial endocarditis
       B. Subacute hepatitis
       C. AIDS (HIV)
       D. Syphilis
       E. Lyme's disease
       F. Intestinal parasites
       G. Tuberculosis
       H. Cytomegalovirus
       I. Toxoplasmosis
       J. *Candida*—yeast infection
       K. Other virus infection
       L. Neuromuscular inflammation/disease

V. NEOPLASTIC—HEMATOLOGIC
  A. Occult malignancy (most commonly: breast, lung, colon cancer or leukemia/lymphoma)
  B. Severe anemia

VI. CARDIOPULMONARY
  A. Chronic congestive heart failure
  B. Chronic obstructive pulmonary disease

VII. IMMUNOLOGIC
  A. Systemic Lupus erythematosus (milder autoimmune syndrome)
  B. Hypogammaglobulinemia (genetically related)
  C. Subacute allergic reactions

VIII. TOXIN—POISONING
  A. Poisoning from heavy metals, pesticides, hydrocarbons, etc.
  B. Environmental illness

The laboratory workup is the third step in the information-gathering process.

As I have said, CFS is one of the diagnostic dilemmas of our time. It's hard to see the beast. One can only follow its footprints.

CFS weaves a path of destruction that generally runs through the body's immune system, striking primarily at the B cells. The B cells make the antibodies against everything, including the virus. If the infection is particularly severe, it disrupts the function of both the B cells and the T cells, clearing the path for *Candida* and other opportunistic infections.

The main diagnostic problem is that the blood tests currently being used to detect the virus are measuring the types and amounts of antibodies made by the B cells. The problem comes in three parts:

1. In the worst possible case (when you feel like you're going to die and sometimes you're afraid you won't), the content in the blood of antibodies against the virus is very low because of massive damage to the B cells.

2. In an intermediate situation, the antibody titers tend to be very high because large numbers of B cells are still alive and functioning.

3. In an early infection, the antibody factories are just coming into production and the titers are low.

If one looks only at the titers, the worst case is indistinguishable from an early infection. Charlie Pellegrino, in the summer of 1985, displayed one of the highest titers on record. He was probably at the border between an intermediate and a worst case, and more on the intermediate side of the line because the high titers themselves were an indication that his immune system was still at war (perhaps on the very edge of throwing in the towel, but still fighting neverthe-less). If the titers alone are considered, Charlie's case, in July 1985, could easily have been mistaken for a worst-possible case. How-ever, it could have gotten much worse. I have since seen patients with lower titers than Charlie, who suffer from the severest ravages of the disease, including cancer, multiple visceral ulcers, anegia, paralysis, and dementia. They are literally crawling with EBV and overwhelming yeast infections. What makes CFS particularly fasci-nating is that, as a worst-case patient begins to recover, the titers rise, almost to Charlie's extraordinary levels, before declining. In other words, if one looked only at the rising antibody titers and ignored the fact that the patient's symptoms were abating as the immune system kicked back into gear, one would guess from the blood charts that the patient was actually getting sicker, which is clearly not the case.

In diagnosing this disease, one must always look at a constella-tion of signs and symptoms, such as the history of the disease in the patient, physical findings (swollen lymph nodes, *Candida,* sudden onset of allergies to foods, etc.), and finally a series of laboratory tests, of which the antibody titer is only one piece of the puzzle.

Charts of the antibodies present in the different types of EBV disease follow, since they are perhaps the most difficult to interpret and understand. Moreover, EBV is a useful and relevant model because it appears to be chronically active in eighty percent of CFS patients. In the first case, we are looking at a simple positive/ negative profile for the most common manifestation of EBV, acute mononucleosis:

Antibody Type	Acute Mono	Normal Healing Six Months After Acute Mono
Heterophile	Positive (unless patient is Asian)	Negative
Anti-Viral Capsid Antibody (VCA)	Usually positive	Positive
Anti-Epstein-Barr Nuclear Antibody (EBNA)	Negative	Positive
Anti Early Antigen (EA)	Negative	Negative

If the patient can't beat the virus into complete remission, the virus can reemerge if the body is weakened by physical or mental stress. During the acute recurrent phase of EBV disease, the antibody positive/negative profile will appear as follows:

Antibody Type	Acute Recurrent EBV
Heterophile	Alternatively positive and negative
Anti-VCA	Positive
Anti-EBNA	Positive
Anti-EA	Positive

Finally, if the virus dominates and establishes a chronic infection, the antibody profile begins to reflect a progressive erosion of the immune response:

Antibody Type	CFS
Heterophile	Negative
Anti-VCA	Positive
Anti-EBNA	May be negative in severe illness
Anti-EA	Positive

Various diagnostic cutoff points of antibody titers have been arbitrarily used in the literature. By and large, these do not seem to be of help. The titers are but a snapshot of one particular moment in a disease process. If we put a whole series of titers, taken every few months, alongside the varying severity of the patient's symptoms, B-cell activity, antibody levels, alpha interferon level, and liver function tests (if originally abnormal), then the picture, which changes through time, looks like this:

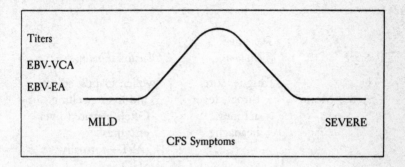

Titers

EBV-VCA

EBV-EA

MILD   SEVERE

CFS Symptoms

Since the rise and fall of the titers reflect the health and numbers of the B cells, the titers (amounts of antibodies made by the B cells) alone do not a diagnosis give.★

The antibodies to the Epstein–Barr virus nuclear antigen (that is, to viral DNA) that play a key role in putting the virus into remission and keeping it there can be almost undetectable, initially, in those who have been chronically ill for a long time. As the immune system recovers, these antibodies will appear and remain for several months (or even years) after the virus has been beaten back. Clearly, then, to assess improvement and the level of disease, other tests are needed to provide a fuller picture.

The spectrum of EBV disease may be correlated with other

★The implications and ramifications of the nuances of the viral titers can be challenging, to say the least. I send most of my patients' blood tests to one or the other of the two most progressive, innovative, and helpful labs in the country. These labs also store all unused blood for two months, which is a great convenience when I have a patient who has come to me from some distance. When I get the initial results back, I can call up the lab, add another test, and obtain a whole workup without having to keep drawing and sending more blood. It also allows me to be more selective when I order the tests, because I know that I have the luxury of considering the results and ordering more if I have to. The two labs are: National Reference Lab under Dr. B. Statland, 1-800-237-7904; and Specialty Labs under Dr. J. Peter, 1-800-421-7110.

laboratory tests (besides the specific viral titers) and described as stages.

The following criteria are most helpful in diagnosing CFS (after ruling out other possible diagnoses based on the patient's history, plus physical and laboratory findings).

Stage	Subjective Symptoms	Objective Findings
I Acute Mono	Fatigue, sore throat, fever, achiness, headache	Swollen glands, spleen and liver swelling. Often elevated liver enzymes (AST—formally SGOT)
II Acute Recurrent EBV	Cyclic recurrence of above symptoms	Cyclic recurrence of above findings
III Mild EBV-related CFS	Above symptoms remain	Above findings persist. C-reactive protein appears, indicating prolonged inflammation. Abnormal glucose tolerance test, indicating hypoglycemia
IV Moderately Severe EBV-related CFS	Recent memory begins to weaken. Concentration poor	RAST tests positive for multiple food and environmental allergies. Antinuclear antibodies may appear. Rheumatoid factor may be intermittently positive

Stage	Subjective Symptoms	Objective Findings

V
Severe EBV-
    related CFS
	Full-blown
	  symptoms.
	  Encephalitis,
	  Guillain-Barre
	  syndrome,
	  transverse
	  myelitis,
	  myocarditis,
	  pneumonitis,
	  hypo-
	  thyroidism,
	  pancreatitis,
	  diabetes
		Thyroid hormone T-4
		  decreasing. Thyroid
		  stimulating
		  hormone increases.
		  Allergy skin test
		  may fail to respond.
		  Anemia appears.
		  Immunoglobulin
		  production begins
		  to fail. Deficiency
		  of IgG subgroup 3
		  and/or 4 and IgA
		  subgroup 2 may
		  occur. T cells may
		  become abnormal,
		  with decreased
		  levels of T-4
		  helpers. Adrenal
		  function tests may
		  be abnormal. Serum
		  cortisol levels show
		  flattening of the
		  normal diurnal cycle

VI
End Stage
  Disease
	Associate cancers
	  may occur	

OTHER CRITERIA FOR CFS

SYMPTOM CRITERIA

To fulfill a symptom criterion, a symptom must have begun at or after the time of onset of increased fatigability, and must have persisted or recurred over a period of at least six months.

1. Mild fever—oral temperature between 37.5°C and 38.6°C—or chills
2. Sore throat
3. Painful axillary, anterior, or posterior (cervical) nodes   *neck*
4. Unexplained generalized muscle weakness, often worse premenstrually
5. Muscle discomfort, myalgia, or fibromyalgia trigger point
6. Prolonged (24 hours or greater) generalized fatigue after levels of exercise that would have been easily tolerated in the patient's premorbid state
7. New or different generalized headaches
8. Migratory arthralgia without joint swelling or redness
9. Neuropsychologic complaints (photophobia, transient visual scotomata, forgetfulness, excessive irritability, confusion, "brain fog," difficulty thinking, inability to concentrate, depression)
10. Sleep disturbance (hypersomnia or insomnia)
11. Description of the main symptom complex as initially developing over a few hours to a few days
12. Frequent findings include:

    (A) Depression (occurring since the onset of illness)
    (B) Recent onset of food and/or environment allergies/sensitivities
    (C) New onset of digestive disturbances
    (D) Increased sensitivity to temperature extremes
    (E) Recent onset of menstrual disturbance

PHYSICAL EXAMINATION CRITERIA

Physical criteria must be documented by a physician on at least two occasions, at least one month apart.

1. Low-grade fever—oral temperature between 37.5°C and 38.6°C, or rectal temperature between 37.8°C and 38.8°C
2. Nonexudative pharyngitis
3. Palpable or tender anterior or posterior cervical or axillary lymph nodes
4. Positive laboratory findings

The laboratory testing can be as varied and complex as the patients who present with the CFS symptoms. To begin with, all other reasonable causes for the malady must first be sought and eliminated. There are many ways to evaluate a patient's immune system, but rarely are all of the tests needed. The selection should reflect the severity of the presenting symptoms, tempered by clinical experience.

Let us begin with a couple of nonspecific tests for inflammation: ESR and CRP. Either one or both can be elevated with CFS. If it (or they) is, then this is a quick, cheap and easy pair of tests to use in monitoring the tide of the war within. More to the point, a lymphocyte enumeration panel will give us a lot of useful information. It will tell us how the B cells are faring. If their population is depleted, then some aggressive B-cell virus hunting is in order; likewise for T-cell populations and T-cell viruses. A frequent finding in CFS is an abnormal lowering of the activity of the natural killer cells (NK), which is significant since the job of these cells is to protect us from cancer, and/or an elevation of some T-cell populations. This inflammation, too, can be gleaned from the lymphocyte enumeration panel.

In the face of frequent colds/flus, sore throats and swollen glands, an evaluation of the functioning and activity of the immune system becomes important. As B cells are destroyed, the levels of the antibodies that they produce drops—which is why, for example, when EBV and human herpes virus 6 (HHV-6) are at their peak, the levels of antibodies against them may be low. Thus, much can be learned from monitoring IgG and IgA antibody levels (and specifically to measure their subclasses). Often in CFS, we find an abnormally low level of one or more of the subclasses, even if the total level of antibodies is within the normal range. As the B-cell virus(es) are beaten back, the levels of antibodies, both subclasses and total, will return to normal.

Another area where we commonly find suppression in the immune system is in the ability of the lymphocytes to replicate themselves and form clones and colonies. A sensitive measure of this ability can be derived using the single lymphocyte immune function (SLIF)* test. In response to all of this suppression, the immune

*DNA Science Labs 1-800-748-6800

lymph system system will frequently start pumping out high levels of lymphokines (alpha interferon, interleukin-1 and interleukin-2) in an effort to stimulate the B cells, macrophages, and T-lymphocytes. At this point, it appears that the lymphokines may have reached an optimum level for supporting the immune system. Too low a level leads to immunological impotence and too high a level can so overburden the immune system that it essentially begins tripping over itself, becoming oversensitized and of no more use than an underproductive system. A highly dysfunctional immune system can easily become confused and begin making antibodies against one's own tissues, leading to an autoimmune syndrome and/or disease. Antibody tests such as ANA and protein levels of C3 and C4 are helpful or, with a high index of suspicion, a full ANAlyzer panel* can point toward organs or systems that bear further evaluation and support.

Psychologically Psychodynamically, autoimmune syndromes seem to be associated with major issues of guilt, depression, and/or poor self-esteem.

Allergies typically occur to foods and/or environmental substances during the course of CFS. There are several different pathways that the immune system can follow in response to an allergen. *nuts pop eggs* All of the bases can be covered, including checking for some toxic substance reactions, by using an IgE level (adding more specific RAST tests to suspected triggers) and an Elisa/ACT† panel. Then you can deal with whatever shows up by avoidance, desensitization, short-term use of antihistamines or other supplement use to stabilize and stop the allergic response.

Stepping aside just a short distance from allergies, we encounter the whole subject of toxicology. Toxicological testing can be near to endless, but as a simple yet nonspecific place to begin, just to ascertain whether or not it is an issue for a patient, two simple urine tests are helpful. The D-Glucaric acid and Mercapturic acid** tests will provide a broad picture of how the liver and kidneys are handling various toxins. They are generally sensitive to three classes

*Specialty Labs 1-800-421-7110
†Serammune Lab 1-800-553-5472
**Doctor's Data 1-800-323-2784

THE DIAGNOSTIC DILEMMA   83

of substances: heavy metals (mercury, lead, etc.), organophosphates (pesticides—remember Alar?), or petrochemicals (solvents, hydrocarbon, paint thinners, etc.) The two acid tests are a start, and if the levels don't come down as the patient's health improves, then more specific testing may be in order to see why one's health may not be improving as fast as one would like.

There are many health care professionals who believe that health starts (or ends, as the case may be) in the colon. So if there are digestive disturbances, then a comprehensive digestive stool analysis with an ova and parasite (CDSA/OP)* test may be in order. This is a test that can easily and painlessly be conducted at home.

For some of those with CFS, the loss of memory and concentration can become excessive. Tests such as a BEAM-EEG or a SPECT scan can be useful in quantifying the amount of neurophysiological disruption that has occurred and can be a useful guide in cognitive restructuring therapy.

Last but not least and, one hopes, needless to mention, various viral antibody titer tests are called for. An EBV panel is a good place to start even if used as nothing more than a stress indicator. Nowadays, an HHV-6 test is usually worth conducting, as it often runs with Epstein–Barr virus-related CFS and can contribute greatly to headaches, loss of memory and concentration difficulties. If achiness is a particularly prominent feature then CMV and Coxsackie panels may be indicated if Lyme and arthritis tests are negative.

There are many more tests that can and, depending on the case, should be done to rule out other causes for the symptoms, but this battery is usually more than enough. Tests yielding abnormal, telltale results should be repeated periodically to monitor the healing process. Commonly, we will see the blood tests improve before there is actual clinical improvement in the patient's condition, as the immune system is still acting like an energy black hole. By monitoring the tests at approximately three month intervals (or one month intervals, depending on the severity of the condition), we can demonstrate that healing is occurring, help to bolster the patient's mood, and justify his sense of a positive expectation during the course of CFS.

*Great Smokies Diagnostic Lab 1-800-522-4762

Since the CFS-related viruses can affect the entire person (every organ and system is a potential target), then the entire patient must be considered in making the diagnosis. A checklist is a helpful but mechanical crutch in the practice of medicine. It tends to subconsciously limit diagnostic perspective and, if leaned on too heavily, may even blind the physician to a more humanistic approach to healing.

FROM THE DIARIES OF ELYSE GOODWIN
NOVEMBER 20, 1987

My experience with chronic fatigue syndrome began during the summer of 1985, when I was on vacation from a stressful job. For twelve years I'd been organizing music classes throughout the New York City school system. In addition, I gave private lessons after school, took classes of my own, and tried to maintain an active social life.

In July 1985, I took a vacation at my country house in Stockbridge, Massachusetts, where I played tennis for hours on end, swam, and relaxed. I never dreamed of what was to come. By August, when I should have been feeling rejuvenated after a month-long vacation, I was feeling more tired than ever and noticing a lack of enthusiasm for everything, including sex and food. I tried to ignore these symptoms and carry on, since I had always been the epitome of health and ambition, with mountains of energy and a determination to be successful, fulfilled in my work, and financially well off. I didn't know how to be sick. But by the end of August, I knew something was wrong and I decided to have a checkup and blood tests, hoping to pinpoint the problem.

My initial medical consultation was with an NYU Medical Center–affiliated internist who conducted a routine physical exam and (at my request) drew off some blood to determine whether or not I had a thyroid problem. His interpretation of the results was that everything was within normal ranges and nothing was wrong. I walked away feeling like a hypochondriac.

As the fall semester began, I went back to work feeling progressively worse. My chronic fatigue was soon accompanied by a feeling of being "spaced out," as if I were high on drugs.

Since I drove to work every day (thirty-five minutes each way), my experience on the highway became a daily nightmare. I was extremely tense and had to drive slowly, with my foot on the brake all the way home because that was the only way I could feel that I was in control of the moving car, but even then I had my doubts. At work, I was functioning on automatic pilot while experiencing problems with energy, decreased ability to concentrate, and a growing depression.

My first experience with complementary medicine began in October 1985, during a weekend in the country. After a full week of lower back pains that refused to go away no matter how much aspirin I took, I called a good friend whom I respect a great deal and knew to be a passionate believer in holistic health. I asked her where I could get help. She suggested that I see Dr. Jesse Stoff, a homeopathic M.D. in Great Barrington.

I made an appointment with him to have my thyroid checked; at least, that's what I thought I was making an appointment for. I saw him in early December 1985 and felt at once that I was in good hands. He had a wonderful laugh, but he was very serious about investigating my symptoms. He took notes and asked questions about my physical problems, and then went beyond them to questions about my dreams, my lifestyle, and emotional attitudes. He took blood tests and recommended nutritional supplements. When I returned two weeks later, he explained the test results and verified that my thyroid was no longer functioning at normal levels. He prescribed Armour thyroid pills and then further explained that my body was in fact producing antibodies against my thyroid. He suspected that one virus or another was at work, and explained that a further analysis of my blood might identify the beast.

By February 1986, a very abnormal response to EBV was verified. I let out a sigh of relief, knowing that my illness was a known reality and that information was available about it.

My initial reaction to the treatment was one of shock. I never dreamed that I'd be changing my eating habits and taking vitamin pills, along with extracts from strange plants with names like Echinacea. But then, I'd never dreamed of feeling so ill for so long. I was miserable and more than willing to try this, if there was a chance that it would help.

I was amazed at my progress. I thought I was going to feel

lousy for years, but little by little, I felt more like my old self and was able to gradually resume sports and social activities. Now, more than a year later, I feel great and have had no return of my symptoms.

And one thing strikes me as strange when I look back upon my illness: this experience has changed my life—changed it for the better. Through a combination of circumstances, I have left my job in New York City. I have made health practices my top priority, since without health nothing else really matters. I am living in the Berkshires four days a week, and I am planning to move here full time. I no longer push myself to work too hard. I am happy to take a break now and then, even if it means I will make less money. Epstein-Barr virus has taught me about the simplest joys in life—how very important they are.

6

STRESS: THE CAPACITY
TO ADAPT HAS BEEN EXCEEDED

Tending to a relative with Alzheimer's disease is not just psychologically stressful—over the long run, say researchers at Ohio State University College of Medicine in Columbus, it can undermine the caregiver's immune responses. Janice K. Kiecolt-Glaser and her colleagues compared 11 men and 23 women caring for family members with Alzheimer's disease with controls matched for age, sex and education. Subjects caring for an Alzheimer victim reported more distress and poorer mental health than individuals with no such responsibilities. Caregivers also had indications of poor immune function: lower percentages of T-lymphocytes and helper T-lymphocytes than controls, as well as a lower ratio of antibody-stimulating cells to antibody-suppressing cells. In addition, there was evidence of poorer immune system control of the latent Epstein-Barr virus among caregivers.

—SCIENCE NEWS, SEPTEMBER 12, 1987

Adrenal exhaustion could be caused by emotional tension, such as frustration or suppressed rage . . . the negative effects of the negative emotions on body chemistry. The inevitable question arose in my mind: what about the positive emotions? If negative emotions produce negative chemical changes in the body, wouldn't the positive emotions produce positive chemical changes? Is it possible that love, hope, faith, laughter, confidence and the will to live have therapeutic value? Do chemical changes occur only on the downside?

—NORMAN COUSINS, *ANATOMY OF AN ILLNESS*

WHEN YOU CAN'T SAY YES TO ANOTHER EXCESS

Stress is an interesting and elusive subject. The difficulty in studying it arises from trying to distinguish between the stressor (the event) and the stress (a harmful internal response to the event).

Most of us tend to believe that a man who pumps gas in a small, peaceful Massachusetts town is not under stress, and that one who works on Wall Street is. Boy, are we wrong!

There is a CFS patient who pumps gas in rural Massachusetts, and he is one of the most stressed-out people you will ever meet. He is an artist who spends most of his time trying to support his family. There is very little time left over for his artwork, and this frustrates him. By the time he sought medical attention, he had dug quite a hole for himself—literally: he had a stomach ulcer. At that point, even when he found time to paint, he couldn't, because he was so ill and bitter about his predicament. And yet he lives in a place that city dwellers dream of escaping to.

If you've ever spent a day on the floor of the Stock Exchange, you can see immediately why many people would like to be living in the country, pumping gas, spending quiet days with friends and family, and painting a picture now and then. The Exchange is a zoo! There are people running everywhere, yelling back and forth to each other. It's so noisy and chaotic that many of the traders don't even try to yell. Instead, they've adopted a complex series of hand signals to communicate back and forth across the room. Pieces of paper cover the floor. Electronic monitors flash information at you, seemingly from every direction. Yellers and hand-signalers sometimes appear on the verge of seizure. Hundreds of time clocks punch down simultaneously on trade tickets. People wearing different-colored coats and badges threaten to run you over if you happen to be standing in their way as they hurry to record a trade. This place would not seem to be conducive to quiet meditation. Yet you'll notice a few people who are very much outside the pandemonium, untouched by it even as it surrounds them. We recall one fellow who sat very calmly in the lounge area just outside the big room. He smoked a pipe and watched numbers and symbols shooting across a monitor. Every few minutes he got up to punch some keys on the quotron to find out how a particular stock was doing. Finally, when everything seemed right, he walked onto the floor, joking with some of the harried traders that he passed. As if merely selecting food from a menu, he made his trade. Then he walked back to his chair in the lounge.

By the time the Exchange closed, he had made $380,000 on that trade. He told us that he didn't always do as well and that sometimes he even lost money, but he was right on the majority of the trades. He explained that there were weeks when he would make only one trade. At times he actually found it boring, but he was happy and content with his work. He had clearly put the mayhem and the financial risks into perspective, balancing them with the rest of his life.

So why is it that in an apparently tranquil setting, one man is eating himself up while in the middle of an electronic monetary jungle, where one wrong move can mean debt forever, another man sits content and happy?

What is the difference?

Stress- the capacity to adapt has been exceeded

What is stress?

Let us begin with some definitions. Stress is an often used and often misunderstood term. Physiologically, stress is the state produced within an organism in response to a demand made upon it that requires some readjustment or adaptation. Since circumstances and the environment are always changing, we are always under some stress. From a clinical perspective, stress may be defined as the internal state that results when the capacity to adapt to what is has been exceeded. This definition is the more useful of the two, and will be what we mean when we refer to stress. *STRESS*

During the course of our lives, we are all exposed to changing circumstances. Those circumstances may be physical (a car accident), emotional (a loud disagreement with your spouse), or mental (a job deadline). If we accept a new circumstance, deal with it, and move quickly toward our goals in life (assuming we are lucky enough to have goals—a lack of them can also lead to stress), then all is well. But if we don't move, if we feel stuck and become in some way overwhelmed by circumstances, then an internal state of stress results.

The internal state of stress may be described subjectively and physiologically.

Subjectively, because of how our nervous systems are constructed, there are two possible responses to stress. The less common of the two is what Dr. Phil Nuernberger, director of the Himalayan Institute, calls the possum response. Some people respond to a threat by passively withdrawing. Metaphorically, they just roll over and play dead. Their response to fear is inhibition and a decrease of all physiologic functions, loss of muscle tone, mental lassitude, and eventually depression. In this response, the body's biochemical arsenal remains untouched. The more common reaction to stress is that of stimulation—often called the fight or flight response. We are activated and prepared to either fight the stressor or to flee from it. This response mobilizes all of the body's systems and resources, but if sustained for a long period, results in overload and burnout. Stress, then, can be further defined as an internal state of imbalance, disease, or unhappiness. This state may lead to impaired physiological and/or cognitive functioning. What can cause the initial internal imbalance that prevents us from dealing with circumstances in a healthful way?

Disasters, whether natural or man-made, can come without warning and are often outside our control, yet they do not themselves cause stress. We carry with us various attitudes, thoughts, and beliefs that mold our emotional response to disaster. Our emotional response, in turn, dictates the physiological response of the body. By controlling the emotional response and thus the physical response, we can avoid the negative effects of stress.

There are several ways in which we can respond to the multitude of events around us, and the method we choose will dictate how much stress we generate for ourselves. If we respond inappropriately, we create a dire state of imbalance (or confusion) within us.

To a society, the potential toll of stress is large. To individuals, the cost can be lethal. Consider the following:

Cardiovascular disease is responsible for one million deaths per year in the United States, amounting to 54.8 percent of deaths from all causes. About forty-two million Americans have high blood pressure. Americans consume nearly fifteen tons of aspirin per day. One out of every six Americans takes some form of tranquilizer regularly. The most prescribed drug in the United States is Valium; the second most prescribed is Librium. A conservative estimate is that 10 percent of the work force can be labeled as either alcoholic or as problem drinkers, and that one out of every twenty drivers on the road is impaired by alcohol or some other drug. Alcoholism costs $13 billion annually for health and medical costs, and $20 billion for lost production costs. Last year Americans spent some $200 billion—more than twenty times NASA's budget—on cocaine (and that's only one of many recreational drugs).

Right . . . our responses to events should be chosen carefully. There are four main ways of responding:

1. We _surrender_ to the flow of circumstances (life) fatalistically. The oceans of the world have no choice but to surrender to the pull of the moon and to rise in a tide. The ocean cannot influence the moon, merely respond to it.
2. We _ignore_ life as we pass through it, until an accident makes us conscious of our circumstances.
3. We attempt to _resist,_ which often wastes energy and fuels stress.
4. We _use_ our circumstances to help us achieve our goals.

WHEN ILLUSIONS FALL

People often enter into marriage foolishly, expecting the person they love to be the same person four or five decades later, a little grayer, perhaps, and a little the worse for wear and tear, but still the same in all essentials. Ten years later they end up in divorce court, pointing accusing fingers at each other. "He changed!" she says, and "She changed!" he says—as if change were the most unexpected thing in the world, which it is not. If a relationship with a spouse, a parent, a child, or a friend is to endure, change must be expected, even encouraged.

We cannot chain someone down and expect him to remain the same forever. We should be surprised at ourselves, considering how often we do this. What we expect of our politicians is a common reminder. If a congresswoman learns more about a certain subject and, as a result, reverses her stance on a key issue, we call her inconsistent. But consistency of thought, it's been pointed out, is the hobgoblin of small minds.

What many of us perceive, and occasionally try to instill as a sense of stability and predictability in our lives, is merely an illusion, albeit a stubborn one.

Putting aside our desire for permanence and accepting the inevitability of change will dissipate stress and augment health. We must have the courage to trust ourselves as we participate in the parade of life that marches over this planet. We need creativity to find ways to draw from and learn from every circumstance. If you were unsatisfied with the changes in a loved one, or they were unsatisfied with the changes they saw in you and, in the end, you lost each other, nothing good can come from mourning endlessly about the loss. Good can come only from looking honestly at what went wrong, and trying to avoid those same mistakes next time. You may very well make new mistakes, but it is not making mistakes that limits the extent to which we can be happy, it is the frequency with which we make the same mistakes. We must seriously approach misfortune with the desire to discover what we can learn from it in order to make our future happier. As Ann Landers (who has probably had more impact on two generations of Americans than any other single voice) is so fond of saying, "When life gives you lemons, make lemonade." It may be cliché, but it's good medicine for stress reduction.

WHEN THE LIST MAKES YOU SICK

Now, let us consider what causes stress. There are two ways of looking at this subject. Classically, there is an approach to rating stress developed by psychologists Thomas Holmes and Richard Rahe. As a result of their work with people under a wide range of stresses (including the death of a spouse and changing jobs) who appeared to be suffering from high blood pressure, heart disease, ulcers, and other varieties of physical deterioration, they were able to construct a stress scale. What they learned was that different events or changes (either positive or negative) trigger different grades of stress in most people.

You can rate the stress potential in your own life by running down the list and checking off the values for the stressors that apply to you. Think back over the last twenty-four months.

There is a second way to consider the effects of circumstances or stressors. For more than five thousand years the Chinese have spoken about the circulation of what might be called the "doing-willing" energy of the body. They have described pathways or meridians to indicate where this energy may be felt and influenced. According to Chinese practice (as with the acorn exercise described in the previous chapter), anyone can train himself to feel the warmth or tingling of this so-called energy at the acupuncture points, which lie on the meridians. Theoretically, negative emotions (guilt, anger, fear, worry, etc.) put a "crimp" in the circulation of this energy, creating areas where the energy backs up and causes pressure or tension. Eventually the tension can build up to a point where it causes pain, first psychologically, and ultimately, if not corrected, physically. The more energy we have circulating in our bodies, the faster it can back up and enter our physical consciousness. Most of us therefore find ways to bleed off some of the tension so as not to feed the pressure around the crimps. This can be accomplished via any method that deadens our energy. Various chemicals fit the bill, such as nicotine, alcohol, and other recreational drugs. Foods such as deep-fried potatoes and refined white sugar, exercise past the point of exhaustion, or Olympic sex will produce the sought-after deadening effect. The extra energy required to move a very obese body, too, will sap the living energy. By killing off some of our life force, we reduce tension around the crimps in our energy flow. These techniques quickly become addictive, because they deaden our inner awareness that something is dreadfully wrong.

Since such methods, in effect, kill us a little bit each time we indulge in them, they are a very insidious form of stress "reduction" that can ultimately decrease not only the quality of life, but the quantity. In accordance with Chinese philosophy, the way to deal with addictive behavior, and thus avoid dying by inches, is to

Life Event	Value	Your Score
Death of spouse	100	_____
Divorce	73	_____
Marital separation	65	_____
Jail term	63	_____
Death of a close family member	63	_____
Personal injury or illness	53	_____
Marriage	50	_____
Fired at work	47	_____
Marital reconciliation	45	_____
Retirement	45	_____
Change in health of family member	44	_____
Pregnancy	40	_____
Sex difficulties	39	_____
Gain of new family member	39	_____
Business adjustment	39	_____
Change in financial state	38	_____
Death of a close friend	37	_____
Change to a different line of work	36	_____
Change in number of arguments with spouse	35	_____
Mortgage over one year's net salary	31	_____
Foreclosure of mortgage or loan	30	_____
Change in responsibilities at work	29	_____
Son or daughter leaving home	29	_____
Trouble with in-laws	29	_____
Outstanding personal achievement	28	_____
Spouse begins or stops work	26	_____
Begin or end school	26	_____
Change in living conditions	25	_____
Revision of personal habits	24	_____
Trouble with boss	23	_____
Change in work hours or conditions	20	_____
Change in residence	20	_____
Change in schools	20	_____
Change in recreation	19	_____
Change in church activities	19	_____
Change in social activities	18	_____
Mortgage or loan less than one year's net salary	17	_____

Life Event	Value	Your Score
Change in sleeping habits	16	____
Change in number of family get-togethers	15	____
Change in eating habits	15	____
Vacation	13	____
Christmas	12	____
Minor violations of the law	11	____
Enter your total here		____

If your total is over 300, then you have an 80 percent probability of a serious change in your health within the next year.

go after the cause of the crimp and uncrimp it. This allows energy to flow, reducing the pressure from back-up and creating an inner sense of balance. We saw an example of this in chapter 5 when one Charlie Pellegrino built a city of sand and became so engrossed in the work that all the pain and tiredness seemed to go out of bones and muscles. For one afternoon there was no trace of illness, though the illness was at its peak.

Before we examine specific ways to uncrimp the blockage and induce energy flow (as we will in chapter 9), it is important to understand that stress, and blockage of energy, can be self-inflicted. In addition to the Holmes-Rahe scale of externally identifiable stressors, recreational drug abuse (the term "recreational drug," as used in this book, refers to mood-altering substances ranging from nicotine to alcohol and cocaine) and physical self-abuse are powerful internal stressors that act to weaken the body. Many people, among them CFS sufferers, complain to physicians of fatigue on one hand while clearly adopting behaviors that drain them on the other. We must ask such people, if they complain of a lack of energy, why they want more energy. What would they do with it? If one has a strong sense of purpose, such as raising a child, writing books, creating works of art, or helping other people, this is an easy question. But there are a lot of people walking around who hate their jobs, hate their families, and who even hate themselves. In an attempt to escape, that is, to become less conscious of their lives, they turn to chemical or physical self-abuse to reduce their energy.* As energy levels drop, the immune system weakens and the Epstein-Barr virus (or some other disease) appears. Illness is often a socially acceptable way of becoming a hermit and trying to ignore life. In order to discover a possible psychological underpinning for sickness, there are several difficult questions that anyone suffering from CFS, or any other chronic disease, should ask themselves:

- Am I using my illness to get the care and attention that I felt I deserved and wasn't getting?
- Do I enjoy not having to deal with people and situations I dislike, such as my job?
- Am I using my illness to avoid the possibility of failure, or even success?
- Do I feel sorry for myself as a victim?

If you are ill and can answer "yes" to any of the above questions, then you have a decision to face. You have to decide that you really want to be well. Before we proceed any further, the power to make this decision should not be misinterpreted in any way as blaming the victim. For a start, not all CFS patients—indeed, probably only a small number of them—have as a primary immune system stressor their emotional environment, and consequently a greater opportunity for control over an eventual recovery than, say, a patient whose primary stressor is a genetically-linked autoimmune disease or some past overexposure to a toxin in the workplace.

On a cellular level, we have defined (stress) as an instance of energy being expended faster than it is replenished by the body in which the cell is embedded. To the individual cell, it matters not whether a person is stressed because of lupus, excess exposure to mercury or radiation, excess consumption of sugar and caffeine, or hatred of a boring job. All the cell knows is that its energy resources are being depleted, therefore decreasing its capacity to adapt.

In today's environment, the residue of carbon-burning unloaded

*Almost everyone we know who has developed a chronic drug or alcohol problem will admit that they did so because they really did not like themselves. They also describe their binges as an attempt to get as close as possible to unconsciousness without passing out, and to sustain that state of mind indefinitely.

pollution
&

into the air we breathe may very well be as great a stressor (or even a greater one, depending upon where you live), than an unhealthy diet. Like the individual cell in an overstressed body, those who live beneath mile-deep lenses of filth can do little except try to adapt—at least until new solar-collecting technologies eventually remove the atmospheric stressors. In parts of Manhattan, the air is laced with asbestos particles from automobile brake shoes. None of the automobile engines or power plants that burn petroleum do so with 100 percent efficiency, meaning that in addition to lead and oxidized gasoline, microdroplets of unburned petroleum and partially fried carbon products enter our lungs, ride into our bloodstreams and slick our skin. They come down with every rain and wash into the lakes and rivers from which most of our drinking water is drawn, water often used to wash down meals rich in wheat products, which are usually contaminated by mercury-bearing fungicides.

While we can reduce some environmental stressors with changes in eating habits, we simply cannot avoid breathing. So if you answered "yes" to one or more of the questions above, view this merely as an opportunity to reduce yet another source of stress. A yes answer is no cause to blame yourself or to run about beating yourself up any further. Quite the opposite: it is a signal that you should *stop* beating yourself up. Do not under any circumstances adopt the belief, based upon an honest yes, that you have created the disease. At worst you have only created an emotional environment which supports a disease that in all probability would have developed anyway. Correcting that emotional environment, much like eliminating certain dietary habits, will simply push you a little further up that hill toward recovery. The push may amount to "only" a 5 percent tipping of the odds in your favor. If this does not sound very significant, consider how you would feel about a 5 percent increase in your rent or mortgage payments. Five percent can amount to an awful lot. (If your emotional state is such that you really do believe no one in this world even knows you exist, or cares, just try missing a couple of rent or mortgage payments.)

Again, if you are able to answer yes to any of the four questions, the decision to be made is: Do you really want to be well? Why do you want to be well? What will you do with the rest of your life when you are well?

You will not find the answers to these questions in this book or in any other book. You can, however, find signposts. The acorn exercise (chapter 5) is a signpost, an indication of a process that would probably be helpful to follow. In the chapters that follow, others will be glimpsed. But the answers themselves must come from you. Without a central purpose or goal to your life, it is easy to become lost, unbalanced, and overstressed. People without purpose often feel like rudderless ships with the engines burning at full steam. Without purpose, a feeling of being trapped can set in despite seemingly infinite options in every direction. Without a rudder, it is easy to fall prey to petty worries, fears, and self-doubts, which often lead to failure, depression, disease, and/or addictive behavior. Until your rudder becomes a strong and sure guide, it is a helpful exercise (in terms of stress reduction without energy loss) to focus your thoughts upon the faultless performance of a task immediately at hand (such as a school term paper or a project for the home), even if the task may seem rather insignificant at the time. By learning to gather and focus your thoughts, your resolution and energy can be developed. Having accomplished this, you will find that there is little else that cannot be accomplished. (P.S. This is another signpost.)

When you seek purpose and direction, consider this: you don't have to have the aspirations of a Lee Iococca. Probably no one has the opportunity to do more good for the world in a single year than the average schoolteacher, nurse, or firefighter. One proof of the impact that a few very special teachers can have (especially when added to the example of very special parents) is the existence of this book. You see, both of us had severe reading disabilities.

We are sure that, at the time, the task of teaching a troubled boy how to read must have seemed tedious, if not downright insignificant. But our teachers and our parents had a clear purpose and direction in mind.

Lucky us.

WHEN CARDS AND ACORNS FALL

Did you ever build a house of cards? If not, let us briefly explain the process to you. First, you need a deck of new, perfectly flat, unbent cards. Stand the cards on end, at sharp angles to one another, laying cards across the top to brace the first level of cards and hold them upright. Do the same with the second and third levels of cards, expanding as much as you want, depending on how many decks you happen to have with you. It's just one more thing to do in a quiet New England emergency room, at three in the morning, with three feet of snow outside.

It is probably worth your trying to build a simple two-level house of cards once just so you can experience what we are talking about. What we are going to say about the nature of humans is based upon observation and direct experience, not some vague metaphysical philosophy. In many ways a house of cards is an excellent analogy for human nature and the function of humans. The lower, upright level of cards supports the layer of cards lying flat on it, while these in turn give structure and function to the lower cards, keeping them in place. The balance is based on a certain amount of tension, yet there is a flow to the entire form. If we introduce a sudden change (say, a sneeze), then a new balance must be found or the house may collapse.

Now let us narrow our sights on the nature of man from an experimental perspective. For consistency's sake, and so we can all compare oranges with oranges, we will refer to a method discussed in the previous chapter: the acorn exercise. If you can approach a simple acorn with a fresh eye every day, you will develop a non-judgmental perspective that can free you of preconceptions and allow you to learn from observation and experience. If you do not do the acorn exercise, then you may have difficulty understanding what we are about to say, because you will not have directly and personally experienced it for yourself. Just as it takes practice and experience to construct a house of cards, it takes practice with the acorn to fully experience the paradigm of the nature of humans.

When we study the nature of humankind, we come first, most basically and obviously, to the physical body. It is filled with spirals and ropes of DNA, stitched together from elements coughed into the galaxy by dying stars. We know our bodies through our physical senses, and find that we are built from materials found in nature. As we encounter the body more fully, we realize that it has various colors, shapes, textures, strong and weak areas, sounds (if we tap it), and so on. These findings will be virtually identical whether the person happens to be talking to us or has just died. The physical body alone is just a container that we move around in. We like to view it as being devoted entirely to the service and pleasure of the brain, but if macrophages were gifted with a voice, they would probably beg to differ with us.

The physical body is but the bottom level of upright cards, an indispensable precondition for us to be alive and human; it is not the limit of our humanness. There are, of course, our thoughts. How is it that certain cells arranged in certain ways allow you to think? A lot of matter from diverse places (salts from Antarctica, calcium from a Triassic pond) was assembled, not very long ago, into your body. Yet from the moment of birth (and even before birth, while you floated and twitched in the womb), the part of you that is truly you has been conscious, and is now able to read this book. and to ask questions. You read these words because of the special arrangement of cells in your brain. Your mind is reflected in specific chemical and electrical signals that are somehow separate from the cells themselves.* Which is just as well for you, for the elements in your body could have been assembled in such a way that you were born a brain cell, or a macrophage, and then you would not be thinking at all.

The exact microstructure and physiology of thought remains an unsolved problem for the anatomist and the neurophysiologist. However, through our observations, we notice something quite important. When the general structure of the brain is not devel-

---

*Jesse Stoff comments: This is the technocrat's view of the spirit of humankind. The other half of this team, the physician, does not fully agree. According to Charlie, the mind is in the brain and the brain is you, and that's that. Thus, if I could somehow obtain a photograph of the position and motion of every electron in Charlie's brain at a specific instant, I should be able to determine exactly what he was thinking at that instant—which gives new meaning to the principle of uncertainty, because I'd probably have to destroy his brain to do this, and I'd never know if my determination was correct.

oped properly, as in microcephaly, we can expect very little in the way of original ideas and complex thought. It is also apparent that a large, well-developed brain is not in itself a guarantee of genius. There are obviously other factors to consider with respect to consciousness. This is where observation and direct experience become crucial, so keep practicing with your acorn.

Our society generally accepts and understands whatever can be analyzed or measured, a disease Bennett Goodspeed refers to as *analexia*. The renowned physicist Werner Heisenberg said, "With our experiments what we observe is not nature itself, but nature exposed to our method of questioning." Fortunately, we are not limited by and to our rational intellect. But with a nonjudgmental, receptive attitude, we can transcend our subject-object mentality. No longer limiting ourselves to be merely "independent, objective observers," we are free to experience our humanity with the perceptions of an artist. By making a science out of the art of describing human beings, anatomists and physiologists are opting to be precisely wrong rather than generally correct. By creating the illusion of certainty where there is none, doctors are continually surprised by a change in condition, such as when a little boy overcomes his autism through nothing more high-tech or scientific than the love and support of his parents. So let us proceed, through experience, and discover a fuller understanding of the nature of humankind.

WHEN JESSE STICKS HIS NECK OUT

Jesse Stoff explains: I am writing this subchapter alone because the subject makes Charlie Pellegrino uncomfortable. You see, he is the technocrat of this team. He likes to see tangible evidence and hard data. I have become somewhat of a spiritualist. Any devoted healer cannot help but do so. A technocrat and a spiritualist . . . at first glance we may seem to be poles apart, but when we work together on a project, the result is often an interesting fusion of ideas. Besides, I suspect Charlie is more of a spiritualist than he cares to admit; it bleeds through in every one of his books. (I wonder if he is aware of it.)

In any case, he's bowing out of the next few paragraphs.

"When you go on about forces and energy and the nature of

man," he says, "I think you are sticking your neck out."

"But what's a neck for if not to stick it out now and then?"

"Not my neck," says Charlie.

Fine. So, let's talk now, just you and me. Let's talk about will, and stress, and the nature of man. Let's talk about things Charlie cannot directly touch or quantify.

Two men were lying in adjacent beds in a cardiac care unit. Both had suffered heart attacks, and both had approximately the same level of elevated enzymes, indicating a similar amount of damage. They were about the same age and otherwise in good health. One was pensive and the other depressed. One walked home after being discharged. The other went to "the eternal care unit." I heard the cardiologist mutter to the family of the deceased something about the will to live.

The will to live. Charlie can tell you about it. He'll admit to you that he had too many books to write, so he couldn't fall over and stop living, and that his determination had a lot to do with his getting better. He'll tell you about the friend of his who was shot during a hold-up, from both barrels of a sawed-off shotgun, through the diaphragm, bladder, liver, and intestines from about four feet away. When the rescue team got to him, his blood pressure was undetectable and a man announced that he was dead. Charlie's friend looked the man in the eye and said, "Goddammit, I'm not dead yet!" The rescuer ran away and vomited. The next day, in the hospital, Charlie exchanged jokes with his friend: "Well, at least it cured your colitis."

"No," the friend said, "that's the part of my intestine the robbers blew away. My bad part is now my good part."

A doctor explained to Charlie, out in the hall, that his only concern was that the spray of feces from his friend's demolished colon might cause an infection during the coming week. "But," the doctor added, "there's no way he should be alive today. What he's come through—I'm not a very religious man, but there's something about this. If anyone is going to make it, it's him. He must have an incredible will to live."

The doctor was not at all surprised when Charlie's friend developed not the slightest trace of infection.

And Charlie will tell you also of the student who was stabbed near Victoria University in New Zealand. The young man looked up at the people who came to aid him, asked, "Why me? Why me?" and died. It was only a superficial wound.

Without the intangible will to live, what is otherwise a corpse becomes a corpse. This is the force of what the Chinese call the "chi" and what we refer to as the "doing-willing" energy of the body. It actually and perceptibly exists, yet it is no more visible to our eyes than are colors to those born blind. As stated earlier, you can, with practice, feel this energy at the acupuncture points. It manifests itself as a slight warmth or tingling sensation. If we hook very sensitive meters and temperature probes to our fingers, with a bit of practice we can, through the force of our will, raise the local skin temperature and change the conductivity of our skin. The temperature and electrical changes, I'm sure, are secondary to the actual movement or flow of this doing-willing energy, because the energy itself is not detectable with machines.

Physiologically, our will seems to be responsible, to one degree or another, for the growth, repair, and maintenance of the body. When the liver is stressed or inflamed, the activity of this doing-willing energy diminishes. A victim of hepatitis becomes the antithesis of Prometheus.

Back to our house of cards metaphor. If the bottom level of upright cards is allowed to represent the physical body, and the roof the doing-willing force that holds the cards upright, then above the doing-willing force we have the realm of emotional-feeling activity. This is the level from which our daily consciousness arises. Man is much more than a physical being. Our thoughts depend on the structure of the brain for their manifestation, but neither their origin nor their content lies in the realm of matter or physical energy. However intangible thoughts and feelings may be, they are nevertheless real. We live in a world of ideas and of tangible objects. If we lose confidence in the reality of either world, we automatically destroy the validity of the other. What remains is chaos, and stress.

Our feelings and emotions are characterized by duality, by the qualities of attraction and repulsion (for example, joy and sorrow, love and hate, aggression and patience). These opposite qualities supplement each other and provide a rich resource for us to draw upon in order to reach a state of balance (that is, a state of minimal stress). Just as the doing-willing energy enlivens the physical body and is supported by it, the emotional-feeling activity gives color, direction, and form to the doing-willing energy. Through our emotions we can guide our will. Above, and supported by the emotional-feeling level, is the realm of thinking—not just any kind of thinking, but the kind that can be free of instinct and impulse, the kind that provides the potential for selflessness and self-consciousness. Such clarity of thought transcends have-to's, guilt, and analytical thought. Analytical thought alone cannot lead to happiness and a sense of fulfillment, because love, freedom, and truth are ideal realities that exist nowhere except in the world of intuitive experience.

If we avoid acting on impulse, if we favor civilization over instinct, we can penetrate and to some degree direct our emotions, which in turn can penetrate and direct the lower levels in our house of cards.

Again, at center stage, should be a definition of our essence and purpose in life. For me that's easy. I love spending time with my friends. I love spending time in my office helping people. I love spending time on my hobbies (there really are people in this world who collect molds, fungi, and black rocks, and I'm one of them). To define purpose, each of us has to find our own way, following signposts. But without a central purpose or dream, there is little to hold on to when things don't seem to be going our way. We have increased difficulty adapting, and we suffer stress.

WHEN STRESS HOLDS SWAY

What does stress actually do to our systems?

Since the overwhelming majority of people respond to stress by being stimulated (the flight or fight response), stimulation-related changes are the ones we will now describe.

When we are under stress, whether momentary (trying to steer your way out of a car accident) or prolonged (divorce), the involuntary part of our nervous system, called the *autonomic nervous system,* kicks into gear. This system is divided into two parts. The *parasympathetic* portion, which induces glandular secretion and increases the muscle tone of internal organs, as well as that of the heart, works to slow down body reactions due to stress, and, if overstimulated, allows the body to adopt the possum response. The second part is called the *sympathetic* portion. This system depresses glandular secretion, causes the contraction of blood vessels, and decreases the contractility of smooth muscle tissue. When activated by stress, the immediate effect of the sympathetic nervous system is to produce a general condition of heightened arousal. This allows the mind and body to function at an abnormally accelerated rate. We know a submarine pilot who, on the morning of October 16, 1968, was taking the Woods Hole submersible *Alvin* out for a dive to a chain of volcanoes more than a mile and a half under the Atlantic. Ed Bland stood inside the sail (the dorsal fin) directly atop *Alvin*'s spherical crew compartment. The submarine dangled from the support ship *Lulu* like a giant sea creature in chains. The following account* is a vivid example of how we experience the flight or fight response.

> The first indication of trouble is a peculiar tilt backward and to the right . . . jolt! A cable has snapped—*Alvin*'s nose pitches up fifty degrees—there's a terrific load on the starboard forward cable—SNAP!—and here we go!—the sub dunks down forty feet—it's dark outside, and strangest of all, there is time to sight-see—the brain has switched automatically into overdrive, taking every possible measure to help me live. All pain receptors have been cut off. A flood leaps down at me through the open hatch; it also spurts up through seams in the floor, because the sail is meant to fill with water during a dive—leave it airtight and it squashes like a beer can. There are bubbles outside the Plexi-glas—I hear them hiss. The brain is snatching up every image, every sound, pulling in all the information it can get, spreading it out on the floor of the skull and analyzing the pieces for a way out. The mind is crowded with so many new experiences that a second is stretched to the outermost limits. I live in a netherworld of slowed time—my eye pauses at a crack in the Plexiglas. My head must have hit the front of the sail as I ducked when the

*This account is excerpted from *Her Name, Titanic* by C. R. Pellegrino (Avon/ Morrow, 1990).

cables snapped. The flood is drifting in, falling down into the hollow sphere at my feet. If the sphere can be kept from filling, the sub won't die. The sphere has a hatch—Close the hatch!—I kick it down—it won't go down! A cable is stuck in the hatch—the fall did more mischief than I'd thought. My mind doesn't want to believe that this is going to happen: I'm going to lose my ship, perhaps even my life—and now there is sunlight. Five, maybe seven seconds have passed—*Alvin* has popped back up to the surface. I scramble out the top of the sail—amazing, I've uttered no words—*no words at all*. The sail settles lower and lower—I jump off and swim away. For five full seconds I listen to water lapping at the sail and tumbling in with an awful sucking sound. In those five seconds the sail vanishes—but I'm safe, and I know it, and the brain shifts out of overdrive. As time begins to speed up again, I become aware of a hot knot on my head . . . my ankle appears to be sprained . . . I'm jerked up by the shoulders . . . it's a diver fitting a lifejacket under me . . . he's come from *Lulu*.

"Are you alright?"

"Yeah. Fine. But I'm afraid I've lost *Alvin*. I've lost my ship."

During the weeks that follow, the loss of his ship becomes a long-term stress, as opposed to the short-term stress he'd experienced on *Alvin*. Ed's brain shifts to maximum overdrive—repeatedly. Each day seems to endure for a month.

Throughout both the short-term and the long-term crises, one of Ed's key experiences has been massively stepped-up adrenal secretions. The *adrenal glands* are crucial in focusing our force of will. Located above each of the kidneys, the adrenals are built from an outer mantle (called the *cortex*) laid over an inner core (called the *medulla*). These two regions secrete different classes of hormones, which under normal circumstances balance and complement each other, but during periods of prolonged stress have a synergistic effect that can wear the body down.

Nerve fibers from the sympathetic nervous system terminate in the adrenals, allowing for an extraordinarily rapid response to potential threats. The inner part of an adrenal gland, the medulla, manufactures and releases, among other substances, *epinephrine* (adrenaline). Adrenaline flow is responsible for most of the hyperactivity we associate with the fight or flight response. The cortex of the adrenal gland is the site of *cortisone* production. Chronic elevation of cortisone will dramatically reduce the stomach's resistance to its own acid, leading to gastritis and ulcers. Bones may become more brittle. Cortisone also triggers the retention of sodium, resulting in elevated blood pressure. Among other functions, this substance protects us from short-term allergic reactions by toning down or calming immune response. Thus a long-term stress, leading to chronically elevated cortisone levels, may suppress the immune system. Then EBV and other invaders can come to the fore.

Cortisone can influence virtually every aspect of the metabolism. The liver responds by gearing up for long-term endurance. It increases its stores of the complex sugar glycogen. It manufactures and ships out more cholesterol, which, under normal conditions, provides for long-term energy needs. Under abnormal conditions it deposits inside our cardiovascular system with life-threatening potential. Cortisone can also slow down the digestive system almost to the point of stopping it. This diverts blood to the muscles and is useful if you have to get out of a submarine in a hurry. But if for weeks thereafter you worry about the loss of the submarine, bringing yourself to the verge of adrenal exhaustion, a slowed digestive system outlives its initial usefulness.

The thyroid gland is like the gas pedal of our metabolism. Like the adrenals, it produces and releases more of its hormones during times of stress. In the short run, this provides extra energy. If the stress is not eliminated quickly, however, an inner shakiness develops, along with insomnia and an intolerance to heat. Exhaustion and burnout soon follow. Then the thyroid finally slows down— abnormally so—and a state of depression will probably result. People suffering from adrenal and thyroid exhaustion often experience a depression so powerful that they do not want to get out of bed. They find themselves fighting an urge to stay there for days on end.

The cardiopulmonary system is perhaps the most acutely sensitive to changes in our emotions. With anticipation and stress, the pulse quickens and the blood pressure increases. This is beneficial in times of stress because it means fresh oxygenated blood is being brought to the muscles. Again, in the short term this is highly useful but under long-term stress, chronically elevated blood pressure just helps fill coronary care units and morgues.

In considering some of the major effects of stress, let us end with the organ that causes the whole damned mess—the brain itself. Our thinking process (the top level of our house of cards) creates various beliefs and attitudes that are translated into emotional responses. These have physical effects on the body, and these effects are aided by that part of the brain called the *hypothalamus*. If an event is perceived as threatening, this is communicated from the higher centers of the brain to the hypothalamus, a walnut-sized body under the cerebrum, where most thought activity actually occurs (making the cerebellum the part of the brain where we really live). The sympathetic portion of the autonomic nervous system is then activated via columns of nerves extending from the back of the hypothalamus. These neural pathways run down the spinal cord, ultimately winding their way into such places as the lungs and adrenal glands. The release of adrenaline, of course, feeds back to the brain, elevating awareness and stimulating the small pineal gland located there. This gland plays several key roles, including the production of a substance called *melatonin* and the regulation of circadian cycles.

Melatonin has many effects, including an anticancer effect. Guess what substance isn't produced during periods of prolonged stress? Right! Between the suppression of melatonin production and the general suppression of the immune system by cortisone, the health of stressed and depressed people is understandably vulnerable to all infections.

As you might have guessed, circadian cycles are also disrupted by an adrenaline-stimulated pineal gland. Sleep-wake cycles and the production of sex hormones, growth hormones, and liver enzymes—all controlled by the pineal—may be drastically altered. What writer Norman Cousins calls the negative emotions—frustration, confusion, and suppressed sorrow or rage—have ripple effects that resound through the entire body, shattering an otherwise orderly biochemistry.

Clearly, prolonged and untreated stress has a variety of effects that ultimately predispose us to greatly increased risk of illness. The illnesses (such as Epstein-Barr disease, a clear example of a multidimensional disease affecting many levels of function) act as stress accelerants and thus propel the disease process into a vicious cycle. To break the cycle most quickly and decisively, a strategically implemented, multidimensional approach must be used. This approach has been applied successfully in several hundred cases of chronic fatigue syndrome and continues to be applied, with remarkable success, to ever-growing numbers of sufferers.

Let us begin.

7

THERAPEUTICS 101

I want you to walk two miles a day. . . .
And take my dog with you.

—Doctor to patient

A BIRD'S-EYE VIEW OF MEDICINE

Over three thousand years ago, ancient Egyptian priests approached their patients with a powerful diagnostic tool: empathy. After talking with their patients, they literally experienced what the patient felt and would directly perceive from their own natural processes what the appropriate remedy was.

The Greek physicians were among the earliest to evolve an objective science of medicine. They were the first to record specific uses for various medicinal substances. For example, they knew that the herb chamomile alleviated cramps. Thus, if a patient went to an ancient Greek physician and complained of cramps, and, further, if the general expression of his health ("constitution") was somehow "crampy," chamomile would be given.

Both of these approaches were "holistic" in that the entire impression the patient presented was taken into account before diagnosis and prescription. Over the succeeding centuries, with the evolution of human society, people felt less and less an integral part of nature. This led to an increasingly objective-analytical reductionist approach to nature and medicine. In the Middle Ages, medical practitioners tended to use rather coarse substances, many of which, then as now, were concocted experimentally—apart from nature—and were often quite toxic. Some practitioners still used herbal recipes that had been handed down through the ages, the rationale for their use having been long forgotten. Notable exceptions to this rule were the physicians Culpepper and Paracelsus, who still incorporated atavistic insights into their practice of medicine.

In the eighteenth century, Dr. Samuel Hahnemann systemized a highly complex approach to medicine called *homeopathy*, which we will discuss later in this chapter. Briefly, Hahnemann studied the effects produced by various natural substances and developed a system for matching them to the symptom "picture" presented by an ailing patient. Implicitly trusting the body to respond, he deliberately exacerbated the symptoms with the appropriate homeopathic substance in order to help trigger the body's natural healing processes.

Hahnemann's approach has this in common with that of the ancient Egyptians and the Greeks: all were built upon holistic principles, meaning that the entire patient, not just the symptoms, was considered. Since the early 1900s, modern medicine has diverged dramatically from this millennia-long holistic approach. Today's standard diagnostic procedure involves gathering "relevant" data about the presenting symptoms—relevant having come to mean objectively quantifiable through X rays, cardiograms, and laboratory tests. The physician then prescribes a treatment based on the "relevant scientific information" about the symptoms. Little or no effort is made to explore the initial causes of the health problems, as they are not usually organically based and therefore cannot be quantifiably verified. This approach has resulted in a fragmented form of health care that has departed greatly from that practiced throughout most of the history of medicine and the recorded history of man.

The paradigm for treatment presented in this and the following chapters is based upon the historically-rooted "artistic" approach to medicine, which has been further clarified through the insights of Dr. Rudolf Steiner. The artistic dimension involves the physician's first gathering the subjective information that the patient reports, along with the necessary objective laboratory information. Then, guided by the insights and experience, the physician synthesizes as complete an image as possible of the individual and of the illness. This approach was discussed in chapter 5; now we will explore it in detail.

TAKE A DEEP BREATH

The Epstein-Barr virus causes multilevel and multisystem dysfunction. At this time there are no drugs that specifically home in on and dismantle EBV or any of the other CFS-related organisms. Even if there were, it is doubtful that the disruption created at all levels would vanish as soon as the virus was eliminated, as drugs do not stimulate the natural healing process. This is why any therapeutic strategy must match each of the levels of disruption or imbalance in order to strengthen and correct them so the condition does not return.

Even with the best-case scenario, when someone recovers from CFS in a very short time (a few weeks to months), since most of the viruses implicated with CFS (including EBV) belong to the herpes family, at best the virus will be brought down to a normal state in the blood: permanent latency/remission. The normalcy can last a lifetime, and will, unless the patient gets into a situation of unrelenting and unendurable stress. Unemployment or even career setbacks can stress otherwise healthy people to the point of minor immune dysfunction. Add a high-stress diet, including up to six colas a day (as used to be the norm for one Charles Pellegrino), and a few strange habits (such as dousing one's lawn, immediate surroundings, and the water table with organophosphates and, even more disruptive, insecticides, while at the same time protesting the infinitely smaller disruptions of nuclear or hydroelectric power), and a weakened, misfiring immune system may be in the cards. Thus, a proper strategy for the treatment of CFS is to adopt a long-term (life-long) program for the prevention of relapses, not merely stimulating the immune system and supporting the metabolism to deal with the current mayhem. In a nutshell, this means that both patient and physician must focus on the *quality of life*.

The job is not complete once you have recovered from an

encounter with CFS. If one is interested only in short term results and, having regained normal health, reintroduces the stressors over which all of us have some control (such as six cans of cola per day!), the illness may return. For most of us, there is no pay off in short-term thinking. Far from returning to old habits, we must hold dearly to the new habits acquired on the road to wellness. Ignore your health and it will go away.

Now, keeping the long-term view in mind, we can start talking about therapeutic strategies. The game plan calls for more than the reading of blood test results, writing prescriptions and patching up leaks. It calls for a great deal of good old preventive medicine, and reflects an understanding of the different levels of function/dysfunction of the individual.

Let us begin with the bottom level of our house of cards, the physical body, and let us start with something simple: sleep. As we saw in chapter 3, we should, especially if we are sick, try to maximize the amount of sleep we get between the hours of 9:00 P.M. and 3:00 A.M. (that's local time). Remember the liver and its anabolic, regenerative cycle? By sleeping, or at least resting, during these hours we give the liver a chance to "catch its breath." A healthy liver affords an opportunity for the elements of the immune system that are located within it to repair and regenerate themselves. This will lead to two things: a stronger immune system and increased levels of energy.

For most of us, going to bed at 9:00 P.M. (10:00 P.M., at the latest) is very "early." You might find yourself staring at the ceiling, but in time, your circadian cycles will reset themselves (with the help of certain therapeutic strategies that we will soon discuss), especially if you set your alarm clock and get up at the same "early" time every morning—7 A.M. seems to work well. You can get up later, and even take afternoon naps if you want to, so long as it doesn't interfere with your sleeping at night.

Exercise is the next ingredient. For a CFS sufferer who may be too exhausted to get out of bed on most days, even the idea of exercise sounds ludicrous! However, exercise stimulates the metabolism, especially the digestive process, and thus increases the efficiency of the absorption of nutrients and the elimination of toxins. Make time to walk a few blocks to the neighborhood whole-foods store instead of taking the car. And when you do drive to the mall, park at the far end of the lot and walk the extra few yards. You can use the exercise, and you'll notice that you are able to find a parking space almost immediately. (We've yet to understand why people drive in circles for ten to fifteen minutes, looking for a space near the front door, building up stress with each passing minute, and sometimes fighting for two or three additional minutes when someone steals a space they have been waiting at for five minutes, hoping the man in the station wagon would stop yelling at his children and vacate the stall—when they could have walked from the back of the lot in only three minutes.) Walk up the stairs instead of taking the escalator or elevator. When you go to the bank or post office, take the bicycle into town and leave the car at home. Start slowly, maybe just five minutes per day, then *gradually* increase your activities.

Ultimately, the kind of exercise you want to do is the aerobic sort—fast walking, swimming, bicycling, hiking, or cross country skiing. Don't laugh, CFS sufferers, you *can* get there!

Until you can do the more active exercises, start with something gentle, like yoga. We have found that yoga classes are generally available all over the country (frequently at village recreation centers) and are a useful way to get started.★

The techniques and uses of yoga have been recorded since the second century A.D. through short verses or aphorisms. Currently, there are several living yoga masters of which, perhaps, B. K. S. Iyengar is the most distinguished. Although in his mid-seventies, he still instructs classes at his school in southern India and travels extensively around the world giving lectures and demonstrations.

Iyengar's unique contribution to the practice of yoga is in the integration of his detailed understanding of the physical/structural alignment of the body and the healing power of the exercises. He uses yoga poses as tools for transforming consciousness and generat-

---

★Jesse Stoff comments: To paraphrase Amanda, our acupuncturist, as she explained it to me and teaches to our patients: Yoga continues to be a time-honored and powerful tool for transformation, promising the realization of physical health, psychological well-being, and spiritual peace. It allows us to develop focused awareness of our beings, encourages us to quiet our brains and delve more deeply into the wisdom of our body.

ing maximum vitality through restructuring the physical body. Iyengar works primarily with people who are ill by teaching them specific restorative poses. According to Iyengar, practicing the poses is a spiritual act, a sort of worship within the temple that is our body. His teachings are an attempt to unite the empirical and analytical with the spiritual and the intuitive.

Iyengar instructs people who are ill to perform an elaborate system of restorative poses designed to augment healing at the deepest levels of our house of cards. These poses are 100 percent passive and relaxing, and "props" or "tools," such as blocks, belts, and blankets may be used to assist in attaining the correct position. No muscular tension is generated. The body is invited to relax, to release tension and thus open onto a profoundly healing level. Although passive, yoga is still a dynamic approach, inspiring those who practice it to examine and transcend their perceived limitations. Through various poses, Iyengar challenges us to move deeply within ourselves, one direction or type of posture at a time, to maximize our openness and awareness.

The restorative series of poses allows us to first open or "spread" our internal organs. Through the sequence of positions, the organs are then "squeezed," by a stance, such as bending forward and resting on bolsters. Finally, they are "soaked" with a fresh supply of blood, allowing them to detoxify and be nourished so as to support their regeneration. This simple series of postures has demonstrable and dramatic positive effects on the course of many illnesses, including CFS. So check your community bulletin boards and local newspapers and try to find someone who is teaching yoga classes. Ask them if they know, and can teach you, restorative Iyengar yoga. Books are available but illustrations and captions are difficult to learn from. A reasonable second best to an actual class would be a videotape (available form 1-800-SOLSTICE [765-7842]). Try it. You'll probably enjoy it as well as profit from it (in terms of improved health).

The yoga poses are very gentle and easy to do. In time they should increase your stamina, bringing you to the point where you can begin the heavier, aerobic exercises, such as walking to the local grocery store. But when you do start swimming or taking short hikes, don't rush it. And never, *never exercise to the point of exhaustion*, let alone past it!

For the yoga to be maximally effective, your attention must be focused and not wandering. Mind, body, and pose must be coordinated. You must train your mind to pay attention to the activity at hand because the yoga, in addition to strengthening your body, will sharpen your awareness and align your will.

Awareness of yourself and the environment around you can translate confusing circumstances and events (such as being ill and working toward recovery from illness) into useful knowledge. Most illnesses occur because of an overburdened system. As self-awareness grows, the patterns and errors that contributed to the state of overload become apparent. This is not merely an intellectual exercise. (True awareness cuts through the illusions [of control] and assumptions in one's life—such as expectations of permanence and predictability in others). It is only fair to warn you before you read any further, that with practice, as awareness grows, your human weaknesses will become as apparent to you as they may already be to others. This may result in a momentary drop in self-esteem, but will empower you to correct the traits you find wanting. Thus, on a fundamental level, learning a new exercise or moving from the exercise to, say, the mastery of a complicated swimming dive begins the process of coming to terms with yourself.

"At Oberlin College," explains athletic trainer Dan Millman, "I once had the pleasure of coaching a dedicated diver named Margaret. Her progressive growth of awareness in learning a particular dive parallels the stages we all go through in training—and in daily life.

"After her first attempt, she had no awareness of what she had done wrong, and had to rely entirely on my feedback.

"After more attempts, she could tell *me* what she had done incorrectly *after* the dive was finished and the errors had been made.

"Before long she was becoming aware of her errors *during* the dive.

"Finally, her awareness was integrated with body, mind, and emotions *before* the dive, and the errors were corrected before they were made. The dive was beautiful.

"This example has profound implications for daily life, because we go through the same process in all kinds of learning situations.

"There is a great difference between recognizing an error, which comes after a simple explanation, and accepting an error *as an error*, which implies full responsibility for its correction."

FIBRO WHAT?

While we're on the subject of muscles, poses, exercises, and the like, there exists an inflammatory muscle ailment called fibromyalgia that often occurs during the course of CFS.

Fibromyalgia ("fibro" as in fibrous connective tissue, and "myalgia" as in muscle) is a chronic disorder of the muscles and the connective tissue (the gluey tissue that holds our cells together). The condition induces the formation of fibrous lumps, which can trigger painful muscle spasms, which may in turn cause tissue congestion, decreased mobility, and recurrent low-grade fevers. One inevitable by-product of chronic localized muscle pain is sleep disturbance (insomnia), leading to a constant state of fatigue, which leads to inactivity. When muscles aren't used, their tone decreases and they become even more sensitive to pain. A cycle develops and becomes self-sustaining. Fatigue and increased pain deter one from exercise. Decreased activity increases the pain and worsens the insomnia. Lack of restorative sleep increases the sensitivity to pain and the perception of fatigue. Ultimately, many suffers become depressed and develop headaches and a generalized flu-ish feeling just from the inflammation.

Like many other symptoms of disease, fibromyalgia is a sign that something is very wrong on a deeper level. The cause is often directly attributable to the virus that is causing the CFS or to some secondary autoimmune process from your overstressed and now misdirected immune system. However, less common causes (including a tumor, slipped disc, or local infection) should be investigated and ruled out, as indicated by your doctor. In any case, the final result is the same: muscle spasm, pain, secondary fibrous (scar) tissue formation, and loss of function.

The areas affected by fibromyalgia are often referred to as trigger points, and generally occur in predictable locations as illustrated in Figure 1.

Now, what is to be done?

DON'T EXPECT A CURE FROM A DRUG

If there were a pill, you and most everyone else would take it. There is no easy way, but there are many things that you can do to begin improving the situation almost immediately. It's up to you. A note on therapeutic drugs and fibromyalgia: Elavil, an antidepressant, and/or any one of a number of antiinflammatory drugs can provide some measure of relief. However, they do have a number of unpleasant side effects and do nothing to actually

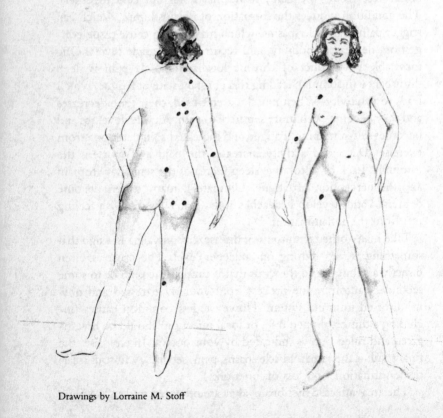

Drawings by Lorraine M. Stoff

"cure" the problem. Therefore, we recommend them only as a supplement to (not a first resort or replacement for) other treatments, and then only when absolutely necessary.

As for those other treatments, let's start with the relationship between fibromyalgia and myotherapy. Both deal with muscles: one reports pain and the other says, "Let's fix it!"

Myotherapy* is a system for locating fibromyalgic trigger points, which are the irritable, painful spots in your muscles. Myotherapy is applied in two steps. First, it locates the trigger points whose main effect is to throw their host muscles into painful and often disabling spasm. Secondly, it is used to defuse the trigger points, stretch out the kinks, and reeducate the muscles back to their normal resting length and condition. This assures painless and efficient function. As a secondary plus, any muscles that have been substituting or taking up the load of the spasmed muscles are released from duties they were never built to perform. Too much of that sort of effort puts the substituting muscles at risk of developing the very same tendency for spasm that caused them to be substituted for in the first place, thus spreading the problem.

Myotherapy exercises (see the recommended reading list, pp. 347–348) provide easy stretching movements for the once kinked muscles. They should be practiced at regular intervals. This provides the essential qualities of strength and flexibility which lead to coordination . . . and prevents the build-up of unnecessary tension. All of the muscles are closely related and, as close relatives often do, they influence each other's behavior.

Myotherapy works to erase spasm and pain. The problem is, people tend to vary in their responses to pain. What to one person might be excruciating would be described by another as "smarting." People are often not very clear as to where exactly the discomfort originates when describing chronic pain. This may be complicated by the fact that trigger point discomfort has a tendency to move around, sometimes shifting even to the other side of the body. There is, however, one thing patients with chronic pain are never confused about, and that is what they can and *cannot* do.

*You may be able to get a referral to a local myotherapist by calling the Bonnie Prudden Pain Eraser Clinic at 413-298-3781.

If you have symptoms of chronic pain, make a list similar to the one that follows, using whatever applies, adding those that are specific to you:

I can't get my hand up to comb my hair.
I can't fasten my bra.
I can't get my coat on without help.
I can't open the mayonnaise.
I can't get the dog's leash on.
I can't practice (piano, tennis, other) for more than a half hour
   at a time.
I can't carry trays.
I can't wash and cut my hair.
I can't do a decent sewing job or tie surgical knots that hold.
I can't change the baby.

You now have a first-class picture of whatever limits your own, individual threshold of pain is setting for you. You already know your symptoms. The combination of individually applied myotherapy along with specific exercises can dramatically accelerate your healing of the areas of fibromyalgia. The gentle exercises allow you to work the damaged areas just cleared of trigger points *without* further injury or pain. They should be done at regular intervals. They are designed according to pain, occupation, sport or hobby, and can be individually recommended by your myotherapist.

Most people work at something and often the work that they do contributes to their pain. A typical example is overstressing of the wrist by keyboard operators. Gentle exercise should be done daily to both counteract the limiting postures of the workplace and provide the needed warmup, stretching, and release of tension. Tension builds up during the work day, and *every two hours* something must be done to relieve it.

ADD VITAMINS AND MINERALS

We turn now to medically therapeutic assaults on CFS. To strengthen the vital systems of the body (the liver and associated immune defenses), we must use similarly vital therapies.

The first of the vital therapies is vitamins. Until about 1980, the field of nutritional supplementation (increased doses of vitamins) had been largely ignored, if not attacked outright, by physicians. Now the expanding study of intermediary metabolism—the biochemical reactions that occur within cells and the crucial role played in them by vitamins—has come into its own. This is due in part to the development of new methods and more sensitive laboratory probes. One piece of the jigsaw puzzle of intracellular biochemical reactions in the defeat of disease was contributed by Massachusetts Institute of Technology biologist Susumu Tonegawa. In 1987 he won the Nobel Prize for his piece of the puzzle, which was built around those millions of antibodies we send out to cage viruses, toxins, and other elements of nonself.

Researchers once believed that we carried a different gene to manufacture a tailor-made antibody for every variety of pollen or virus that might invade us. Tonegawa realized that the millions upon millions of different irritants to be kept at bay would require so many millions of human genes to be dedicated to this effort that, under rules requiring the matching of one gene to one foreign substance, there could not possibly be enough genes left over to build retinal cones, or toenails, or the columns of the neocortex, and humans should therefore not exist. Tonegawa discovered a mechanism by which bunches of genes coding for antibody cages shuffle about and recombine to form different genetic sequences in B cells. Given the ability to constantly shift their genes, B cells can manufacture a billion antibodies, each specific for a different virus or substance, from only a thousand genes. This process, by the way, uses up a lot of zinc and vitamins A and C.

During a lecture at the Massachusetts Extension Service, we heard about an important and timely study by the U.S. Department of Agriculture. While it is true that plants grown on synthetic fertilizers tend to be bigger and heavier, this is merely because they retain more water than plants grown without synthetics. When all the water is evaporated and their dried remains are analyzed, grains, fruits, and vegetables grown on synthetic fertilizers contain significantly lower concentrations of protein, vitamins, and trace elements (particularly zinc and manganese) than those harvested from plants grown by organic gardeners or simply allowed to grow wild.

We do not use the word "significant" lightly; in many cases the difference is more than 50 percent. This means that the vegetables in your local supermarket are not only twice as big and twice as expensive as those grown before the "green revolution" (the widespread use of synthetic fertilizers), but you'll probably have to eat about twice as many of them to get the same nutritional value.★

Interestingly, many of the nutrients found in decreased amounts in synthetically fertilized vegetables are now being revealed as essential to the intracellular metabolism in fighting off a variety of disorders and diseases including cancer. Thus eating "good" foods alone will not ensure adequate levels of vitamins and minerals anymore. And remember, if you are ill, your need for particular vitamins and minerals is greatly increased due to the increased activities of repair and regeneration. Certain nutritional supplements can not only increase the supply of essential nutrients, but also have specific therapeutic effects.

If you've ever stepped into a health food store or pharmacy, you've no doubt seen more different bottles of vitamins than there are species of fish in the Atlantic Ocean. We're going to keep things simple to encourage compliance and to avoid the "maracas syndrome" (which is what happens when you take so many pills that you rattle when you walk).†

Let's begin with *beta-carotene*. You'll find it in most yellow, orange, and dark-green vegetables. It is the pre- (pro-) vitamin form of the active *vitamin A*. Vitamin A soaks up free radicals. These are substances with unpaired electrons, which means they are attracted like magnets to cell membranes and enzymes. Where

---

★If you can get to a health food store that offers organically grown vegetables, you probably won't have to eat twice as much, so long as you're willing to pay four times as much. Of course, for the price you're also getting the seller's word that no insecticides or herbicides were used (this is generally true), but be as certain as you can that the supplier does not use human manure as a fertilizer. This can have consequences far more immediate than insecticides. If you do come across a store owner who extols the virtues of human manure (they're a rare breed, but they do exist), give back your groceries and walk away fast. The only good "parasites" we know of live in France.

†Prior to taking the vitamins recommended in this or any other book, we suggest that you consult a nutrition-conscious physician.

they bind, they cause damage. In addition to limiting such damage, vitamin A also enhances the function of lymphoctyes. The amount of beta-carotene converted by the body into vitamin A is directly proportional to the body's need for vitamin A. What is not immediately converted is stored in the liver and processed when necessary. The advantage of consuming beta-carotene rather than dosing yourself directly with vitamin A is that you don't have to worry about the possible toxic effects of leftover vitamin A in the blood.

As a starting point, we recommend 10,000 IU once a day. The source can be either a capsule or any of the following: one large raw organically grown carrot (which must be prepared as a fresh juice because humans lack the enzyme to break down the cellulose [the cell wall] that encloses the nutrients), four 15-centimeter (6-inch) pieces of raw or very lightly cooked broccoli, one cup of spinach, one sweet potato, one mango, two apricots, or two wedges of watermelon or cantaloupe. Other useful but less potent food sources include: watercress, tomato juice, parsley, Brussels sprouts, and cherries. Two direct sources of vitamin A include: one teaspoon of cod liver oil or 28 grams (one ounce) of beef liver (which is *not* recommended unless it was definitely an organically-raised animal).

However, if you are *still* smoking, 25,000 IU per day is more appropriate, as much of your vitamin A intake will be directed toward undoing (in so much as it can be undone) the damage caused by cigarettes, which includes the introduction of free radicals contained in the smoke itself.

The range of commercially available forms of *vitamin C* is a good example of the advantages of natural vitamins (and those derived from food) over synthetic ones. The more we learn about vitamins, the more we see that it isn't just one easily synthesized chemical in, say, orange juice, that produces a desired effect. In most cases, a complex group of substances or cofactors work together. Vitamins derived from natural sources have all the associated cofactors intact; synthetic vitamins do not. Ascorbic acid (the laboratory-produced, naked core of the vitamin C complex), for example, may produce kidney stones if taken in large quantities without enough water and magnesium. Natural vitamin C will not. We recommend that you read the fine print on the side of the vitamin bottle. If it says vitamin

C *with* rose hips (roses are one of the main natural sources of vitamin C), then what you are probably holding in your hand is a bottle of 99.9 percent synthetic ascorbic acid powder that someone showed to a rose hip. If it says vitamin C *from* rose hips, then you are generally dealing with natural vitamin C, which is more gently absorbed by your body. Pure ascorbic acid, in addition to potentially upsetting the kidneys, is more likely to irritate the stomach and cause diarrhea than is natural source vitamin C. *ALL* substances, natural and synthetic are potentially toxic; it's just a question of the quality and the quantity of the material in question, and its interaction with the individual's biochemistry, which determines the effect it may have.

Another point illustrated by synthetic versus natural vitamin C is the huge difference between the minimum amount of a vitamin required to prevent deficiency-related disease (for example, scurvy) and the amount necessary for optimum body function. The U.S. RDA (recommended daily allowance) to prevent scurvy is 60 milligrams of vitamin C, but in many instances, such as when ankylosing spondylitis and CFS are at work, thousands of milligrams per day may be needed for optimum health.

During the early 1980s, in the *Proceedings of the Society of Experimental Biology and Medicine,* Dr. M. P. Dieter demonstrated a positive correlation between vitamin C intake and the weight and vitality of the thymus gland and lymph nodes. Dr. R. Anderson reported in the *American Journal of Clinical Nutrition* that macrophages act more quickly against bacteria when serum levels of vitamin C are increased. Such increases also diminish the severity and duration of allergic reactions while, at the same time, they appear to stimulate all the major aspects of immunological function. As in the celebrated case of Norman Cousins (who was diagnosed as suffering from ankylosing spondylitis), a slow intravenous drip of as much as 25,000 milligrams of vitamin C over a period of four hours per day for several months has helped thousands of patients suffering from collagen disease. As of this writing, a slow intravenous drip of vitamin C, along with other vitamins and trace minerals is becoming a more widely used, if not yet a fully accepted, supportive treatment for CFS. Fortunately, such extreme measures are generally not necessary.

No one is quite sure how vitamin C assists immune response. There is no doubt, however, that clinically it is an extraordinarily helpful vitamin. Being water soluble, it passes quickly out of the body without being stored. Deposits can be found in such obscure places as the adrenal glands and the cornea of the eye, but even there you will not find much. The vitamin is much more efficiently used if the dosage is spread out over the course of the day. Knowing this, some vitamin producers are mixing natural vitamin C in a hard, chlorophyll matrix that dissolves slowly. If you suddenly dump one gram (1000 mg) of vitamin C into the bloodstream, the body will take only what it can use from the surge and excrete the rest. If the dosage is spread out over time, keeping an almost constant supply in the blood, the body can metabolize it as needed and less of it goes to waste.

We recommend a starting dosage of at least a half gram (500 milligrams) three times per day, taken orally. Vitamin C is best taken with meals (that way it's easier to remember the pill). Again, people fighting CFS and other diseases use higher than normal amounts of vitamins C and A, and thus have a tendency to become vitamin-deficient.

The third leg of our basic supplement regime is *zinc,* an essential cofactor for over seventy enzyme systems, all of which play key roles in protein synthesis. This metal increases the number of T cells in the blood and helps them to function more effectively. It helps B cells manufacture antibodies and increases the appetite of macrophages for foreign substances.

Like vitamin C, zinc is not stored in the body, so a constant, easily absorbed source is needed. The easiest form to use, from the body's point of view, is zinc combined with (chelated to) an amino acid—it doesn't really seem to matter which amino acid, so long as it is bound to one. Look at the fine print on the side of the bottle and find out how much zinc is actually in each pill; each one should have the equivalent of 25 milligrams of zinc. Take one per day (with breakfast).

Two other supplements—B complex and magnesium—are necessary, particularly if there is active liver impairment (which most people with CFS have to one degree or another). Taken with the other supplements, they will further help the healing process.

The vitamin B complex is perhaps the clearest example of a group of substances that work together to have a desired effect. The actual number of B-complex members has never been settled, but we know that there are more than a dozen. To keep things simple, when shopping for vitamins, pick a bottle that is labeled "B complex 50," which means that the average dose of most of the B vitamins is 50 milligrams or more. Take three of these per day, one with each meal, as with vitamin C. You may notice that your urine takes on a deeper color. This means only that you are not using all of the B vitamins and the excess is being dumped overboard. Don't worry about it.

The B vitamins act as cofactors in more than sixty essential enzyme reactions. They are crucial in hormone production, nerve conduction, and liver function. They play a role in the transformation of glucose (blood sugar) into energy, and assist in the absorption and metabolism of other vitamins. The proper production of antibodies is dependent on the availability of B vitamins.

Magnesium should be taken with the B vitamins, as it works in concert with them to help the liver. Like zinc, magnesium is easier for your body to absorb and use if it is bound to an amino acid. You want a dose equivalent to 400 milligrams of elemental magnesium, which may be two to four pills, depending on the brand. Magnesium works best if taken in the morning, so that it is pumped into the liver's circadian cycle when it is needed most.★

Insomnia is a common effect of CFS. We mentioned in chapter 3 that calcium can help. Calcium, like zinc and magnesium, is a metal. You could actually build gleaming cities out of it on the moon, so long as the metal remained in a vacuum and never came into contact with moisture. On Earth, the buildings would rust instantly, crumbling into white powder resembling the substance of our bones. Like zinc and magnesium, calcium is absorbed and used

★There are many horse pill–sized multivitamins on the market which seem to have the necessary amounts of vitamins in them. Unfortunately, some of the pills are so hard that your weakened digestive system can't dissolve them. Also, properly tailored vitamins will not be found in the typical multivitamin tablet. If you have trouble finding a good source of vitamins locally or for further information on specially prepared vitamin combinations for supporting the treatment of CFS call 1-800-765-7842.

more efficiently if bound to organic molecules, such as lactose. Take 500 milligrams of calcium lactate an hour or two before bedtime. The timing—magnesium in the morning, calcium at night—is important, so don't confuse them. The benefits of this combination are not instantaneous. It may take six to eight weeks to refill your reserves before it can take full effect, but it has proved helpful in most cases of insomnia.

POWDER OF THYROID AND NECTAR OF *ECHINACEA*

When one is under stress, the thyroid becomes more active and pumps out more of its hormones. If the stress lasts long enough, the gland may be unable to maintain the increased levels of production and can begin to fail. Often in cases of CFS, the confusion of the immune system will lead to the production of antibodies against the

TYPICAL VITAMIN Rx*

Beta–carotene	10,000 IU	1x daily
	25,000 IU	1x daily for smokers
Vitamin C	500 mg	3x daily
Amino-chelated zinc	25 mg	1x daily

With associated liver problems which are common, and/or premenstrual tension

Vitamin B complex	"50 mg"	3x daily
Chelated Magnesium	400 mg	1x in the morning only

With associated insomnia

Calcium lactate	500 mg	1x in the evening only

*Jesse Stoff comments: In my practice, we also recommend different essential fatty acids, including gamma-linolenic acid and eicosapentaenoic acid. They are crucial for normal cell membrane function. As they can cause upset of the gastrointestinal tract, we prescribe these on an individual dose schedule. For those people with AIDS (not to be confused with CFS, this more extreme immune dysfunction results only from infection by the human immune deficiency virus), we add AL721 (a special combination of lipids) and often cholesterol if the patient's level is below the normal range, as it often seems to be. In these cases, specially prepared eggnogs are very helpful.

thyroid, almost guaranteeing its failure. As the thyroid falters, metabolism slows. The patient may gain weight—too much weight—and experience a general feeling of chilliness. Even before hormone levels fall below normal ranges, depression usually sets in. In women, this effect is amplified near their menstrual periods, due to increased metabolic demands that the system cannot fulfill. Based on this clinical scenario, a natural *thyroid supplement* is appropriate in that it seems to distract the confused immune system from attacking your thyroid gland. Such supplements are produced by some vitamin companies, and a stronger version is available by prescription. (Armour thyroid tablets are the most common form.) One grain or less should be taken in the morning. Talk to your doctor about specific dosages because you want to be careful to support, not suppress, thyroid activity.

We also recommend, based on our combined experience as doctor and patient, herbal extract of *Echinacea*. Known for centuries as a native American garden plant, *Echinacea* is a member of the daisy family, growing up to a meter in height and producing beautiful, cone-shaped flowers. The pollen granules form a pentagram on the purple flower head.

Native Americans based several folk remedies on the plant, and they seem to have known what they were doing. In a laboratory setting, animal cells incubated with extract of *Echinacea* for six hours prior to being exposed to flu, herpes, and vesicular stomatitis viruses became 50 to 80 percent resistant to infection. Such results show *Echinacea* to be almost as effective as interferon in inactivating some viruses (and without the toxic side effects that the drug version of interferon may produce).

There are two or three species of *Echinacea*, of which *Echinacea angustifolia* is said to be the most potent. *Echinacea* extract can be purchased in or ordered from most health food stores. We recommend fifteen drops three times daily, and find it to be very helpful. If you don't like the taste, simply dilute it in orange juice or some other cool liquid.

Numerous studies published in Europe suggest that *Echinacea* is effective in stimulating the immune system into action against viruses, bacteria, and chemical toxins. The herb has proved effective in challenging CFS-related viruses, *Candida*, and chronic inflammatory conditions. It increases the activity and rate of replication of the helper T cells, the generals of your immune system. It increases the number and activity of the macrophages and their amoeboid cousins, including the B cells. All in all, *Echinacea* is quite a useful adjunct to our protocol.★

It is with *Echinacea* that we enter into the realm of prescription-strength herbal/homeopathic medicines.

Hippocrates once said that most diseases can be cured through the very same factors in which they originate. Like the American Indians, who recognized the therapeutic value of *Echinacea,* he might have been on to something. Thousands of years later, in the eighteenth century, Dr. Samuel Hahnemann began paying attention. He systemized a very complex approach to medicine called homeopathy.

First, Hahnemann studied various substances prepared from plants, animal sources, and minerals. He gave them to healthy people to see what kinds of symptoms they generated, a process he called "proving." He also studied many cases in which large doses of certain substances were given, either accidentally or deliberately, that produced cases of poisoning. Again he studied the symptoms. He thus accumulated a great deal of information about the range of symptoms generated by a particular substance when given to healthy people. From this he synthesized a sort of remedy "picture." He noticed, for example, that while bee venom caused localized swelling, beekeepers, who suffered more bee stings than the rest of the population, very rarely (seemingly never) developed arthritic swellings. Perhaps the swelling associated with arthritis was actually an attempt by the body to correct a problem, and very dilute solutions of bee venom might increase the efficiency of the response.

The second step in Hahnemann's process was to approach a sick individual, take a very meticulous history, and perform a physical

---

★Jesse Stoff comments: *Echinacea* is not only a wonderful stimulant for the immune system, but can also provide a gentle stimulus for the metabolism. Gentle and effective metabolic stimulation can also be given by way of the ginseng herb *(Panax quinquefolium)*. Ginseng has been used medicinally by the Chinese for over five thousand years, and it still works very well.

exam. As a result of his findings, both objective and subjective, he created a "picture" of the patient's current illness. Finally, he matched the medicine picture he had synthesized with the picture he observed in the patient and gave the appropriate medicine (for example, bee venom for arthritic swelling), specially prepared, to the sick individual. By giving a mild, symptom-inducing remedy to the patient, Hahnemann was, in a sense, trying to make more of the symptoms of which the patient had complained, using them to raise the body's immunologic "thermostat," to engage the body's own healing processes. He implicitly trusted what he called the wisdom of the body, believing that in this way the symptoms would help it correct the underlying illness.

Today we know that fever is actually the body's way of repairing damage and knocking out infection; and swelling, though not an earmark of good health, is a sign that reconstruction is in progress. In fact, unless a fever rages so high as to become life-threatening, taking aspirin to break the fever is merely good news for the infective agent. (Stricken with flu, you are better off *raising* your temperature by taking a hot bath.)

What we will now describe are some modern homeopathic remedies, along with their clinical effects in fighting CFS.★

WHY DID CHARLIE PELLEGRINO SHOOT HIMSELF FULL OF BELLADONNA AND BEE VENOM?

Jesse Stoff explains: No, I'm not writing another subchapter alone because Charlie disagrees with the subject. Charlie can't help but agree. He believes in data, and his improved blood values (serum iron, indicators of inflammation, and viral capsid antigen among them) satisfy him as objective data. The fact that he recently beat me to the top of Monument Mountain and feels fit enough to take up surfing probably qualifies as subjective data. The main reason

★These homeopathic medicines are specially prepared and are available now without a prescription from: 1-800-765-7842. The reader shall note that we are not talking in this case about ultradilute substances (what most people think about when they think about homeopathic remedies), in which one wonders if they are receiving even a single molecule of *Echinacea* or whatever substance is to act as a remedy. The substances are present in quantities great enough to be tasted.

I'm writing alone is because we have to shift voice. I have to step back and recommend remedies. But first, I have to tell you a few things about Charlie, and it is very difficult for both of us to write in the third person about Charlie when one of us *is* Charlie.

Charlie was given most of the remedies I am about to recommend, plus other, more specific remedies that were taken by injection. Most CFS sufferers will not require such measures. Charlie's was a special case of CEBV with very severe complications. In such situations, the injectable form works faster and more intensely, quickly stimulating the immune system to push back the virus. Charlie was also the "laboratory rat" on whom I used new combinations of remedies. The fact that this particular rat had been a best friend since childhood strengthened my determination to see him get better. I threw everything I could at him.

I have since discovered that less-severe cases of CEBV can be treated with less-powerful combinations of remedies, taken orally. I have had hundreds of patients with CFS in whom only the remedies that follow were given (orally), along with the aforementioned vitamin and mineral regime. They recovered predictably well.

For the average CFS patient, I start by prescribing:

1. Argentum Nitricum 30/Echinacea 2/Ferrum Phosphoricum 8, also called Immunaid (available from 1-800-SOLSTICE), and
2. Erysiodoron I, also called Inflamaid (available from 1-800-SOLSTICE)

Both are in liquid form. What I recommend is that you take seven drops of each three times a day. Taking them before or after meals is an easy way to remember them, but they work best if you don't take them *with* food—five to ten minutes before or after a meal is fine. Take them one after the other; they work better if you don't mix them together on a spoon. They don't taste very good, so you may want to dilute each in a tablespoon of water. Clinically, they have the effect of stimulating the immune response and reducing inflammation. CFS-related sore throats, swollen lymph nodes, and tender joints will all be helped.

In the first remedy, the Argentum Nitricum and Ferrum Phosphoricum seem to amplify the effects of *Echinacea*. This remedy also helps in the overall regenerative process. Under the best conditions, the end result of inflammation is the repair and regeneration of whatever was inflamed. The inflammation that accompanies infection is a reaction, a healing process aimed at eliminating the foreign invader and the abnormal conditions that allowed it to take hold initially. Thus, to truly heal any infection, the immune system must be stimulated and supported. *Echinacea* does indeed stimulate the immune system. However, if you ate about 50 pounds of *Echinacea* flowers (which would qualify as a massive overdose), the immune system would be overstimulated and serious inflammation might result. (Any substance is potentially poisonous, even water. It's just a question of the dose.)

In addition to stimulating (but not frying) the immune system, we must at the same time correct some of the problems that fostered the infection. The second remedy, Erysiodoron I, helps the metabolism to plow out accumulated waste products, relieving the need for an inflammatory process.

It is important to follow up on these two remedies by supporting organ functions. Perhaps the most important function to support is that of your liver. As Charlie and I mentioned in chapter 3, the liver is the warmest organ in the body. Putting warm castor oil compresses (heated to 37.7–38.4°C or 100–101°F) over the upper right part of the abdomen can slightly increase the liver's temperature and efficiency. Twenty minutes twice per day while listening to soothing music, meditating or reading is sufficient.

As a specific remedy to help the liver, I recommend the combination of: Choleodoron/Hepar Magnesium 4/Mercurius Viv. 8/Taraxacum 4 (also called Livaid; available from 1-800-SOLSTICE).

Seven drops three times per day (ten minutes before or after meals) should be given. Clinically, this medicine has a "decongestive" effect on the liver, as French homeopaths have noted for some time. It is essentially a combination of magnesium with extracts of beef liver and the celandine plant. Developed by Dr. Rudolf Steiner, the preparation seems to stimulate the anabolic metabolism of the liver and, in doing so, supports not only the immune system but also the digestive system. The abdominal pains and bloating often noted by CFS patients will generally subside when it is taken.

The next remedy is helpful in supporting the activity of the pancreas, which will also further healing of a virus-ravaged digestive system: Ferrum Hydroxydatum 5%/Kali Aceticum 6/Pancreas 3/Quercus 3 seven drops orally three times a day (also called Pancaid; available from 1-800-SOLSTICE). As with the other three remedies, it should be taken ten minutes before or after meals. Again, all these homeopathic medicines should be taken sequentially (one after the other), not mixed together on a spoon and gulped down.

Together, these four remedies constitute the basic homeopathic protocol for treatment of CFS sufferers. Two additional remedies may be indicated, depending on the symptoms experienced.

As the battle against the CFS viruses follows its course, the body's energy reserves are slowly drained. Clinically, when fatigue becomes overwhelming, one can assume that the adrenal glands aren't as healthy as they should be, even if the serum cortisol levels are within normal ranges. Since this is common in patients with CFS, the following remedy is quite helpful and often needed: Sepia Comp./Gl. Suprarenales 4/Prunus Sp. Sum. 2/Levico 4. Seven drops, three times a day, will help with energy loss (also called Energaid; available from 1-800-SOLSTICE). You'll usually notice over the course of several weeks a lessening of fatigue and irritability, and even a clearing away of the bags and dark circles under the eyes.

The other additional remedy is designed to help the thyroid. You will recall Epstein-Barr and other viruses can attack this gland directly, or may confuse the immune system to the point that it starts producing antithyroid antibodies. When the thyroid is damaged, much of the stimulus to the liver and overall metabolism is lost, contributing to the general lethargy, even pushing body temperature down as low as 36.1°C (97°F).

The remedy, Gl. Thyroidea 4/Ferrum Ars. 6/Spongia Tosta 3/Equisetum 4, is very helpful (also called Thyraid; available from 1-800-SOLSTICE). It is a thyroid supporter and gentle stimulant, not a thyroid supplement, so in more advanced cases, Armour thyroid (as discussed earlier in this chapter) may also be needed. In practice, however, the liquid (to be taken as seven drops, three times a day, like the others) does help the thyroid work more efficiently.

IN SUMMARY FOR PHYSICIANS:

STEP 1:

RX 1: Argentum Nitricum D30/1:Echinacea D2/1: Ferrum Phosphoricum D8

q.s.ad. 50 ml
Sig: 7 drops PO TID

RX Erysiodoron 1

50 ml
Sig: 7 drops PO TID

STEP 2: Once the diagnosis is confirmed, to support the liver, pancreas and digestive system.

RX 1: Choleodoron/1: Hepar Magnesium D4/1: Mercurius Vivus D8/1: Taraxacum D4

q.s.ad. 50 ml
Sig: 7 drops PO TID

RX 1: Kalium Aceticum Compound D6 Trit/1: Pancreas D3 Trit/1: Quercus D3 Trit/Ferrum Hydroxydatum 5%

q.s.ad. 50 ml
Sig: 1 peasized portion PO TID

STEP 3: To support the adrenal glands.

RX 1: Sepia Compound/1: Glandula Suprarenales D4/1: Prunus Spinosa Summitates D2/Levico D4

q.s.ad. 50 ml
Sig: 7 drops PO TID

To support the thyroid gland, if needed.

RX 1: Glandula Thyrodea D4/1: Ferrum Arsenicosum D6/1: Spongia Tosta D3/Equisetum D4

q.s.ad. 50 ml
Sig: 7 drops PO TID

These medicines are well known homeopathic substances. The ingredients of the compounds are as follows:

1. Erysiodoron 1—Apis and Belledonna
2. Choleodoron—Chelidonium and Curuma
3. Kalium Aceticum Compound—Kalium Aceticum, Antimonite, Crocus Sativus and Coralium Rubrum
4. Sepia Compound—Calcarea Carbonica, Ignatia and Sepia

These remedies will indeed prove beneficial in conjunction with the nutritional supplements already described and the techniques soon to be described. They are fairly tough remedies—as long as you keep them out of the sun and away from high temperatures (like you should be doing for yourself anyway), they can remain potent for years. So it's time to have a little talk with your doctor.*

There are two products on the horizon that may be very helpful in stabilizing, supporting and protecting the immune system, much as the natural Armour thyroid tablets help the thyroid gland. The first is a natural extract that was patented some years ago but has

*As we go to press a new interest and acknowledgment of CFS emerges: HEM pharmaceuticals has "leaked" a shred of information about a drug that they have under investigation, in a therapeutic trial, called Ampligen. Ampligen seems to be helpful (even though the studies at this time are still very small) for people who are in the immunohyperstimulation phase of the illness. During this time, due to damage to the normal feedback inhibition loops of the immune system, the level of lymphokines produced seems to be far greater than the body can physiologically process. These high levels can cause a variety of the flu-like symptoms. Ampligen may help the immune system come back to a more steady state of balance faster. It doesn't repair any of the damage that was caused but it may reduce some aspects of stress on the immune system long enough to allow it to "catch its breath." If future studies support the early findings then Ampligen will be a very helpful supplemental therapy for a wide number of viral infections, if one's immune system swings into hyperactive ranges—including the treatment of AIDS.

only now entered the last phases of testing. It's made by INNOVA, Inc., and is called UNISUN 11-9. They haven't released much information about it yet, but from the studies I saw, it looks like it will be a very helpful adjunctive therapy because it can allow the immune system to take a little "rest." It has immunomodulation effects which means that it helps the immune system come back to a balanced and normal level of reactivity. Thus, the hyperactive symptoms of autoimmune antibodies, increased allergies and swollen glands will subside as will the hypoactive symptoms of frequent colds and secondary infections.

The second product is a natural broad spectrum interferon preparation made by the Borroughs-Wellcome company. It is available in an oral tablet that is allowed to dissolve under the tongue once per day. It's being used extensively in Europe as an adjunctive therapy for CFS and is also in clinical trials in Africa to help in the treatment for AIDS. Again, there isn't a lot of information available yet but more is expected very soon. For up to date information call 1-800-SOLSTICE (765-7842) or Dr. Stoff's office in Tucson, Arizona, 602-323-2244.

FROM THE DIARIES OF CHARLES R. PELLEGRINO
NOVEMBER 6, 1987

Back in the dark days of 1985, before we knew exactly what was wrong with me, Jesse had recommended that I cut out of my diet red meats and several other items, particularly fats, refined sugars, and liver-insulting alkaloids.

"Oh, no," I said. "No ice cream?"

"You don't need it. Not unless you're suffering from some rare disease that can only be cured by coating the insides of your arteries with cholesterol. And that's not your problem, Charlie."

So I cut out ice cream and steak, Big Macs and Coca-Cola. And we added homeopathic remedies to the antiinflammatory drugs, hoping to cut back on the arthritis and fatigue. A long winter stretched toward spring. The last snows came and went. Spring itself came and went. The sickness came on again higher and stayed.

In July, blood test results convinced us that the Epstein-Barr virus was probably the root of my illness, or in the very least a powerful cofactor. Jesse began formulating a new protocol of homeopathic remedies.

"You still eating that wicked ice cream?" Jesse asked.

"No. I stopped that months ago."

"No drinking, of course."

"I don't drink."

"And no smoking."

"I don't smoke. I never have. You know that."

"That's your problem," he said quickly, that familiar Cheshire cat grin on his face. "You see, you're the worst kind of patient. You haven't been living up to your immoral obligations. Most people, when they're sick, they're like a balloon going down. They have some bad habits they can jettison and they float up. You're going down and down and you have nothing to jettison."

FROM THE VERY LAST PAGE OF CHARLES R. PELLEGRINO'S ACCOUNT OF THE BALLARD EXPEDITIONS TO THE ROYAL MAIL STEAMER *TITANIC* 2:20 A.M., April 15, 1987

There.
It's done.
I think I'll go have some ice cream now.

FOOD, GLORIOUS FOOD

Our next step on the therapeutic path is diet.

There are two priorities in choosing what to eat: (1) choose foods high in nutrient value to supply the basic building blocks the body needs to repair itself, and (2) be as certain as you can that the food you eat is not going to put any additional stress on the liver or immune system.

The basic, simple diet should be mostly vegetables, grains, fresh fruit, and as the main course of one meal per day, chicken, fish, or turkey.

If you really love ice cream and hot dogs and steaks, shifting to moderate consumption is the new rule. Since most of us can't judge for ourselves what moderation is, especially after we have exceeded it, we will give you numbers to go by. You may treat yourself to, say, one of the above (not one of each) once every other week, or once every month if you can hold out that long. If you absolutely have to, you can allow yourself that special treat once a week. But don't exceed this limit. And don't delude yourself by saying, "I haven't had a hot dog in a month, so I'll have one now," and then wash it down with beer, which you also have not had for over a month. And then, on the way home, you stop at an ice cream parlor for dessert because you haven't had an ice cream sundae for over a month. And the following day, you have a steak for lunch because you haven't eaten steak since last month. A rotating diet of foods from the reduced consumption list can be just as bad as eating hot dogs every day. This is an important thing to remember, especially during the early stages of your retaliation against CFS.

On the list to "restrict or cut out completely" are: red meat (beef, veal, lamb, pork), deep-fried foods, caffeine (coffee, tea, most soft drinks, and chocolate), and alcohol. (A note on moderation: if you get drunk or wasted more than once a month, you are crossing the line from moderation into serious trouble no matter what your physical condition; if you're a weekend warrior, you're already in trouble.) Dairy products should be limited to no more than a half glass of low-fat milk or a piece of cheese once per day. Sugar should be limited to a couple of teaspoons per day *at most*. All of these substances either put a toxic stress on the body or slow down the immune system. Dairy products seem to increase the production of mucus; if you suffer from recurrent EBV blooms and related sore throats, then an increase in the production of mucus can increase the risk for a secondary bacterial infection.

Smoking, of course, is totally out.

(—*but I'd rather die than quit all those things, and live on fruits and vegetables*—)

(*Be careful what you wish for. You may get it.*)

Sorry to bring this up, but if you happen to be troubled by recurrent yeast-fungal infections, then a low-yeast or yeast-free diet must be added to the basic regimen, and/or some temporary anti-yeast drug like Nystatin powder or Diflucan may be helpful.

Yeast Avoidance List

A. Baked goods made with yeast. (Goods made with baking soda or baking powder are "acceptable.")

B. Fermented liquids and aged foods:
   —beer, wine, liquor
   —malt-containing foods and liquids
   —cheese, saurkraut, etc.
   —vinegar

C. Juices. The juices of all fruits and berries contain yeasts that reside on the skin of the whole fruits. Fresh juices made from peeled fruits, if quickly consumed, are acceptable.

D. Dried fruits and things they end up in, such as condiments, dressings, sauces.

E. Mushrooms, which are essentially large fungi.

F. Vitamin B is often made from yeast, so if yeasts are a problem, be careful to seek a yeast-free vitamin B complex.

This list should help you to evaluate how sensitive you are to yeast and its products by avoiding and then reintroducing them. If you have recurrent yeast-fungal infections, then it is clear that you have a problem fending off these organisms. Yeast sensitivities are not as easy to see objectively as, for example, a severe case of athlete's foot. Recurrent headaches, stomachaches, even chronic pain may be yeast-related complications layered on top of a CFS viral condition. Since many people with CFS do have secondary yeast problems, it wouldn't hurt to adhere strictly to the yeast avoidance list for about two weeks to see if any of the symptoms diminish.

As we saw in chapter 4, one possible result of a CFS-confused immune system is the onset of allergies, particularly to certain foods. Special blood tests, called RAST or ELISA/ACT tests, can identify various allergic problems. In addition to these blood tests, there are numerous clinical symptoms that generally occur within two hours of eating the offending agent.

COMMON REACTIONS TO FOOD ALLERGIES*

The following list includes conditions that may be caused and/or exacerbated by food allergies.

JOINTS
Achy-painful
Stiff
Swelling
Erythema-warmth-
   redness

SKIN
Itching: local, general
Hive reaction
Moist-sweating
Flushing-hives
Pallor: white, ghostly

HEAD PAIN
Headache: mild-moderate
Severe migraine
Ache-pressure
Tight-exploding
Throbbing-stabbing

FATIGUE
Tired
Generalized heaviness
Sleepy-yawning
Exhausted
Falls asleep

STIMULATED
Silly as if intoxicated
Grimacing
As if going to faint

Chilly-cold
Warmth-hot flashes

DEPRESSED
Withdrawn-listless
Vacant-dull faces
Negative-indifferent
Confused-dazed
Crying-sobbing

CONTACT
Poor contact
Surroundings unreal
Disoriented-catatonic-
   stuporous
False belief-delusion
Hallucinations
Suicidal-feel like hurting
   self
Maniacal-very high

EYES
Itch-burn-pain
Lacrimation-tearing
Injected-foreign body
   sensation
Allergic shiners
Feel heavy

NASAL
Sneeze-urge to
Itching-rubbing

Feels as if obstructed
Discharge
Stuffy feeling
Hearing loss
Hyperacusis (abnormal
   sensitivity to sound)
Itching

LUNGS/HEART
Coughing
Wheezing
Reduced air flow
Retracted-shortness of
   breath
Heavy-tight
Not enough air
Hyperventilation (rapid
   breathing)
Chest pain
More alert-talkative
Hyperactive
Tense-restless
Anxious-apprehensive
Fear-panic
Irritable-angry

SPEECH COMPREHENSION
Mentally sluggish
Concentration poor
Memory loss (acute)
Speech slurred
Stammering-stuttering
Speech paralysis
Reads aloud poorly
Reads and hears with
   poor comprehension

MUSCLES
Muscle tremor-jerking
Muscle cramps-spasms
Pseudoparalysis-weak
Tight-stiff
Achy-sore-painful

GENERALIZED
Dizzy-lightheaded
Imbalance-staggering
Vertigo-blackout

THROAT/MOUTH
Itching
Sore-tight-swollen
Dysphagia (difficulty in
   swallowing)-choking
Weak voice-hoarse
Salivation-mucus
Bad, metallic taste

VISION
Blurring
Acuity decreased
Spots-flashes
Darker-vision loss
Photophobia
Diplopia (double vision)
Dyslexia (transposition of
   similar letters)-difficulty
   reading
Letters or words
   becoming small or
   large
Words moving around

GENITAL/URINARY
Voided-mild urge
Frequency
Urgency-pressure
Painful or difficult
  urination
Dysuria-genital itch

EARS
Full-Blocked
Erythema of pinna
  (reddening)
Tinnitis (ringing in ears)
Earache
Tachycardia (rapid pulse)
Palpitations (rapid,
  violent, or throbbing

pulses, often occur
within minutes of
ingesting the offending
substance)

GI/ABDOMEN
Nausea
Belching
Full-bloated
Vomiting
Pressure-pain-cramps
Flatus-rumbling
B.M.-diarrhea
Gallbladder symptoms
Hunger-thirst
Hyperacidity

*Based on the work of William H. Philpott, M.D., published in *A Physician's Handbook on Orthomolecular Medicine*.

If food allergies are suspected but not yet confirmed with blood tests, then a "cave man," or *elimination diet* can be very helpful. Here's how it works: Start with a simple diet of low-stress foods (see below), perhaps even eating the foods separately, one food only per meal. After two weeks, begin adding other foods and food combinations. If one or two items seem to cause problems, eliminate them again and see if you notice an improvement.

As your CFS condition begins to improve, your body will produce more digestive enzymes. Food will be more completely digested before being absorbed, thus decreasing the severity of allergic reactions.

SIMPLE LOW-STRESS FOODS

Animal protein: Chicken, turkey, fish (trout, salmon, sardines)

Vegetables: Green peas, beans and other legumes, sweet potatoes, cabbage, lettuce, carrots, squash, asparagus, cauliflower, onions, radishes, beets, celery, greens (beet, mustard, spinach, kale, collards), cucumbers, okra, brussels sprouts, avocado, broccoli, parsnips, rutabaga.

Fruits: Apples, bananas, grapes, peaches, pears, pineapple, cantaloupe, watermelon, figs, dates, cherries, apricots, plums, nectarines, persimmons, blackberries, blueberries, cranberries, dewberries, boysenberries, raspberries, loganberries. Fruits are very easily digested (and therefore put the least stress on the body), especially if eaten in the afternoon.

Baked Goods: If a wheat allergy is indicated, you'll want to bake your own wheat-free bread, carrot cake, and so on, because almost all commercially available breads, cakes, and crackers contain wheat. Good wheat replacements include oat, rice, and soy flours. In baking cakes, sugar is best replaced by raw honey.

Miscellaneous: Nuts (cashews, pistachios, almonds), raw honey, pure maple syrup, safflower oil. In general, margarine is not recommended because most brands contain a single chain length of fatty acid, which puts a big stress on the liver. An exception, Willow Run brand, includes multiple fatty acids.

You will notice that citrus fruits are not on the list. If all is well after a week on a low-stress diet, add oranges and other citrus fruits first (including limes, grapefruit, flavorings in desserts). If an upset stomach or other adverse reactions to citrus fruits are not noticed within three days, add corn-containing foods (corn bread, batters, cereals, and peanut butter, and the many other processed and refined foods containing corn oil, starch, or syrup).

If all goes well again, add eggs next. (Egg-containing foods include: macaroni, salad dressings, noodles, pancake mixes, and other manufactured or processed foods. Please keep processed foods to a minimum, though.)

Then add wheat (breads, crackers, soups, cereals, pancake mixes, batters, salad dressings, gravies).

Finally—but only in small amounts, once per day—you can add margarine and dairy products (cheese, butter, breads, certain soups).*

A second diet strategy for dealing with food allergies is much more "interesting." It is an especially useful approach in the treatment of multiple sensitivities, if you are one of those few people who are clinically and antibody-positive to nine out of ten foods. This strategy can be challenging to your culinary creativity, but it is very helpful in improving health.

If multiple food allergies are troubling you, as they often do people with CFS, then for now the *diversified rotation diet* is your answer. In this diet, you rotate your foods, so that every day for four days you consume only certain vegetables, grains, fruits, and sources of protein. After four days, the cycle begins again, so that what you eat on Day One you can eat again on Day Five, and what you eat on Day Two you can repeat on Day Six. By rotating your foods, you are calling on only certain enzyme systems on a given day, which gives the other systems a chance to recover. Also, like the elimination diet, the rotation diet makes it easy for you to see which foods are causing you problems. However, for most people, a rotation diet is a stressor in its own right, so keep it simple and, unless rotation is specifically indicated (as confirmed by your physician), use the elimination diet.

The therapeutic strategies described in this chapter are merely a first step designed to support the basic physical structure. If you are a CFS sufferer, you should notice an increase in energy within three to six weeks of beginning this program. Let's review what else you can do to get the ball rolling for yourself.

1. Sleep—bedtime as close to 9:00 P.M. as possible
2. Exercise—simple movements, perhaps as directed by your myotherapist, leading ultimately to aerobic activity
3. Myotherapy (if fibromyalgia is present)
4. Vitamin protocol

*See chapter 11 for a detailed diet plan and some *good* recipes.

5. Herbal/homeopathic medicines—under a doctor's direction. These do not present toxic side effects and can greatly speed up the healing process.
6. Diet—simple, low-stress (no red meat, fried foods, alcohol, caffeine, etc.), elimination, or diversified rotation

AND NOW A WORD OF WARNING

As people begin to recover from CFS, and as they begin to have more energy, there seems to be an almost universal reaction. They look back over their lives of the past six months, or two years, or five years, and recall everything they wanted to do but did not have the stamina for. Now, with the first glimmer of renewed energy, rather than guard, protect, and nurture it, they almost invariably shoot out the door and try to make up for everything they "missed" while they were ill—*and they blow it*. All we can say is, please don't.

Please, don't do that. Be careful. You can ruin weeks of effort. This is a time to practice balance in what you do. Have a bit of faith in yourself and trust in your body's ability to heal; the best is yet to come. Generally, energy gain is not linear, but to some extent cyclic, with four steps forward and one step back.

Remember, that taking it slow is the fast track to healing from CFS and you'll get there.

My Journey

I thought my life was over.

My body wasn't working.

My stomach didn't digest my food.
My chest hurt and rasped.
My limbs were weak.
My ligaments and muscles didn't support my knee, hips or back.
My legs twitched without control.
My throat ached all the time.
My eyes were sore, tired and too weak to use most of the day.
My concentration was gone.

My sleeping pattern was upside down.
My memory seemed sporadic and unreliable.
I was no longer able to do the simplest of tasks.
Driving showed me how my reflexes had slowed.
Even brushing my teeth was an arduous chore.
Leaving the house became almost impossible.
Crawling up the stairs was a mini-marathon.
But I, angry and frustrated, finally acquiesced and accepted.
I rested, prayed, learned to visualize.
I became productive in my daily spirituality.
I worked at becoming a vehicle for God's energy . . . since mine
    was gone.
I overcame fear of needles.
I learned about alternative healing methods.
I listened to others who had made this journey successfully.
I'm learning new nutrition and implementing.
I take it one-day-at-a-time, sometimes faltering but most often not.
I started painting.
I've begun to learn how to change me—not just my surroundings
    to heal.
I look inward, not outward, for change more often.
I allow music to soothe or energize me.
I practice therapeutic yoga.
I've become more tolerant.
I'm learning humility—a very humbling experience.
I learned to ask for what I need—most of the time.
And I learned that my life's journey thru enlightenment hasn't
    ended, it's just beginning.

It starts with the first step . . .

                                        Katherine Sarah (Soskin)
                                        June 1991

8

WILL

Drawing by Josh Stoff

One of the most ancient archetypes is the image of the sword. Countless other weapons have come and gone but even today, in the age of missiles and nuclear fission, the image of the sword is more than a weapon against foes of flesh and blood. It symbolizes willpower, the power which, if used correctly, can conquer the evil existing as a possibility in all men. Its slender, radiant blade is an image of the rays of the sun, bringing light into darkness. With its point turned downward, it has always been a symbol of peace. It is not by accident that its hilt is shaped like a cross. Thus, since time immemorial, the hero's sword appears in legends and myths as an image of creative will, its blade of light subduing the dragon on earth. If man wants to be free and to subdue the dragon in himself, he must learn to wield a sacred sword.

—DR. FRANZ WINKLER

A WORLD OUT OF CONTROL

"I don't want to go out tonight," Charlie said.

"It's a good movie. Come on!" Jesse urged.

"I'm too tired," came the reply. "I really want to go to sleep."

"Look. I've got some new rocket engines. We can pack a five-pounder together, give it a payload of flares, and launch it off the beach after the show."

Charlie grinned, and slowly stood up.

Along with fatigue, depression and an overall feeling of ill health, the virus brings an ominous sapping of the will. The will to get up, to do, and often to live is seriously undermined. But what exactly is the will?

If Aristotle could somehow be snatched out of the past, what would he think of Manhattan on this November afternoon? Standing amidst a mighty forest of skyscrapers, he would see immediately that it could not have been shaped by nature, that it had been put there by human hands. Miracles everywhere. Volvos and Mustangs—and *aluminum*. God's teeth! They couldn't even smelt aluminum in ancient Greece. It was rarer than silver, and yet here are buildings actually covered with it today, and flying machines seem to be made of it. (*Flying* machines?)

At last, he might guess, man had exerted his total will over the elements, perhaps even tamed nature itself, and emerged into a utopian age.

Look around you. Office buildings with great halls and plush carpeting . . . electric heaters, air conditioners . . . humidifiers, dehumidifiers . . . the businesswoman's coat, the bag lady's rags . . . and over there, a foul-smelling woman holds a paper cup stuffed with bills. A cardboard sign around her neck begs passersby to help her get home to Alaska.

"Alaska?" a young man asks.

"Yes," she says. "They put me and my friends on a bus and sent us all here. They said, 'You want welfare, go to New York.'"

At night, scores of cars are lined up in front of the Jacob Javits Convention Center. Prostitutes surround them and business looks good. "You've got to be crazy!" someone shouts from a car window. "Don't you realize there's an AIDS plague out there?"

"Aw, c'mon," a young man shouts back. "It can't happen to me."

Tens of centuries have passed. The elements are tamed. Man seems so in control, seems to have learned so much that it would not surprise Aristotle to hear that people were living outside the Earth aboard a space station or that man had set foot on the moon. Everything has changed—everything except man himself. So much knowledge and so little learning, so little self-control. No, it would probably not surprise him to hear that there were ten thousand artificial suns poised to fly out against the world, that without warning this city could simply vanish in a searing white glare—gone forever, a vapor in the heavens.

Although man has attained an impressive amount of power over his surroundings, his self-knowledge and inner control are very poor. Instinct and impulse, rather than direction and wisdom, are the means by which many (if not most) people lead their lives. We know men and women who put more forethought into which VCR movie they should rent than into, say, choosing the right spouse.

The rift between the near-total human control of the environment and the lack of inner control causes tremendous personal stress. We have paid dearly for our worldly accomplishments. The constantly shifting Manhattan skyline is the wonder of the world. Huge buildings are thrown up in less than a year, each beautiful in its own way, and the whole so densely packed that in places you cannot see the sky. But cut off the oil from Alaska and the Persian Gulf, shut down Indian Point, stop the inflow of food, and the labor of centuries would be gone in a single day. The tall buildings provide only the illusion of solidity and permanence. The city is, in fact, incredibly frail. It is only two meals away from total collapse, only two meals away from civil war. We may indeed have created an architectural marvel worthy of the envy of Olympian gods, but even the loftiest of its inhabitants live forever on the edge of losing it all, and most of them don't even know it. In an effort to make life richer, more exotic, more full of zest, life has become more complicated, more fragmented, more . . . exhausting.

One needs tremendous strength to maintain perspective on and enthusiasm for life. When afflicted with CFS, the task becomes even more difficult. Apathy and cynicism bite down hard. The inclination to look for fault outside of oneself is often unstoppable.

The means of narrowing and bridging the rift between self-control and control of our outer conditions must be sought in two areas (whether or not we happen to be suffering from CFS). The first area is the simplification of one's outer life. This includes such things as not trying to chain other people down and prevent them from changing, setting a direction in life (yours, not someone else's), recognizing your errors as errors and taking full responsibility for their correction, and having enough self-control—if not self-love—to avoid addictive, impulsive behaviors (the future AIDS victims parked in front of the Jacob Javits Convention Center late at night being cases in point).* The things we discussed in the previous two chapters had to do with making such changes in one's outer life, avoiding toxins, dietary changes, exercise, sleep rhythms. The second area of development, one's inner self, is what this and the next two chapters are about.

So what exactly is the will?

Rather than pursue long, dull philosophical and psychological discussions about the will, we can discover its nature through direct clinical experience. Let us begin by saying what the will is not.

Puritans and Victorians saw the will as something stern, condemning, and repressive, like their image of God, which inhibited the full enjoyment and expression of life. That may be the way people were expected to control their will then, but suppressive behavior is not a function of the will itself. The function of the will is not to act against the personality of the individual; instead, it is the activity through which we are able to do what we want—even to design nuclear weapons and plant them in the Earth. The will is an instrument of our thinking that allows us to carry out our

*Let's not think only in terms of individuals. This advice could apply just as easily to nations. Clearly, the great American and Soviet tribes spent nearly half a century behaving contrary to every one of these guidelines. There are some slight differences, however. Instead of parking in front of the Jacob Javits Center late at night, their leaders adopted an even more dangerous addictive behavior. It was called an arms race.

intentions. We call it choice, without which we might just as well be cold and stiff. After the physical body we inhabit, the will is the next level of our house of cards, and the next most important aspect of CFS therapy.

MEMORIES

As a diseased liver falters, the whole body falters with it. This, of course, has an emotional toll. Apathy and depression settle on top of fatigue. The will diminishes. Someone with acute hepatitis, for example, will do almost anything you tell him to do. He cannot make decisions. He may start twenty different projects at once and not finish one of them, or he may just spend the day sitting in a chair, content, staring off into space. Inner impulses and external influences dominate the personality, while the strength to be one-self fades into an elusive dream.

Another expression of the will is the memory. With both the liver and the will impaired, the memory is weakened (even without signs of CFS-related inflammation in the central nervous system). If you have ever tried to recall a name or a phrase, only to have it dangling "on the tip of your tongue," you'll understand what living with CFS can be like. The concentration that goes into trying to dredge up information (usually to have it slip away) is an expression of the will.

As CFS patients heal, the will is strengthened and the memory, too, recovers.

CRISES IN THE HISTORY OF LIFE

It sounds extremely odd, we know, that something as downright unpleasant as chronic illness can provide an opportunity for personal growth. We're not saying you ought to be elated by the prospect of a CFS virus bloom, but it is important to understand that crises do create favorable circumstances for experiencing the will. Sometimes, when we are confronted by overwhelming danger, something in us awakens—a surge of unsuspected strength. Its expression can range from the spectacular (surviving a double-barrel shotgun blast or lifting the back end of a Buick that fell off its jack and pinned your father down) to the not-so-spectacular (climbing out of an abusive relationship without letting your humanity drain away). We are able to generate such power only through the activity of the will, and only through intense concentration and motivation.

Simply put, enthusiastic motivation is an irresistible desire to accomplish something. Honestly appraising what you *want* is half of the battle. The other half comes from our observation that people rarely truly heal unless they have *fun* doing it, and have developed a love for life, such as it may be at the moment. Willfully moving toward what you want (health), as opposed to moving away from what you don't want (illness), can give a powerful boost to the immune system. "The will to live," said Norman Cousins, "is not a theoretical abstraction, but a physiologic reality with therapeutic characteristics."

In order to fully activate and profit from your will to heal, you have to maintain an honest perspective and sense of reality of what is possible, right now. Your loved ones and your physician can be helpful sources of feedback regarding what may be currently possible for you, but only if they have an honest sense of empathy for your predicament. Pity from those around you is not powerful and is in fact useless.

We have observed that people heal fastest if they're surrounded by love and understanding. If your husband or wife does not understand and is not supportive, then counseling is necessary in order for you as a couple to start building your healing team. You should not require a blood test result or a doctor's pronouncement to get your family on your side. We have seen countless relationships in which the healthy spouse kept pushing an ill mate far beyond what he or she was reasonably capable of, often creating an overwhelming sense of guilt. Apparently, and ironically, this arose out of a sense of pure love, a desire for the partner to be well. But the desire can run out of control, leading to a logic that goes something like this: "If she could just do . . . this . . . she'd be okay."

Communication is critical, whether or not a spouse is ill. But first, you must be clear about what you are communicating, even to yourself (especially to yourself). What do you really want from the years or decades that stretch ahead of you? To continue an unhealthy lifestyle? To continue exposing yourself (perhaps inadvertently) to a variety of toxins? To push to new levels of stress ("achievement") where no one has gone before? Or to recover your health? It's all a matter of how you direct your will. Is yours the will to heal?

There are now emerging from some quarters hints that we may be able to exert conscious control over body functions once believed to be automatic and totally beyond our control. Now comes word from dozens of researchers that heart rate, blood pressure, even the rate at which the liver produces bile are changeable by a simple act of will. You can be trained to dilate the blood vessels and raise the temperature of either hand. In much the same way you would concentrate your attention on the action of each muscle as you performed a complicated dive into a swimming pool, it has been reported, you can remove warts through hypnosis. Hypnosis, according to Hollywood myth, is a state in which one essentially sleepwalks and surrenders his will to someone else. Nothing could be further from the truth. It is, in fact, a very powerful state of concentration, a heightened expression of the will. An Olympic diver is in a similar state of trance when she is performing; you can call her name aloud and she will not hear you.

It is, of course, easy to understand how a diver controls her muscles. They are connected by nerves directly to her brain. The cells that release wart-destroying chemicals, the cells that cage and dismantling wart-causing viruses, are not directly connected to the brain. How, then, does one merely will warts away?

The phenomenon may seem insignificant next to explaining how one survives when a shotgun has blasted half the abdomen away and reduced the blood pressure to undetectable levels. But it is, at second glance, no less spectacular. It seems unthinkable that you can herd free-roaming white blood cells like cattle to a specific point under your skin simply by thinking about sending them there. Yet such control exists. It's as real as flexing a muscle, or dredging a name up from memory. It is another expression of the will.

We might want to take pause and think about that . . . for a very long time.

MORE NOTES OF A VIRUS WATCHER

Jesse Stoff comments: I'm stepping out again, in my own voice, because I will soon be recommending some exercises designed to strengthen your will. With refined control of the will, we can generate our own internally guided motivation based on a fuller sense of ourselves. We can do things because we want to, not because we need to.

At first, if you are ill, you will find it easiest to guide your motivation when some minor event (a family member complaining to you, about you) causes you to feel tense and stressed. What you are feeling then is a surge of excess energy. This is a time to use and guide some of that tension or energy, with your will, to do something you want to do—preferably something constructive and fun. Some people simply go off alone and arrange music on a cassette tape or work on a coin collection or on a collection of black rocks and fungi—whatever. If you enjoy writing letters and someone has offended you, then write a nasty letter (but put it away and don't mail it). In fact, researchers at Ohio State University have learned that when someone writes about a stressful or traumatic experience, the heart beats faster, blood pressure and hand perspiration decrease, and immune function becomes stronger. Interestingly, psychologist James Pennebaker of Ohio State University has found that writing on a pad or even speaking into a tape recorder produces stronger physiological changes than talking to a person who just sits and listens. "It would follow that people are holding back or controlling some of the emotion that could be detected by a listener," Pennebaker says. "Inhibition can be viewed as a source of stress that, over time, is cumulative and increases the probability of disease."

I am not suggesting that you run away to write nasty letters at every little stress, ignoring people or events that you don't like. Caves are lonely places if you try to live in them. What I am suggesting is that you *use* the tension and energy, direct it toward some activity that is both enjoyable and constructive. You should then find yourself calming down (the release of energy), while at the same time feeling a sense of accomplishment in a piece of carpentry, or a piece of writing, or a new arrangement of pictures in the family album (it can be anything so long as it is something you enjoy). You'll probably notice, as you divert your attention and quiet down, that you are able to go back to the cause of the tension and see it in a different way (because you are different), and perhaps come up with a creative solution.

As an exercise, or signpost, draw a line down the middle of a piece of paper. On one side, make a list of people and/or events to which you respond with a buildup of internal tension or stress. On the other side, make a list of things that you like to do, things that you really want to do.* *Keep this list in your pocket.* If or when something from the stressful side occurs, take the list out of your pocket, see what's on the side opposite the stressful items, and as soon as you can, go and do one of them. And, if at all possible, do it *today.* This will balance the stress against some beneficial activity that you enjoy. The point, however, is not merely to balance and neutralize the stress, but to do something that you want to do *through an act of your will.* Initially, this extra energy created by the exercise of will can be diverted from becoming stress and tension.

The list, and most of the exercises that follow in this chapter, never really applied to Charlie Pellegrino. He had already developed many of the skills I am going to teach you—developed them to an extreme—from the time he was a child. In his case, I think it was a matter of survival. Teachers assumed he was stupid because he read very poorly and was inattentive in school. And he had far too much energy (and still tends to be "high strung"), which made him seem not only stupid but a nuisance as well. He tells me that when he was eight years old, he saw a man filling a pipe set in the ground; the man pumped in too much water too fast, and the pipe burst and gushed. He tells me that is how he always felt as a child, as if he were filling up and wanted to burst. He was, I think, what Pearl Buck once described as:

> the human creature born abnormally, inhumanly sensitive. To him, a touch is a blow, a sound is a noise, a friend is a lover, a lover is a god, and failure is death. Add to this cruelly delicate

*Use your common sense. Exclude from this list such things as getting drunk and overeating.

organism the overpowering necessity to create, create, create—so that without the creating of music or poetry or books or buildings or something of meaning, his very breath is cut off from him. By some strange, unknown, inward urgency, he is not really alive unless he is creating.

Fortunately, Charlie discovered creative outlets in his early school years—and none too soon, for he was heading toward expulsion at age nine. Instead of disrupting the class, he began drawing cross sections of large, spherical underwater buildings in his notebooks. He became obsessed with protozoa, and tried to trace backward what came before amoebae. At age nine, he concluded that there must once have existed very simple "noncells." And, though he read very poorly, he began writing a story about a man trapped alone on an island, where he saw beautiful meteor showers at night, and regretted that he had no one to share them with. Into his first clumsy attempts at science and writing, he diverted a great deal of the excess energy that had, for two years and more, made him "want to burst." His fourth-grade teacher didn't seem to mind that Charlie wasn't paying attention in class. He was quieter, and that was all that mattered. Her opinion of him had swung from extreme annoyance to utter indifference in the space of a few months.

Two years later, despite a great deal of progress and the help of three extraordinary teachers, Charlie was still one of the slowest readers in school. As he entered junior high, a guidance counselor called him to a private meeting and advised him not to take certain science and math courses because he did not have the aptitude. According to the IQ test, Charlie was mildly retarded, and the counselor told him so.* At a very impressionable age, Charlie defied the counselor's assessment, loudly and to his face, and ended up spending an afternoon in the principal's office. He had, after all, shown extreme disrespect to a teacher who was "only trying to make things easier." Science remained absent from his schedule. His protests grew louder, and when all else failed, he brought his parents in to fight for him. And they won for him. Though the

*Charlie Pellegrino is, to this day, a vocal opponent of IQ testing in schools.

reading proved difficult, Charlie's sheer love of science carried him through. (This is a signpost: Don't let anyone determine your limits. Given a will of your own, only you can test the waters; only you can find out where your limits are.)

Directing his attention to things he loved—the stars and the ocean depths—Charlie eventually overcame his reading problems. Having to climb that hurdle strengthened his will. He emerged with an unusual love of books, and I think the hurdle, much like EBV, gave him more than he'd ever have had otherwise.

He's lucky. Creativity is Charlie's most driving instinct. I think the only way to truly stop him would be to put him in a room where he was not allowed to create. Then he'd be dead in two weeks. Exploring and books and art are more important to him than food.

Faced with a runaway EBV bloom, he began writing faster.

Faced with a dear friend's loss to addiction, he sailed with explorer Robert Ballard and began pouring all his conflicting feelings of love and anger into a novel about the *Titanic*. By example, Charlie shows us that when tensions build up, rather than dig ourselves an ulcer, we can creatively divert the energy, diffusing the tension and helping ourselves to feel better all at the same time.

With refined control of the will comes the ability to *concentrate*. Concentration is produced by attention to a thing or event as a result of a need or interest. Lack of concentration can be one of the most troublesome aspects of CFS, especially to professionals. Without the ability to focus intently, when necessary, even the strongest of wills becomes ineffectual. When the subject of the attention is not particularly interesting or important, focused concentration can only be produced with consciously sustained effort, which can be very tiring. For example, a lawyer patient of mine with CFS can only concentrate on his work for an hour a day, after which he feels completely exhausted. However, when it comes to his coin collection, he can focus, in detail, for hours and feel refreshed. The difference is *enthusiasm and passionate feelings*—a most powerful fuel for the will. When you put your "heart" into it, with enthusiasm, almost anything is possible. The entire system responds. The metabolic rate increases. Breathing and pulse quicken. The body temperature can rise by 1°C (1.5°F)—which, as you may recall, has the result of stimulating the immune system. Anything worth doing is worth doing with a sense of joy and purpose. You'll be healthier, and you'll find your will and powers of concentration improving. With practice, an increased power of concentration can be extended beyond the coin or rock collection, or whatever enjoyable activity you use as a fuel source. Focusing the will consciously is also helpful in decision-making. With CFS, even simple decisions can become monumental obstacles. Strengthening the will allows the decision process to flow.

Another manifestation of the will is *persistence*. Whether we are talking about rewriting a manuscript or breaking a smoking habit, your ability to endure and persist is another will activity. I've had the good fortune of knowing two examples of sheer persistence. Charlie is one, but long before Charlie, there was my grandfather Sam. He worked for three years in his little candy store in Brooklyn until, after hundreds of trial-and-error formulas, he figured out the process for making a chocolate malted. Along the way, he learned about food chemistry—enough so that patents for preserved frosting, chocolate sprinkles, and numerous other sweets quickly followed his initial breakthrough, leading to an inevitable family pun about "the sweet taste of success."

My grandfather went to work every day until he was ninety-four, not because he had to but because he loved his work and was enthusiastic about it. Not all of his chocolate inventions were a success (the chocolate-chip bubble gum endeavor sticks in my mind as firmly as it stuck in my brother's hair!), but he kept working on them nevertheless. The best defense against a failed idea was a dozen new ideas, so long as he persisted and carried every project through to completion.

Patiently staying with what you feel to be important requires *courage*, which is another activity of the will—courage to stand up for what you believe in, to stand alone if necessary and fight for your dreams, courage to get out of bed in the morning and see what new experiences the day offers, courage to look at yourself in the mirror and ask, "Why am I sick with CFS? Can I learn from this?" And courage to stare down the virus and reclaim your life.

Every time a fire fighter imagines an unconscious child on the other side of a wall of smoke, a surge of courage is summoned up. The energy activity of courage, persistence, concentration, and motivation are all manifestations of the will. If you are suffering through a viral assault on your liver, the doing-will force is diminished, and you must consciously reclaim it. Any measure taken to regain the full potential and resources of your will speeds you along the road toward complete recovery. The support given to your liver and immune system (by homeopathic remedies, food supplements, and changes in diet) makes this an easier task, but not an automatic one. You must still take command of your life.

There are a number of interesting and helpful methods that can specifically aid in strengthening your will. The fact that you are continuing to read this book is one example of persistence (will), with positive implications for your health and future. Good start! Now let's move along.

One helpful method of charging up your batteries and strengthening your will is the use of *affirmations*. An affirmation can be as simple as a single word, such as *strength, confidence, courage, tenacity, determination, energy,* or *concentration*. Feel free to think of a different or better word or phrase, so long as it is positive and health-inspiring. A single word can be a meditative focus, but only if it leads to an activity or change in your behavior. This is a simple yet powerful technique for beginning to engage your will. More lengthy affirmations can also be used. In your local library, you will probably find half a shelf of books containing affirmations or maxims. You may wish to leaf through some of these and pick out a few that really move you. In order for it to be helpful, the phrase or word you choose must be clear and meaningful to you. Repeat your affirmation several times at about the same time every day. Soon the word or phrase may bring images, perhaps even obviously meaningful ones, bubbling up from the subconscious—*courage* (a white tiger walking into a cave) . . . *determination* (my grandfather) . . . *persistence* (getting your work done and handing it in on time). Let the images come. They can keep the affirmations from becoming boring, and a useful thought may come along with them.

Affirmations are a wonderful way of replacing negative thoughts with positive ones. This is an old idea that I can't claim credit for.

It seems that Homer wrote about it centuries ago in *The Odyssey*. During his legendary voyage, Odysseus (Ulysses) had to sail past the Sirens, whose music had the power to lure men overboard or to make them steer their ships into the rocks upon which the Sirens lived—"for with the music of their song, the Sirens cast their spell upon him, as they sit there in a meadow piled high with the mouldering bones of men." To block out the Siren's deadly song, sailors put softened beeswax in their ears, but this made it difficult to follow commands, and many ships ended up on the rocks anyway, with their crews devoured by the Sirens. Odysseus found a better way. He took on board his own, better musician, Orpheus. So sweet was his song, none bothered to listen to the Sirens.

Transforming negative thoughts into positive thoughts is not merely a matter of saying "no" to the negative thoughts. It is a creative process of generating positive feelings from within. As a point of focus and a signpost along the path, affirmations can be helpful.

There is an old saying that applies very well to self-development and other kinds of training: "Fake it until you make it." When someone has been chronically ill for months or years, depression and lethargy can become a psychological habit as well as a physiologically based condition. Habits by their very nature have a tendency to linger, so it is generally helpful to practice casting yourself in a strong, healthy, happy light. Don't overdo it, and keep it in perspective.

As with physical exercise, when you exercise your will, do not attempt to exceed or even to approach the point of exhaustion. That can wipe out days of gains. But don't just say your affirmations; *be them*. This is a wonderful way of reeducating and engaging the will. At first you may feel a bit unlike yourself, or even phoney or silly, but stick with it because this is a powerful way of breaking old habits and cycles. The attitudes and activities you adopt for yourself will automatically evoke corresponding images and ideas, which in turn can change or intensify the feelings you experience and make them real. The psychological habit of depression can be broken while you are uprooting its physiological cause. The whole healing process is thus accelerated.

At this point, I am going to suggest using inspirational biographies and literature (and/or tapes*). What an opportunity to make friends with your local bookseller or librarian! There are many wonderful books that can cultivate and reinforce your determination and will. Ralph Waldo Emerson's essay on self-reliance is relevant and timeless:

> There is a time in every man's education when he arrives at the conviction that envy is ignorance; that imitation is suicide; that he must take himself for better or for worse as his portion; that though the wide universe is full of good, no kernel of nourishing corn can come to him but through his toil bestowed on that plot of ground which is given to him to till. The power which resides in him is new in nature, and none but he knows what that is which he can do, nor does he know until he has tried. Not for nothing one face, one character, one fact, makes much impression on him, and another none. This sculpture in the memory is not without pre-established harmony. The eye was placed where one ray should fall, that it might testify of that particular ray. We but half express ourselves, and are ashamed of that divine idea which each of us represents. It may be safely trusted as proportionate and of good issues, so it be faithfully imparted, but God will not have his work made manifest by cowards. A man is relieved when he has put his heart into this work and done his best.

Read and reread this passage; it can help you to create the inner conditions that are a prerequisite for you to be able to commit the time, energy and effort necessary for the development of the will.

When you feel ready to read and concentrate on a whole book, autobiographies and biographies can be very helpful. Let me point

---

*Tapes are the easiest course of action if you don't particularly enjoy reading or if CFS has made reading exhausting. They don't require a great deal of time and energy. There is a company that specializes in the kinds of inspirational (autobiographical and/or self-help) tapes I have in mind: the Nightingale-Conant Corp., 7300 North Lehigh Ave., Chicago, IL 60648-9951. You can call for information toll free at 1-800-323-5552. This is an excellent and reasonable resource well worth looking into. Another wonderful source of practical and inspiring tapes is The Option Institute, R.D. #1, Box 174A, Sheffield, MA 01257. More about this gold mine later.

out a few inspirational examples of those who overcame odds through force of will. Thomas A. Edison was labeled retarded as a child. Chuck Yaeger and Norman Cousins also overcame adversity. (Charlie and I both recommend Cousins's *Anatomy of an Illness* and *Head First*.) *Life and Death in Shanghai*, bound to become one of the classics of the twentieth century, is Nien Cheng's personal account of her perseverance through solitary confinement and torture during China's Cultural Revolution. It is a haunting tale told by a woman of indomitable will, who maintained her uncommon compassion for humanity even after the murder of her daughter.

Dennis Overby's award-winning (1978) *Omni* story about Stephen Hawking is also worth looking up. Imprisoned in a wheelchair, unable even to move his hands and barely able to speak, Hawking sent his mind where no one had gone before—into the horizons of black holes—and came back with discoveries that revolutionized astrophysics. (See also the recommended reading list on pages 347–348).

All of these people are examples for the rest of us. If Aristotle could stand here today, and know of them, he would nod and agree that perhaps humanity in the twentieth century is not so bad after all, if such people can exist. And if he looked a little closer, he would probably see that such people can be found everywhere, that they are far more common than one would ordinarily think, and he'd probably quip, "Most people are like tea bags: they don't know their own strength until they get into hot water."

With these initial steps as preparation, we have just begun to strengthen the second level of cards in our house: the will. Having learned to walk, with the exercises that follow, we can now begin to run. A point to keep in mind: Your attitude toward these exercises is crucial. Roberto Assagioli, M.D., in his book *The Act of Will* says, "The important point is not in doing this or that exercise, but the manner in which it is performed." They should be done willingly, with interest, precision, and style. Most important, they must be done happily and with enthusiasm. Otherwise, don't bother. Some of you may not have to. If you find it easy to focus your will to accomplish tasks, if you are, like Charlie, the kind of person who, when you set a goal, will get there no matter what is thrown in your way, then, like Charlie, you can probably get by without the exercises.

These exercises, like those in chapter 7, are based upon the insights of the Austrian philosopher Dr. Rudolf Steiner. There are six of them, each to be performed for a full month if they are to be effective.

To some people the word *exercise* conjures up images of some overwhelming obstacle that must be overcome. That is not what I mean. For these particular exercises we could just as easily substitute the word *experience*. These experiences that you create for yourself, over the next six months, should come as naturally as eating, or writing a letter to a friend, or watering your plants. There should be no obstacles in your path except those you arbitrarily cast there.

After this lengthy introduction, you may think I am going to ask you to scale the north face of the Matterhorn. Nothing of the sort. These are simple experiences/exercises, yet repetition of them brings a supportive and strengthening effect on your will. The guidelines for them are vague, and deliberately so; I am merely giving you skeletons to fill out with your own experience. As your will becomes stronger, so too does your concentration and memory. Most people notice improvements during the first month. They are subtle, so be alert.

First month: This exercise is for strengthening your control of your thoughts. For five minutes, at about the same time every day, allow yourself to concentrate on one thought only. The thought should be a rather insignificant one. The goal is to acquire the power of clear, analytic thinking unencumbered by outside influences or internal strife. For example, concentrate on something as simple as a pin, (though not necessarily a pin) and then, through your own initiative, connect that object to everything you can think of that is related to it. Again, I am deliberately keeping the instructions vague because I want you to generate these thoughts all by yourself.★

★The acorn exercise described in chapter 5, a more complex version of this exercise, is a two-fold experience that requires you to generate a sense of awe and

After two or three weeks of performing this exercise, you should notice a subtle but growing inner sense of firmness and clarity of thought. You may use the same thought every day, or a new one each day—as you wish. Just keep it simple, and remember that in order for it to be a helpful experience, you must do it consistently every day for a month.

Second month: Add a new exercise, but continue with the first exercise as often as possible (recommended: every other day). Remember, each exercise leads to and supports the next.

The idea of the second exercise is to initiate an action or activity just for the sake of initiating an action or activity. Think of, and then follow through with, some simple act that in and of itself is useless. Watering your plants, walking the dog, and taking out the garbage do not qualify. An example (and only an example) of something that does qualify is to look at your keys or a piece of paper across the room on top of a dresser, walk over to the object of choice, pick it up, and move it to the other side of the dresser—a simple, useless act, but one born out of a deliberate inner impulse. Choose a different act each day. Again, the crucial point is to perform the new exercise daily, at about the same time, for a month. Over the course of the month, you should notice that you have less and less difficulty initiating and carrying out the various activities of daily living.

Third month: You are now ready to undertake an exercise designed to cultivate a sense of equanimity and balance toward fluctuations of your emotions. Pleasure and sorrow, joy and pain,

---

wonder during the second stage. This engages and strengthens your intuitive powers, which adds another layer of richness to life. If you wish to experience it, you should do it separately from these six. Note that you need not think only in terms of the meditative exercises outlined in this book. Do not underestimate the power of prayer. There are emerging well-documented cases in which charismatic prayer produces what can only be described as medical mysteries. During the autumn of 1991, in Jerusalem, Charlie Pellegrino personally witnessed the spontaneous reassembly of a knee so undeniably damaged as to be inoperable, a total loss. This was no magic show, no illusion. It was the knee of a devout agnostic very close to Charlie. We'll make a spiritualist out of Charlie yet.

should be consciously and deliberately replaced by a more balanced mood. What we are working toward is simply this: Your awareness of your inner emotional state should grow so that no joy carries you away, no sorrow depresses you, no circumstance leads to uncontrolled anger, no expectation fills you with anxiety or fear.* This experience does not make you into an unfeeling machine. Your emotions simply become experiences that, to one degree or another, are under your control. You can be happy or sad as appropriate, without these emotions overwhelming and controlling you.

Continue to practice the first two exercises at least every other day.

At least once every day, stop what you are doing and just consciously experience a new, inner sense of calmness. In your own way, allow it to grow from your heart and radiate through the rest of your body. As you practice this exercise, you will find it easier to avoid addictive behavior, whether it be drinking four cups of coffee, or smoking, or workaholism. As your emotions become clearer to you, your appreciation for them will grow, with a sense of gratitude toward them and all of life's experiences.

Fourth month: This month, practice taking what might be called a positive attitude toward all of your daily circumstances. Seek the good, noble, praiseworthy, and beautiful. Look—really look—for the so-called silver lining in every dark situation. (Well, within reasonable limits. We don't expect you to go around reminding people that Hitler was nice to dogs.) Understand that the first step in this exercise is to attain a nonjudgmental attitude; I do not want you to automatically adopt a polar reaction to a stressful circumstance. During this month, it is important to consciously remain in control and neutral, and then to pursue the positive sides of some person or event that troubles you.

By concentrating on—and in a sense creating—the positive aspects of all that life has to offer, your will becomes stronger. Gradually, as you become more attentive to the subtleties and full potential of your experiences, a feeling of happiness and fulfillment will emerge.

---

*I refer here to everyday joys and sorrows. By all means, allow yourself to be carried away by the joy of winning $40 million in the lottery.

As always, it is important to at least intermittently practice the exercises of previous months. Having worked hard for each experience, you cannot allow it to slip away until the entire series is completed and you are feeling better.

Fifth month: We aim again at your attitudes. This month is a time to practice cultivating a feeling of openness when engaged in a new experience. That is not to say that you should cultivate gullibility; rather, what you are striving for is an open-minded consideration of the experience before you. Our ability to consider things in an open-minded way has progressed very little since Galileo ended up in trouble with the Vatican for proposing that the moons of Jupiter were not studded in the surface of a crystal sphere. A lack of openness to observed phenomena and new experiences leads to a mental rut and a paralysis of the will.

Here's the exercise: When someone tells you something that you offhandedly consider to be impossible, reserve judgment and allow yourself to say, "Anything is possible and he might be right." Then gather together all the facts you can before reaching your final conclusion.

Sixth month: Practice the preceding exercises in a systematic rotation until they become an automatic part of your daily thinking and way of acting. As you perform them, you should notice your inner strength, your will, breaking boundaries imposed by disease. The only limitations that remain are those you choose to keep. You are your own expert.

All of the above experiences are deliberate acts. They are thus manifestations of your will, signposts for personal growth and development. The third, fourth, and fifth exercises have an impact on your attitudes and emotions. The order of the exercises is very important and should be followed carefully. The strengthening of your will supports a new level of emotional stability, maturity, and insight—which forms the next level of our therapy and is the subject of our next chapter.

9

CFS AND DEPRESSION: IF YOU DON'T GO AWAY AND LEAVE ME ALONE, I'LL FIND SOMEONE ELSE WHO WILL

The patient, treated on the fashionable theory, sometimes gets well in spite of the medicine.

—THOMAS JEFFERSON

A merry heart doeth good like a medicine.

—PROVERBS 17:22

A VERY BAD MEAN NASTY UGLY HORRIBLE DAY

This chapter deals with a common result of chronic disease: depression.

Any long-term illness, simply by inflicting pain and weakness for years or months or weeks on end, will cause a reactive depression. With CFS, the depression can be particularly devastating, because there are factors that magnify it. The disease is subtle and severe, often operating inconspicuously, yet with debilitating effect. You will recall that a whole constellation of signs and symptoms must be considered in making a diagnosis. One can only track the footprints of the disease, meaning that it can be difficult to identify. A result of this is that many CFS sufferers are told that their illness is psychosomatic, that they are merely under stress, and that their best course of action would be to visit a psychiatrist. Professional counseling may indeed prove helpful, if only symptomatically.

You may also recall that an EBV-ravaged immune system can actually begin manufacturing antibodies agains one's own thyroid. Hypothyroidism (a slowing down of thyroid function) may result, leading to a drop in body temperature, a general slowing down, and amplification of the ever-present fatigue and depression. Hence, there are several reasons for CFS-related depression—which brings us to the third level of treatment, the emotions.

Depression is felt as an overwhelming sense of despondency or dejection, or a great weight of internal sadness. This inner sense of lifelessness may result in a feeling of doom and despair—clearly not the way one wants to walk through life, assuming one can crawl out of bed in the first place.

There is a simple test that we can use to accurately and reliably translate your subjectively experienced moods into a quantifiable number. The CFS Emotional Symptom Scale (CFS-ESS) can be completed in three to five minutes and will help you to gain some perspective on your current emotional state. When you take the test, respond to each self-statement with the qualifying number that applies best.

Now add up the numbers circled for all twenty-five questions. We'll get to what the score means in a moment. But first, as you can see from a quick glance down the list, there are many symptoms of depression. The feelings to which these questions refer overlap with the symptoms of CFS and thyroid disease. This explains, in part, why it is important to gather all of the clinical evidence, to look at the entire constellation of signs and symptoms, before venturing a guess as to which came first: the disease or the depression.

The purpose of this scale is to help you chart your progress toward recovery. This scale does not compare you to other people because everyone's level of emotional experience is different. Therefore, we have delineated no absolute standards for comparative emotional health. We recommend that you use your scores to monitor your emotional condition over time.

Clearly, the higher your total, the better you must be feeling. For

CFS EMOTIONAL SYMPTOM SCALE

	Almost Always	Frequently	Sometimes	Rarely/ Hardly Ever
1. I feel lethargic	1	2	3	4
2. I feel sad	1	2	3	4
3. I feel discouraged about my future	1	2	3	4
4. I feel unable to concentrate	1	2	3	4
5. I feel unattractive	1	2	3	4
6. I feel unable to accomplish anything	1	2	3	4
7. I feel worthless	1	2	3	4
8. I feel irritable	1	2	3	4
9. I feel disappointed in myself	1	2	3	4
10. I am afraid of dying	1	2	3	4
11. I feel like crying	1	2	3	4
12. I feel physically vulnerable	1	2	3	4
13. I feel anxious	1	2	3	4
14. I am moody	1	2	3	4
15. I feel uninterested in sex	1	2	3	4
16. I feel disconnected from other people	1	2	3	4
17. I feel that my body is out of control	1	2	3	4
18. I feel uninterested in other people	1	2	3	4
19. I feel helpless	1	2	3	4
20. I feel like killing myself	1	2	3	4
21. I am forgetful	1	2	3	4
22. I sleep poorly	1	2	3	4
23. I feel tired	1	2	3	4
24. I feel unmotivated	1	2	3	4
25. I feel indecisive	1	2	3	4

objective feedback on your progress, we recommend that you repeat this test every two months. If you stick to the techniques and methods described in this book, you will notice, over time, a clear, quantifiable improvement. This alone should be encouragement enough to continue the program.

If your score is over 64, the self-help skills described later in this chapter will probably be sufficient to deal with and diminish the depression aspect of CFS. Of course, since you'll be doing many other things to help yourself (diet, vitamins, homeopathic remedies, exercise, and sleep), resulting in an improved metabolism and immune response, you will soon be feeling better physically and your mental outlook is simply bound to improve.

If your score is under 64, then your improvement will be accelerated with psychosupportive assistance. (If you are feeling so depressed that you want to hurt yourself, then professional psychological help is a must—NOW!)

Depression has traditionally been considered a purely emotional disorder. Therapy aimed at getting in touch with and repeatedly expressing the feelings associated with the depression has traditionally been the accepted course of action. A number of recent studies have shown that, at least when the depression (or a large part of it) is connected to a chronic illness, merely getting in touch with the symptom of depression and expressing it serves to rehearse the negative emotions and imprint it. This is unlike the depression that results from our own behavior and from our interactions with others (such as an impending divorce), which can and should be treated by a professional guide helping you to come to terms with and further learn about yourself. But the depression that results from CFS is not primarily an emotional disturbance. In the same way that fever is a symptom of the flu, depression is a symptom of CFS. Like any other symptom, we don't want to suppress it, nor do we want to rehearse it. Instead, we want to find and cure what causes it. A thyroid in need of support is one common cause to consider. The weakening of the liver and immune system are others, and these can all be treated. But the deteriorating health that precedes treatment causes a buildup of negative emotions, and rather than dwell on these or rehearse them, attention should be shifted, as much as possible, to positive emotions.

It's easy to lose control. It's easy to let lost time from work decrease your feeling of self-worth. If the process of the illness is not quickly put into perspective—if you do not accept the fatigue and sore throat for what they are—then negative beliefs about yourself may become self-fulfilling prophecies, and these may in turn amplify the depression. There is a direct causal relationship between what you think and the way you feel: "I feel useless and terrible" (therefore I am useless and terrible), "I feel overwhelmed and hopeless" (therefore my disease must be impossible to resolve). Emotional responses nearly always play a role in CFS-associated depression.

There are at least two ways to intervene in this depressive, self-perpetuating cycle. To begin with, we must balance the negative emotions with the most positive of emotions, love.

Dr. Bernie Siegel, Yale University's renowned cancer surgeon, has this to say about love: "If I told patients to raise their blood levels of immune globulins or killer T-cells, no one would know how. But if I can teach them to love themselves and others fully, the same changes happen automatically. *The truth is: love heals.*"

"To love others you must love yourself," says Dr. Leo Buscaglia, who actually teaches a course on the subject at the University of Southern California. "You can only give to others what you have yourself. This is especially true of love. You cannot give what you have not learned and experienced. Since love is not a thing, it is not lost when given. You can offer your love completely to hundreds of people and still retain the same love you had originally. It is like knowledge. The wise man can teach all he knows and when he's through he'll still know what he has taught. But first he must have the knowledge."

All negative emotions and feelings stem from a lack of self-love. Loving oneself and others is perhaps the most creative use of one's energy. And, as Dr. Siegel has noted, love invigorates the immune system. It has been reported that when we feel love, the production of antibodies increases, often dramatically. People involved in stable relationships characterized by genuine caring and mutual tenderness have a significantly lower incidence of high blood pressure, arterial deterioration, and illness in general.

This goes beyond health issues. To bring something of yourself to others with no expectations of anything in return, or to reciprocate to another who has brought something of himself to you—this is love. And if you are the kind of person who puts another's needs above your own (not as a martyr), and if you are (oh, so lucky) to be living with another who places your needs above his own, then this is magic, this is healing. This is not just a signpost. This is a billboard!

This prescription for life springs from an attitude: *To love is to be happy with . . .* with yourself and with those around you. It is a growing awareness that "I love myself by being happy with who and what I am" and "I love you by being happy with who and what you are." When we love without judging, without directing another to live according to some inward, self-made plan, we are more secure with ourselves. Add to this an acceptance of ourselves without, for example, letting our jobs become our whole identity, and we grow stronger yet.

This attitude can become a way of life, a new perspective from which to view our beliefs. It forms the basis of what author and educator Barry Neil Kaufman ("Bears" to his friends) calls The Option Process®.*

We're going to step aside now, Charlie and I. We're going to let Bears describe in his own words the adventure in happiness that the Option method offers. It has turned out to be a powerful tool for helping people break the cycle of depression that often accompanies CFS disease.

SOME NOTES OF A BELIEF BUSTER

She leaned toward me, squeezing my hands while pleading silently for help through her eyes. Her current episode of arrhythmia, one of hundreds, had continued now for almost thirty-three hours. Although she was sitting, her heart raced at almost 180 beats a minute in a dizzying dance of changing rhythms and missed beats. An ache radiated from the center of her chest into her arms. Her

*The Option Institute is located in the Berkshire Mountains, at R.D. #1, Box 174A, Sheffield, MA 01257.

fingers tingled with a fluctuating numbness. She panted, taking shallow breaths . . . fighting to the point of exhaustion the sensation of suffocating.

"I can't bear the thought of going to the hospital again," she whispered, "but I can't stand this anymore." She had held off, hoping it would change, yet simultaneously acknowledging what the cardiologists had insisted, that once it begins, emergency room medical assistance provides the only real help. And yet the "correction" of the arrhythmia is only fleeting. Many times, hours after the emergency room trauma, the rhythm breaks again. On occasion, the medical intervention creates a heart block, which can have dangerous, even deadly consequences.

I released one of my hands from the vise of my daughter's fingers and stroked her face gently. Just two weeks before, we had celebrated her twentieth birthday. "If you want to go to the hospital, that's fine," I said softly. "I'll be there with you—with whatever you decide."

She pushed out a half smile. "I want to do it myself, Daddy, but I can't. They said I can't." The cardiologists viewed her condition as congenital in origin, and arrhythmia as under the control of the autonomic nervous system. Thus, they concluded, no act of will could change the arrhythmia once it had begun.

Nevertheless, I asked her, "Bryn, do you believe them?"

"Un-huh! But it's been almost three years and I've never been able to do it."

"Okay, let's say that's true. Why, if you have never been able to do it thus far, does it mean you couldn't do it now?"

"It doesn't. I guess I could try again. But we have tried so many times before." She shook her head. "This will never work unless I really think I can do it."

"Can you?" I asked gently.

"I want to believe I can. There I go again, doubting myself." She stopped speaking, struggling to pull in enough air. "Okay. I can. I will. I guess I should get the stethoscope."

I winked and pulled it from my back pocket. We had tried this many times before and I had come prepared.

She giggled for the first time in two days as she adjusted the instrument in her ears and placed the listening cup over her heart.

I held her hands as she closed her eyes and concentrated. Ten seconds passed, then twenty, then a minute, then several minutes. Her eyes opened limply. "It's still going wild. Nothing's changing."

"Bryn, as you're listening, what are you thinking?"

She sighed. "How one wild beat follows another. Even when it beats regular for one or two beats, I kind of listen for the next series of crazy beats."

Suddenly I realized she had conditioned herself always to anticipate the arrhythmias rather than to visualize a smooth, regular rhythm. "Honey, what about waiting for the next regular beat, anticipating the next regular beat, and then visualizing one regular beat followed by another?"

She nodded, closed her eyes, and continued to monitor her heartbeats. Her hands gripped mine tightly, then began to quiver abruptly. I held my breath, staring at her, not knowing what was happening. The quivering increased, but her face appeared paradoxically serene. Then, quite suddenly, she opened her eyes and tears began streaming down her face. "I did it. Oh my God, I did it."

She placed the stethoscope in my ears. What I heard was the most amazing music . . . a steady, even rhythm of heartbeats.

For Bryn, this would be one victory among many more to come.

What's possible for you, for me, for any of us? Perhaps the most useful way to explore such a question would be to look at how we see the world and the limits that can come from our perceptions.

"I can't help it, that's the way I am." This familiar idiom, which many of us use casually to explain feelings, behaviors, and physical states, suggests an out-of-control relationship between us (the thinking/decision-making self) and our emotions, actions, and bodies. Many would have us believe that we are aliens inhabiting physical units that we do not control. In essence, we become victims rather than initiators, responders rather than creators, adapters rather than masters.

What if all of these notions were simply cultural myths rather than facts? What if who we are, what we have become, and how we can change are arenas under our complete personal jurisdiction? What if being happy or unhappy is an experience we can choose? And what if that choice has enormous impact on our body chemistry and electrophysiology? What if we are in charge, and have always been so, but have never found a useful way to understand, acknowledge, and harness that power?

One aspect that distinguishes us from others is our beliefs. Our emotions and behaviors follow from those beliefs. Parents, priests, teachers, corporations, and politicians busily compete to teach us or sell us beliefs. They know (and we soon learn) that the game of power (personal and political) depends on what we choose to believe. Nobel Prize winners, army generals, physicians, lawyers, journalists, carpenters, masons, truck drivers, secretaries, and homemakers have this in common: they operate from their beliefs (how they vote; what sort of army they support, if any; what purchases they make; where they live; whom they marry; what clothes they wear). We understand immediately the power of beliefs in the political arena and in the marketplace, yet we do not readily apply that same clarity to ourselves.

The Option Process acknowledges our beliefs as the heart of the matter. To be happy (and to foster physical well-being) becomes more than a debatable philosophical construct for some distant time, but an actual living possibility, a choice that we can make right now. We become happier and healthier by exploring and changing our beliefs.

From the attitude *to love is to be happy with* comes the method for helping ourselves to become happier in every way. An unhappy person is a person reacting to his beliefs of unhappiness. The self-discovery involved in finding the clues (or beliefs) that fuel our unhappiness points out the opportunity we have to change. This realization comes simply from approaching ourselves with honesty and acceptance, from opening ourselves to our beliefs. Often the journey has exciting and unanticipated twists and turns as the person exploring becomes the master sleuth of his or her own beliefs and motivations. Each self-discovery becomes an opportunity for change and re-creation. Sometimes the effects, though profound, are internal and unspoken. On other occasions, the result of changing a belief or judgment can be quite visible and startling.

*There are no good or bad beliefs, no good or bad behaviors or feelings. We
are what we are, and in every way we do the best we can, the best we
know how, based on our present beliefs.*

When a young boy in a wheelchair, suffering from a progressive
and fatal neuromuscular disease, began to entertain the idea (the
belief) that he could help himself improve despite the prognosis of
experts, he began to regain the use of his hands. After a thirty-five-
year-old woman discarded her beliefs about the burdens of adulthood, she experienced dramatic relief from years of chronic back
pain. Once a business executive forgave his dishonest partner, a
bleeding stomach ulcer began to heal. When a homemaker stopped
judging her husband, dropping the belief that she needed him in
order to survive, her lingering viral infection abated. These are not
infrequent events or feats by only the courageous or intellectually
gifted; these are everyday miracles that all of us can perform in an
everyday world.

Thus, exploring our beliefs and changing them (either through
formalized dialogues with a guide, or just by confronting them
ourselves) can have a definite impact on our physiological systems.
Beliefs and their accompanying feelings translate into neurological
responses, which in turn affect one's immune system and general
physical well-being. If depression and unhappiness cause a dampen-
ing and diminishing of the health process, then joy and happiness
can result in a strengthening of the physiological system. Often,
discarding the belief that created the unhappiness opens the doorway to comfort, an enhanced sense of "wellness," and a more
healthy bodily process. Option provides a gentle, loving, user-
friendly technique and lifestyle perspective that has far-reaching
implications.

The Option perspective begins with an attitude of trust and
acceptance. In such an environment, people worldwide demonstrate continually their ability to be their own experts, to find their
own answers, and ultimately, to transform themselves and their
bodies. Any of us can begin that process by listening and accepting
and trusting what we know. And we do know!

Many years ago, one of our six children (our son) was diagnosed
as incurably ill, afflicted with a syndrome known as *autism*. He

spent his waking hours spinning in circles, mute, self-absorbed, and pushing away from all human contact. Viewing this severe developmental impairment and brain dysfunction as a lifelong condition, the well-meaning "experts" told us that eventually he would live out his days in some nameless state institution. Hospitals, clinics, and the medical and psychological literature supported this view (belief).

In contrast to such guidance, we chose to see our son very differently—not as a sad, hopeless case, but as a unique and beautiful little boy doing the best he could. Adopting the attitude of acceptance that we had been teaching, we approached him nonjudgmentally. Instead of forcing him to join our world, we entered his universe (spinning with him, rocking with him) and tried to express our love and communion with him. In an intense program that we devised, and with the help of our other children, we worked with our son twelve hours a day, seven days a week for almost three and one half years. When we finished the journey, the mute, autistic, retarded (under 30 I.Q.), self-absorbed toddler blossomed into a highly verbal, extraordinarily intelligent (near genius I.Q.), extroverted, and happy youngster. Today, at fifteen years of age, he maintains a straight A academic average at a neighborhood school, loves astronomy, computers, baseball, and people, and bears no traces of his earlier difficulties.*

Had we accepted and adopted the beliefs of those trying to guide us, no doubt this child would have been condemned to an institution, and those beliefs would have become self-fulfilling prophecies. If we hadn't believed we could effect change, we would not have tried. Instead of following experts, we opened ourselves to the possibility that our internal systems—neurological, biochemical, electrophysiological—are not fixed and inflexible, but are everchanging, self-regulating, and self-adjusting, capable of being influenced by our motivation, our wants, and our beliefs. What we witnessed in our child was either his somehow repairing neurological systems that were not operating effectively, or his creating new neural pathways so that he could learn, participate, be open to loving and to being loved.

*The inspiring journey of the Kaufmans' rebirthing of their son is told in *Son-Rise* by Barry Neil Kaufman (New York: Warner Books, 1985).

Our son's wondrous journey became a pivotal experience that reaffirmed the power of beliefs and of a willingness to approach a situation or person without any preconceived judgments or expectations. The only limitations are the ones we create!

We acquire beliefs in order to take care of ourselves in the best way possible. Beliefs are so numerous in our culture and language process that often we articulate them without question or review: "This is the best country in the world . . ." "We have a right to free speech . . ." "Death is inevitable . . ." "College prepares you for life . . ." "You have to take the good with the bad . . ." "Life is a series of ups and downs . . ." "Feelings are like instincts; you don't choose them, they happen to you . . ." "Nothing lasts forever . . ." "Good health is a matter of good genes and good luck."

To question beliefs like these does not necessarily mean they are erroneous or invalid. An inquiry simply creates an opportunity to understand more fully *why* we believe what we do and whether we want to continue believing it. Do the beliefs we hold serve us? Do they empower us or make us feel impotent? Do they lead to happiness or unhappiness? Do they promote health or sickness?

Frequently we reformulate what other people say into conclusions (beliefs) about ourselves. The avalanche of commentaries begins in childhood. "Be seen but not heard." (Conclusion: What I say doesn't matter.) "I know better than you." (Conclusion: I'm not intelligent enough to know.) "You are too young to understand." (Conclusion: When I get older, I'll get smarter—I hope.) "Don't question what I say, just listen." (Conclusion: Other people's statements are more important than my own.) "You make me unhappy." (Conclusion: I have the power to cause unhappiness in others.) "If you loved me, you'd keep your room neat." (Conclusion: If I don't do what someone wants, it means I don't love them.) "Take the medicine or you won't get better." (Conclusion: Outside intervention is the only thing that will save me; I have nothing to do with my healing process.)

Once childhood and adolescence give way to the more mature years, then the messages appear to change—or do they? "If you loved me, you'd be more caring or sexually active." (Hmmm— Conclusion: I still have to do what someone wants in order to prove I love them.) "You'll never understand me." (Conclusion: I must lack insight or compassion.) "When will you change?"

(Conclusion: It's not okay to be me.) "You make me furious." (Conclusion: I determine what others feel.) "Can't you do it right?" (Conclusion: I'm ill-equipped; there must be something wrong with me.) "You can't expect to be healthy forever." (Conclusion: I have no control; disease and sickness are inevitable.)

Our beliefs are learned from others or deduced from our own experiences. In effect, they are interpretations and conclusions. What others say and teach us tells us about their thought processes and beliefs. What *we* decide to "buy"—adopt and empower—tells us about our processes and our beliefs.

Despite all this belief-consuming, we do not believe all that we are told ("The stock market is a good place to invest your money"—some of us believe it, some of us don't). We choose our beliefs freely; therefore, we are free to discard them if we decide to. Nevertheless, our beliefs tend to be constant. We hold onto them for a long time, usually because we don't explore or challenge them. Option opens the doors to questioning any belief, not as a sign of disrespect or indictment, but as an opportunity to review, to reaffirm, to change, and to be happy.

The impact of the beliefs we hold is profound. The ramifications can be empowering and liberating, but they can also be devastating. If I think something is wrong with me or that I am unlovable, I will probably have corresponding feelings associated with such beliefs—sadness, isolation, and impotence. My actions will follow from such beliefs. For example, I might leave a relationship or bury myself in work to find meaning or a sense of self-worth. Ultimately, my body process (sluggishness, suppressed immune system, vulnerability to disease and viruses) will reflect my mind-set. Without implying that I am to blame, it becomes clear that I precipitate my susceptibility to illness. I can divert my body, with my beliefs, from working properly. The realization that we are responsible for our health is not to be construed as an indictment or reason for guilt, but rather a realization of our own power to determine what happens to us. With this realization comes the hope, strength, and opportunity to create ourselves anew, with vim and vigor and a wonderful state of complete health.

Why, then, do we rush to judgment, to create interpretations or beliefs? The answer is quite simple: beliefs are created and held to support what the believer thinks is best. A pertinent example is beliefs about unhappiness. We teach the value of discomfort as a medium of growth, learning, and enlightenment. "No pain, no gain." Our scriptures echo the vision of suffering as a method of purification. No wonder we teach unhappiness.

We use unhappiness to motivate ourselves and others. We use the fear of cancer to induce others to stop smoking, but more cigarettes are being sold than ever before. We hate our fat so we diet, yet more people are overweight now than in any other period. We spank our children to teach them, and we express anger toward lovers to get them to change—all of which usually leads to resistance rather than compliance.

Nevertheless, we push on! We teach misery as a sign of caring (if I am unhappy, you should be unhappy to show you care) and as a sign of intelligence (conscientious people would be rightly unhappy about famine or disease; any opposing position would be unthinkable). It is no accident that we use the phrase "happy idiot" to suggest the inappropriateness of sustained good feelings.

Finally, if all else fails, we threaten ourselves with the promise of future unhappiness. (If John doesn't get home on time, I'll be angry. If I don't get that job, I will be heartbroken. If this Epstein-Barr virus doesn't go away, I'll hate my body.)

Once they are articulated and itemized, our beliefs begin to sound somewhat bizarre and self-defeating. This is why a careful review of them provides each of us with a wonderful opportunity—something we affectionately call "belief-busting." Using the Option dialogue, we unearth our beliefs (like those stated above) to make ourselves conscious and aware of why we think, feel, and do what we do. If we discard the belief (belief-busting), we change those thoughts, feelings, and behaviors and give ourselves room to be happier. If we choose to keep them, we usually do so with strengthened conviction. Either position becomes a victory; the decision is ours. Option presents only the *opportunity* to change, to re-create ourselves and to be happy. We do the rest.

How do we unearth our beliefs and provide ourselves with the possibility for such sweeping and dynamic changes? Questions! Simple, nondirective and nonjudgmental questions! Often we pursue answers before we have even clearly formulated what it is we want to know. As I teach the Option dialogue to others and use it for myself and my family, I become more and more aware of what a gentle, loving, and joyful gift a question can be when confronting doubts, confusion, and despair.

Imagine becoming the happy detective exploring your own feelings and behaviors in order to uncover the clues (beliefs) to your discomforts. Imagine taking an impartial position, doing the best you can not to judge what you come to know. The attitude with which you pose the questions—an attitude of acceptance—is, in effect, a crucial part of the process. The more we discover and the more we come to understand about ourselves, the more powerful we become in resolving issues and living a happier and healthier life. We have nothing to lose, but so much to gain!

Where do we begin?

The Option dialogue, in essence, can be viewed as a progression of three simple, essential questions. Remember, we are sleuthing through our mind-set in search of beliefs—our beliefs! The first question: *What are you unhappy about?*

Suppose your answer is: "My severe case of CFS." The next question, really just a variation of the first, might be: *What is it about it that makes you unhappy?* Wait, you may want to protest, how could anyone ask such a silly question? More than absurd, you might want to argue, it's offensive. Anyone would be unhappy if he were sick! Perhaps, but that doesn't invalidate asking you or anyone else what specifically the unhappiness is about.

I am often surprised and amazed, in dialogues, by the varied and unique perspectives people have on their unhappiness with their particular malady. Frequently, therapists, helping professionals, and teachers believe they know the answers (your answers) in advance; that's how they make diagnoses and predictions. But only you can know your answer!

Back to the question. What is it about your CFS infection that makes you unhappy? No one is saying that you should not feel unhappy, or that if you become unhappy, you should suppress it or not vent it. The probe is to identify the underlying belief. Here is a sampling of answers to the question given by different people dealing with the same illness. "I am unhappy because I have suffered so much." "I am unhappy because I am not able to work."

"I feel guilty about not taking care of the house and not having any energy for my children." "I am unhappy because I am so difficult to love and will end up alone if this continues."

Each answer followed from that first simple question. There are no right or wrong answers; there is only your answer, and the dialogue follows from your answers. There are no preset goals; this is your journey. As for varying the question, remember that "unhappiness" is a catchall word. You might find that the words "anger" or "anxious" or "depressed" or "sad" seem to best describe your mood or state of affairs. Then the question gets a simple adjustment. What are you "angry" about? Or what are you "sad" about? Again, this is your dialogue. Make it fit you! You are in charge!

The second question is: *Why are you unhappy about that?* Or more specifically, why are you unhappy about being chronically ill? Again, no judgments are implied by the question. We are just trying to understand. The first question helps define *what* we are unhappy, concerned, disturbed about. The second asks us to explain *why* that state of affairs results in these feelings. Here are some possible answers to the second question: "I am unhappy about being chronically ill because I feel I have no control over what is happening to me." Or, "I have been cursed with damaged genes."

Ah-ha! Beliefs have surfaced, which leads us to the third and final question: *Why do you believe that* (that is, why do you believe you have no control over your illness or why do you believe you are cursed with damaged genes)? Now you have an opportunity not only to view your belief, but to explain to yourself why you believe it. If it doesn't make sense, you can drop it—here and now! If you do, your perspective about your illness and what you might choose to do about it could change quite dramatically.

But let's suppose you find you have good reasons to hold your belief. No problem! You can just ask another question. For example, suppose you said: "I have bad genes because my parents were always sick." We can stay with the belief question. "Why do you believe your parents' illnesses mean you have bad genes?" There are also many questions you could ask about what, in fact, you think "bad" genes means.

If you think you are getting stuck, an alternate question might be helpful. "What are you afraid would happen if you weren't chronically ill?" Or, "What are you afraid would happen if you didn't believe you had bad genes?" Some possible answers: "Then I would have to work harder and be more responsible." Or, "If I didn't have bad genes, then I couldn't blame anyone else for my illness." Thus the detective, in a dialogue with him or herself (or with an Option Mentor), often discovers that there are payoffs to our problems and illnesses. Once we discover this, we can change the dynamics of our self-manipulation and find healthy ways to achieve our goals (like taking time off, getting attention, soliciting the love and caring of another).

Another helpful note: Write your dialogues on paper or say them aloud if possible. Why? So that you can see or hear them, making them more concrete in your mind. Fears and beliefs alike are easier to grasp once articulated. It's also exciting to hear yourself say aloud something you didn't know you believed until you said it.

Belief discovery and "belief-busting" can have profound effects, permeating every area of our lives. The Option Process dialogue helps us literally to re-create ourselves.*

Now, a tight recap. There are three basic questions (with some sub questions or alternatives to help clarification). The more specific we can be, the more visible the underlying beliefs become:

1. *What* are you unhappy about? (What do you mean by that or what is it about that that makes you unhappy? Do you have an example?)
2. *Why* are you unhappy about that?
3. *Why* do you believe that? Or, Do you believe that? Or alternately, What are you afraid would happen if you weren't unhappy about that?

---

*For an expanded presentation of the Option Process and the dialogue, see *To Love Is to Be Happy With,* by Barry Neil Kaufman (New York: Fawcett Crest Books, 1984).

MORE NOTES OF A VIRUS WATCHER AND HIS LABORATORY RAT

Jesse Stoff and Charlie Pellegrino comment: Both of us have come to know this belief-buster who calls himself "Bears." As a result, the physician-spiritualist has found himself reassessing many old beliefs, asking many new questions about incurable illnesses and the power of mind over body. Bears's impact on Jesse's thinking has been major. The explorer-technocrat is more cautious. He asks many questions, but he has not changed many beliefs. His overall response is fascination, especially with the impossible recovery seen in Bryn and Raun, and he'll definitely keep them in mind as he goes out into the world with an eye open for more examples (more data). As for the dialogue process, one of us (Jesse) has experienced it, with Bears himself as a guide. It was a wonderful adventure in self-discovery.

This much we both agree on: beliefs and the emotional responses arising from them are acquired, or created, during the act of thinking. Through the Option Process (beginning with the basic questions and following whatever meandering path springs from each ensuing answer), you can really begin to understand your emotions, and need no longer be enslaved by them or subject to the impulses they create. Understanding and recreating your emotions in a positive way, thus overcoming depression, is an important process to learn from CFS (or any other illness). By the time you recover, you should no longer need the lessons that the illness has to offer. Because of its varied symptoms, because CFS affects people on many levels, it provides a rich set of circumstances to learn from. It actually affords one the opportunity for rapid personal growth. As you pull in the reins of your emotional life and become its master, a new sense of inner strength and security will emerge. With this comes a new level of maturity that allows for much richer and more fulfilling interpersonal relationships and often a genuine love of humanity. Love heals. The growth potential of belief-busting is fascinating to observe. As an example, we give you the following Option dialogue between Bears and a CFS sufferer.

KATHY: I feel stupid. I'm thirty-three years old and yet I feel like a hundred. I mean it. You couldn't imagine what I go through just getting out of bed in the morning. Exhausted before I begin. Dead on my feet. And that's not the half of it! My husband, Al, keeps saying if I don't pay more attention, be more involved—and he means sexually, of course—then he wants to consider a trial separation. Ha! My boss makes impossible demands on me. We are submitting a brief for an upcoming case and he really wants it yesterday! My kids drive me crazy. Really, that sounds silly, but they keep asking and asking for more, and when I don't deliver, they just cry and moan and groan. God, sometimes . . . well, sometimes . . . (a long pause, she turns away)

BEARS: Why didn't you finish the sentence?

KATHY: (begins to cry) Just listen to me. I'm ashamed. I have twice what most people have and I am overwhelmed. I want to be able to handle it, but how could I? Now with this!

BEARS: What is the "this" you are referring to?

KATHY: (sighs, then manages a smile) My diagnosis.

BEARS: And what is that?

KATHY: Well, I've been around, from doctor to doctor. I mean, I haven't just been this way for the last two weeks or two months. This feels like years. Anyway, the diagnosis is something called Epstein-Barr virus.

BEARS: What does that diagnosis mean to you?

KATHY: That I am really sick. That my immune system is shot. That I am going downhill.

BEARS: In what way do you see yourself going downhill?

KATHY: (laughing) Where do I begin?

BEARS: Why did you laugh?

KATHY: (demeanor changes abruptly) To keep from crying.

BEARS: Kathy, why do you want to keep yourself from crying?

KATHY: (looks up) I am afraid to let go!

BEARS: To let go of what?

KATHY: (begins to cry) That's—that's what I can't figure out. I just keep holding on. To my work. To my husband. To my kids.

BEARS: (gently) How do you do that? How do you hold on?

KATHY: Well, take Al. Whatever happens, he wants more. If it's dinner, then he'd like it hotter or colder or more varied. If it's the house, he'd like it cleaner or better decorated. And if it's sex, he'd like me more willing, more aggressive. Well, I'm not a human dynamo. I just can't please everyone. And I am tired of it.

BEARS: In what way?

KATHY: What about me? What about a quiet moment to rest at night? What about someone cooking me a goddamn dinner for once? What about someone saying I am doing okay and then getting off my case? (Her face becomes flushed.) Well, now they'll have to get off my case!

BEARS: Why is that?

KATHY: (She pulls a prescription from her purse.) This is why! I am sick. Something is really wrong! (She begins to cry again.)

BEARS: Kathy, why are you crying?

KATHY: I never intended to act like this. I'm sorry.

BEARS: Why are you sorry for crying?

KATHY: You mean I don't have to be?

BEARS: What do you think?

KATHY: (As the tears still run down her cheeks, she begins to smile.) I don't have to be. Yeah, I don't have to apologize.

BEARS: How do you account for your change of position?

KATHY: I just realized I do that all the time. Assuming I am always doing something inappropriate. This is me! This is the best I can do.

BEARS: How does that feel?

KATHY: Great! But that won't make me well.

BEARS: What do you mean?

KATHY: Well, this virus. I guess it could be anything. When I was an adolescent, it was asthma. When I was in my twenties, it was PMS. Now, a virus. I guess it just increases that terrible feeling of being a victim.

BEARS: A victim of what?

KATHY: Of me. Of my body!

BEARS: How are you a victim of your body?

KATHY: I didn't ask for this! I am just trying to make it through the day . . . doing my duty—my wife duty, my mothering duty, my employee duty. (she sighs)

BEARS: Why did you sigh?

KATHY: I just realized that it's my ticket.

BEARS: What's your ticket?

KATHY: My virus. I have been wanting to quit this job for years. Well, now I have a good reason.

BEARS: How is this a good reason?

KATHY: The doctor said I had to rest, take care of myself (another smile). Now he can't fight me on it!

BEARS: Who can't fight you on what?

KATHY: Al. He said we needed both incomes. He said I had to share some of the responsibility. Ha, just like him. I work. He works. But I cook and clean and handle the kids. Once in a while, his highness helps. Big deal. I guess I was afraid to say no. No, I am not going to work for a while! It's just too much for me now.

BEARS: Why were you afraid to say that?

KATHY: He'd . . . well, he'd stop loving me.

BEARS: Why do you believe that?

KATHY: It's always been that way. If I didn't perform, I'm out. It happened in the school band when I had my asthma attacks. I played the flute and had no breath left for anything. It happened with my first boy friend. When I didn't "perform," he dropped me. So why wouldn't Al be just the same?

BEARS: Do you believe he would be?

KATHY: I truly don't know. I never really looked at this before. I was too afraid.

BEARS: Afraid of what?

KATHY: I just couldn't handle being alone, especially with two kids.

BEARS: Why couldn't you handle it?

KATHY: Why? Well, money firstly.

BEARS: What about money?

KATHY: (She smiles.) Well, that's probably not too real. With my income and Al helping—I am sure he would help—I could get along.

BEARS: If you can get along financially, then is there anything else you would be afraid of in being alone . . . with two kids, as you said?

KATHY: I'd have no one to talk to! (Another smile.) That's not true either. There's Arlene, Sandy, my brother Jake. Okay, I'd have someone to talk to. I guess it doesn't look so scary when I take it apart.

BEARS: What does that mean to you?

KATHY: Maybe, I have to start taking things apart more.

BEARS: Like what?

KATHY: Like this whole virus thing!

BEARS: What about it?

KATHY: Well, you know before, when I said they would have to get off my case because I'm sick, well, I guess I needed an excuse.

BEARS: What do you mean?

KATHY: I don't know if people cause their own viruses or whatever. Maybe they do. Maybe they don't. But I know that if there's a good reason for being tired, like an illness, people will be more sympathetic.

BEARS: Like what people?

KATHY: (She shakes her head again.) Like Al.

BEARS: Why do you want him to be more sympathetic?

KATHY: So he'll go along with my not working and maybe give me some space sexually. I really love him. I just feel so pushed. If I didn't feel so pushed, I would be there more—for him, for me. Funny!

BEARS: What's funny?

KATHY: In my family, sickness was the only truly valid excuse. If you ever wanted attention, just get a fever. If you ever wanted someone to stay with you at night, just get an asthma attack. If you were healthy and happy, you just got ignored. Wow, I never said that before. Huh! This is great.

BEARS: What's great?

KATHY: Seeing me. Understanding me. I keep complaining about Al, but look at me. I haven't been a picnic to live with.

BEARS: Why do you think that is?

KATHY: Because I don't say what I feel or what I think. I just complain. And then, well, every once in a while, I get sick. And when I am sick, I give myself permission to ask or say what I think.

BEARS: What are you wanting to ask or say to Al now?

KATHY: Just love me. Let me rest for a few months. Ease off and I will be there. (Tears start to flow again.)

BEARS: (Softly.) Why are you crying?

KATHY: I feel like I love Al so much now. More than I have allowed myself in months.

BEARS: How come?

KATHY: I am letting go of blaming him and I don't feel scared anymore.

BEARS: What has changed for you that you don't feel scared?

KATHY: I guess seeing that I am not so stuck. It's almost like I've been afraid of things that don't make any sense when I talk about them now. I kept thinking I'd be rejected if I didn't keep performing. Well, maybe that's true, and if it happened, I'd be okay. Really I would. But somehow, from this place, I don't think that will happen. I will find a way to make him understand.

BEARS: How will you do that?

KATHY: (She holds the prescription up again.) Not with this! I am not going to use my virus, my diagnosis. I am just going to explain how I feel, that I love him and I want some space so I can be there for myself, for the kids, and really, for him.

BEARS: How does that feel?

KATHY: This is going to sound silly, but it feels great. (Pause.) I feel great! (Another pause.) What does this all mean about my virus?

BEARS: What do you think it means?

KATHY: Maybe I haven't been much help to my immune system. (She stretches her arms out to her sides.) I kind of feel like I am waking up. What would happen if I really liked life and liked living?

BEARS: What do you think would happen?

KATHY: I think I can help make me healthy.

BEARS: How?

KATHY: You're going to laugh.

BEARS: Why do you believe that?

KATHY: (She looks sharply into Bears's eyes.) I don't. That's another one of my "supposes." I can help myself by not only

taking my vitamins and remedies but by being more reasonable with myself.

BEARS: How would you do that?

KATHY: Talking honestly to Al. Taking a leave of absence from
my job. It's all too simple.

BEARS: What's too simple?

KATHY: This! Why didn't I do this before?

BEARS: Why is that a question for you?

KATHY: There I go again, beating myself up for not performing.
To answer your question—I didn't do it before because I
wasn't clear enough to act. Now I feel I can. So that's why I
can do it now and not before. That seems simple too, but not
too simple. (She laughs.)

Immediately after the session, Kathy reported feeling a surge of
energy that dissipated the extreme fatigue she had been experiencing. At her request, we custom-designed a cassette tape for her
through which she could remind herself daily about her own
power and her own evolving desire to be authentic. Kathy used the
homeopathic remedies prescribed by her physician, engaged in
some additional dialogues, and continued with her tape. Within
two months, the virus began to abate substantially. She enjoyed a
renewed sense of well-being and an invigorated perspective on life.

GETTING STARTED WITH THE OPTION PROCESS

One way to begin your journey with the Option Process is by
taking a personal "belief inventory." As you reflect on and answer
the following questions, you'll begin to recognize some of the
beliefs that may be influencing your state of health and happiness.
Often we can begin moving toward a healthier vision of ourselves
just by recognizing the self-limiting beliefs that have stood in the
way.

- Do you believe you can be happier than you are now? If yes,
why? If no, why not?
- What do you believe is the relationship between your
thoughts/attitudes and your state of health?

- Do you see yourself as healthy or sickly? Clarify your reasons for seeing yourself this way.
- Do you view sickness as an isolated problem or as a total expression of your body/mind/lifestyle? Why?
- Do you fear disease and/or death? If yes, what do you believe about them?
- When you feel unhealthy, do you approach your condition by trying to fight the problem or by trying to restore harmony? Why?
- Do you believe your illness has a message for you? If so, what is it?
- Do you "get" things by being sick? If yes, what do you get?
- Are you unhappy about being sick? If yes, why?

Some beliefs serve our unhappiness, others help to generate peace of mind and well-being. The following series of belief statements is assembled to help you recognize specific perspectives and conclusions you may have drawn that could be impacting dramatically on your state of health. If you do not hold these beliefs, then you have just had the opportunity to reaffirm what you know. If you do possess these beliefs, ask yourself why you believe them and consider the implications of changing.

BELIEFS TO CONSIDER DISCARDING

- My body is against me.
- Sickness and health "just happen" to me; I have no control.
- The best way to treat disease is to fight disease.
- If I'm not unhappy about being sick, it means I don't care.
- If I don't fear being sick (or getting sicker) I won't take good care of my body in the present.
- It's not okay to be sick.
- My body operates independently of what I think or feel.
- I need to be sick in order to take care of myself (rest more, eat well, take time off, etc.).
- The best way to get love, caring or "space" from others is to get sick.
- Good health is a matter of good genes and good luck.

Finally, you could reflect on a third list . . . a list of health-promoting beliefs that you might consider adopting. As you review these statements, ask yourself whether you agree with them and what reasons you have for agreeing or disagreeing. Then consider the possible effect on your health which might come from adopting some or all of these beliefs:

Beliefs to Consider Adopting

- Physical illness is a signal of imbalance and an invitation to restore balance.
- Physical symptoms are messages, not accusations.
- Everything that happens in my body is an opportunity.
- Thoughts do not simply take place in the brain; they occur body-wide.
- My mind is my body/my body is my mind. There's no separation.
- My current state of health is a reflection of my beliefs and choices. I can change my health by changing my beliefs and choices.
- My body is always working to take care of itself. Even disease or pain are expressions of my body's efforts to take care of itself.
- Illness is one possible consequence of unhappiness.
- I can be happy with my body "as is"—and still work on improving my health.
- I can be everything I've ever wanted to be.*

Jesse Stoff comments: In addition to belief-busting as a tool for helping to put depression into perspective, let me recommend laughter. As Umberto Eco writes in *The Name of the Rose,* "I don't believe the doctor cured him. He taught him to laugh at his illness. Illness is not exorcised, it is destroyed. . . . Perhaps the mission of those who love mankind is to make people laugh at the truth, to make truth laugh." In *Anatomy of an Illness,* Norman Cousins

*The material contained in this section is excerpted from *Happiness Is A Choice* by Barry Neil Kaufman, Ballantine Hardcover Books, 1991.

describes how he rented Groucho Marx films and laughed himself silly. After every round of movies his physicians noticed that his blood tests improved. He describes laughter as a form of internal jogging that enlivens the body and lightens the soul.

Depression can occur when, as a result of self-recriminations, feelings of guilt, and loss of self-esteem, perspective is lost. Inner and outer conditions become a blur of doom and gloom, and the ability to discriminate between oneself and one's illness is lost.

There are many ways to begin restoring a sense of humor, which is our next signpost. One way of beginning to put some distance between you and your illness is to try the following exercise, regardless of how corny it seems. Go to your local five-and-dime or K mart and buy a Groucho Marx nose-moustache-glasses set. Put it on, then sit in front of a mirror, shake a finger at yourself, and spout out every feeling of guilt and self-criticism you can think of while looking yourself right in the eyes. This should be done daily until the things that you're saying about yourself sound as ludicrous and foreign to you as you look sitting there in this get-up. If you don't start to smile and laugh soon, you need serious professional help.

Our sense of humor further develops as we acknowledge and appreciate the positive aspects of our lives. As a sort of affirmation, praise the good things that you are already doing, no matter how small, because they are the seeds of happiness and are the key to a renewed sense of perspective. To acknowledge and appreciate what's working in your life is perhaps the most powerful way of transforming your depression and unlocking the door to the uniquely human characteristic that is laughter. Through this signpost you can begin to create a lifestyle that offers the opportunity for greater health and happiness. A sense of humor and sustained joy are things that come to you by seeing them, through a sense of gratitude for life, not by arbitrarily creating them.

10

PSYCHONEUROIMMUNOLOGY: MIND OVER VIRUS

I can't die! I have too many books to write.

> —PALEONTOLOGIST STEPHEN JAY
> GOULD, 1982

I can't die! I have too many books to write.

> —ASTRONOMER GERARD K.
> O'NEILL, 1984

I can't die! I have too many books to write.

> —CHARLES R. PELLEGRINO, 1985

THE LADY AND THE TIGER

BOOM-BOOM-BOOM! BOOM-BOOM-BOOM!

Suddenly Ann heard a drum begin beating, three times as fast as her pulse.

"Close your eyes," said her friend, her shaman. "Go to a cave."

As she eased back in the chair, images came to her mind of places she knew, places where she might find a cave. And there it was—from her girlhood days in Guatemala. As she took her first hesitant steps toward the cave, a tiger appeared at the entrance. She was startled and frightened, and then the tiger turned the purest white. It did not threaten. Instead, it walked straight past her toward a tall stand of trees, seeming to ignore her completely. It paused there, at the edge of the jungle, as if waiting for her to follow.

The stiffness in Ann's back abated a little, and she followed behind the beast. They traveled on foot, the white tiger leading the way. The jungle was dripping. Shafts of sunshine slanted through the tree ferns, and where they pierced through to the jungle floor, heavy dew sparkled in a million points of light. It was morning— mid-morning, Ann guessed. By noon the dew had gone, the air was sticky and close, and she was still trotting behind the tiger, feeling overwhelmingly exhausted.

The sun was climbing down the western sky when they came upon the clearing. In the center was a lighted candle, shaped, it seemed, as a symbol of Ann. The bright flame of her spirit still burned, but the wax, her body, was deformed by chronic viral disease.

BOOM-BOOM-BOOM!

The shape of the wax shifted, shifted into something ugly and strange. Ann watched the flame sputter. "My God!" she cried, her words echoing in the clearing. "I'm going to die!"

The tiger looked directly at her from the other side of the candle, and she understood what she must do. She understood that she must let her fear go. As she did, her eyes filled with tears, and the flame became brighter, stronger.

BOOM-BOOM-BOOM!

Slowly, deliberately, the tiger licked the candle. Now, a strong, straight pillar of wax stood where moments before had crouched a shocking apparition—the more shocking because it was familiar. Ann looked at her hands and they seemed to glow.

She heard her name being called from somewhere far away and knew that it was time to leave. She knelt down to hug and thank the tiger. He licked her face. Then, with unbounded energy, she quickly retraced her steps through the jungle to the entrance of the cave. She turned to wave good-bye to her feline friend but the tiger was gone. So, too, was the jungle. In its place was a stunning view: quartz crystals, whole forests of them stretching to the horizon, tall and clear-cut and bright. At her feet was a particularly beautiful one with a point on both ends, which she knew to be her tiger. She picked it up, put it in her pocket, entered the cave, and stepped back into the room where she had started.

Boom-boom-boom! Boom-boom-boom! . . . and then silence . . .

Nothing had changed. The room was the same—except that on the table a candle was burning. Ann wondered. She thanked her friend, the shaman, and stood up to leave. As she stood, she felt a lump in her pocket, reached for it, and pulled out a quartz crystal. She laughed. Dr. Stoff sometimes gave little presents to his patients as tokens of affection, and he had given her this one the day before. She turned the crystal back and forth between her fingers. It was a rare one, with a point at both ends. It was special. And Ann knew that she, too, was special.

Ann had a particularly severe case of CFS. When we met her, she'd been sick for three and a half years. A rising tide of virus-induced fatigue and confusion had already cost her a career in accounting. Her lymph nodes felt like squashed golfballs. Her liver and spleen were swollen and tender, and her lymphocyte subpopulation was hauntingly reminiscent of an AIDS victim's blood, although there was no hint of the AIDS virus. But there was fear. As long as she could remember, there had been fear: fear of disappointing her parents, fear of not getting into a good school, fear of getting poor grades, fear of not landing the proper job, fear of not getting a promotion, fear of life in the big city. And now this virus had staggered her with all the force of mortality.

Jesse Stoff comments: In addition to the remedies described in previous chapters, I recommended visualization exercises (experiences) to Ann. They can be a powerful adjunct in stimulating the immune system. In her case, I believed they might assist in confronting and conquering her fears as well. I discussed this with her, and she felt that it would be worth a try. But she asked if she could use a visualization like those used by her Guatemalan ancestors, a shamanic journey. I thought that that was a great idea, and I gave her the name of a biochemist friend of mine who was studying these journeys. They quickly became friends, and then he led her to a cave, where she met a white tiger.

I was quite concerned about Ann and asked her to come back in two weeks (instead of the usual four to six weeks between early visits). When she returned, the transformation in her was miraculous. In two short weeks her swollen glands had diminished to normal size. There was life in her eyes, and she had so much energy that she almost seemed to glow from within. She also had a whole new outlook on life that could be summed up in one word: perspective. I asked her what had happened, and she told me that she had simply decided that she really wanted to live, no matter what. So she took the vitamins and funny-sounding remedies and visited my friend the day after she left my office. Then she told me of her journey and her realization that she had the power to re-create herself through her thoughts and attitudes. It was quite a lesson.

I noticed a little cloth bag hanging from a chain around her neck. When I asked about it, she told me it contained a special reminder: a quartz crystal, with a point on both ends.

MORE NOTES OF A LABORATORY RAT

Charles Pellegrino comments: Shamans are often referred to by us "civilized" types as third world (Quick! Where are the other two worlds?) medicine men or witch doctors. Yet some of them, at least, are keepers of an extraordinary body of ancient practice and wisdom, which they use to achieve healing and maintain well-being. These techniques predate history and are strikingly similar among cultures that are quite different in other respects, and separated by oceans and continents. Through trial and error, or perhaps as the result of a different world view, they arrived at the same conclusions about engaging the visualization experience.

In his book, *The Way of the Shaman,* Yale University anthropologist Michael Harner writes, "Shamanism is a great mental and emotional adventure, one in which the patient as well as the sha-man-healer are involved. Through his heroic journey and efforts, the shaman helps his patients to transcend their definition of them-selves as ill. He calls forth a commensurate emotional commitment from his patients, a sense of obligation to struggle alongside the shaman to save one's self. Caring and curing go hand in hand."

Bringing this ancient wisdom up to date, Western physicians and scientists have become all too familiar with psychogenic healing in what is known as the placebo response.

We are accustomed to reading in the medical literature claims that during the testing stages, a new drug worked, say, 25 percent better than the *placebo* (a substance given with no expected thera-peutic response, such as ordinary water or a pill containing sugar). If you look closely at the reports, you will notice that the placebo generally works 10 to 25 percent better than nothing at all. Often the placebo works better than the drug being tested, but when this happens the drug is judged to be a failure, and such reports only occasionally see publication in the medical journals. The placebo effect is often regarded as a nuisance that gets in the way and makes drug testing more tedious. What nature is really up to should be as obvious as your big toe; but the placebo is ignored, perhaps because it is so obvious. The medical journals fail to mention that the placebo does quite a lot.

The mechanism of action of the placebo is largely unknown, but the placebo effect itself seems to be on the verge of gaining respect-ability through the science of *psychoneuroimmunology*, which views the immune system as capable of behaving like a sensory organ and therefore potentially under our conscious control. In my case, getting better was largely a matter of thinking, "I've got too many books to write." I couldn't just drop dead. I had all those projects ahead of me—and I wanted to finish every one of them.

"That's why you're alive," says paleontologist and author Ste-phen Jay Gould. And he knows what he is talking about. In the autumn of 1982 I had returned to the United States from New Zealand. During one of my visits to Princeton, Donald Baird, a former advisor on my master's thesis, reminisced about two of the clumsiest paleontology students he had ever known: me and Steve Gould. Before we had completed our degrees, we had, between us, dropped hundreds of fossils, ranging from trays of snails to petrified crabs. Gould broke the tyrannosaur's teeth. I stumbled on and crushed its toes. "Many people now believe that nature wiped the dinosaurs out with an asteroid," said Baird. "It took you and Gould to finish the job."* Then Baird told me that Gould was ill with a particularly deadly form of cancer and that the word spreading through the scientific community was that he would be dead within three months. Baird could not help noticing that I did not look so well myself.

Two years later, Gould met me at Brookhaven National Laboratory. Chemotherapy had reduced his weight (he had needed to drop some ballast anyway), and he complained about having to buy a whole new wardrobe, but he was optimistic that his remission would extend until his death by natural causes at an advanced age. "Attitude clearly matters in fighting disease," said Gould. "We don't know why—from my old-style perspective, I suspect that mental states feed back upon the immune system—but match people with the same cancer for age, class, health, socioeconomic status, and in general those with positive attitudes, with a strong will and purpose for living, with commitment to struggle, with an active response to aiding their own treatment and not just passive acceptance of anything doctors say, tend to live longer. I've asked Sir Peter Medawar, my personal scientific guru and a Nobelist in immunology, what the best prescription against cancer might be. You know what he says? A cheerful, hopeful personality. That's it."

No, that is not entirely it. Thirty percent of it, perhaps, but I do not think a sanguine personality, a strong will, and a purpose in life are the be-all and end-all. These things alone cannot get you through. If they could, then some people would live for hundreds of years. The mind and the body have their limitations. But when you come right down to it, 30 percent is pretty significant. If all the tools that modern medicine could summon were capable of noth-

---

*I still live up to this reputation. In 1987, I added to my credits falling overboard from the research vessel *Atlantis II* onto the deck of a passing boat, and breaking the Great Wall of China. I have made a promise never to go anywhere near the Leaning Tower of Pisa.

ing more than pushing you close to the edge of recovery, then 30 percent (a little application of the will) can surely push you that extra few feet and put you over the hump. In that case, 30 percent can make all the difference in the world.

One of the first researchers to begin quantifying the mind-body connection (the mutual effects the mind and body have on each other) was Dr. George Solomon, a psychiatrist at Mount Sinai School of Medicine in New York City. Using the knowledge that such major immunological organs as the thymus gland and the lymph nodes were wrapped in nerve fibers, Solomon discovered during the 1960s that by electrically stimulating certain parts of an animal's brain, its ability to fight infection could be improved. By damaging those same parts, its immune function could be impaired. Seeing some indications that macrophages and other defensive cells had specific binding sites for neurotransmitters (including the mood-altering endorphins) on their outer membranes, Solomon and many of his contemporaries began to suspect that feedback from the immune system might even affect the emotional and rational centers of the brain. This would explain, in part, why people get irritable when they are sick and why mental capacity often deteriorates in parallel with resistance to disease.

But no one was really paying attention in the 1960s. Infatuated with technological wizardry and looking ahead to new drugs that were believed (a bit optimistically) to be capable of putting an end to all disease, the medical community simply was not interested in mind-body effects. Dr. Solomon laments, "I left the field of psychoneuroimmunology for ten years because no one would listen."

The noted psychologist Robert Adler was fascinated by what Solomon at first dubbed psychoimmunology. He was convinced that herein lay a whole new dimension of medical science, where the nervous system played an intermediary, connecting role in immune response. He therefore inserted the prefix "neuro" into Solomon's term to create a true tongue twister—*psychoneuroimmunology*—which can be shortened to PNI.

Already in the course of this book we have seen several fascinating and well-documented cases of mind over body, including a miraculous recovery from a double-barrel shotgun wound and control over an often fatal cardiac arrythmia. Two others we know of are particularly interesting and appropriate. Jesse will tell you of an experience he had in Copley Square, downtown Boston, on an autumn evening in 1985. And then I'm going to tell you about the strange case of the *Titanic*'s chief baker.

FIRE AND ICE

Jesse Stoff comments: A couple of years ago, while I was lecturing at an Expo in Boston, someone asked me to attend a special evening seminar: a fire walk. That afternoon, when I paused for lunch, I told a stockbroker friend of mine that I planned to try it and asked him jokingly if he'd like to join me. "Why not?" he said. "If I get cooked, at least I'll have my doctor there."

A man named Tony Robbins was in charge. He began by lighting a huge bonfire in Copley Square, with the fire department and press on hand. We then went into a small room, forty of us, where for three hours we were lectured to by Mr. Robbins. He spoke somewhat like a television evangelist, against a backdrop of music, and he eventually brought most of us to a state of frenzy. The effect was hypnotic.

When we finally went outside, we ran and yelled and danced barefoot. I noticed that my friend did not appear to be all that excited. (I guess there was no percentage to calculate.)

A cinder bed about fifteen feet long had been prepared from the bonfire, and we lined up in front of it. On cue we stopped our yelling, raised our right hands to shoulder height, looked up, and began chanting "cool moss." I did not notice the people in front of me walking across. When it was my turn, Robbins made sure my pants were rolled up so they would not burn, looked me in the eyes, tapped me on the shoulder, and I was off—walking directly on top of the bed of glowing hot coals. From somewhere far away I could feel and hear the coals crunching as I walked, and then it was over. And the most uncanny thing was that I did not realize it was over and that I had done it until one of Robbins's helpers stopped me on the other side and straightened out my arm.

Quickly, I ran under one of the big lights and examined my feet. When I brushed off the black, charred wood fragments—including a pea-sized one that had stuck to my foot without causing harm—I saw that there were no blisters and no reddening of the skin, nothing at all to indicate that I had just walked over a fire hot enough to melt aluminum. A thread hanging from the bottom of my pants had burned, but the hair around my ankles was not even singed.

I looked around for my friend and found him sitting under a light, with tears in his eyes. He had suffered several first- and second-degree burns. He looked up at me and said, "I didn't really believe that I could do it and I was right."

I agree that that is why he failed. And I think that what I experienced that night was a vivid demonstration of the power of the mind to create a protective reality.

Charlie comments: I think there are a number of physical explanations for Jesse's fire walk, including the Liedenfrost effect. There is a trial by ice, however, that continues to intrigue me. On the night the *Titanic* made its acquaintance with the iceberg, chief baker Charles Joughin, like so many others aboard the liner, was awakened by a sickening jolt. Joughin had not been hired for his leadership abilities, but he showed enormous initiative and courage that night. He organized his little staff of bakers to ransack the kitchens and carry provisions up the grand stairway to the lifeboats. He was offered a seat in boat number 10, but stayed on deck and launched it instead, while all around him many of those in charge stood by wringing their hands or seeking the safety of the lifeboats.

During the last five minutes of the *Titanic*'s life, he was in the pantry on the stern's starboard side, preparing himself a drink. The ship was listing so heavily that stairs, by that time, must have become impossible to ascend. He reclined against a wall that seemed on the verge of becoming the floor when he heard crashing and groaning iron—"as if something had buckled." The liner had in fact snapped in half, and the afterpart was no longer plunging down, but actually seemed to be floating back up and settling toward the stern. The floor was suddenly down again. Joughin shot out the pantry door, found a set of stairs, and emerged onto the well deck. And then the *Titanic*—what was left of her—rolled gently onto her port side. The baker hauled himself over the starboard rail and began running along the actual side of the ship. In the dim light of the flagstaff lantern, he could see a man ahead of him, descending the six-story rudder. He ran toward the man, but the rudder glided under and he never did see him again. The little island on which Joughin stood was descending like an elevator. He stopped running, tightened his life jacket, and stepped calmly into the water. He didn't even get his hair wet. He was puzzled and thankful that the sinking ship had not created the anticipated whirlpool.

Now, Charles Joughin was a man of average build, and he was not wearing exceptionally heavy clothing. The −3°C (28°F) water in which he was bathed should have killed him. Fifteen hundred people had gone into the water with him, and most of them were dead or unconscious within a half hour. Those few who survived contact with the cold water described a feeling like many sharp knives biting in at once. When it first touched them, it kicked the air out of their lungs.

During the *Titanic*'s final hours, Joughin had been drinking whiskey, knowing that the liner was doomed, and expecting nothing except death. The alcohol might have had something to do with his survival for more than four hours in the freezing water (Jesse and I generally view alcohol as being unnecessary and harmful; here is the exception that proves the rule). Experiments have shown that people sitting in ice baths or lying on cots in chilled rooms lose heat faster if they drink alcohol, which increases circulation and therefore brings more blood to the skin surface, where it is cooled and then carried down to the core of the body. But volunteers for such experiments usually sit back calmly listening to music and/or reading. They are not participating in a major shipwreck, an event that is bound to fill one with dread, if not outright panic. If you are sinking and sober and aware, your heart will beat faster, and your circulation will be considerably more rapid (which translates to a more rapid decrease of the core body temperature) than if you are too drunk to care.

But the calming effect of alcohol alone cannot fully account for Joughin's survival. For two hours he paddled alone in the cold Atlantic. By then everyone else in the water had died. Shortly before dawn he saw thirty men standing on an upside-down lifeboat and swam over to them. There was no room for him on the keel, so he held on, with fist–sized chunks of ice bobbing around him. Two of the men standing on top of the boat eventually froze to death, and only after their bodies were lowered over the side did the baker climb out of the water. My only explanation for his survival is that he simply did not know he was supposed to die. He must have had extraordinary will. In other lifeboats, men who were merely wet, who had spent the night in relative safety, died, their last words being, "I'm going to die. I'm going to die."

Oh, yes, the body does respond to our beliefs, although the mechanism of response is not yet well understood. When we turn our focus to the immune system response, we see that the mind-body connection can extend even to the level of personality. Dr. Bennett Braun has studied people with multiple personalities and discovered that when victims of this disorder shift character, their bodies shift along with them. Braun has noted all sorts of physiologic and immunologic changes, including a dramatic case involving a woman who was hospitalized for diabetes. Her blood sugar surges were particularly difficult to treat because the symptoms appeared only when a specific personality was in charge.

Not everyone is comfortable with such news. One physician likens the possibility of being able to control our heart rhythms, our insulin secretions, and our macrophages to being handed the controls of a plane when we are perfectly comfortable riding in the back as passengers. From my perspective, that's not so bad. And it's an apt analogy. In 1984 I had the very poor judgment to board a plane that truly belonged in an Indiana Jones movie. As a passenger I had no control. As it turned out, neither did the pilot. Lucky for me that one of my fellow passengers knew how to land an airplane; otherwise I might now be just another permanent fixture in the jungle that overgrows Mayan Coba. A little control can be a healthy thing, whether we are talking about airplanes or macrophages.

MINDING YOUR BODY

Among the first to apply clinically the concepts of psychoneuroimmunology (PNI) were Drs. Carl and Stephanie Simonton of the Cancer Counseling and Research Center in Dallas, Texas. They began in the 1970s by teaching cancer patients different kinds of visualization exercises, with the idea of stimulating the immune system. The exercises were not unlike Ann's shaman journey. In one case, a boy imagined fleets of X-wing fighters bombing the daylights out of his tumor. He conducted the exercise every day, and the tumor eventually shrank out of existence.

By simply adding visualization to their patients' overall treatment strategy, the Simontons have repeatedly demonstrated that the survival times of terminal cancer patients can be doubled. And in anomalously high numbers, their patients have undergone spontaneous remissions.

Another leader in the PNI field, and a powerful patient advocate, is Dr. Bernie Siegel of Yale University. He combines visualization exercises with a healthy dose of common sense and wisdom. His goal is to help his patients gain perspective on their lives, and to know the peace of mind that results from it.

"My message is peace of mind, not curing cancer or paralysis," says Dr. Siegel. "In achieving peace of mind, cancer may be healed and paralysis may disappear. These things may occur through peace of mind, which creates a healing environment in the body."

Modern medicine is predicated on the idea that one should try to prevent death. This is why, for example, the U.S. RDA (Recommended Daily Allowance) of vitamins is so low, as we mentioned in chapter 7. The RDA is based upon the minimum amount of vitamins necessary to prevent disease and death, not the amount necessary to maintain optimum health. Any system of medicine based on preventing death rather than improving the quality of life (modern medicine being the first such system to adopt this approach in the history of humankind) is going to fail because, try as one may to keep brain-dead people alive by assaulting their bodies with tubes and pumps, no one can live forever. Instead of accepting perpetual failure, let us adopt a new goal or purpose for medical intervention: to live life. Medical intervention then becomes a means to maximize the creative potential of each individual, to allow patients to fully explore and manifest their individuality to whatever extent the limitations of their bodies allow

To be happy and fulfilled, with a sense of purpose; to accept, support, and love oneself, one's family, and one's neighbors; to be human; to be

authentic—In preceding chapters we passed signposts pointing to these goals. Among them are focus, control, enthusiasm, gratitude, love, balance, happiness, and perspective. To find perspective in one's life is often the reward of an illness. Suddenly you find yourself standing, as if on a mountaintop, looking out over the telephone bills, the electric bills, and the ache in your throat, and seeing opportunity. You can, in a sense, re-create yourself. The signposts are but a skeleton of the full range of human potential. You have to create the image of yourself.

"That is what PNI is all about," says Dr. Bernie Siegel. "Psychological and spiritual development are capable of reversing the disease process. In the figurative sense, it is as if all the destructive power that the disease unleashes is channeled into self-discovery, and the virus is in turn attacked by a rebellious immune system. The disease process is now estranged and unnecessary, as though the victim has been reborn and rejects the old self and its disease. When a patient with a physical illness makes a thorough and positive personality change, the body's defenses may now eliminate the disease, which is not part of the new self."

Jesse Stoff comments: Charlie's reality seems to be a sea of ideas and images—especially images. I understand that he designs and tests antimatter rockets (starships), without actually building them, by putting coils and tethers together in his head and letting gamma rays and muons run through them. Then he mentally dissects the machine, seeks out the parts that have worn down or heated up too much, redesigns them, and runs them again until they break. I think he walks this Earth in what many of us would call a hallucinogenic state. Charlie is the only person I know who seems to have movie pictures perpetually running in his head. Mention some thought to him, such as the view from the Moon, or from a planet circling Alpha Centauri A, and he will spontaneously respond with a beautiful description of what it must be like to stand there. No need for visualization therapy or shamanic journeys here. When I told Charlie that he had a fascinating disease, I got his attention. When I told him he did not have to be sick and crippled for the rest of his life, he trusted me enough that he didn't see himself as sick and crippled anymore, and he isn't.

The mind is the key.* Everything else—vitamins, remedies, and exercises—can only help you to stop the progression of an illness, until in your mind you learn what you need to learn and you decide to be well. No one really becomes healthy unless he wants to be and sees himself so. Health is nothing more than the full, positive, creative expression of yourself. Argue for your disease and its limitations and they are yours. It's your choice. You are in control. If and when you realize this, then you will become a member of the limited and exclusive club that Bernie Siegel calls "exceptional patients." These people, he says, "manifest the will to live in its most potent form. They take charge of their lives even if they were never before able to, and they work hard to achieve health and peace of mind. They do not rely on doctors to take the initiative, but rather use them as members of a team, demanding the utmost in technique, resourcefulness, concern, open-mindedness, and love." Imagine this statement from a surgeon!

I find the Option dialogue process discussed in chapter 9 an excellent way of gaining insights into why a person is sick to begin with.

Bears Kaufman comments: First, we can open the doorway to the PNI connection by using the Option dialogue process to foster an entirely new perspective on ourselves, our bodies, and our health. We do this by questioning and, ultimately, changing our beliefs. "Am I fearing sickness or wanting to be healthy?"—these are two very different notions. "When I am physically unhealthy, do I fight

---

*Charlie tells me that if he'd taken the same shotgun blast his friend took, he'd have been lying on the floor estimating his falling blood pressure, the damage to his bladder, liver, intestines, major arteries, kidneys, and so on. He'd probably have concluded that he could not survive for very long, and he thinks he would have, in his mind's eye, seen himself as dead and died on cue. His friend had little knowledge of the organs that had been damaged, did not "know" he was supposed to die, and lived. Charlie says, "If ever a little learning can be deadly, *that* is a classic example. My friend was far better off not knowing the house rules, not knowing what 'can' and 'cannot' be done."

the problem or try to restore inner balance and harmony? Do I see myself as healthy or sickly? Is my body in or out of my control? Am I waiting for some disease (cancer, a heart condition, CFS, etc.) to 'get' me?"

The answers to those questions tell us much about how we handle ourselves in the face of illness. Change one of those answers (beliefs), and our experience or physical imbalance will change radically. Also, what we decide to do for ourselves will be profoundly altered. Instead of being a "victim," we can participate actively in the healing process by developing and empowering an attitude of well-being (I know I can make a difference, and I will!). This in no way means that we shouldn't find all the support (medical, homeopathic, etc.) that we can to assist us; it simply means we should become engaged in our own healing process.

Once we discard the self-defeating beliefs and fears about health and healing that don't serve us, we can consider new ones that do. "Disease" means not at ease or moving away from our natural flow. Put ourselves in a state of comfort and we help restore the possibility of health. By becoming happier, in addition to the crucial physical remedies suggested in this book, we help ourselves pursue a state of wellness.

The second step in the process of activating the PNI connection is to create a mechanism for reminding ourselves (and giving direct messages to ourselves) about what we want and what we can do. Many (though not all) people find that guided visualizations can provide that helpful daily reminder. Once we have used the Option Process to discard some of those old beliefs and, perhaps, to create new, more useful ones, we can put into action our new awareness, tailoring each visualization to our individual beliefs and wants.

Visualization involves creating a safe internal space. It can be done in a bedroom, or while jogging or riding the bus. In that solitude, we can visualize energizing that portion of the physiological system (brain, neurons, heart, glands, the immune system) most crucial and pertinent in helping restore and maintain health. In one case it might involve designing a clear metaphor for letting go of muscle spasms in the lower back, for example, pouring a warm river of sunshine down the spine. For another person, it might mean learning about and then imagining the multiplication of B cells, T cells, and macrophages as they neutralize a deeply entrenched virus.

The possibilities are endless; each person evolves as his or her own best expert, structuring (with the help of a physician, psychologist, or counselor, or simply working by themselves) his or her own vehicle to health and healing.

Illnesses and their symptoms are signs for us . . . in effect, questions that can lead us to our beliefs. They are not indictments that we are bad for ourselves (my body is not my enemy). They are not accusations that we don't want to be healthy and happy (truly, each of us does the best we can). They are not statements about the future. Anything is possible! There are always exceptions! "Hopeless" is just another belief and a way of choosing death.

In choosing our beliefs and therefore their consequences, we influence our physical destiny profoundly. Once we embrace the implications of this understanding, we can truly take charge, with a renewed sense of power and optimism. My body, my friend!

Jesse Stoff comments: Our thinking is the uppermost, and perhaps the most important, level of our house of cards, for it gives form and function to the lower levels. The lower levels provide substance. Our thinking provides the blueprint or direction.

The most powerful visualization exercises are those that are individually crafted to include new beliefs that you want to assimilate. The visualization itself is but a metaphor to awaken your positive, creative potential and direct it toward the part of you that is ailing. Hence, there are as many correct visualizations as there are patients and health issues, and a number of visualizations can be constructed for (or by) any particular person. To get you started, and to give you an idea of how the process works, we have included below a visualization that I find to be generally helpful to people with CFS. Feel free to add to it from your own thoughts, beliefs, or ideas that you find to be personally relevant.

To begin, buy or borrow two audiocassette recorders. On the first, play some relaxing music that lacks lyrics. The music you choose should be soft and nondirective. For most of you this probably means "boring stuff" from the classics, or from the "new age" artists.* Place a blank tape in the second recorder and set it on "record."

Play the music at a low volume in the background and then, into the second recorder, slowly read aloud the visualization that follows, with whatever additions you like. This should take about fifteen minutes. Play the tape back to guide your visualizations, setting aside fifteen minutes for them at about the same time every day.

HEALING VISUALIZATION

Make yourself comfortable in a quiet room, free from distractions and interruptions. You may want to dim the lights to create an atmosphere that will help you to relax very deeply. Ease yourself into a comfortable position, either sitting up or lying down. Loosen any tight-fitting shoes or clothing and feel free to shift your position or gently move any muscles to prepare yourself for deep relaxation. Allow yourself to enjoy this peaceful time. It is a time to care for yourself and to let your body release its own natural capacity for healing and renewal.

Take a slow, deep breath, let it out slowly, and gently close your eyes. Become aware of your breathing, feeling the air as it enters your body as you inhale, fills your lungs, and then leaves your body as you exhale. As you become totally aware of your breathing, allow it to become slow and rhythmic, like waves rolling in from the ocean. With each inhalation, breathe in a wonderful sensation of peacefulness and calm. Then, as you exhale, slowly breathe out any tension or concerns. Let your attention remain on your breathing as you sink deeper and deeper into a feeling of relaxation, breathing in peacefulness and calm, savoring the feeling of relaxation, and breathing out any tensions or concerns.

Now, turn your attention to your right foot. Slowly curl your toes under and clench the muscles in your foot. Hold

*A tape catalogue can be obtained by writing to: Kripalu, Box 793, Lenox, MA 01240.

that tension as tightly as possible for about five seconds. Be aware of all the sensations in your toes, foot, and ankle. Release the tension and take a slow, deep breath, feeling the difference in your foot between tension and relaxation. Clench your foot again for five seconds, noticing the tension. Then release and become aware of the relaxation, which you may experience as a feeling of warmth, heaviness, or a tingling sensation.

Now turn to your left foot. Clench it for five seconds and then relax. Notice the feeling as you release. Tighten it again for five seconds and then release. Feel the pleasant sensation of relaxation in your feet and ankles. Imagine the sensation as a warm, light-green liquid that begins to spread upward into the rest of your body, filling up your calves and knees with a comfortable heaviness and warmth, filling up your thighs, hips, and pelvic area, the entire lower part of your body now feeling pleasantly heavy and warm. Allow the green liquid to spread further, into your abdomen, back, and chest. And now into your shoulders, arms, and hands, your body feeling relaxed and peaceful. Now allow that warm green liquid to spread into your neck, head, and face, so that your whole body is feeling peaceful, heavy, and warm.

As you enjoy this feeling of deep relaxation, imagine yourself in your favorite outdoor place on a warm, sunny day. You are by yourself, noticing the beauty of the blue sky and the natural scenery that surrounds you. Pick a comfortable place and lie down. Allow yourself to let go, your body held firmly by the soft ground beneath you. As you breathe slowly and naturally, take in the calmness and tranquility of this peaceful, beautiful scene.

See the yellow-orange glow of the sunlight and feel its warmth on your face and body. Its gentle golden glow brings you healing energy from the heavens. This is the energy that supports all life and restores health and wholeness. As you inhale, breathe in the golden light that warms your body, bringing health and vitality. Allow the energy to intensify in the area of your solar plexus. As it does so, experience the wonderful sense of well-being and vitality. Nothing to do here, only the savoring of the peace and beauty of this moment. You can experience this feeling whenever you choose, when you become deeply relaxed and centered within yourself.

Now, allow the energy to intensify in the right side of your abdomen, in the area of your liver, a major organ of your immune system. Feel the golden healing light warm the liver and restore its power to cleanse and protect the body. Imagine your liver strong and functioning perfectly, helping to heal your body and bring you to a state of health and vitality.

Now, take a moment to imagine yourself as a child again, feeling happy, healthy, fully alive. It's springtime and you're filled with enthusiasm as you take out your bicycle after a long winter. Dust it off, pump up the tires, and take it outside into the warm sunshine. Gripping the handlebars confidently, put one foot on the pedal and then swing your body up comfortably onto the seat. Feel the joy as you begin to pedal in an easy, rhythmic motion, moving forward slowly at first, then picking up speed as your pedaling becomes faster. Feel the wind as it brushes against your cheeks and ruffles your hair. Feel the air filling your lungs with each deep breath and the energy surging into every part of your body. Let yourself flow with the easy, natural rhythm of your pedaling, your breathing, and the beating of your heart. It's so effortless you can even stop pedaling and still glide smoothly, easily. No need to push yourself. Just the pleasant sensation of motion and the beauty all around you, gliding easily, perfectly balanced, and in control—changing direction with a simple turn of the handlebars, controlling speed by deciding how fast to pedal, and always feeling free to choose where you want to go. This exhilarating feeling of freedom and mastery is yours to experience now and whenever you choose. Take a moment to become fully aware of this feeling. Notice your breathing and how energized your body feels. You can evoke this feeling in the future by tuning in to your breathing and remembering the images and sensations you have just experienced. Tapping into this relaxed energy not only feels good, it also helps to support the healing process. Take a few moments to complete your bike ride, savoring the sights and sounds as you head home, and enjoy the energized, exhilarated feeling in your body. As you arrive home, put your bike back in a place where you can find it easily again. Prepare to return to the present moment, no longer a child, but feeling the enthusiasm, joy, and vitality that you felt during your bike ride. Take a few slow deep breaths; wiggle your fingers and toes, and feel the energy flowing to all parts of your body. Imagine the furniture and other objects in the room around you. Very slowly open your eyes, feeling refreshed, energized, and alert.

This visualization script was written by my friend and colleague, Dr. Jeff Rossman, a warm and talented clinical psychologist with a great deal of experience with CFS patients, who shares an office with me. A more extensive visualization tape is available from our office.*

Diane is a very creative "exceptional patient" of mine who had a powerful experience as a result of her CFS disease. I asked her to write about it in her own words. This is what she wrote:

Four and a half years ago I awoke from a nightmare in a cold sweat, with a pounding headache, a sharp pain below my breastbone, and almost completely out of breath. Groggy and still wheezing, I fumbled for the pen and tablet in my nightstand drawer and began to scratch out my all-too-real experience, in which my life energy seemed to be locked in a bloody battle with my physical body:

> A wild dog lives off my body
> and feeds on the small bones I sacrifice
> to protect my vital organs.
> I am nauseous from her hollow panting;
> her yellow eyes eat into my stomach.

*Rather than resort to shamanic drumming, classical music, or the like as a background, we employ sophisticated state-of-the-art technology using subliminal sound patterns to help you relax faster and deeper and to create a more powerful experience for you. For information about the tape, call Solstice at 1-800-765-7842.

I tempt her with my heart
to make her stop.
She circles there for hours,
until the fiery ring of her motion
seals her permanently from what
she wants. Now she is more crazed:
one lung then the other shudders
like a river crossed by moonlight.
As she tears into my throat
ghostly sounds rasp out in all directions.
My tongue leaps from the dark hole
in my face—her tongue.

We are howling for our lives.

I had the distinct impression that this wild animal had literally followed me out of my nightmare and was lying in wait for me in my own body! The most terrifying part of it was that I somehow knew my life depended on her overcoming me, that I had to lose the fight in order to win it—I had to die in order to live. But I also knew with a certainty that I have seldom experienced before that I could not simply surrender to her either. I was deeply shaken and confused.

It was almost six-thirty in the morning: my husband would be stumbling toward the shower momentarily and I would be stumbling after him, both of us hurrying toward our respective busy days. However, when the alarm clock sounded and broke my reverie, I could not lift myself out of bed, nor could I have imagined then that the nightmare was just beginning.

I spent the rest of the week in bed with a particularly nasty cold that never seemed to go away entirely. Like the nightmare that accompanied it, this persistent ailment coincided with my intimation that something in my life had irrevocably turned.

For the next several months I was wholly absorbed in what I considered then to be a full-scale psychospiritual transformation. At twenty-six, I was happily married, working full-time as an educational consultant at a psychiatric hospital, and taking graduate courses in psychology and theology. Yet, within the familiar structure of an over-extended life, my normally vibrant and resilient personality seemed to be unraveling. I grew increasingly despondent, restless, absentminded, and aloof. I felt as though my life forces were being sucked up through my head into a glowing balloon which hovered above me and seemed to want to pull my consciousness with it.

At the same time, my daily meditation, which had frequently been perfunctory and effortful, became infused with an intensity and vitality so compelling that all of my previous experiences paled in comparison. My nights became enlivened by richly textured dreams that disrupted my sleep and made it increasingly difficult to attend to my daily responsibilities.

While I was aware of being constantly tired and light-headed and feeling like I was always battling a lingering flu, it never occurred to me that I might be suffering from a physical illness. Rather, I assumed that I was simply unable to contain both the intense energy of a spiritual opening and the intense pain I was absorbing from students—many of whom were chronically suicidal. Convinced of my inadequacy as a helping professional, I quit my job. My husband, my family, and my friends recognized that I was very depressed and, like me, attributed it to human service "burnout." They were characteristically supportive and encouraged me to relax, write, and prepare for the birth of our first baby.

It was only after I miscarried nine weeks into the pregnancy that I began to suspect that I might have a serious medical problem. However, my gynecologist assured me that I was in relatively good health and that by continuing to eat healthfully, exercise, and relax, I would soon become pregnant again.

Over the next several months, as my inner life continued to deepen and expand, my physical health continued to deteriorate. In addition to feeling sluggish, nauseous, and achy, I began to experience excruciating gallbladder attacks and chronic bronchial asthma. My menstrual periods stopped altogether.

On the one hand, as a longtime student of human development and growth-oriented psychotherapy, I was naturally drawn to and stirred by the process taking place within me. On the other hand, as it grew increasingly difficult to do even menial tasks like grocery shopping and housecleaning, I began to wonder if I could pay the price of personal growth.

I remember one lovely spring morning when a friend stopped by to see if I wanted to go for a walk. When she arrived, I was still in my nightgown. "I'll just help myself to some juice while you get ready," she called from the kitchen. Twenty minutes later she poked her head into the bedroom; I was curled up in a ball on my bed, crying. "I know things haven't been easy for you lately," she said gently. "Would you rather just stay here and talk?"

For the first time, I revealed to my friend the agonizing fear underlying my experiences over the past two years. "Annie," I sobbed, "I think I'm dying."

She peered into my eyes and tenderly but firmly replied, "I can't stand to see you this way anymore. Please let me take you to a doctor."

"I've already been to the doctor—twice, in fact—and he assured me that everything was normal. He just told me to take aspirin for my aches and pains and to find a good psychotherapist for my depression."

"Well," she asked matter-of-factly, "how long are you going to wait before you get a second opinion?"

Finally, unable to deny it my attention any longer, I dragged my depleted body to my friend Jesse Stoff and asked if he would help me figure out what was wrong with me. Within a couple of weeks, after extensive testing, he gave me the diagnosis: chronic active Epstein-Barr virus disease. While I had no idea what CEBV was, I was relieved to learn that what I was suffering from had a name and that he could treat it. This lovely friend, a rare embodiment of brilliance and generosity of spirit, had always inspired my confidence. Now, with him as my doctor, I felt doubly blessed.

Since my illness was diagnosed eighteen months ago, I have been engaged in a multifaceted treatment program, designed by my doctor, comprised of homeopathic remedies, traditional drug treatments, nutritional supplements (including vitamins and minerals), dietary changes, therapeutic eurythmy, therapeutic massage, visualization, psychotherapy, and a lot of rest.

It is virtually impossible to describe the specific effects of the various components of this therapeutic regimen, because my experience suggests that they work in concert with one another in a synergistic fashion. I can, however, briefly describe the course of my recovery over the past year and a half.

Initially, my doctor prescribed homeopathic remedies and therapeutic eurythmy in order to support my immune system augmented by traditional medications to improve the functioning of my lungs and thyroid. He also recommended specific dietary modifications to relieve the painful disturbances of my gallbladder and digestive system.

I experienced little improvement during the first few weeks, and because of my continued low energy level (the most incapacitating symptom of the illness for me), I questioned the treatment's effectiveness. Moreover, I felt frustrated as I began to suspect that there was no instant cure for my chronic condition.

The following three or four months of my recovery were probably the most challenging. Not only had the initial enthusiasm generated by having what was becoming a recognizable and mediaworthy illness subsided, but I also began to experience how slow and inconsistent my progress would be. I was definitely improving: the gallbladder attacks had stopped, I was no longer catching every cold and flu bug that came around, and my menstrual cycle had resumed, although it was still somewhat irregular. Nevertheless, I was discouraged. Ironically, as I began to experience short periods of relative wellness, I became more acutely aware of how miserable I felt the rest of the time.

More discouraging, though, was the cumulative effect of chronic illness on my self-esteem. At this point, I was a full-time graduate student in a creative writing program. Having previously excelled in other academic settings, I expected graduate school to be an exciting and rewarding experience. Instead, I found that getting myself from class to class was exhausting, that concentrating on assignments required an unprecedented act of will, and that writing itself was practically impossible. This writer's block, which reflected my overall sense of stagnation, eventually led me to seek counseling. I began working with an extraordinary woman who integrates her medical training and her capacity for deep spiritual insight into a therapeutic process which continues to be one of the most valuable aspects of my healing. At the same juncture, I also incorporated creative visualization and kundalini yoga into my already extensive repertoire of daily therapies.

By the end of the first year of treatment, my life, as well as my health, had undergone a profound transformation. In addition to my improved energy level and self-esteem, my husband and I realized that we had opened to and made room for a new way of doing and being in the world. Subtly, but unmistakably, as we both made the conscious effort to understand and overcome my illness, we discovered that our daily activities began to flow in a more natural rhythm. We slowed down, lightened up, and took better care of ourselves and each other.

My level of health reached a new plateau. Most of my original symptoms were gone, and there were moments in which I felt more energized, more purposeful, and more grateful to be alive than I had ever felt before. However, I still had chronic asthma and occasional periods of low energy. And I had not become pregnant again. At the suggestion of a friend and with the support of my doctor, I made an appointment with a renowned physician whose primary method of therapy is acupuncture. After four treatments over a period of eight weeks (during which time I continued to take the remedies, medications, and supplements I had been taking all along, as well as the Chinese herbs this new doctor prescribed in conjunction with the acupuncture), my asthma disappeared. My energy level continues to improve and my husband and I have great confidence in my acupuncturist's opinion that we will be able to conceive this spring.

Over four years ago I was amazed to find that my sunny, active life had turned into a nightmare from what I eventually learned was a chronic illness. And, since that time, I have continued to be amazed by the intensity and promise of pain and the paralyzing effects of fatigue, by the effectiveness of "strange" medicines and the ineffectiveness of unfocused effort, by the saintliness of some husbands and the loving concern of family and friends, by the skill and wisdom of my health practitioners and the skill and wisdom of the human body, by the exquisite unfolding of the human soul and the exquisite awareness that the wild dog of my nightmare has become my beloved companion. Now, she is walking beside me out of the nightmare into a life we had only dreamed of.

· ★ ★ ★

Jim L. is another "exceptional patient" whose healing journey took him through a transformational experience as he learned to co-exist with his HIV infection. After one of our sessions he sent me this note:

> To all those medical people who offered me no way out, to all the newspeople on television and in the press who have totally destroyed the hope of anyone ever surviving with AIDS, I offer myself as living proof that AIDS, or any other "terminal" illness, does not mean an automatic death sentence. In fact, many of us have made our transition through this disease, some consciously and some unconsciously, by using our illness to change our lives and live quality not quantity.
>
> It wasn't always like this. I didn't just find out one day four years ago that I was harboring a disease, and the next day put a big smile on my face and claim, "I am in charge of my life." It took quite a while for me to get to that point in my healing process. And healing *is* a process, a process to which I pay a great deal of attention. I've learned that healing takes place on so many levels beyond the physical.
>
> The story of why I am still alive is simply *my* story. It is what has worked for me. It is not meant to be a list of shoulds and should nots, but rather as an offering of hope to my brothers and sisters who have been told their time is over . . . IT IS NOT! It is only over if you *believe* it to be so. Just think of all the life-force that is drained from us when we put all this energy behind negative thought patterns. The more we believe such patterns, the more energy we give to the disease. And the more energy the disease has, the more it manifests itself.
>
> If I wake in the morning and tell myself it is going to be a great day, and if I allow myself to believe it, then indeed, it will be a great day. However, if I awake with a "victim consciousness," then I will attract things to myself that victimize me. The seed that I plant within me in the morning will grow and grow, all day long. And just like a tiny seed that is planted in the ground, the more you water it, the more it grows. I realized that I allowed myself to be victimized in my lifetime to the point where my body revolted and I walked right into an awaiting disease.

For the first three-and-a-half years of my diagnosis, I walked, lived, ate, drank, and slept in fear. There was not a waking or sleeping moment I was not in fear. Why me? What had I done to deserve this? Every answer to every question reinforced my guilt. During the first two years, I went to more doctors than one can imagine. I did experimental drug programs in New York City. I even went to a pharmacist who claimed AIDS was a latent syphilis virus. It all sounds so silly now, but at the time, I was desperate. I wanted to live. I would have tried almost anything.

All I had ever asked for was to have my body healed, but I placed too much attention on being healed physically when I needed to go so much deeper. I learned that physical healing came about as a result of healing the whole being—body, mind, and spirit. The emphasis was to be placed on the process, not the product: a process that would bring about inner peace. If the outcome was physical health, great! If not, that would be okay, too.

About two years ago, I was coming pretty close to ending my life. I attempted to bear all this pain on my own. I was so ashamed of who I was and of this "ugly" disease. When I felt as if I could not handle one more day of this hell, I reached out and said, "God, I need your help. I can't do this on my own anymore." It was at this point of total surrender that this power greater than I'd ever witnessed went to work in my life. This was not an "instant" healing, but later, as the pieces began to fall in place, I could see that my life's direction had turned around that day and my healing went into its next phase: learning to trust in this Divine Guidance.

I went to work rethinking my life and applying pure, simple love to every situation. It was not always easy. Learning to love the IRS auditing agent was a major challenge. If I could see love in myself, then I could see that this same love must be in everyone else—even the IRS man. To accept people for who they are, without judgments, was always a big issue for me. I was finding out that love was the most powerful, healing balm ever and was available to *everyone everywhere!* They just had to say "yes" to it.

Sometimes our real healing, that which we will take with us, takes place at another level of our being, and when it is done, our time is simply up. We've completed our stay here. To me, that is important to remember because it means if I die during the process, *I did not fail.*

It is a pretty amazing thing when we conceive that our thoughts are responsible for all that we are. It is even more amazing to me that each one of us has the power within us to change our thoughts and thereby change our whole expression of life. Simply by starting the day with an affirmation, like "Today I choose to be a more loving person" can have a profound effect on our immune systems. So imagine what an affirmation each day like "Every day in every way, I am growing healthier and stronger" can do.

Another major helper for me was joining groups that loaned me support. I found that dealing with an illness by myself was just too tough. Loving guidance and support were needed. I am surrounded by medical professionals now who offer me alternatives. I get solid nutritional counseling, I am learning about the healing power of Chinese herbs, and I attend holistic health meetings so I am always attempting to be one up on new therapies. Homeopathy has played a major role in my healing, through the guidance of my doctor, Jesse Stoff.

I am forty-five years old at the time I write this. It was only thirty years ago that no one who contracted cancer was given any hope of surviving. And so, thirty years ago all those people died because they were told they would. They bought into that belief system and succumbed. I am sure that a few did make their transition with a clear and free conscience, however, the majority just died.

Today, people who have cancer are hearing about a thing called hope and many are buying into that hope and surviving. Many are even into total remission. We are choosing to take charge of our lives and not give in. And so, I believe the same scenario I have just described about cancer is now proving itself true with AIDS. Seven years ago, if you were diagnosed with AIDS, you were told you had eighteen months to live, at most. And just about everyone died right on schedule. Then a few brave afflicted said, "Hey, wait a minute, folks. I am not ready to die!" Well guess what? These folks started to live longer than eighteen months. And many, myself included, are still alive. And, I just might add, are quite healthy.

Every day, more and more people are buying into this hope and are making some of the most important growth steps in their lives, even while dying.

The process of living each day is important to me now. I love to laugh and I am not afraid to cry. And most important of all, I meditate and pray every day as often as I want. Getting up a little earlier to spend some quiet time with my Creator sets the mood for my day. Thank you God for giving me one more beautiful day to live. Today I choose to see love in everyone.

God Bless You!

—Jim L.

11

TO SERVE MAN: RECIPES FOR HEALTHFUL LIVING

Don't get on that spaceship! Don't get on that spaceship! We've translated the book the aliens left behind: To Serve Man—it's a cookbook!

—FROM A CLASSIC *TWILIGHT ZONE* EPISODE

Upon what meat doth this our Caesar feed,
That he is grown so great?

—WILLIAM SHAKESPEARE, *JULIUS CAESAR*

The food strategy we present here contains simple combinations and recipes based upon the simplification/"cave-man" diet outlined in chapter 7. For some CFS patients, food sensitivities (usually temporary) require an easily digested diet that can be used by almost all people working toward conquest of CFS, whereas the reverse, a more liberal diet, is not universally applicable. Hence, if you are not suffering from food allergies, you can mix the food combinations recommended here as you like.

Our strategy probably requires some changes in your eating habits. As we pointed out in chapter 7, you can and probably should treat yourself to that occasional (small) ice cream sundae or hot dog, but heed the advice we gave: do not splurge to excess, especially if you are not yet well. You will be doing yourself the most good if you regard these guidelines as a lifetime change of eating habits. Lifetime, of course, means never having to say never to Häagen Dazs. Any diet that drives you crazy, you are not likely to stick to. So when you do treat yourself to an old favorite, do savor every bite, and do so guilt free.

Follow our advice and you will be helping your liver while reducing any possible contribution to symptoms arising from food allergies. Your body and immune system should function more efficiently, giving you increased stamina and an added edge against the Epstein-Barr, Coxsackie, and other CFS-related viruses. The menus that follow are but guidelines. They will provide a foundation upon which you can exercise your own judgment and creativity. If you are already using a yeast-free diet strategy, the menus will require only minor changes in your habits. We encourage you to add new fruits, vegetables, and grains in the appropriate areas, but remember—avoid red meats and deep-fried foods.

The recipes have been designed to be flexible, appealing, and easy to prepare. If *we* can prepare these dishes (and we're not cooks), then we're certain that you'll have no trouble sticking with the diet (however, we must admit, Donna Astion, a professional chef, did advise and guide us). You should note that we emphasize using ingredients in a form that is as close as possible to whole, natural, and unprocessed (for example, if not fresh vegetables, then frozen, and then, only as a last resort, canned). In general, additives and preservatives may prolong the life of vegetables and their products, but they won't prolong yours. (Rule: if it won't rot, it isn't worth eating.) There are, of course, exceptions to almost every rule. Certain artificial preservatives, including BHT and other antioxidants, mop up free radicals and may thus have a slight cancer-preventative effect. But BHT may cause undue liver stress, and since you should already be taking vitamin C, vitamin E, and other antioxidants that do not stress the liver, you can probably live without BHT.

Processed or refined foods have been literally smashed to pieces and then reassembled. Unfortunately, not all of the pieces have been put back in. Some manufacturers will then "enrich" the food, which means that someone poured in vitamins (usually synthetic) and minerals to make up, in part, for what was lost. For example, when white flour is manufactured, the fiber and bran portions of the wheat are stripped away and discarded. The end product, refined white flour, is little more than ordinary starch with loads of calories but little nutritional value. Similarly, the manufacturing process that yields white sugar results in a dead, crystalline substance that, in order to be metabolized, causes the body to essentially waste energy. The human body was never built to handle as much sugar as most of us eat. A can of soda contains what in the wild would amount to a megadose, and most sodas are now being sweetened with the ever-cheaper fructose derived from corn sugar—which can cause heart problems if you are not getting sufficient amounts of copper in your diet. Since sugar (particularly high fructose corn sweetener) often inadvertently finds its way into our diets in everything from spaghetti sauce and salad dressing to bread and canned carrots, copper supplements may eventually become a necessary addition to the American breakfast table. (The amino acid phenylalanine—marketed under such names as NutraSweet and Equal—is now widely used as a sugar replacement in soft drinks, and large doses of this may be worse than sugar.)

Since refined sugar has a mild suppressive effect on the immune system, please keep its use to a minimum. This may be difficult, even if you have no raw sugar in your home, because so many of the foods we eat have been presweetened (especially the processed foods, which is another reason for avoiding them).

Another advantage of whole, natural foods is that they are high in fiber. Fiber is the indigestible (unless you are a cow or a termite) part of grains, fruits, and vegetables, made predominantly of cellulose. Although it has no nutritional value, it is far from inert. It slows the absorption of sugars and fats in our diet, and thus helps to stabilize blood sugar levels and reduce the likelihood of fat-aggravated heart disease and certain cancers. Bran flakes, all grains, and crunchy fruits and vegetables contain significant amounts of fiber. Oat bran and rice bran are apparently among the most interactive of fibers and may therefore be very helpful in stabilizing blood sugar, which can in turn prevent reactive hypoglycemia, a common condition among CFS sufferers. Drs. Cheraskin and Orenstein (clinical biochemists) have demonstrated that one cup of whole grain (particularly oat bran), prepared for breakfast daily, can reduce the blood content of a fat that causes cardiovascular disease by 10 percent in one month, in part because when you fill up on a whole grain breakfast, you are less likely to be eating a lot of other, higher-stress foods.

Remember that the vitamin supplements discussed in chapter 7 are important, even though the vitamin content of your diet will probably be higher than it was in the past. Remember also that vitamin supplements are merely that: supplements. They cannot take the place of a balanced diet. They simply add good immunologic support.

When shopping for food, a useful habit to get into is reading the labels. Labels are now required by law to list nutritional information (the amount of protein, fat, sodium, and so on, per serving), which is important if, for example, you are trying to limit the amount of fat and sodium in your diet. Ingredients are listed in descending order of the percentage they make up in the product. The first ingredient listed makes up the highest percentage of the contents and the last ingredient the lowest. The list of ingredients is vital, especially if you are on an elimination diet (in which case you must look for "hidden" ingredients: fermented products, corn products, and citrus flavorings).

As a rule, you want food in the purest, freshest possible form. Organically grown vegetables are more expensive than supermarket vegetables, but they will contain fewer (or no) pesticides, herbicides, fungicides, or cleaning fluids. (Winter tomatoes imported to the United States from Mexico, for instance, are actually washed in bleach before shipping.) If fresh fruit and vegetables are in short supply locally, frozen or dried foods are the next best thing. (Warning: dried fruits usually contain very large doses of preservatives.) Canned food is the least desirable because the cooking and canning process boils off most of the nutrients and boils in traces of aluminum and other potentially toxic metals. If you must resort to canned foods, seek out those that are packaged in glass jars.

Keep a little diary of what you eat and, if allergic symptoms occur within a few hours, take note of them. These include: headache, worsening of fatigue, bloating and gas; and a worsening of aches and pains. If these symptoms appear to repeat with certain foods, then these should be avoided for several weeks.

If you do experience extreme discomfort resulting from a food reaction, we recommend two first-aid remedies. First, you may want to try an aspirin-free antacid. Alka-Seltzer "Gold" would do nicely. Drop one tablet in a glass of water (preferably spring water) and let it dissolve. Then drink the solution and repeat with a second tablet. The tablets are very rich in sodium, so don't use them more than once every two or three days, because sodium causes you to retain fluids. Second, vitamin C, taken in crystal form, can be a big help. Pour a teaspoon of crystals (in this form, you will probably only be able to find synthetic vitamin C readily), about 2,000 milligrams, into a glass of spring water, stir until dissolved, and drink the solution. You may repeat this every two hours for six to ten hours. Taking vitamin C in this way can cut short food reactions, chemical sensitivities, even bee sting reactions.

If a food reaction is powerful and prolonged, then there may be (rare) occasions when you will want to get the offending agent out of your system quickly. A laxative is then in order. For such emergencies, we recommend citrate of magnesia, also known as "liquid dynamite." It is available over the counter in single-dose bottles at your local pharmacy. We recommend using only a half bottle the first time because it can cause cramps in some people. Maximum dose is one bottle per day for no more than three days in a row.

There are a few more rules that should be kept in mind. You may eat any or all of the foods listed (here and in chapter 7) for a particular day, and as many of the different recipes as you want to try for that given day. Do not omit any food groups (for example, protein) described in the diet. You must, every day, eat a balanced diet.

For reasons of cardiovascular health, you will notice that the recipes are low in fat, with little or no salt added. If you must use a bit (and only a bit) of salt, at least try to use sea salt, since it has traces of useful minerals in it.

Drinking plenty of fluids is recommended. We suggest drinking six glasses of water or juice per day. You can make fruit and/or vegetable juice fresh, daily, too. Bottled spring water (not distilled water which is a "dead" liquid) is worth buying and storing because it is, in most cases, superior to municipal water, even if your town taps a groundwater supply (as does much of Long Island, which used to have the finest water in the United States until salt, industrial waste, and contamination from graveyards began encroaching on the overpumped water table).

Fluoride is one of the most powerful enzyme inhibitors known. More and more of it is being added to municipal supplies, in part because some industrial processes produce fluoride as a by-product; hence, industry has lobbied to get local governments to buy some of the excess and dump it in the water supply. This is probably the first time in history that humans have been used as industrial waste dumps. There have been calls to double and then double again the amounts of fluoride permitted (or rather, required) in city water supplies. Yes, it is undeniably good for teeth (in very small quantities), but it also liberates aluminum from cookware when heated, and there are hints that aluminum toxicity plays a leading role in such conditions as Alzheimer's disease. Fluoride is itself capable of breaking down collagen, the body's glue, and is a known accelerant of ankalosing spondylitis and other autoimmune diseases. In towns where water has been overdosed with fluoride (there have been cases in Turkey, India, Sicily, and, in the United States, in Texas and Colorado), there is evidence that resultant collagen breakdown, enzyme inhibition, and immune suppression can speed up the aging process. In Kizilcaoein, Turkey, where the fluoride content of drinking water reached 5.4 parts per million by 1978, residents had been aging at approximately twice the normal rate. Men at the age of thirty needed walking sticks, and their wrinkled facial skin made them look sixty. Upon falling, their bones tended to shatter like glass and few ever reached the age of 50.* So, if you're trying to support your metabolism and immune system, keep your intake of fluoride as low as possible.

Also bear in mind that there is an intrinsic rhythm to the digestive system, and this should be supported, not resisted. Eat your

---

*Charles Pellegrino comments: There is increasing evidence that dental mercury/silver amalgam fillings contribute to an already high human intake of mercury from contaminated wheat and fish. A flurry of news reports on dental mercury in 1990 sent people to dentists requesting removal of silver fillings and replacement with new composite materials. Such procedures are invasive, expensive, and, in most cases, unnecessary. Unless you are clearly identified as someone who responds excessively to even small amounts of mercury, you need only have mercury-free composites put into *future* fillings, or replaced in old fillings as they naturally erode and outlive their usefulness.

meals regularly, three times a day, at about the same time. The largest meal of the day should be either breakfast or lunch. Eating a big meal in the evening and then going to sleep does not allow the food to digest very well and can contribute to sleep disturbances.

So, without any further ado, *mange!*

Bread and Crackers: You'll usually need to bake your own breads if wheat is a problem. Most commercial products contain wheat. You can use oat, rice, potato, or soy flours. Rice crackers and Wasa "lite rye" crackers do not contain wheat or yeast (read labels!). Also "Essene Rye Bread" contains no wheat or yeast.

Beverages: Tap water, bottled water. Fresh vegetable juice (not fruit juice if yeast may be a problem).

Miscellaneous: Tofu (but not fermented soy products, such as soy sauce, just to be on the safe side). Cashews, pistachios, English walnuts, black walnuts, hickory nuts, pecans, almonds, Brazil nuts, hazel nuts (but no peanuts). Be absolutely sure nuts are fresh and not moldy. Safflower oil, Canola oil, sunflower oil, flaxseed oil, olive oil (no corn oil or mixed vegetable oils). *Do not cook with or heat polyunsaturated oils. Cook only with olive oil.*

FOODS YOU NEED TO AVOID
These are hidden in processed foods. Be sure to read labels. To lessen your chances of making mistakes in planning, shopping, and carrying out an elimination diet, avoid packaged and processed foods wherever possible.

Milk-containing foods: Cheese, butter, yogurt, cream soups, ice cream, margarines, breads, cookies, candies, salad dressings, ovaltine, luncheon meats, and other manufactured or processed foods that may contain milk.

Egg-containing foods: Cakes, cookies, ice cream, pies, macaroni, salad dressings, mayonnaise, noodles, pancake mixes, and other manufactured or processed foods.

ELIMINATION DIET
FOODS YOU CAN EAT

Vegetables	Fruits	Meats	Grains
White potatoes, onions, cauliflower	Apples	Fish	Brown Rice
Eggplant, peppers, mustard greens	Bananas	Chicken, turkey	Oats
Cabbage, bok choy, turnips	Peaches	Beef, pork	Millet
Tomatoes, radishes, rutabagas	Pears	Veal, lamb	Buckwheat
Broccoli, asparagus, watercress	Pineapple	Clams, lobster, crab	Amaranth
Green peas, beans and other legumes	Cantaloupe	Oysters, shrimp	Barley
Sweet potatoes, yams	Watermelon	Squirrel, rabbit	Rye
Collards, lettuce (dark leaf)	Strawberries	Quail, duck, goose	
Kohlrabi, kale, horseradish	Cherries	Game birds, pheasant	
Carrots, squash, okra	Apricots, coconut, persimmons		
Celery, cucumbers, beets	Blackberries, blueberries		
Avocado, parsnips, brussels sprouts	Cranberries, raspberries		
Spinach	Loganberries		

Wheat-containing foods: Breads, cookies, crackers, soups, cereals, batters, luncheon meats, pancake mixes, salad dressings, gravies, bouillon cubes, postum, and other commercially prepared foods. "Rye" and other breads usually contain wheat flour.

Corn-containing foods: Candies, breads, pastries, batters, cereals, ketchup, peanut butter, bacon, envelope and stamp adhesives, toothpaste, and many other processed and refined products that contain corn oils, starches or sugars.

Sugar-containing foods: Candies, soft drinks, cookies, ice cream, salad dressings, ketchup, and countless other packaged and processed foods.

Chocolate and cola-containing foods: Avoid chocolate and cola drinks of all kinds. Also, candies, snack foods, cereals, and desserts that contain chocolate or cola.

Citrus-containing foods: Oranges, lemons, limes, grapefruit, Sprite soda, flavorings in desserts, and other processed foods.

Coffee, tea, and alcohol: All coffee and tea (including instant and caffeine free) products. Also, all alcoholic beverages.

Yeast and foods made from yeast: Mushrooms, fermented foods (such as miso soup or soy sauce), brewer's yeast, dried fruits, grapes, and peanuts (which tend to be "yeasty"), vinegar and condiments such as prepared mustard and ketchup. Alcohol is also in this category.

Foods containing coloring, including flavoring and additives: Processed and packaged foods, cereals, soft drinks, ketchup, mustard, hot dogs, luncheon meats, and many others: especially avoid benzoic acid and sodium benzoate preservatives. In addition, avoid foods that contain tartrazine (yellow no. 5) dye.

Adapted from *Tracking Down Your Hidden Food Allergies* by William Crook, M.D., 1980, Professional Books, P.O. Box 3454, Jackson, TN 38301 (800-835-6368).

If you are going to try a rotation-elimination diet, here are some ideas.

BREAKFAST: DAY 1

Fresh Pineapple makes a wonderful breakfast. When you buy it, make sure that it is on the soft side. One way to test for ripeness is to pull out a leaf or two; they should come out easily. And smell the bottom, looking for a sweet pineapple aroma. When you cut off the leaves, make the incision 1 1/2–2 inches from the top (if you put this chunk, with the leaves, on a sponge that you keep wet, it will usually root, providing you with an unusual house plant).

To cook *plantains,* begin with a little bit of butter melted in a frying pan. Cut the plantain in half lengthwise and fry gently. As it is cooking, add a dash of vanilla and cinnamon. Cook until lightly browned on both sides. Fried plantains with a glass of soy milk make a delightful breakfast or snack.

The recipes here have been designed to be simple, appealing, and relatively easy to prepare. Through our experience with the elimination diet, we have found that it proves to be most enjoyable when the foods chosen are wholesome and familiar. If you are not naturally adventuresome with your food choices, stay with the basics. Simple broiled meat or fish, served with a steamed vegetable and a choice of grain constitutes a delicious and satisfying meal.

Labels are particularly important reading material while on the elimination diet. Many foods contain "hidden" allergens, such as corn starch, corn syrup, citrus flavorings, fermented foods, and milk solids.

When planning your daily food choices, it might be helpful to keep in mind that sweets are best consumed in small amounts toward the end of the day. Breakfast can be a substantial meal without excess sweetness. Try pairing your favorite traditional breakfast food with a savory food, such as home-fried sweet potato for a refreshing change, or a bit of leftover broiled fish filet from a previous meal. Eating savory food for breakfast rather than sweet food is not such an unusual idea; we have come to accept ham, bacon, and smoked fishes as traditional breakfast fare.

It may also help to bear in mind that if your digestive system proves to be reactive, you can adjust the seasonings you add to food to suit your taste. Add herbs and spices in small amounts. You can always add more seasoning to a dish just prior to serving, but it's impossible to remove any offending flavor once it's been added in too great a quantity to your entree.

ABOUT GRAINS

Grains can be a tremendous addition to your every day diet. They are easy to prepare and are incredibly versatile. Extra grains cooked at one meal can be used for a salad, a porridge the following morning, a stuffing for poultry or vegetables, or a creamy grain pudding for dessert.

Cook the grains in water if you plan on using any leftover amounts for either breakfast or dessert. Otherwise, a vegetable or chicken broth can greatly enhance the flavor of cooked grains for a savory dish.

For a more robust taste, some grains can be dry-roasted in the pan prior to adding liquid. This toasting imparts a nutty flavor and keeps the grains separate during cooking.

While your grains are cooking, resist the urge to stir them. Grains need to cook gently without disturbing the tiny steam holes formed while on the stove. Unless you are making the classic Italian comfort food, risotto, stirring causes the grains to become sticky rather than fluffy.

The following guide may help you get more familiar with cooking times and yields of common grains.

	Uncooked	Liquid	Finished
Barley—pearled variety	1 cup	2½ cups	3 cups
Kasha★	1 cup	2 cups	3 cups
Millet★	1 cup	2½ cups	3+ cups
Rice—Brown	1 cup	2¼ cups	3 cups
Arborio	1 cup	2 cups	3 cups
Bulgar (cracked wheat)	1 cup	2 cups	2½ cups
Couscous	1 cup	2 cups	3 cups

★Toasting in a pan first enhances their flavor.

ALLERGY/ELIMINATION SUBSTITUTION CHART

For 1 cup *white* or *whole wheat* flour, substitute:
  ½–¾ cup barley flour, or
  1 cup oat flour, or
  ¾–⅞ cup rice flour, or
  ½ cup ground nuts and ½ cup oat flour
For 1 cup *milk,* use:
  equal amount of soy milk or nut milk
For *butter:*
  use equal amount of soy margarine
  to saute, use olive oil or safflower oil
For *eggs:*
  There are a few types of "egg-replacers" on the market,
  available at most natural foods stores. If you are craving baked
  goods while on the egg-free elimination diet phase, you can
  try to use this product in your baking. While it will bind the
  product in a manner similar to that of eggs, it will not provide
  the lightness that egg whites do in a finished baked goods
  product. Use "egg-replacers" as indicated on the product
  package.

A FEW WORDS ABOUT SWEETENERS

Instead of sugar, the recipes listed in this chapter contain honey,
molasses, maple syrup, or succanat. As a rule of thumb, recipes that
call for sugar can be converted to a natural sweetener using the
following guideline:

1 cup succanat, or	½ cup honey, or
	½ cup maple syrup, or
	½ cup molasses

There will be a difference in texture and taste with each substitu-
tion. If you use honey, you might reduce the oven temperature by
25°, as honey causes baked goods to brown more quickly. Also,

you might find that when using a liquid sweetener rather than sugar, you can reduce the other liquids in the recipe by up to 1/4 cup for each 1/2 cup of honey/syrup used.

BREAKFAST RECIPES

Natural sweeteners are the rule here, as are whole grain flours. Expect a more dense, hearty product than when white flour is used.

Homemade Granola   MAKES 4 CUPS
(DF, YF, WF, EF, CF, CIT.F)*

Many granola varieties on the market are a less-than-healthy choice because of the addition of sweeteners and fats. This is a basic granola recipe that you may embellish with your own choices of dried fruit, raisins, or nuts once the granola has been baked and cooled.

4 cups old fashioned oats	1/3 cup honey
2 teaspoons cinnamon	1/4 cup safflower oil
2 teaspoons vanilla extract	

1. Preheat oven to 325°.
2. Mix all ingredients together and stir until well blended and oats are thoroughly coated with oil/honey.
3. Spread onto a 9 x 13" sheet or edged cookie sheet.
4. Bake for about 30 minutes, stirring frequently to promote even browning.
5. Cool and store in an airtight container.

Serve the granola with soy or nut milk for a dairy-free breakfast.

*As a quick guide to help you plan:
  DF–Dairy Free
  YF–Yeast Free
  WF–Wheat Free
  EF–Egg Free
  CF–Corn Free
  Cit.F–Citrus Free

Nut or Seed Milk
MAKES 4 CUPS

Nut or seed milk can replace a dairy-based liquid for general cooking, baking, and eating purposes.

1 quart water   *1 ½ cups nuts and/or seeds*

1. Soak the nuts/seeds overnight in the water.
2. Blend the mixture in a blender or a food processor and refrigerate for future use.

Honey Date Scones
MAKES 1 DOZEN

(DF OPTION★, EF, CF, CIT.F, YF)

6 ounces butter (unsalted, chilled)
3 ½ cups whole wheat pastry flour
1 tablespoon baking powder
2 teaspoons baking soda

2 tablespoons honey
1 cup buttermilk
½ teaspoon salt
½ cup chopped dates
2 teaspoons vanilla

1. Cut butter into flour until mixture resembles coarse meal.
2. Mix remaining ingredients with flour/butter mixture with a few swift strokes. Do not overmix this or the texture will be more breadlike than delicate.
3. Press dough out onto a floured surface to a 1-inch thickness and cut with a round cookie or biscuit cutter. (Add some extra flour, if needed.)
4. Place on greased cookie sheet about 2 inches apart and bake at 400° for 25 minutes or until the tops are golden brown.

Great served with a fresh fruit conserve or honey butter.

These scones can be made dairy-free by using soy margarine in place of butter and 1 cup nut/seed milk in place of buttermilk.

Muesli

(DF, YF,* CF, CIT.F, EF, WF OPTION†)

Muesli is a nutrition-packed cold cereal option. Its roots are Scandinavian and it is very simple to prepare. Packaged muesli is available on the market but their cost is usually prohibitive. Paired with a whole grain muffin or fresh fruit, this breakfast is a taste of the Alps. Serve with nut/seed milk or soy milk.

Mix in large bowl:

2 cups old fashioned oats
1 cup barley or rye flakes
1 cup wheat flakes (for
   wheat-free variety,
   substitute rice flakes)

1/4 teaspoon nutmeg
1/2 cup chopped nuts
1/2 cup each chopped dates
   and chopped dried apples

*YF: Use fresh fruit instead of dried fruit.
†WF: Do not include wheat flakes in your muesli mixture.

Corn Muffins

(DF OPTION, CIT.F, YF)

These muffins are not very sweet, so they may easily be paired up with a salad later in the day.

2/3 cup cornmeal
1 cup whole wheat pastry
   flour
1 tablespoon baking powder
1/2 teaspoon salt
1 egg, slightly beaten

2/3 cup melted butter (or soy
   margarine)
1 cup buttermilk (or
   nut/seed milk)
1 tablespoon maple syrup or
   honey

1. Preheat oven to 400°. Grease muffin tins.
2. Mix dry ingredients together, and add wet ingredients to dry, quickly, without overbeating.
3. Fill muffin tins three-quarters full, and bake for about 25–30 minutes, until muffin edges are golden and center is firm.
4. Let cook on a rack. Serve with fresh fruit.

Oatmeal Muffins

MAKES 1 1/2 DOZEN

(WF, DF OPTION, CF, CIT.F, YF)

1 1/2 cup oats
1 1/2 cups buttermilk (or
   dairy-free choice)
1 cup oat flour
1/2 cup rice flour
1 tablespoon baking powder
1/2 teaspoon baking soda

1/8 teaspoon nutmeg
2 eggs
1/2 cup melted butter (or soy
   margarine)
2 tablespoons honey
1/2 cup slivered dried fruit
   (optional)

1. Preheat oven to 400°. Grease muffin tins.
2. Soak oatmeal in buttermilk.
3. Combine remaining dry ingredients, and add wet ingredients, including oatmeal mixture.
4. Stir in dried fruit slivers and fill muffin tins three-quarters full.
5. Bake for 25 minutes or until tops are gold brown and center is set.

Any Grain Porridge

MAKES 2 1/2 CUPS

(EF, YF, CIT.F, DF OPTION, CF OPTION, WF OPTION)

This recipe is great for using leftover grains. As mentioned earlier in the chapter, any grain can be an appropriate and appealing breakfast dish. Mixed grains can also be used here.

2 cups leftover cooked grain
1 cup liquid (soy, nut/seed
   or cow's milk)
1 teaspoon vanilla extract

1/2 teaspoon cinnamon
1/8 teaspoon nutmeg
2 tablespoons honey or
   maple syrup

1. Put grains into a saucepan over low to medium heat.
2. Slowly add cooking liquid and stir constantly until the grains have absorbed the additional liquid and become creamy and thick.
3. Add honey, vanilla, cinnamon, and nutmeg, and serve with your choice of condiments.

Buttermilk Pancakes

MAKES 2 ½ CUPS

(CF, CIT.F, YF, WF OPTION)

1 ½ cups whole wheat pastry flour	1 ¼ cups buttermilk
1 ½ teaspoons baking powder	1 egg
½ teaspoon baking soda	2 tablespoons safflower oil
½ teaspoon salt	1 tablespoon maple syrup
	1 teaspoon maple (or vanilla) extract

1. Preheat griddle, lightly oiled, if not nonstick.
2. Mix dry ingredients together in a large bowl.
3. Blend wet ingredients together and add to dry. Do over over stir. A few small lumps may remain.
4. Pour a small amount of batter onto prepared cooking surface. When bubbles appear on the surface of the pancake, turn it over and cook until the upper surface is soft. Color is the key to doneness also, as long as the heat has not been too hot.
5. Serve with fruit conserve or yogurt, and a bit of maple syrup or honey.

Sweet Potato Home Fries

SERVES 2

This is a good way to use leftover sweet potatoes.

1 tablespoon olive or
safflower oil
1/4 cup chopped onion
2 cups cubed boiled, cold
sweet potatoes
1/4 teaspoon paprika

1/2 teaspoon dried thyme
Fresh ground black pepper,
to taste
2 tablespoons fresh parsley,
minced

1. Heat skillet over medium heat, add oil and onions.
2. Sauté onions until soft, then add sweet potatoes. Don't stir the potatoes. Use a spatula to turn them over so they don't break apart. Sprinkle paprika on them.
3. Cook onions and potatoes until potatoes begin to get crispy, about 15 minutes.
4. Just before removing them from heat, add the thyme and fresh ground pepper to taste, and toss with parsley to finish.

Fruit Shakes

MAKES 2 SHAKES

(WF, CF, CIT.F, YF, EF, DF OPTION)

Fruit smoothies are a quick and nutritional breakfast, perfect for warm weather days.

1 cup yogurt or 1 cup
nut/seed milk
1 cup chopped fresh fruit
(especially good here is
banana, strawberry or
mango)

1/8 teaspoon nutmeg
1/2 teaspoon fresh chopped
mint
1/2 teaspoon almond extract

1. Blend all ingredients in blender or food processor until smooth and thick. Pour and enjoy.

For added frothiness, add 2 ice cubes, one at a time, to blender while processing.

A couple of *bananas* all by themselves certainly qualify as a breakfast.

Did you ever eat a *pomegranate*? It's a bit of a challenge, with all the seeds, but the fruit is very sweet and succulent. Add a handful of pecans or walnuts alongside, and again you have the makings of an easy, simple breakfast.

Currants or *gooseberries* are wonderful all by themselves. You can also mix them in a bowl with sesame seeds or pine nuts. Pour some soy milk over them, and you have an instant, nutritious, delicious breakfast.

For a hot breakfast, mix ¾ cup of currants, add 1 tablespoon of sesame seeds and 1 ounce of pineapple juice. Bake the mixture for 15 minutes at 300°F, and enjoy.

LUNCH AND DINNER*

A good source of protein is *tofu,* or soy bean curd. For those of you who are not familiar with it, let us tell you something about its origins and uses. Tofu has been widely appreciated in Asia for thousands of years. It is made by cooking soybeans in water until they turn into a creamy "soy milk." Then a natural thickener is added to allow "curds" to form. The curds are strained and pressed into blocks, which can be diced for cooking. Tofu is a rich source of protein, calcium, and vitamins. It is low in calories and sodium, and is completely free of cholesterol. And if that's not enough, it is also highly economical and versatile. Soybeans themselves are deficient in three of the eight essential amino acids that your body needs to make complete proteins. However, the curdling process that yields tofu adds the missing amino acids. Tofu protein is as good as the protein found in meat, fish, and poultry, and in some respects even better. Throughout Asia, tofu is often referred to as "meat without bones."

There is really nothing exotic or difficult about cooking with tofu. Think of it as analogous to pasta. Both foods are rather bland and uninteresting by themselves, but they make a wonderful backdrop for the textures and flavors of other ingredients. Furthermore, tofu can be barbecued, stir-fried, broiled, crumbled onto salads, steamed, mashed, chopped, or puréed to make wonderful dips for vegetables.

---

*Remember to make lunch the larger of the two meals.

Tofu Soup
SERVES 2

4 cups vegetable stock (see
   page 246)
8 ounces tofu, cubed
½ cup sliced leeks
½ cup chopped onions

½ cup chopped mustard
   greens
Garlic (fresh or powdered),
   mustard, and horseradish,
   to taste

Place the stock in a heavy saucepan. Add the remaining ingredients, bring to a simmer, and cook over low heat for 5 to 10 minutes. The vegetables should be tender yet still on the crisp side.

Tofu Scramble
SERVES 2

Unsalted butter
8 ounces tofu
¼ teaspoon minced garlic

¼ teaspoon prepared
   mustard
Pine nuts (optional)

1. In a shallow pan over medium heat, melt a little bit of butter, just enough to coat the pan.
2. Crumble the tofu into the pan and add garlic and mustard. Stir continuously until golden brown.
3. Pine nuts may be added for additional flavor and crunch.

Tofu Stir-fry
SERVES 2

2 garlic cloves
1 medium onion
1 leek
Unsalted butter
1 medium turnip

8 ounces tofu
1 tablespoon sesame seeds
½ small red cabbage,
    shredded

1. Chop the garlic, onion, and leek and sauté them in a small amount of butter, until they become soft.
2. Dice the turnip and tofu and add them to the vegetables. Cook over medium heat for 5 to 8 minutes, or just until the turnip begins to soften.
3. Add the sesame seeds and shredded cabbage. Toss well and cook for 1 minute more.

A baked yam and steamed asparagus, broccoli, and/or cauliflower would complement the stir-fry very well.

Grilled Tofu
SERVES 2

8 ounces of extra firm tofu   Minced garlic, to taste

Cut the tofu into four or five slices (about 1 inch thick). Sprinkle the minced garlic on a large plate and press the tofu slices on it, first on one side, then the other. Put the slices on a preheated outdoor grill and allow them to cook until evenly browned. Turn and brown the other side. Serve with vegetable of the day.

We enjoy adding soaked mesquite wood chips to the coals. They add a very pleasant smoked flavor to the tofu.

Tofu Salad   SERVES 2

8 ounces pressed tofu, cubed
½ cup broccoli florets
½ cup cauliflowerets
½ cup shredded mustard
  greens
½ cup shredded kale
½ cup sliced radishes

1 medium Bermuda onion,
  sliced
1 tablespoon sesame seeds
¼ cup minced garlic
¼ teaspoon dry mustard
1 tablespoon sesame oil
Pecans, walnuts, or pine
  nuts (optional)

1. Toss the vegetables and sesame seeds in a large container.
2. In a small bowl, mix together the garlic, mustard, and oil.
3. Sprinkle the dressing over the salad.
4. Nuts may be added for taste and crunch.

Jennifer Judelsohn's Stuffed Peppers   MAKES 4 SERVINGS

¼ cup scallions, chopped
  fine
2 cloves garlic, minced
2 teaspoons olive oil
2 onions, chopped
2 stalks celery, chopped fine
2 carrots, chopped fine
16 ounces soft tofu, drained,
  rinsed, and crumbled fine

1 yellow squash, chopped
  fine
1 zucchini, chopped fine
¼ teaspoon each: red
  pepper, cumin, sea salt,
  and nutmeg
3 cups cooked brown rice
8 medium-sized bell peppers
paprika

1. Slice tops off bell peppers and clean out insides. Finely chop the tops and set aside.
2. Blanch peppers in boiling water for 2 minutes. Then rinse quickly in cold water.
3. Sauté onions, garlic, and scallions in olive oil until translucent. Add tofu, celery, carrots, squash, zucchini, and green peppers. Sauté until vegetables are crispy and tender.
4. Add seasoning and rice. Mix well. Cook covered on low heat for 10 minutes, stirring occasionally.

5. Fill peppers with vegetable/rice/tofu mixture. Sprinkle tops with paprika. Place filled peppers upright in a baking dish.
6. Bake for 30 minutes at 350°.

Vegetable Stock

MAKES 4 CUPS

1 cup chopped carrot
1 cup chopped potato
1 cup chopped turnip
1 cup chopped onion
1 cup chopped celery

2 sprigs parsley
1 clove garlic
4 or 5 peppercorns
2 quarts water

1. Place vegetables, garlic, and peppercorns in water, bring to a boil, and then simmer for 1 hour.
2. Strain broth and use as a base of soups or pilafs.

Vegetable Stew

SERVES 2

4 cups vegetable stock (see page 246)
½ cup tofu
½ yam, diced

1 cup chopped asparagus
1 cup cauliflowerets
1 cup broccoli florets
1 small onion, chopped

1. Place the vegetable stock and tofu in a blender and purée well.
2. Transfer to a saucepan and bring to a simmer over low heat.
3. Add the vegetables, cover, and allow the stew to simmer for 45 minutes.

Note: Varying the amount of tofu will alter the consistency of the stew, so feel free to experiment.

Stuffed Cabbage

SERVES 4

2 pounds green cabbage
1 tablespoon unsalted butter
1 clove garlic, minced
1/2 cup chopped onions
1/2 cup puréed tofu

1 tablespoon flour
1/2 cooked yam, mashed
3 cups vegetable stock (see page 246)

1. Cut out the core of the cabbage, keeping the head intact. Blanch the cabbage in boiling water for 6 minutes or steam it for 10–12 minutes. Allow it to cool enough so that you can comfortably handle it. Remove the ten or twelve best leaves and trim the ribs so that you can easily bend them.
2. Melt the butter in a skillet and add the garlic.
3. Combine the onions, puréed tofu, flour, and mashed yam. Add them to the skillet and sauté over medium heat for 10 minutes.
4. Place a heaping tablespoon of the tofu stuffing in the center of each cabbage leaf. Fold in the sides of the leaf and roll it up.
5. Place the stuffed cabbage leaves in a large pot and add the stock. Bring to a boil and let simmer for 30 minutes.

Sweet and Spicy Cabbage

SERVES 2

1 small red cabbage, shredded
2 medium onions, chopped
1/2 cup pineapple juice

1 garlic clove, minced
1 teaspoon sesame seeds
1/8 teaspoon cinnamon
1/2 teaspoon dry mustard

1. Place all ingredients in a nonstick frying pan.
2. Stir well, cover, and cook over low heat for 15 minutes, stirring occasionally.

Candied Carrots
SERVES 2

2 pounds baby carrots
1/4 cup maple syrup

1/4 cup sunflower seeds

1. Steam the carrots until just tender.
2. Transfer to skillet and pour in syrup.
3. Gently simmer until carrots are coated and syrup has reduced slightly.
4. Serve sprinkled with seeds.

Applesauce
SERVES 2

4 large apples, cored and
   peeled
1 tablespoon water

1 teaspoon maple sugar
1/4 teaspoon ground allspice
1/4 teaspoon ground cloves

Place the apples in an ovenproof dish and bake at 350° for about 20 minutes or until tender. Combine with the other ingredients and purée in a blender or food processor. Chill overnight and serve.

Fruit Compote I
SERVES 2

1/2 cup fresh strawberries,
   hulled
1/2 cup fresh raspberries
1/4 cup chopped apricots
1/4 cup chopped apples

1/2 cup sunflower seeds
1/4 cup shelled whole
   almonds
Maple syrup to taste
   (optional)

Combine the fruit and nuts in an ovenproof baking dish and bake at 350° for 15 minutes. Serve hot. Maple syrup may be drizzled on to taste.

Asparagus Soup

SERVES 2

¼ cup chopped onion
1 tablespoon oil
2 cups cooked asparagus,
  chopped

2 cups vegetable stock (see
  page 246)
2 tablespoons chives
Fresh ground pepper, to
  taste

1. Sauté onions in oil for five minutes.
2. Add the asparagus and cook for five minutes.
3. Add stock and simmer until asparagus is soft, about 10 minutes.
4. Add chives and pepper.

Vegetarian Chili

SERVES 4

(WF, DF, EF, YF, CF, CIT.F)

3 tablespoons olive oil
1 medium onion, diced
2 cloves garlic, minced
1 carrot, cut into ¼-inch
  slices
1 green pepper, chopped
1 zucchini, cut into ¼-inch
  slices
1 large (2-pound) can
  Italian plum tomatoes
  with their liquid
2 tablespoons chili powder

1 teaspoon cumin
2 teaspoons thyme
2 teaspoons oregano
2 tablespoons parsley,
  minced
1 can kidney beans, drained
  and rinsed
1 can chick-peas, drained
  and rinsed
1 cup vegetable stock (see
  page 246)

1. Sauté onion and garlic in oil for five minutes. Add carrots and cook for two minutes.
2. Add peppers and zucchini. Saute for another five minutes and stir in tomatoes and seasonings. Simmer.
3. When vegetables are tender, stir in beans and enough stock for a stew-like consistency.
4. Toss in parsley, stir. Serve over a bed of brown rice.

Chick-pea and Vegetable Cassoulet

SERVES 4

(WF, CF, CIT.F, EF, DF, YF)

1 medium onion, diced
3 tablespoons olive oil
2 cloves garlic, minced
2 carrots, cut into ¼-inch slices
1 medium zucchini, cut into ½-inch slices
½ red pepper, cut into strips
2 teaspoons cumin

1 teaspoon coriander, minced or ground
2 teaspoons thyme
Fresh ground pepper, to taste
1 16-ounce can Italian plum tomatoes with liquid
1 can chick-peas, drained and rinsed
2 tablespoons fresh parsley, minced

1. In large skillet, sauté onion in oil until soft. Add garlic and carrots. Cook for three minutes.
2. Add zucchini, red peppers, cumin and coriander. Cook another three to four minutes. Add thyme and pepper.
3. Add tomatoes with their liquid and chick peas. Cook until the vegetables are soft but still toothsome.
4. Finish with parsley and serve with grains.

Sesame Fish Fillet

SERVES 2

(CF, WF, DF, CIT.F, YF, EF)

These pan-fried fish fillets are unusually tasty. They are easy to prepare and can be grilled outdoors as well.

2 tablespoons soy sauce
2 tablespoons olive oil
1/2 teaspoon toasted sesame oil

3/4-pound salmon fillet or other firm, mild fish
1/2 cup sesame seeds, untoasted

1. Mix soy sauce, 1 tablespoon olive oil, and sesame oil. Next, use a pastry brush to coat the fillets with the mixture.
2. Press the fillets into the sesame seeds to thoroughly coat both sides.
3. Heat 1 tablespoon olive oil in a large skillet.
4. Place fish in pan and cook on medium heat. (Ten minutes each side for a 1-inch thick fillet, less for a thinner fillet.) Be careful to turn fish once to avoid breaking and to allow even browning. Fish will be done before it is dry enough to flake.

Note: Sole cooks quite quickly, about 7 to 10 minutes total cooking time, while a thicker fish, such as salmon or halibut, will take 7 to 10 minutes per side.

Poached Chicken with Three Spices

SERVES 2

(WF, DF, CF, CIT.F, YF, EF)

This recipe is especially suited to chicken but you could easily substitute sole or flounder in its place and reduce the cooking time for the fish by one-half.

1 small onion, minced
2 tablespoons olive oil
1 garlic clove, minced
1 teaspoon ginger
1/2 teaspoon cumin
1 tablespoon ground coriander
2 chicken breasts (or

3/4-pound sole or flounder fillets)
1 1/2 cups chicken or vegetable stock (see page 246)
2 tablespoons chopped fresh parsley

1. Saute onion in oil until translucent. Add garlic, ginger, cumin and coriander. Cook for three to five minutes to blend flavors.
2. Add chicken to the poaching liquid and cook on low/medium heat for 25 minutes, or until chicken is cooked but still moist.
3. Just before removing from heat, toss in fresh parsley.
4. Serve over a bed of grains.

Colcannon   SERVES 4

(WF, EF, CF, CIT.F, YF, DF OPTION*)

The ultimate Irish comfort food.

4 large potatoes	1 teaspoon caraway seeds
2 tablespoons olive oil	½ cup light sour cream*
4 cups chopped cabbage	1 teaspoon paprika
1 medium onion, chopped	Salt and pepper, to taste

*Substitute ¼ cup nut milk for DF option.

1. Cut potatoes into cubes and sauté in oil under tender. Mash lightly with a fork.
2. Saute cabbage and onion in oil. Stir in caraway seeds. Sauté until cabbage is wilted but still green.
3. Mix potatoes with cabbage-onion mixture. Stir in sour cream and adjust salt and pepper to taste.
4. Spread into a 9 x 13-inch baking pan and sprinkle with paprika.
5. Bake at 400° for 20–25 minutes until heated throughout.

Risotto

(DF, YF, CF, CIT.F, EF, WF)

Risotto is a creamy Italian dish which can be served as a side dish or as a one-fork supper, with the addition of vegetables or seafood. It is easy to prepare, but does require stirring during the cooking process. This can be as basic or elegant an offering as you choose. (Note that Risotto calls for arborio rice.)

1 small onion, chopped	*stock (see page 246),*
2 tablespoons olive oil	*heated*
1 ½ cups arborio rice	*1 teaspoon dried thyme*
1 clove garlic, minced	*2 tablespoons fresh parsley,*
4 cups chicken or vegetable	*minced*

1. Sauté onion in oil for five minutes over medium heat.
2. Stir in rice and garlic. Cook for two minutes.
3. Add 1 ½ cups of the stock and stir. Simmer until almost all liquid has been absorbed. Add a little more broth and continue to simmer until rice is tender. Keep adding liquid and stirring until you've reached a creamy, porridge-like consistency, about 30 minutes.
4. Toss in thyme and parsley prior to serving. Adjust seasonings to taste.

This dish can be enhanced by adding diced vegetables, seafood, or grated parmesan cheese.

Stuffed Potatoes

(YF, WF, CF, CIT.F, EF, DF OPTION)

Potatoes can be either a robust side dish or a light entree. Here are two suggestions for stuffed potatoes. Let your culinary instincts guide you to your own creative stuffings. Stuffed potatoes are a good way to use leftover vegetables.

  2 Russet baking potatoes, cleaned and dried and pricked with a fork

Filling #1: Broccoli-Cheese Potatoes

1 cup broccoli florets, steamed and cooled (steam only until bright color emerges)
¼ cup chopped scallions
½ cup grated Vitalait or similar low-fat cheddar cheese
2 tablespoons low-fat milk
Salt and pepper, to taste

Filling #2: Zucchini Dill

¼ cup minced red pepper, ⅛ cup minced red onion, and 1 cup grated zucchini, sautéed in 1 tablespoon olive oil and drained
1 tablespoon chopped fresh parsley
1 tablespoon fresh dill

1. Bake potatoes at 425° for one hour. Let cool slightly.
2. Cut a lengthwise oval from the top of each potato and scoop out potato pulp from the jacket.
3. Mash potato with a fork and stir in broccoli, scallions, cheese, and milk or zucchini and dill mixture. Season to taste.
4. Refill jackets with potato-broccoli or zucchini-dill mixture and bake for another 15 minutes.

Cashew Sauce with Steamed Vegetables   SERVES 4

(YF, DF, WF, CIT.F, CF, EF)

This sauce is excellent made with cashew butter but any nut butter works well. Try the sauce warm or cold, on fish, chicken, noodles, or vegetables.

1 small onion, chopped
1 tablespoon olive oil
2 teaspoons minced garlic
2 teaspoons minced ginger root
1 ½ cups water or mild stock (chicken or vegetable)

⅔ cup cashew butter
2 tablespoons chopped scallions (green stems included)
2 tablespoons minced fresh parsley
Fresh ground pepper, to taste

1. Cook onion in olive oil for three to four minutes or until it begins to soften.
2. Add garlic and ginger. Cook another minute or two.
3. Add broth and nut butter. Cook slowly over low heat until the sauce has thickened, about 15–20 minutes.
4. Toss in scallions. Cook another five minutes and finish with fresh parsley.
5. Serve over steamed vegetables of your choice.

When steaming vegetables, bear in mind that the size and density of the vegetable will determine how long it will take to cook. Carrots cut into ¼–½-inch slices can cook evenly with broccoli and cauliflower florets. Asparagus is best cut into 1 ½–2-inch lengths. Zucchini and yellow squash cut into ½-inch slices on the diagonal look very appealing. Steam vegetables only until crisp-tender and vibrantly colored, about 10–15 minutes, depending on your choices and cuts. Garnish the dish with sunflower seeds and a handful of nuts.

Mixed Grain Salad   SERVES 4

(DF, EF, WF OPTION, YF, CIT.F, CF)

2 1/2 cups cooked grains,   1 garlic clove, minced
  cooled   1 carrot, grated
2 scallions, chopped (green   2 tablespoons sunflower
  stems included)   seeds

Dressing

2 tablespoons soy sauce or   1/2 teaspoon toasted sesame
  Dr. Bonner's Mineral   oil
  Bouillon   1 tablespoon water
1 tablespoon vinegar or   1 tablespoon honey
  apple juice   1 tablespoon sesame butter
                                     or tahini

1. Mix the grains, vegetables, and sunflower seeds together in
   a bowl. Whisk the dressing ingredients together in a bowl,
   pour over the salad, and toss.

Gingered Salmon Cakes

SERVES 2

(DF, WF, CIT.F, CF, YF)

These salmon croquettes are surprisingly easy to make and are packed with flavor.

1 ¾-pound salmon fillet
1 scallion, chopped coarsely
1 tablespoon minced ginger
   root or ½–1 teaspoon⁻
   ginger powder

1 egg, slightly beaten, to
   bind
¼ cup chopped celery
1 tablespoon minced fresh
   parsley
2 tablespoons olive oil

1. Place salmon, scallion, and ginger root into food processor. Process until salmon is coarsely ground, about 30 seconds.
2. Add egg, celery, and parsley with a few on/off turns.
3. Form salmon mixture into patties about 4 inches across and ½-inch thick.
4. Heat olive oil in skillet and pan-fry until golden brown on each side, about 5 minutes per side, depending on the thickness of the patties.
5. Serve hot from the pan with your choice of vegetable and/or potato.

Basic Grain Pilaf   SERVES 4

(CF, CIT.F, DF, EF, YF, WF OPTION)

Any grain can be used as a delightful pilaf when a change of pace is needed. Use the grain guideline we've provided (see page 233) for the correct proportion of liquid to grain. Cold pilaf makes a good base for a salad the following day or use it as a stuffing for red and green peppers or zucchini boats.

½ cup chopped onions	*2 cups cooked grain of choice*
1 tablespoon olive oil	*Savory broth or water*
1 celery stalk, chopped	*Fresh ground pepper, to*
1 carrot, diced	*taste*
1 ½ teaspoons dried thyme	*2 tablespoons fresh parsley, minced*

1. Sauté onion in oil for two to three minutes until it begins to soften.
2. Add celery and carrot. Stir until still crisp but tender. (Cook a bit more for quick cooking grains, less for longer cooking grains.)
3. Pour grain into pan and stir for a minute or two to lightly coat grains.
4. Add cooking liquid and seasonings. Cook gently until liquid is absorbed and grain is tender. Toss in fresh parsley.
5. To serve, fluff with a fork and scoop out pilaf with a large serving spoon.

Herb Vinaigrette

The amount of oil in this dressing is kept to a minimum, without sacrificing flavor. There is an optional yeast-free version of this dressing, using a replacement of Dr. Bonner's Mineral Bouillon for the vinegar.

3 tablespoons olive or walnut oil	2 tablespoons minced shallots
2 tablespoons vinegar (or Dr. Bonner's Mineral Bouillon)	1 tablespoon minced fresh basil
2 tablespoons water	1 tablespoon minced fresh parsley
3 tablespoons raspberry juice	1 tablespoon honey
	½ teaspoon mustard powder

Whisk all ingredients together in a small bowl or place in a jar with a tight cap and shake vigorously.

Yamana

This is a great side dish for one.

1 yam	1 banana

1. Bake the yam at 450° for one hour or until soft.
2. Scoop out the "meat" into a mixing bowl, reserving the skin.
3. Slice the banana. Add it to the yam and mash together well.
4. Stuff the mixture back into the yam skin and let it bake for another 5 minutes.

Banana Ice Cream
SERVES 2

2 overripe bananas, frozen   1/4 teaspoon vanilla extract
2 ounces tofu, frozen

Run all ingredients through a powerful juicer (a Champion or a machine of similar quality). What will come out will be a creamy, rich, and very tasty frozen dessert that is nutritious enough to serve as the centerpiece of a meal. Serve immediately.

Fruit Gelatin
SERVES 2

1 package Knox gelatin   1 tablespoon pineapple juice
2/3 cup hot water   1/4 cup currants
1/3 cup cold water   1/4 cup gooseberries
2 teaspoons vanilla extract

1. Dissolve the gelatin in the hot water and stir well.
2. Mix in the rest of the ingredients, pouring into a serving dish and refrigerate until completely set.

Frozen Bananas
SERVES 1

1 banana   pine nuts

1. Roll an overripe banana in toasted pine nuts (roast them for 10 minutes at 350°).
2. Freeze the banana overnight and enjoy as a snack or dessert the next day.

Frozen Carob Bananas

SERVES 4

(DF, CF. CIT.F, EF, WF, YF)

1 1/2 cups carob chips
2 teaspoons soy margarine
4 bananas, ripe but not
   mushy

1 cup coconut and/or
   chopped nuts

1. Melt carob chips in a double boiler over simmering water. Stir in soy margarine.
2. Using the back of a spoon, coat the peeled bananas with the melted carob chips.
3. Sprinkle on or roll in coconut and nuts.
4. Place on wax paper on a small pan and put into freezer. Allow to freeze until firm, six to eight hours.

VARIATION: Pineapple chunks work well with this recipe too. Pat the chunks dry with a paper towel before coating with carob.

Trail Mix I

SERVES 2

1/2 cup dried banana slices
1/2 cup diced dried pineapple
1/4 cup pecans

1/4 cup walnuts
1/4 cup pine nuts

Combine all ingredients and enjoy as a snack.

Date Squares

MAKES 12–16

(CF, WF, DF OPTION*, EF, CIT.F)

Filling:

1/2 lb. dates

1 cup apple juice

Crust:

2 cups oatmeal
1 cup oat flour
1 teaspoon baking soda
1/2 cup honey

1 1/2 sticks butter or soy
   margarine, melted

1. Simmer dates for 30 minutes in apple juice.
2. Stir oats, flour, baking soda, honey, and butter (or soy margarine) together. Press half of this mixture onto the bottom of a 9-inch square baking pan.
3. Spread the date mixture onto the crust. Spread the remaining oat mixture on top of the dates, covering the dates gently.
4. Bake at 350° for about 35–40 minutes until golden brown. Cut into squares when cool.

VARIATION: In place of the dates, use ½ pound dried apricots or peaches and use apricot or peach juice in place of apple juice.

Indian Pudding   SERVES 8
(WF, DF OPTION*, CIT.F, YF OPTION*)

The quintessential whole-foods dessert. Deliciously rich and spicy. *

½ cup corn meal	1 teaspoon cinnamon
3 ½ cups milk	¼ teaspoon nutmeg
½ cup molasses	¼ cup each nuts and raisins
1 tablespoon butter or soy	(optional)
margarine	2 eggs, beaten
1 teaspoon ginger	

1. Preheat oven to 350°.
2. Cook cornmeal in milk until it begins to thicken, about 10–15 minutes.
3. Stir in all remaining ingredients, except the eggs, and remove from heat.
4. When mixture has cooled, add eggs and bake in a 9 X 13-inch pan for one hour or until set.
5. Serve while still warm from the oven.

*You can easily make a dairy-free version of this recipe by using soy or nut or seed milk (see page 236) in place of cow's milk.

Rice Pudding

SERVES 6

(WF, CIT.F, CF, YF OPTION, DF)

Use any leftover grain that has been cooked in water for this recipe.

2 cups cooked grains
1 ½ cups soy or nut milk
¼ cup maple syrup
1 tablespoon vanilla extract
½ cup cooked apples

¼ cup chopped dates
   (optional)
¼ cup chopped walnuts or
   slivered almonds
2 eggs, slightly beaten
1 teaspoon cinnamon

1. Mix all ingredients together in a bowl.
2. Pour into an 8 x 8-inch baking pan and bake until pudding has just barely set, about 40–45 minutes.
3. Serve warm from the oven.

Apple Walnut Cake

SERVES 8

(WF, DF, CIT.F, CF, YF)

1 cup oat flour
1 cup rice flour
¾ cup barley flour
1 ½ teaspoons baking soda
1 teaspoon cinnamon
½ teaspoon allspice
½ teaspoon salt
1 ¼ cup safflower or

vegetable oil
1 cup honey
1 tablespoon vanilla extract
2 eggs and 1 egg white,
   slightly beaten
1 ¼ cup chopped walnuts
2 apples, cored, seeded, and
   chopped

1. Mix dry ingredients in a large bowl. Add oil, honey, vanilla, and eggs.
2. Stir in walnuts and apples.
3. Pour into a greased 10-inch ring pan or 2 greased medium loaf pans. Bake at 350° for about 1 hour or until cake is golden and set.

Apples with Nut Crust

SERVES 4

(DF, WF, EF, CIT.F, CF, YF OPTION)

A comforting end to a meal, combining whole foods with traditional flavors.

6 Granny Smith apples
4 tablespoons soy margarine
   (or butter)
1 teaspoon cinnamon
1/4 cup succanat
1/4 cup maple syrup

3/4 cup ground walnuts or
   pecans
1/2 cup apple or apricot juice
1/2 cup mixed dried fruits
   (apricots, dates, raisins)

1. Preheat oven to 350°.
2. Slice apples in eighths and remove seeds. Leave skin on for added texture and fiber.
3. Melt margarine, then add remaining ingredients and mix until crumbly.
4. Transfer apple slices to a small baking dish (8 X 8 inches).
5. Top with crumb mixture and bake for about 45 minutes or until apple slices are soft but not mushy. Serve warm.

Poached Pears

SERVES 4

(DF, YF, CF, WF, CIT.F, EF)

1 1/2 quarts peach or apple
   juice
1 cinnamon stick, about 4
   inches long
3 cloves

4 or 5 peppercorns
1/3 cup honey or maple
   syrup
4 Bartlett pears, ripe but not
   overly soft

1. Place juice in large saucepan with cinnamon stick, cloves, peppercorns, and honey or maple syrup. Bring to simmer.
2. Peel skin from pears and place pears into simmering liquid.
3. Cook on simmer until pears are soft and pierced easily with a skewer, about 45 minutes.
4. Serve warm or chilled with a bit of the poaching liquid.

Peach Upside-Down Cake

(YF, CF, CIT.F, WF, DF OPTION)

Bottom:

6 tablespoons butter or soy
  margarine, melted

⅓ cup honey

2 peaches, sliced

Top:

1 peach, puréed, and apple
  or peach juice added to
  equal 1 ½ cups

½ cup butter or soy
  margarine, melted

½ cup honey

2 eggs

1 tablespoon vanilla extract

1 cup rice flour

1 cup oat flour

1 teaspoon ginger

1 ½ teaspoons baking soda

1. For the bottom, stir together the butter and honey and place at bottom of 10-inch cake pan.
2. Arrange peach slices in concentric circles on top of honey and butter mixture. Set aside.
3. Mix puréed peach and juice with melted butter (or margarine), honey, eggs, and vanilla.
4. Stir in dry ingredients. Mix until smooth.
5. Bake at 350° about one hour or until cake is golden brown and set.
6. Remove from oven. Let cool for 10 minutes before inverting onto a cake plate.

FOR SNACKING

For many people, tofu is still a foreign four-letter word. For those of you who are still resistant to the low-fat, high-protein qualities of this food, we offer the following recipe. The beauty of this recipe is that it capitalizes on the best of tofu and completely disguises the taste and texture of the bean curd. This recipe significantly reduces the fat and calories associated with nut butter spreads.

> 1/4 pound custard-style tofu   nut butter
> 1/4 pound of your favorite   1 tablespoon honey

1. Blend tofu and nut butter in blender until smooth and creamy. Finish with honey.
2. Use as a spread on crackers or bread. Leftovers can be refrigerated in an airtight container.

BREAKFAST: DAY 2

Breakfast for Day 2 is easy in that there is a wealth of fresh fruit that can be eaten separately or diced together for a fruit salad. A stick of celery and a carrot are another quick and easy way to start the day.

LUNCH AND DINNER

Shrimp Salad

SERVES 2

1 pound shrimp, shelled and
  deveined
1 head lettuce
2 large carrots, sliced

2 celery stalks, sliced
1 tablespoon sunflower oil
1 teaspoon dill
Cumin and anise to taste

1. Bring 2 quarts of water to a boil, add the shrimp and boil
   for about 5 minutes or until they turn pink.
2. Drain the shrimp and allow them to chill in the refrigerator.
3. Assemble the salad and toss with the oil, seasonings, and
   shrimp.

Bar Harbor Appetizer

SERVES 2

1 tablespoon safflower oil
1 pound baby sea scallops
1 cup finely chopped celery

1/2 cup sunflower seeds
1/4 cup quince juice
Parsley sprig for garnish

1. Heat the oil in a frying pan over medium-high heat.
2. Add the remaining ingredients and stir until the scallops are
   evenly cooked and white, about 10 minutes.
3. Pour off the excess liquid and serve garnished with a parsley sprig.

Celery Consommé

SERVES 2

6 cups cooking broth from
  clams and/or scallops
4–5 cups chopped celery
  leaves and stalks

2 sliced carrots
Caraway and fennel seed, to
  taste (optional)

Combine ingredients in a heavy pot, bring to a boil, and allow
to simmer for 30 minutes. May be served with a tossed salad
or the vegetables of the day or a baked sweet potato.

Shellfish Soup
SERVES 2

3 cups Vegetable Stock
(made as on page 246,
but using artichokes,
celery, parsnips, carrots,
and chicory)
1/2 cup minced raw clams

1/2 cut shrimp, shelled and
deveined
1/2 cup chopped scallops
2 tablespoons chopped
parsley
1/4 cup chopped celery
1–2 teaspoons arrowroot
Fennel, to taste

1. Heat the stock. Add the other ingredients and bring to a boil.
2. Allow to simmer for 30 minutes. The arrowroot acts as a thickener, so vary the amount depending upon the consistency that you like.

Barbecued Shrimp
SERVES 1

6 large shrimp, shelled and
deveined

Fresh raspberry juice
(optional)

1. Butterfly the shrimp by cutting them along the back, almost all the way through, and flattening them out.
2. Put them on the grill. You may wish to add wet mesquite chips for a rich, smoky flavor.
3. While they are grilling, sprinkle fresh raspberry juice on them for added flavor.
4. Cooking time is only 4 to 6 minutes, so watch them carefully. Serve with a tossed salad made with the vegetables of the day.

Boiled Lobster

SERVES 1

1 2-pound live lobster

1. Bring 3 quarts of water to a rapid boil and add the lobster. (This will quickly kill the bacteria in the lobster's gut and prevent it from putrefying and becoming somewhat poisonous.)
2. Cook for four to five minutes, shell, and enjoy with a tossed salad made with the vegetables of the day and a baked sweet potato.

Note: Shellfish are high in cholesterol, so vary your diet in order not to eat them too often.

Stir-fried Shellfish

SERVES 2

*1 cup shrimp, shelled and
    deveined*
*1/2 cup clams, raw, shelled
    and deveined*
1/2 cup scallops
Safflower oil

1/2 cup chopped carrots
1/2 cup chopped celery
1/4 cup chopped parsnips
*Fennel and anise, whole or
    ground, to taste*
Parsley sprig for garnish

1. Combine the shellfish.
2. Pour just enough oil into a frying pan to coat bottom of pan.
3. Add shellfish and cook over medium-high heat for 2 to 3 minutes, until scallops and shrimp just begin to turn white.
4. Add vegetables and continue to cook, stirring constantly.
5. Add fennel and anise. Garnish with a sprig of parsley and serve.

Scallop Casserole
SERVES 2

1 pound parsnips, diced
½ pound carrots, diced
1 pound baby sea scallops
1 teaspoon dried dill weed

1 teaspoon fennel, whole or
  ground
1 large sweet potato, diced
1 tablespoon sunflower oil
Parsley sprig for garnish

Combine the ingredients well in an ovenproof dish, cover, and bake at 350° for 1 hour. Remove cover and lay a fresh sprig of parsley on top of the casserole before serving.

Scallops and Fennel
SERVES 2

2 pounds fennel bulbs
2 pounds scallops

1 tablespoon quince juice
1 teaspoon dried dill weed

1. Cut off bottoms of fennel bulbs, slice them lengthwise, about 1-inch thick and spread the slices evenly in a shallow baking pan.
2. Scatter scallops over the fennel slices.
3. Sprinkle quince juice and dill on top of scallops and bake at 350° for 15–20 minutes or until fennel is tender.

Stuffed Fennel
SERVES 2

½ cup minced clams
½ cup chopped carrots,
  puréed
½ cup chopped celery

½ cup chopped parsnips
2 tablespoons safflower oil
1–2 teaspoons arrowroot
6 large fennel bulbs

1. Combine the clams, vegetables, and oil in a large bowl, adding enough arrowroot to bind the mixture.
2. Cut the fennel bulbs in half lengthwise.
3. Scoop out the middle of the bulbs and add 2 tablespoons of the stuffing to each.
4. Bake at 350° for 15–20 minutes or until tender but not mushy.

Endive Dip

4 large endives
1 teaspoon fennel, whole or
 ground
½ cup safflower oil

1–2 teaspoons arrowroot
 (optional)
Celery and carrot sticks for
 dipping

1. Cut off and discard ends of the endive.
2. Place endive in a blender or food processor and purée.
3. Add remaining ingredients and blend well. Arrowroot may
   be added to thicken the mixture.
4. Serve with celery and carrot sticks.

Endive Salad

6 large endives, cleaned and
 cored
2 peaches, sliced

4 nectarines, sliced into
 wedges

Alternate layers of endive leaves and fruit in a circular pattern
on a platter. Chill and serve.

Waldorf Salad

3 large apples, cored and
 diced
4–5 celery stalks, sliced
½ cup sunflower seeds
½ cup almonds, whole and
 shelled

1 cup fresh cherries, pitted
2 nectarines, peeled and
 sliced
¼ cup raspberries, puréed
¼ cup strawberries, puréed
½ teaspoon arrowroot

Combine all ingredients in a large mixing bowl and toss well.
Chill in the refrigerator for at least one hour and serve.

Baked Parsnips

SERVES 2

This makes a great side dish with Barbecued Shrimp (page 268) or Stir-fried Shellfish (page 269).

1 pound parsnips, peeled
  and diced
1 nectarine, peeled and
  sliced

2 apples, diced
1 tablespoon quince juice
1 tablespoon maple syrup

Combine ingredients in an ovenproof dish and bake at 325° for 30 minutes.

Trail Mix II

SERVES 2

¼ cup sunflower seeds
¼ cup almonds, whole and
  shelled

¼ cup unsulfured dried
  apricots
¼ cup dried apple

Mix together for a snack or dessert.

BREAKFAST: DAY 3

How do you like your eggs—scrambled, fried, poached, or hard boiled? Dice up some potatoes and pan-fry them in a nonstick skillet or in a little bit of olive oil, and pour yourself a nice glass of orange juice, and you're all set. Alternatively, a half a grapefruit or a tangerine will likewise get you off to a nice start.

LUNCH AND DINNER

Tomato Sauce

SERVES 2

1 medium beet, puréed
1 quart tomatoes, puréed
4 fresh tomatoes, diced
4 bell peppers, diced

1 tablespoon molasses
1 tablespoon olive oil
Powdered ginger and
  cayenne, to taste

1. Combine all ingredients in a heavy pot.
2. Bring to boil, reduce heat, and simmer for 2 ½–3 hours, stirring every 10 minutes.

Tomato-Rice Soup
SERVES 2

Tomato sauce (p. 272)   ¼–½ cup raw rice

Prepare the tomato sauce as above, adding rice during the last
20 minutes of cooking.

Turkey Soup
SERVES 2

3 cups vegetable stock (made
    as on page 246, but
    using spinach, beet
    greens, and green peppers)

1 pound turkey meat,
    cooked and cubed
1 medium potato, diced
½ cup corn

Heat the stock, add remaining ingredients and allow to simmer for one hour.

Borscht
SERVES 8

4 large beets, with greens   2 sliced hard-boiled eggs

1. Dice beets and boil in two quarts of water for 15 minutes.
   Remove from heat.
2. Chop beet greens and add them to the cooked beets.
3. When cool, add hard-boiled eggs.
4. Chill overnight and enjoy cold or warmed up. Rice cakes
   go well with this.

Sushi without Raw Fish
SERVES 4

Several 7 x 8-inch (18 x
    20 cm.) sheets of nori
    (roasted seaweed,
    available in whole-food
    stores and Oriental
    groceries)
2 cups cooked rice (preferably
    whole brown)

Pickled ginger, sliced Wasabi
    (horseradish powder,
    available in whole-food
    stores and Oriental
    groceries)
Cooked chicken, fish, eel,
    lobster, squid, octopus,
    scallops or vegetables of
    the day

Sheets of *nori* are an excellent source of iron, and there are as many ways of preparing sushi without raw fish, as your imagination allows. (Raw fish, especially shallow-water varieties, carry the potential threat of parasites.) The simplest method of preparing *nori* is to make hand cones. Fold a single or double sheet of *nori* in half. Mix the *wasabi* with a little water to make a thick paste and spread this lightly over the seaweed. (Careful—it is very fiery.) Spread a mound of cooked rice near the center of the sheet. Top the rice with sliced vegetables, cooked fish, or chicken—use any item that is allowed for the day—and top this with slices of pickled ginger to taste. Roll into a cone and eat, much as you would eat an ice cream cone. Soy sauce may also be added to taste, assuming you have no allergy to soy sauce.

Chicken Cacciatore
SERVES 2

2 pounds boneless chicken breasts, cubed

Olive oil

Ginger, powdered, to taste

6 cups tomato sauce (page 275)

Chili powder (optional)

1. Stir-fry chicken in a little olive oil until evenly browned on all sides.
2. Sprinkle with ginger to taste.
3. Transfer chicken and pan juices to a heavy pot. Pour tomato sauce over it and bring to a simmer over medium heat.
4. Reduce heat, cover, and let cook for 30 minutes. The chicken may be served over rice or rice noodles. Add a little chili powder for extra zest.

Festive Chicken

SERVES 2

1 large boneless chicken
  breast
1 cup chopped spinach
  cooked and drained

2 teaspoons lemon juice
1/8 teaspoon powdered ginger
1/2 teaspoon paprika

1. Place chicken breast in a closeable plastic bag or between pieces of waxed paper. With a rolling pin, gently pound the chicken to half its original thickness.
2. Combine remaining ingredients and spread over the surface of the flattened chicken breast.
3. Roll up the chicken like a jelly roll and secure it with toothpicks. You may sprinkle a little more lemon juice and paprika on it, if you like.
4. Wrap in aluminum foil and bake at 350° for 30 minutes.
5. After cooking, allow it to cool for a few minutes. Then remove toothpicks, slice, and serve.

Colleen's Chicken Oriental

SERVES 2

2 pounds boneless chicken or
  turkey breast, cubed
Olive oil
Ginger powder, to taste
2 bell peppers, diced
1/2 cup diced bamboo shoots,

canned or fresh
1/4 cup macadamia nuts
1 orange, peeled and in
  sections
3/4 cup orange juice
1/4 cup cashews, unsalted

1. Brown chicken or turkey over medium-high heat in a frying pan with a little bit of olive oil. Add ginger.
2. Place chicken in a crockpot or a large heavy pot on low heat and add all remaining ingredients.
3. Cook slowly for 1 1/2 hours.
4. Serve over brown rice or rice noodles.

Berkshire Chicken
SERVES 2

1 pound boneless chicken
  breasts
½ cup orange juice

¼ cup molasses
¼ cup chopped unsalted
  cashews

1. Place chicken in an ovenproof dish and bake at 350° for 20 minutes.
2. Combine remaining ingredients and pour over chicken.
3. Bake for another 5 to 10 minutes until golden brown.

Chinese-style Barbecued Chicken or Turkey
SERVES 2

2 pounds boneless chicken or
  turkey breast

1 ½ cups orange juice
1 teaspoon powdered ginger

1. Combine ingredients and allow chicken or turkey to marinate overnight.
2. Barbecue the next day. Wet mesquite chips may be added for a rich, smoky flavor.
3. Enjoy with brown rice and a tossed salad made with the vegetables of the day or corn on the cob.

New England Roasted Chicken
SERVES 2

1 2½ to 3 pound broiler
  chicken
1 tablespoon olive oil

1 teaspoon paprika
1 teaspoon powdered ginger
2 lemons, sliced

1. Rinse chicken and pat dry. Place on a roasting pan and brush with olive oil.
2. Sprinkle with paprika and ginger, and cover with lemon slices.
3. Cook at 325° for 2 ½ hours.
4. Serve with rice and steamed vegetables or salad of the day.

Stuffed Peppers

1 pound chicken or turkey,   *6 cups tomato sauce (page*
   cooked and minced   *275)*
2 cups cooked rice   *4 bell peppers*

1. Combine chicken or turkey with rice and 2 cups of tomato sauce. Mix well.
2. Wash peppers, remove the tops and discard core and seeds.
3. Stuff the peppers with rice mixture and place them in a deep baking dish.
4. Pour remaining tomato sauce over peppers. Cover and bake at 350° for 20 minutes.

South County Deviled Eggs

4 peeled hard-boiled eggs   *1/2 teaspoon paprika*
1/4 cup coconut milk   *8 black olives*
1/2 teaspoon powdered ginger

1. Cut eggs in half lengthwise and remove the yolks.
2. Mash egg yolks, coconut milk, and ginger together until smooth.
3. Stuff mixture back into the hollows of the egg whites. Sprinkle with paprika and place a black olive on each deviled egg.
4. Serve as an appetizer or as a main course with a tossed salad.

Fried Rice

1 tablespoon olive oil   *1 bell pepper, diced*
2 cups cooked rice   *1 tomato, chopped*
2 eggs, beaten

1. Put oil in a frying pan and place over high heat.
2. Add rice and stir until it starts to fry.
3. Add eggs and stir until well scrambled and cooked through.
4. Add remaining ingredients and cook another five minutes on low heat.

Massachusetts Succotash

SERVES 2

1 oz. slice of Chinese-style
  Barbecued Chicken or
  Turkey (page 276)
2 cups chopped spinach,

cooked and drained
3 cups corn kernels, cooked
½ cup water

1. Combine ingredients in a heavy pot and cook over low heat for 30 minutes.
2. Discard the chicken or turkey (only used for flavoring).
3. Put remaining ingredients in a blender and purée until smooth. Serve while hot.

Trail Mix III

SERVES 2

¼ cup unsalted roasted
  cashews
¼ cup unsalted pistachio
  nuts, undyed and shelled

¼ cup raisins
¼ cup chopped dates
¼ cup shredded
  unsweetened coconut

Combine all ingredients. Munch on for a snack.

Mexican Popcorn

SERVES 2

2 ounces popcorn kernels
1 tablespoon olive oil

1 teaspoon crushed red
  pepper

1. Pop the popcorn in oil in a covered pot over medium-high heat or in one of the many commercially available poppers.
2. When kernels are all popped, sprinkle on red pepper and stir in well.

BREAKFAST: DAY 4

Breakfasts for Day 4 are easy and tasty. Just go to the produce department of your favorite food store, pick out a nice, slightly soft melon, bring it home and cut it in half. Scoop out the seeds and enjoy. You can put some blueberries or cranberries in it for a more colorful breakfast treat and squeeze on lemon juice. Smoked salmon or whitefish also make a nice breakfast, and may be easier to digest if you have problems with your blood sugar. (Some people are sensitive even to the natural sugar in fruit and may tolerate it better late in the afternoon or evening.) A can of boneless, skinless sardines packed in spring water also makes a good Day 4 breakfast. Papaya is rich in enzymes that can help you digest your food, especially protein. If your digestion is generally on the upset side, including a little fresh papaya with each meal is helpful. A bowl of hot buckwheat (oh boy!), perhaps with a teaspoon of raw honey and ¼ cup of soy milk makes a good, hot breakfast on a winter's day.

LUNCH AND DINNER

Fish is tasty, nutritious, and easy to cook. As a rule of thumb, cook fish at medium-high heat for 10 minutes per inch of thickness. For example, a one-inch thick swordfish steak will take about 10 minutes to bake at 375° in a preheated oven. The fish should be white and speckled with light brown when cooked and should flake apart easily. Don't wait until it "smells" done, because if it smells like cooked fish then it's probably already a burnt offering. Don't worry about not cooking it enough. There are some people who pay a lot of money for raw fish and claim to like it. (They don't mind the risk and consequences of parasites and, if it has been sitting around too long, bacterial infections.) Cooking fish is primarily a sterilization process.

Pea Soup
SERVES 2

5 cups shelled peas
1/2 cup sliced okra
5 cups vegetable stock (page 246, using vegetables of the day)

1/2 cup diced zucchini
2 tablespoons buckwheat honey
1/4 teaspoon sage
1/4 teaspoon marjoram

1. Steam peas and okra until soft, then purée—the okra acts as a thickener.
2. Add remaining ingredients and cook over low heat for 30 minutes. (Generally we don't like pea soup, but this is good!)

Pumpkin Soup
SERVES 2

7–8 pounds "sugar" pumpkin
4 cups vegetable stock (made as on page 246, using vegetables of the day
1/2 cup uncooked buckwheat groats

1/2 cup raw peas, shelled
1/2 cup diced zucchini
1/2 cup chopped chestnuts, raw
1/2 teaspoon oregano
1/4 teaspoon sage

1. Carefully cut off top of the pumpkin and remove seeds. Then place pumpkin in a large, deep ovenproof pot.
2. Put remaining ingredients inside the pumpkin and replace the lid.
3. Bake at 375° for one hour or until pumpkin is tender but not mushy.
4. To serve, ladle out the soup, scraping out some of the pumpkin with each serving.

Generic Baked, Broiled, or Barbecued Fish   SERVES 2

1 ½-pound fish (tuna,
swordfish, cod, flounder,
trout, etc.), fillet or steak
½ cup raw cranberries

¼ cup cranberry juice
½ teaspoon ground sage
½ teaspoon ground
marjoram

1. Place fish in a baking pan and sprinkle with remaining ingredients.
2. Place in preheated 375° oven and bake for 10 minutes per inch of thickness.
3. Alternately, you can broil the fish 4 to 5 inches from the broiler flame or coils and turn it over halfway through the cooking process. Or marinate the fish overnight in the cranberries and spices and grill it over hot coals. Turn it over halfway through the cooking process

A Note of Caution: Fish bones can be treacherous. They may break apart as you're deboning the cooked fish, so chew well and slowly. Quietly spitting a fish bone into a napkin is considered better etiquette than coughing a whole wad of chewed-up fish across the room, and it's even worse manners to choke to death at a dinner party.

Sole Stir-Fry   SERVES 2

½ pound of sole fillets,
cubed
½ cup zucchini
"shoestrings"

½ cup snow peas
½ cup mung bean sprouts
¼ teaspoon sage
¼ teaspoon oregano

1. Cook the cubed sole over medium heat in a nonstick frying pan until it begins to turn white.
2. Add remaining ingredients and cook for another 3 to 4 minutes, until fish is done and the vegetables are still crunchy.

Fish Gumbo
SERVES 2

½ pound sole or flounder
  fillet, cubed
6 cups vegetable stock (made
  as on page 246, using
  the vegetables of the day)
1 cup dried lentils
½ cup snow peas

½ cup chopped green or
  wax beans
½ cup diced zucchini
¼ teaspoon sage
¼ teaspoon oregano
1 pound okra, cut in
  one-inch lengths
2 cups Cooked buckwheat

1. Place all ingredients in a large heavy pot or crockpot.
2. Cook over low heat for 1½–2 hours, stirring occasionally.
3. Serve with cooked buckwheat.

Poached Salmon
SERVES 2

1 ½-pound salmon steak
1 cup blueberries

¼ teaspoon sage
¼ teaspoon marjoram

1. Place salmon in a deep frying pan, half filled with boiling
   water.
2. Poach for 6 minutes, then add remaining ingredients.
   Cook for 6 more minutes.
3. Carefully lift out the salmon with two spatulas and serve
   with a salad made from the vegetables of the day.

Codfish Cakes

SERVES 2

1/4 pound codfish fillets
1 large winter (spaghetti)

squash
1 tablespoon peanut oil

1. Poach codfish for 10 minutes, drain, and transfer to a mixing bowl.
2. Boil squash for 30 minutes or until tender. Then cut in half and remove the seeds.
3. Scoop the stringy pulp into the mixing bowl and mash well with codfish while still hot.
4. Place oil in a frying pan over high heat.
5. Make flattened golf ball-sized patties of the fish mixture and gently drop them into the hot oil.
6. Turn and cook until evenly browned. Serve with a salad made with the vegetables of the day.

Vegetable Casserole

SERVES 2

2 cups cooked buckwheat
  groats
1 cup cooked kidney beans
1/2 cup chopped butternut

squash
1/2 cup chopped zucchini
2 tablespoons buckwheat
  honey

Combine all ingredients and mix well. Spread in a 9-inch casserole dish and bake at 350° for 30–40 minutes.

Baked Squash

SERVES 2

1 1/2 pounds butternut
  squash
2 tablespoons clover honey

1 teaspoon nutmeg
Chopped hazelnuts
  (optional)

1. Bake squash at 350° for 45 minutes.
2. Cut squash in half the long way and scoop out the seeds and stringy part.
3. Drizzle honey over the squash halves and sprinkle with nutmeg. This makes a great and easy side dish. Chopped hazelnuts may also be sprinkled on top.

Thanksgiving Peas

SERVES 2

1 pound fresh peas, shelled   *¼ cup chopped fresh peppermint*

1. Steam peas for about 5 minutes, so that they are still a bit crunchy and bright green.
2. Mix the chopped peppermint and serve.

VARIATION: For a more festive dish, bake a butternut squash for 1 hour at 375° until tender. Cut the squash in half, scoop out half the pulp and reserve for later. Spoon the peas and mint into the hollow and serve.

Roasted Chestnuts

SERVES 1

This is a simple snack, or even a side dish, that's a favorite of ours. When you buy the chestnuts, make sure that there are no cracks or holes in the shell, or the meat will probably be moldy. Make sure also that the nut is firm with shiny appearance, or you may find a shriveled mass inside.

½ pound fresh chestnuts

Make a half-inch cut in the shell to keep it from exploding when it cooks. Bake at 375° for 15 minutes. Or, shell the nuts and steam them for about 15 minutes. You can eat the chestnuts themselves or mixed with the vegetables of the day as a side dish.

Papaya Royale

SERVES 2

1 1/2 cups blueberries   1/4 cup crushed filberts
1 fresh papaya, diced

1. Place 1 cup of the blueberries in a small saucepan with 2 teaspoons water.
2. Cover and simmer for 15 minutes, stirring occasionally.
3. Strain the juice and discard the solids.
4. Dice the papaya and pour the hot blueberry sauce over it.
5. Top with remaining whole blueberries and sprinkle with crushed nuts.

Fruit Compote II

SERVES 2

1/2 cup fresh blueberries   1/2 cup cranberry juice
1/2 cup diced fresh papaya   Crashed hazelnuts (optional)
1/2 cup chopped figs   Clover honey (optional)
1 cup cantaloupe balls

Mix fruits together well. Sprinkle with crushed hazelnuts and drizzle with clover honey if you have a bit of a sweet tooth to satisfy.

Trail Mix IV

SERVES 2

1/4 cup pumpkin seeds   1/4 cup diced dried figs
1 tablespoon peanut oil   1/4 cup diced dried papaya
1/4 cup filberts

1. Place pumpkin seeds in a broiling pan with oil. Broil for about 5 minutes or until seeds are browned.
2. Transfer the seeds to paper towels and allow to cool. Mix with remaining ingredients and enjoy.

By now you should be well fed. So sit back and listen to some nice music, or read a book and get out of your body's way so it can do what comes naturally . . . heal.

12

PARTNERS IN CRIME: VIRAL COUSINS AND RELATED ILLNESSES

A single death is a tragedy: a million deaths is a statistic.

—JOSEPH STALIN

Captain Trips . . . 99.4% communicability. And that meant 99.4% excess mortality, because the human body couldn't produce the antibodies necessary to stop a constantly shifting antigen virus. Every time the body did produce the right antibody, the virus simply shifted. For the same reason a vaccine was going to be almost impossible to create.

—STEPHEN KING, *THE STAND*
(1978)

SYNDROMES OF RARE DESIGN

It is an old axiom of both the physician and the evolutionary biologist that a virus or bacterium that kills its host is poorly adapted, because it must die when the host dies. Mention viruses and bacteria to most people and they will think immediately of disease. But the fact is that, although our bodies are oceans of viral and bacterial activity, less than 4 percent of these organisms cause illness. Though we exhale them with every breath, though we ingest them with every meal, though they live in our lungs and our blood, slick our skin and our intestines, and migrate by the millions on every fingerprint we leave behind, on every hand we shake, they only rarely make us sick, and for a very good reason.

In the numbers game of evolution, winners achieve increased reproductive potential and sustain it for a very long time. The host that dies is no more or less a failure than the parasite that kills him. The chief difference is that a human has knowledge of death and a standard of failure, whereas the virus is simply unaware that there are winners and losers. An object of the game is to develop a mutual immunity to each other, if not the kind of mutual parasitism (some call it cooperation or symbiosis) that seems to have permitted free-living and occasionally invasive amoebae to become our white blood cells.

In most cases, the Epstein-Barr virus (for example) lives in our bodies for sixty years or more, costing us little more than an occasional B cell. By contrast, the AIDS virus is poorly adapted to humans. Every host that dies kills as many virus particles as there are humans on Earth. The AIDS virus is no better adapted to humans than a new strain of the flu virus that emerged shortly after World War I and killed close to 20 percent of the world population. The 1918 Spanish flu, as it was called, ranked as the most devastating epidemic since the Black Death, until AIDS. It commonly began as fits of sneezing. It produced rosy swellings around the neck, which often blackened and became a hot, suffocating bloating called tube throat. The disease was hauntingly similar to the Black Death, whose symptoms had been preserved for the ages in a children's song, "Ring-Around-a-Rosy" (referring variously to the red marks on bodies, especially around the neck, and to rings of people dancing around funeral pyres); "a pocket full of posies" (signifies flowers thrown on a corpse); "Ashes! Ashes!"* (referring to the bone-fires of the dead, from which the word *bonfire* comes), and "We all fall down!" (we all die).

The 1918 flu killed in days. But those who lived were better able to hold the virus at bay, and the virus, in its most lethal forms, lived for two or three days within its victims and then died with them (mutually assured destruction). In little more than a year, both man and virus had learned to tolerate each other.

Most flu viruses cause only minor illness, but flu cannot be listed

*Another version of the song ends with "Atissu! Atissu!" instead of "Ashes! Ashes!" Atissu replicates the sound of a sneeze, the first symptom, which spawned the tradition of saying "God bless you" to a person who has sneezed.

among the best adapted of human-infecting viruses, because it mutates relatively fast, giving rise to strains that may be more or less harmful than the parent strain. Every century or so, a maladapted mutant kills a great many hosts. EBV and its non-AIDS partners in crime, which include cytomegalovirus, herpes simplex, and human herpes virus 6, are more stable and only rarely kill. They are very old, changing slowly through time. Man and virus have adapted to each other through long years of coexistence.

Of all the odd, haunting diseases in the world today, chronic fatigue syndrome (CFS) and acquired immune deficiency syndrome (AIDS) rank among the most fascinating, partly on account of what they tell us about the coevolution of viruses and man.

Unlike AIDS, chronic fatigue syndrome is only rarely lethal because the viruses usually involved (including Epstein-Barr) have had hundreds of thousands or even millions of years to live and grow with their hosts. Unlike AIDS, the triggers for the basic immune dysfunction leading up to full-blown chronic fatigue syndrome are varied, much as the causes of congestive heart failure are many. The primary immune dysfunction can range from a genetic cause (as we have seen, ankylosing spondylitis will do nicely) to infectious ones (in some cases of CFS an as-yet-unidentified viral trigger is suspected), culminating in unchecked blooms of common and normally benign viruses coursing through the blood of virtually every one of us.

By the time a patient has been presenting symptoms of chronic fatigue for six months or more, Epstein-Barr, and perhaps one or two of the other usual "squatters," have begun massive colonization ventures in the blood as revealed by abnormal levels of antibody production. Eighty percent of all CFS patients are literally crawling with Epstein-Barr antibodies—which makes this particular virus, in most cases, a useful indicator organism. Charting changing antibody levels against the indicator virus can tell us much about the improving health of a patient's immune system, just as charting the decline of an indicator organism (typically coliform bacteria) in polluted waters can tell us much about an estuary's overall health. The indicator organism, while exerting its own influence on the body, is equally important as a means of taking the pulse of immune function.

As we have said, most of us will test positive for EBV. A blood test indicating the mere presence of antibodies against EBV does not a diagnosis of chronic fatigue syndrome make. A positive diagnosis requires *abnormal* antibody levels (as detailed in chapter 5), often accompanied by abnormal blood levels of copper and iron, observed over a period of several months against a constellation of telltale symptoms.

As more and more information comes to light, EBV continues to provide a good working model for how relatively harmless viruses can produce CFS, given the opportunity of an underlying immune dysfunction. We now know, however, that EBV is not the only virus involved. While approximately 60 percent of the patients arriving at the Solstice Clinic with complaints of deep and long-lasting fatigue are expressing chronic active EBV, 25 to 30 percent also present abnormal antibody levels against human herpes virus number 6 (HHV-6). Layered on top of this, 10 to 15 percent will present high concentrations of Coxsackie B and cytomegalovirus (CMV) antibodies, while another layer—about 5 percent—has three or four viruses out of control at once (and an autoimmune syndrome). Not surprisingly, this upper 5 percent tends to be the most ill. The more viruses one presents active in the system, the more difficult the road ahead and the longer the healing period. These are the people who take a year or more (assuming they follow our protocol) to achieve sustained improvement, and to sustain it to the point that working regular hours becomes think-able.

A relatively new group of viruses—the human T-lymphotrophic viruses (HTLV)—appears to be turning up with increasing frequency in chronic fatigue patients, and one of these is not merely an opportunistic colonist, but is, when present, the initial trigger of the colonization. Fortunately, the latter's presence is, at this point in history, rare.

The first member of this viral family is called HTLV-1. Like all other family members, it homes in specifically on the T-cells. Although implicated in certain leukemias, HTLV-1 also seems to favor cells of the central nervous system. It can cause a strange syndrome called transverse myelitis, which is more or less reversible but may, in extreme cases, cause total paralysis. It can be treated as one would treat MEM or EBV, resulting in a reversal of most symptoms. Recent studies suggest that HTLV-1 is implicated in some cases of multiple sclerosis (MS). Other viruses too are being investigated as possible triggers (coconspirators) in the breakdown of nerve sheath tissue (demyelination) that characterizes MS. These viruses include measles, mumps, parainfluenza (a member of the flu clan), canine distemper, and SV-40 (a monkey virus passed on to approximately 60 million Americans vaccinated with polio cultures derived from monkey kidney tissue during the early 1960s).

The newest member of the HTLV group, the most poorly adapted to humans, is the Darth Vader of deep viral infections. In 1991, a very small minority (1.5 percent) of people seeking treatment for what they believed to be chronic fatigue syndrome found that the human immunodeficiency virus (HIV) was the cause of their problem. While this finding is a low probability event (no cause for panic—yet), it is important to note that two years earlier, in 1989, only a third as many CFS patients learned that HIV (the AIDS virus) had brought on their symptoms, reflecting the rapid proliferation of a new viral antagonist within the human population.

Human herpes virus number 6 (HHV) may be even newer than HIV, but as it is suspected to be a mutant strain of the relatively stable Epstein-Barr virus, it is not nearly as destructive. Like HIV, HHV-6 may actually trigger the initial immune dysfunction that allows EBV and other organisms already within the bloodstream to multiply with only limited restraint. When HIV and HHV-6 are both present, HHV-6 will accelerate the development of AIDS by chewing up the B cells, while HIV simultaneously chews down the T cells. Together, the two viruses may be chilling portents of things to come, for, as you shall soon see, their spread through the human multitudes struggling upon this earth arises from the very same environmental misadventures that threaten to turn our rainforests into a memory.

"It is still not comprehended widely that AIDS is a natural, almost predictable phenomenon," warns Rockefeller University President Joshua Lederberg. "It is not going to be a unique event. Pandemics are not acts of God but are built into the ecological relations between viruses, animal species, and the human species; and we had better understand that or we will rue it."

CAPTAIN TRIPS

There was a moment, sometime during the last 50 to 150 years, when an ancient and apparently harmless simian virus embarked upon a genetic excursion away from its forebears to a strange, constantly shifting monstrosity no one had ever seen before. Under normal ecological conditions, the new organism would simply have been contained locally in populations of African monkeys and chimpanzees, but expanding human populations were then encroaching on simian habitats, slashing back the forests, and putting farms in their place. At the edges of receding forests, the farms became bountiful food sources for the simians. As the simians thrived, so too did the immunodeficiency virus residing in their blood. More crops meant more simians, which in turn meant more virus. In West Africa especially, the mangabeys became agricultural pests, household pets, and local game animals. Through bites, scratches, and human contact with simian blood during skinning and cleaning, the virus found opportunities to infect man.*

By about 1950, at least one strain of the simian immunodeficiency virus (SIV) had made the leap to, and acquired the ability to survive in, the human bloodstream. Somewhere along the path from SIV to human immunodeficiency virus (HIV), the organism also acquired an astonishingly rapid mutation rate. The disruption

---

*Witness that the spread of AIDS across Africa closely follows the pattern of immunizations that were given during the 1970s and 80s using vaccines cultured on monkey kidney tissue. Due to its long coevolution with monkeys, the simian T-cell lymphotrophic virus does not kill its older host, as it does man, or even make the simians particularly ill (beyond common coldlike symptoms); hence, the accepted name for the simian T-cell virus—simian immunodeficiency virus (SIV)—is a misnomer, not unlike "yuppie plague" for CFS. SIV, though genetically ancestral to HIV, produces no immune deficiency in monkeys and apes, leaving us with no naturally occurring animal model for the study of AIDS. How the simian immune system controls the retrovirus remains a mystery. The implication is that monkeys must be very good at something humans can't do, and within this anomaly, perhaps if we look deeply enough within the simian genome, we will find one or more hopeful routes to effective treatment.

of African ecology throughout the 1950s paved the way for repeated and apparently very complex cross-infections and incubation phases, with ultimately disastrous results. Through the sacrifice of thousands of simian forebears over as many as 50,000 years, modern animals suffered little or no harm from the virus. Early in the second half of the twentieth century, a new and largely defenseless host—a human host—had made itself widely available through intensive agriculture. In time, a second human activity—rapid global transport—would provide even greater opportunities for spread.

During the spring of 1959, presumably after years of latent infection, a twenty-five-year-old sailor who had once visited Africa checked into a hospital in Manchester, England, with mysterious skin lesions, weight loss, night sweats, and lungs that were literally teeming with cytomegalovirus. His doctors suspected a previously unknown cancer of the immune system, but nobody knew for sure—truly nobody in those days. All they could do was preserve tissue samples when the patient died, and submit a report to the medical journal *Lancet,* hoping some doctor, somewhere in the world, would recognize the syndrome and provide an answer.

Recognition came, but not for some thirty years. In 1990, virologists studying the samples of kidney, bone marrow, and spleen tissue embedded in parafin identified the ill-fated sailor as the world's first known AIDS patient. There must have been other cases at that time because the native term for a debilitating wasting disease—slim disease—first came into use in Africa during the early 1960s. Sooner or later, the mass production of jet engines and the globalization of mankind were bound to scatter the virus out of Africa. Almost overnight, airplanes had supplanted mosquitoes and tse tse flies as the world's most efficient vectors of death, though few seemed to take notice, even as it was happening before their eyes.

The first North American case on record, a boy of fifteen, died in Chicago in 1969. As with the British sailor, doctors, who were mystified by the shutdown of his immune system, stored some of his ravaged tissues for future study. We know now that the boy's body was riddled with the human immunodeficiency virus, and we know also that the boy, like the British sailor, could not have spontaneously generated the virus all by himself. There must have been scattered cases of AIDS around the county by 1969, and we suspect that its rapid spread about ten years later was made possible by a further mutation of HIV that made it easier to catch.

Gaetan Dugas, a twenty-eight-year-old Canadian airline steward, was apparently among the first to contract the mutant strain and might have been one of its primary disseminators. Medical historians would eventually come to call him "patient zero." During 1979 and 1980, before anyone knew that a human immunodeficiency virus existed, Dugas shuttled back and forth between New York and San Francisco, where he passed the silent death to five hundred male lovers. How many those five hundred passed it to is anybody's guess. If you were to use the standard network marketing strategy as an example, whereby each new distributor (theoretically) builds a business by recruiting at least five new distributors, then you'd have at least 2,500 second-level AIDS distributors beneath Gaetan Dugas. Using the same formula, in the third level those 2,500 have gone on to produce 12,000 new distributors, and two levels farther down, the 12,000 have infected 375,000. It threatened to become a pattern of spread any Amway executive would readily have appreciated and envied. Deep in the African wilderness, nature had forged a multi-level marketing plan that could not possibly fail.

In November 1981, the first murmurs of a mysterious new disease reached the public through the pages of *Omni* magazine. The sickness had elements of science fiction: victims' immune systems were shutting off, paving the way for superinfection; people were dying from obscure cancers and bacterial intrusions that few doctors had ever seen before; several men withered into human skeletons, while some unseen predator devoured their brains. By that time, at least one victim had passed the disease to a heroin user, and once the virus struck the intravenous drug-using community, it spread through it with all the rapidity of flu. Many supported their drug habits by prostitution, and as Manhattan's Jacob Javits Convention Center went up frame by frame and years behind schedule, business could not have been better. Volvos and Pontiacs, limos and buses gathered at night. Their occupants got more than sex in the shadows of the unfinished center.

Norris M. was one such occupant. By the spring of 1982, his semen was crawling with death. In May, he infected his wife, two high-priced "escorts" in Atlantic City, his best friend's wife, his worst enemy's daughter, and the "EXTRAORDINARY blonde" whose personal ad he'd answered ("truly beautiful with brains, twenty-three, seeking a very good-looking successful man who's ready for the real thing"). In July, the blonde broke off with him, explaining that she'd just accepted a job offer in London. Her loss troubled Norris barely more than his slight cold, which seemed intent on lingering forever. Everything was looking up. His company was sending him south to oversee new branches in Tahiti and New Zealand, where AIDS was destined to manifest as a heterosexual disease. In September, he flew to the South Pacific, spreading the sickness that some New York physicians had come to call—jokingly, but not so jokingly—Captain Trips.

As with the proliferation of nuclear weapons, everything about the spread of AIDS has been predictable—absolutely predictable. The rate at which the number of victims would double was obvious from the start. Even a child, multiplying pennies by powers of two every few months, could see immediately that starting with only a handful, he'd have millions by the time he grew up; yet in 1987, more than six years into the disaster, leaders in Washington admitted that they were still coming to terms with the "giggle factor" associated with a sexually transmitted disease. Meanwhile, the number of victims continued to double, and these were only the leading edge of an avalanche. For every person dying of the disease, at least forty more had been infected and were infectious, and most of them didn't know it because they did not show any symptoms as yet.

The AIDS virus moves through our civilization much like the approach of a freight train. At first, it appears only as a dark shape on the horizon, and if you happen to be walking on the tracks, this is the time to step out of the way. If you wait too long, by the time the danger is obvious and you can clearly distinguish features, it may be too late to move.

Unfortunately, the virus got a head start, primarily because the person or persons who first contracted it in the United States happened to be a homosexual man or men, and few people were concerned about an epidemic that, in its birth stages at least, seemed to strike only this population. Indeed, there were some even in positions of political authority who expressed a sneaky admiration for what the AIDS epidemic was doing to drug users and minority populations, until they began to realize that in the long term, AIDS is for everybody.

Like most disasters, the epidemic brought out both the worst and the best in humanity: quack profiteers; community leaders who burned the homes of hemophiliac, AIDS antibody-positive children; the hundreds more who, with no apparent leadership abilities, came seemingly out of nowhere and organized to help in any way possible, seeking nothing in return.

Nineteen eighty-seven came and went, and the freight train came even nearer. In Manhattan, virtually an entire floor of Bellevue Hospital filled with victims—drawing nurses, the backbone of the hospital—away from pediatrics and other centers. But there were no new nurses to replace them. Many health-care workers were leaving the profession. At the same time, the numbers of nursing students registering at Hunter College in New York City had fallen off dramatically. Few people had a desire to enter a field where the probability of coming into direct contact with infected blood seemed so high. The low pay simply was not worth the risk. A genuine shortage of health-care professionals was developing at precisely the moment they were most needed. The "AIDS epidemic," as it was now being called, had risen to the status of a lead story on nightly newscasts and became a regular feature in major newspapers.

Amid reports that AIDS appeared to have an early impact on the central nervous system, frequently manifested as dementia, U.S. Navy Surgeon General J.A. Zimble recommended reassigning flight crew personnel who tested positive for the virus. Commercial airlines noted that it violated constitutional rights to require testing of pilots for the virus, and did not comment on the possibility of an AIDS-demented crew winging out of Kennedy Airport in a 747 and taking aim at the World Trade Center. Army officials denied that there was any chance of AIDS-infected personnel launching a nuclear missile toward Russia.

In 1987, even physicians could be overheard from time to time voicing the opinion that AIDS was God's vengeance against whores, junkies, and homosexuals. (They forgot, apparently, that lesbians too were homosexuals and that so far, at least, a lesbian was the safest thing to be.) The victims were villains because they were ill; ill because they were villains. And so, 1987 became the year that $47 million allocated for the testing of new AIDS drugs remained unspent, while the freight train loomed larger and nearer, larger and nearer. Somewhere between 1 and 2 percent of the American population was infected. The virus was spreading most rapidly through a new community: the heterosexual, non–drug using community. And there was increasing evidence that most of the 1 to 2 percent infected would die of the disease. It was impossible to say how many they would infect before they became ill and learned they were carriers of death. Dr. Mathilde Krim, co-chair of the American Foundation for AIDS Research, lamented, "There were many people who knew exactly what was happening, what would happen and has happened, but no one of importance would listen. They still won't listen. This is an epidemic that could have been contained. We definitely could have contained it."

By January 1, 1988, there were severe AIDS outbreaks in San Francisco, Los Angeles, and the New York tri-state area. It had popped up in every major European city, and there were cases in Mexico, Argentina, Australia, New Zealand, Figi, Tahiti, the Philippines, Japan, and China, where it was claimed that the epidemic could not spread as widely as it had in America because there were no homosexuals in China. In the Soviet Union, the public was told that AIDS was an experiment in disease warfare that had gotten out of control in America. In parts of Central Africa, 15 percent of the population was dying, and nations were learning that you didn't have to lose too many sanitation workers or computer operators or telephone linemen before civilization began to crash. By the time 50 percent of a population had died, it was predicted whole countries would simply go silent, vanish from the air waves as if they no longer existed. Three months earlier, the American press had observed that the Africans must be very desperate to be testing vaccines on healthy people at such an early stage. Now that similar experiments were under way in America, the press forgot this observation, or chose to ignore it.

A new year had begun.

★   ★   ★

Early in 1988, a new AIDS variant known as human immunodeficiency virus 2 (HIV-2) turned up in Newark, New Jersey. The new strain had emerged without any warning or explanation, displaying for researchers its distinct and unfamiliar genes. Tracking backward from New Jersey to the coastal forests of West Africa, the virus was found in native populations, and an almost identical cousin to HIV-2—SIV-2—was identified in the blood of sooty mangabeys, local monkeys that were encroaching on farmlands from which they were often harvested as household pets and food.

It was embarrassing when you came right down to it. In New York, the AIDS virus was becoming a leading killer of women in the child-bearing age bracket. According to the latest projections in America alone, by 1990, AIDS would be killing twice as many as the Vietnam War had taken. Virtually every family would know a member or an acquaintance who had died or was dying of AIDS. But the thing that was bringing such calamity into the world arose from nothing so dramatic as a war, noble or wrong. It was too belittling, and almost laughable: *just monkey viruses in humans*. There was no dignity in it.

HIV-2 had become widespread in West Africa and was apparently new only to the west Atlantic. The "new" virus was considerably less lethal than its cousin, but given the fact that HIV-1 seemed to kill almost everyone it infected, that was not saying much. Its arrival in Newark pointed to an obvious complication: standard American blood tests were designed to detect only the older AIDS virus (HIV-1).

The only good news heard that year was that both families of the virus were still transmissible, in almost all cases, only through very intimate contact. The feared CAIDS strain—casually acquired immune deficiency syndrome—had not yet evolved. There was also hope in the fact that the rate at which Americans were falling ill had decreased by about half (the number of new cases was doubling approximately every eighteen to twenty months), apparently reflecting fear of AIDS and resultant changes of habits since 1984, with a corresponding decrease in the rate of infection. But there was no telling what might eventually evolve from the world's most rapidly mutating strand of nucleic acid now that it had broken out of obscurity and isolation to infect a reservoir of millions—each churning out potential new strains.

Nineteen hundred and eight-eight had opened with an aura of fear, and as the year drew on, a whiplash effect began to take hold. People tired of hearing about the epidemic. AIDS no longer sold newspapers or books, and when its victims were featured as subjects on popular talk shows, ratings actually went down. Then the self-proclaimed "experts" came forth, telling people what they wanted to hear—claiming in magazines and on news programs that the disease could not be transmitted heterosexually (this despite widely available documentation that in Africa AIDS was striking men and women equally). Some even pointed to the declining rate of spread in America as an indication that the epidemic was over, that the public had been misled by headline-grabbing alarmists.

The nay-sayers told us more than they knew. They told us more than all of the scientists and health-care workers on the front lines knew. And yet, they spoke as if from highest authority. A chilling murmur began to run through the buses and subway cars of Manhattan: "Have you heard? It's safe to have sex again."

And the train hurtled nearer . . . nearer . . . ever nearer. . . . You could actually watch the deadly complacency settling in. At the beginning of 1988, the personal ads section—singles seeking other singles—had plummeted from three full pages to less than a half page in one major New York newspaper. By the year's end, the personal section was up to a full page. By 1991, it had swollen to nearly three pages again. We suspect the resurgence of the singles pages (and singles bars) can be viewed as a gauge for a generalized return to old habits once the epidemic had become "old news" and once the new wave of "experts" had told America there was nothing for non–drug using heterosexuals to fear. If our suspicions are correct, we should soon see an upturn in the number of infected, non–drug using heterosexuals showing symptoms of AIDS. The three- to eight-year incubation periods will begin running out as this edition goes to press. Should the number of new cases begin doubling every twelve months instead of the 1988 low of eighteen to twenty months, it is our opinion that some of the know-it-alls who should have known better are no less deserving of indictment for murder than one who shouts "Fire!" in a crowded theater.*

Already there are hints that AIDS is spreading rapidly into high
school and college populations (including one particularly tragic
case in which an entire high school sports team, sharing steroids via
needles, contracted the virus). According to the CDC, as of 1991,
2.5 million American teens were acquiring sexually transmitted
diseases every year—a new all-time high, and at the worst possible
time. Fear of AIDS, however distressing, is probably healthy for us.
We should hold to our avoidance of the acts that increase our

---

*Sure enough, as 1991 figures became available, a disquieting picture began to
take shape at the World Health Organization in Geneva. As the year opened, more
than 16,000 women were diagnosed with AIDS in America, accounting for 11
percent of all (reported) U.S. cases. In 1991, 85 percent of women with AIDS
were between the ages of 15 and 44. "In 1982, AIDS wasn't even on the chart,"
said James Curran, director of Atlanta's Centers for Disease Control (CDC) AIDS
program. "In 1987, it was the eighth leading cause of death among women aged
15–44." This for a disease that just five years earlier affected only a couple of
hundred gay men. In early 1991, it became the fifth leading cause of death among
U.S. women of child-bearing age—preceded by cancer (number one), accidental
death, heart disease, and suicide, which was number four. But it is important to
note that the statistics may be somewhat blurred here by the high suicide rate
among AIDS patients. Most alarmingly, AIDS in women increased 29 percent
from 1990–91, compared to an 18 percent rise among men. One World Health
Organization report attributes the dramatic increase in the incidence of AIDS
among women from 1990 to 1991 to a widespread belief, or myth, that the disease
cannot be contracted from heterosexual contact. When State University of New
York AIDS specialist, Jack Dehovitz, began organizing a 1991 study of women
who had no history of intravenous drug use, or other high-risk behaviors, he was
shocked to discover that 3.5 percent of this "low risk" group (although still
asymptomatic) was already infected with the HIV virus—which is perhaps an
ominous indicator of the present U.S. infection rate. In Africa, meanwhile, 75
million are believed to be infected, and for unknown reasons the virus, having
only recently made itself apparent in Asia, appears to be spreading up to 100 times
faster than it has through Africa and America.

"Asia is the sleeping giant of a worldwide AIDS epidemic," says physician-
congressman/AIDS Task Force co-chairman Jim McDermott. "Infection rates are
soaring so fast that data that is more than four months old is useless. It's absolutely
stunning, awesome. And it's a heterosexual epidemic. What I'm trying to do . . . is
raise people's focus, make them pay attention to the fact that this is a global epidemic,
that it should influence our foreign policy, and that all the ingredients are here, in the
United States, for a similar heterosexual epidemic. I call it the Second Wave, and I'm
sure that it's coming both in Asia and the United States."

probability of contracting it. The days of freewheeling casual sex, of frequently changing partners and worrying only about unintentional pregnancy, have been over since about 1981. A new sexual revolution is upon us, one in which commitment is the name of the game; for these days, when two people make love for the first time, one can never be 100 percent certain that the other is not an unknowing, still healthy-appearing carrier. Sex in the latter part of the twentieth century truly does amount to a lifetime commitment—for better or for worse, in sickness and in health. . . .

Even though the virus has been isolated and we can now study it, AIDS always seems to be two steps ahead of science. It is far more mutable—astonishingly so—than, say, EBV. Until recently, the flu virus—which emerges every year with a new strain, as the Hong Kong, the Russian, or the new American one—was thought to be the most rapidly mutating chain of nucleic acids in existence. That title is now held by the AIDS virus, which mutates at least five to a hundred times faster than flu, and possibly as much as a thousand times faster; and even its mutation rate may be subject to mutation. No one is certain how long the virus can survive outside the human body because this feature, too, is changing. Some strains apparently die in seconds, others in minutes, or hours, or days. So far, the only constant is that the virus continues to thwart the efforts of scientists and immune defenses by shifting.

On the average, every AIDS victim seems to give rise to four new strains between the time of infection and death. We know of a patient at Bellevue Hospital who was in a coma and was expected to die at any hour. Suddenly his B cells, shifting from one combination of virus-caging proteins to another, hit upon the right one and started pumping out useful antibodies. He emerged from his coma, regained his appetite, and began manufacturing a new supply of T cells (the primary target of AIDS infection). He put on some weight and eventually walked home, leaving doctors and nurses puzzled about what appeared to be a spontaneous remission from AIDS. Within months, the virus shifted, and he was back in the hospital again. Actually, it had probably shifted even before he got better. Initially, the new variant must have existed in small num-

bers, alongside masses of the old strain—which was being deci-
mated by a flood of virus-destroying antibodies. After passing
through this natural selection filter, suddenly the new strain had a
whole new crop of T cells to attack. And so the new strain,
immune to the patient's newfound immunity, began to multiply
even as he recovered from the previous assault. The immune system simply cannot keep up with a constantly shifting virus.

Four new strains from each infected person, and a reservoir of
tens of millions. In a few years, there will be hundreds of millions
of mutations, and there is no telling how many of them will be
ready to kill in new ways. Our worst nightmare is the—one in a
billion?—chance that one future strain will spread more easily,
through saliva and mucus, just like EBV: 97 percent communicability but with 97 percent excess mortality. Not an entirely unlikely
scenario, given that natural selection, in the short run, will favor the
mutant that spreads most rapidly.

AIDS is the grand master of deep viral infections. Before AIDS,
that title was probably held by EBV. Since approximately 97 percent of the population over age thirty has EBV in its system, victims
of AIDS have a very high incidence of secondary EBV activity. The
two viruses have essentially become partners in crime. The Epstein-
Barr virus wears down the B cells, the antibody factories. In the
presence of HHV-6, the B-cell collapse is further accelerated. The
AIDS virus demolishes the T cells—not just any T cells, but the
generals themselves, the T-4 cells, or helper T lymphocytes.

The chief difference between AIDS and other deep viral infections is that EBV and its occasional partners in crime tend to act
slowly, over the course of decades and appear to do only so much
damage. AIDS acts quickly and doesn't know when to stop. Mortality approaches 100 percent. The virus flunks as a parasite.

Structurally, under an electron microscope, the AIDS virus looks
much like EBV. But it is far, far stranger. It is a retrovirus.* EBV,
like almost every other organism on the planet, carries its genetic

*AIDS and EBV are two of the three most fascinating viral diseases. The third,
known as the laughing sickness, occurs in New Guinea. Like AIDS, it is a
retrovirus and is contracted only through intimate contact—in this case, eating
raw human brains. Its victims literally laugh themselves to death.

code in DNA. The AIDS retrovirus has no DNA. In its core it carries a bundle of RNA—which is normally a mere product of DNA. It does not command anything; thus the AIDS virus, equipped only with RNA, should not be able to pirate cells and throw whole bodies into disorder. But it does. It injects its RNA into the heart of a T cell along with a strange enzyme called reverse transcriptase. What happens next is a miracle of viral evolution. The reverse transcriptase soaks up passing nucleotides (the building blocks of DNA, which can be found floating freely within the cell). If you picture DNA as the die that stamps out a coin (in this case, a coin that makes protein), and RNA as the coin, then the reverse transcriptase is actively packing metal against the face of the coin to make a die from which new coins can be struck. A major metabolic step has somehow evolved in reverse order. The RNA becomes the template, from which a mirror image is cast in DNA.

The virus, in essence, is creating the code of life, and it is an irony of nature that it spreads death through the very process by which life is conceived. The new DNA becomes part of the host cell, and countless RNA copies emerge, wrapping themselves in protein, streaming out into the blood and able to be transmitted to the yet unborn.

There are hints that most mutations occur during the course of infection, when the organism is multiplying most rapidly, meaning that a person infected with AIDS ends up with his own personal strain of the virus. The new strain may consist of only one individual and perhaps a few replicas out of perhaps millions of the virus antigens in the bloodstream. If a surge of antibodies wipes out the millions, the newer, more resistant strain(s) will repopulate the blood. And the virus may change again.

Because of the rapidity of change, a vaccine to stimulate a universally protective antibody response is going to be extremely difficult, if not impossible, to invent. A further consequence of the mutation rate is that those people who reexpose themselves to the virus, time and time again will actually end up with multiple, parallel infections of various strains, and will be capable of passing on all of them through a single sexual encounter or a single sharing of the needle.

The AIDS virus itself does not produce particularly striking symptoms. Early signs resemble a dozen other diseases (particularly CFS).* They include a low-grade fever, generalized lymph node swelling, weight loss, fatigue, loss of appetite, and a low white blood cell count. The opportunistic infections that follow can be spectacular, however. As the immune system loses hold, even organisms that do not normally invade human cells begin to do so, initiating new diseases. AIDS-related pneumonia, for example, is instigated by a usually benign protozoan, *Pneumocystis carinii*. We know of a man who fell prey to a protozoan that caused the entire brain to swell, until it crushed itself against the inside of his skull. Another lost his sight when amoebae began eating away the corneas of his eyes.

There is a curious synergistic collusion between AIDS and EBV. Burkitt's lymphoma is rampant among AIDS patients, along with an aggressive cancer called Kaposi's sarcoma, which may not be a sarcoma at all. Under a microscope, a Kaposi lesion looks more like a benign proliferation of skin cells than a vicious cancer. When Kaposi's sarcoma invades the lungs, it settles in the bronchi, not in the lung tissue itself. It neither looks nor acts like a cancer. It more closely resembles (and is in fact identical to) the aberrant cells seen during an attack of infectious mononucleosis.†

AIDS is now a medical threat to all humanity, so it is fruitless to fix blame on those who suffered first from the disease. Our energy, time, and resources should be focused instead on helping those who have it today, and on trying to prevent its further spread and differentiation.

As with EBV, it's difficult to see the beast. We can best follow

---

*The earliest signs, often felt within days of infection, resemble an ordinary case of flu. Initially, the virus very quickly populates the blood, and is almost just as quickly beaten back by the immune system (curiously, a person may actually test antibody negative during this period). A long remission follows, usually lasting several years. How the immune system brings about the initial overthrow, and why immune defenses eventually erode and fail, are targets for further study.

†Jesse Stoff comments: I have an AIDS patient with Kaposi's sarcoma who has been stable and going to work for the seven-and-a-half years that I have been treating him. For people with AIDS, the appearance of Kaposi's sarcoma is not a reason for giving up, as it may represent only an exaggerated response to yet another viral assault (Epstein-Barr).

its footprints. The presence of the virus in the blood is revealed by the presence of antibodies against it, not by the virus itself. Much like the diagnosis of chronic fatigue syndrome, a whole constellation of signs and symptoms must be looked at in order to arrive at a diagnosis.

As with EBV, HHV-6, or CMV, high antibody titers against AIDS usually mean that the antibodies are ineffective in completely stopping the virus. In the case of AIDS, a sort of Mexican standoff can persist for several months or years. Repeated exposure to the virus (especially to a new strain) or to anything that can suppress T-cell function (which marijuana is now known to do) will greatly accelerate the progression of AIDS. Since the latest evidence suggests that almost everyone infected will at some point develop AIDS, there is no carrier state. As reverse transcription, leading to transcription, leading to more reverse transcriptions unfolds, white blood cells are killed and a leukopenia (an easily seen decline of T-cell populations) may develop, which is a sign that the storm is about to break. The immune system tries to shift into maximum overdrive. Lymph nodes bloat, trying to shore up weakening defenses. As the damage increases, opportunistic infections appear—and it is these, not the AIDS virus itself, that often bring about the final downfall.

Although at this writing there is no cure, no drug which will kill the virus, there is much that can be done to improve the quality and even the quantity of life. The anti-CFS strategies described in this book usually decrease the activity of the AIDS virus in the blood considerably, and appear to temporarily arrest progress.

There are three levels of AIDS treatment.

The first, and "easiest," is the treatment of opportunistic infections. The use of antifungal and antiparasite agents can be life saving—until the next challenge.

The second level of treatment involves the use of antiviral drugs like AZT. Azidothymidine (AZT) was originally developed as an addition to the anticancer arsenal, but turned out not to be particularly effective for this purpose. It works against AIDS by blocking the reverse transcriptase enzyme, thus slowing the virus down.* Unfortunately, it also slows down the patient's bone marrow production of blood cells. Anemia and further loss of some white blood cells is a common side effect of AZT. As a means of preventing much of the bone marrow suppression, dietary supplements of crude liver extract, taken either as desiccated tablets (1,000 mg three times per day) or better yet by injection (Kutapressin, three times per week), and vitamin B complex ("50 mg" three times per day orally) have proved to be quite helpful.

The third level of treatment involves strengthening the body's defenses, preferably at a very early stage, when infection is first detected and before illness results. In addition to *Echinacea* and other immune system supports (including the best possible dietary and sleeping habits), there is AL-721, developed by an Israeli research team. AL-721 is a special lipid combination (lipids are greasy, water-insoluble organic compounds that, along with proteins and carbohydrates, constitute the chief structural components of living cells). It is built from phosphatidylcholine, phosphatidylethanolamine, and neutral lipids. The ratio of these "active" and neutral lipids is 7:2:1 (Active Lipids 7:2:1 = AL-721).

In the laboratory, AL-721 seems to decrease the concentration of cholesterol in the cell membrane, making it harder for lipid-coated viruses (including the AIDS virus, EBV, and other herpes viruses, such as CMV and hepatitis B) to attach themselves to receptor sites on the membrane. Unless the virus can firmly anchor itself, it cannot inject its genes inside and take command.

AL-721 truly does help, and without side effects. And you can make a version of it in your own kitchen that is far cheaper than the imported pharmaceutical preparation and apparently about as effective. To begin, purchase a bottle of PC-55, manufactured by Twin Labs, Inc., Ronkonkoma, NY 11779 (phone: 516/467-3140). Using an electric mixer, blend 5 tablespoons of PC-55 with 12 tablespoons of water in a mixing bowl until smooth. Add 6⅓ tablespoons of butter that has been previously measured out and

---

*After an initial defeat, the virus is now known to shift rapidly to the production of AZT resistant strains, in as few as nine months. Many people now being exposed to the AIDS virus for the first time are receiving the AZT resistant strains.

gently melted (don't burn it!). Continue mixing for about four minutes, until it has an even color and consistency. Divide this mixture into ten even doses. An ice cube tray is a convenient storage device. Store the AL-721 in the freezer, as it spoils rapidly at room temperature.

Prior to use, remove a cube or dose from the freezer and let it sit in the refrigerator for an hour or two. The home brew is best eaten by mixing it in vegetable juice and having it (and nothing else) for breakfast, and again by itself at dinnertime (if lunch is your big meal of the day). After four to six weeks, decrease the dose to once per day. Some people have reported diarrhea, which seems to cease if brown rice is added to the diet.

A natural medicine from Weleda that also provides help without toxic effects is Viscum P 3%. Apply seven drops orally, three times per day, following the therapeutic suggestions for EBV remedies described in chapter 7.

Jesse Stoff comments: I have patients who started off, when they met me, with full-blown AIDS. With these suggestions, most have exhibited improved T-cell ratios and total white blood cell counts. Most of them are stable, holding their own, and leading relatively normal lives. Some people ask what good is there in helping AIDS victims to live longer if there is no cure. While it is true that there is no cure at present, the quality of life can be improved, and perhaps the quantity too can be extended a few years longer—just far enough into a future that might hold a cure or, in the very least, more effective treatments. There is always hope. Anything is possible.

OTHER PARTNERS IN CRIME

The emergence of the human immunodeficiency viruses, human herpes virus 6, and other threatening organisms during the 1980s has heightened concern among virologists and evolutionary biologists about civilization's growing vulnerability to pathogens that have existed undetected, isolated, and relatively harmless in remote animal populations. Given an opportunity to infect previously unexposed human beings, the two HIV strains took it. Had man not bothered the simians, the chances are that immunodeficiency viruses would never have bothered man.

The simian immunodeficiency viruses were there all along. Human agricultural practices, travel, and other behaviors provided opportunities for mutation and spread; and the continued spread of emerging viruses is almost impossible to halt. By comparison, one can stop the spread of malaria-carrying mosquitoes by bug-bombing the wetlands and, as in Singapore, passing laws requiring stiff fines for anyone who leaves empty soda cans or other potential mosquito-breeding grounds on his property. Human sexual behavior is much more difficult to control.

"Some people think I am being hysterical," says Joshua Lederberg, who holds a Nobel Prize in medicine and physiology. "But there are catastrophes ahead. We live in evolutionary competition with microbes, bacteria, and viruses. There is no guarantee that we will be the survivors."

Yale University biologist Lynn Margulis, who views living cells as collections of mitochondria, flagella, and other once free-living organisms whose ancestors colonized each other, and seen in the hind guts of termites and the lining of the human throat symbiotic linkages between individual cells, has proposed that humans, termites, and trees are part of a still larger organization. Margulis is one of the framers of the Gaia hypothesis, in which the earth itself is viewed as a living organism built from the interactions of whole ecologies.

Seen in this light, the history of life upon this planet becomes a progression toward chaos with feedback, with the result that true chaos is never achieved. RPI physicist Ed Bishop has added a haunting and provocative question: "If the biosphere is viewed as a living, unified thing, could not the ever-expanding billions of us be the earth's equivalent of a viral bloom?" If we answer yes, then new diseases emerging from felled rainforests are simply the planet's immune response. Far from being a doting parent, Earth is putting out antibodies against an invading organism. Nature's immune system, as such, becomes a best defense against ozone depletion, runaway greenhouse effects, and descent into chaos.

If we are jolted by the arrival of AIDS, we should be equally alarmed that the conditions may be ripe for similar surprises. "I don't think it is going to be a unique event," says Lederberg. "There will be more surprises because our fertile imagination does not begin to match all the tricks that nature can play."

Perhaps the newest surprise is the arrival of human herpes virus 6 (HHV-6), first identified in the National Cancer Institute Laboratory of Robert Gallo (co-inventor of the HIV antibody test, now adapted to identifying CFS-related viruses). Like HIV, it first interferes with immune responses by attaching itself to a specific protein on the surfaces of white blood cells: the CD4 receptor protein. Unlike HIV, HHV6 does not go on to totally deplete the host's immune system. The origin of HHV-6 is, at this writing, also an unanswered question, though some human activity, some social or environmental change that yanked the virus out of an obscure animal population and began trafficking it through human bloodstreams, seems as good a guess as any. It begins to look as if there is far, far more out there than we know about.

HUMAN HERPES VIRUS 6 (HHV-6)

Formerly known as human B-lymphotrophic virus (HBLV), this member of the herpes clan has many characteristics of EBV and is, in fact, believed by some researchers to pave the way for runaway EBV infection. Others have speculated that it is an unusual "new" strain of the Epstein-Barr virus. First isolated in 1986 (from the blood of patients with adult B-cell leukemia), its origins and significance are not nearly as well understood as AIDS—which "new" though it is, is by comparison an older virus.

Like EBV, HHV-6 is apparently very easy to catch. Like EBV, it is, fortunately, relatively harmless. It differs from EBV in that, like the AIDS virus, it gets inside lymphocytes by attaching to the CD4 protein on the cell surface. Presently, up to 30 percent of the American adult population may be infected—seemingly, in most cases at least, without ill effects. HHV-6 is believed to be implicated (as indicated during rash outbreaks, by a four-fold increase in antibodies against the virus) in roseola, a now-common rash in infants.

Among the human herpes viruses, the ability to regulate CD4 belongs to HHV-6 alone. In the presence of HIV, which also attaches to the CD4 cell receptor—HHV-6 acts as an AIDS accelerant, throwing open new doors and expanding the range of HIV colonization. Why HIV, even when acting alone, is deadly while another CD4 virus is not remains one of nature's unsolved mysteries. There is an emerging picture, however, in which several viruses working together may promote the activity of both AIDS and CFS.

If AIDS is often a death sentence in which emerging technologies provide stays of execution and, assuming continued research, a possible pardon a year or three down the line, then CFS is by comparison a life sentence, in which parole has already become a very real possibility.

Though the cause of CFS is difficult to pinpoint and does, in fact, appear to vary from person to person, the basic result is a misfiring or stumbling of the immune system that allows foreign organisms already inhabiting the blood to run wild. Adding to the mystery, the nature of the misfiring often leads to a hyperactivity of the immune system, in which the production of antibodies and a specific clan of virus-fighting white blood cells (called the CD8 cytotic T cell) is stepped up. This is combined with declining numbers of another T-cell clan that normally reins back immune responses. Predictably, tossing away the reins further increases immune activity. Yet, evidently it is the quality of immune response and not the quantity that counts in our favor. One would ordinarily predict that increased activity translates to increased efficiency and produces a more virus-free system. We suggest that the real picture more closely resembles a factory with a reputation for producing quality products which, due to one financial pressure or another, tries to expand too quickly. Mismanaged and overworked, trying to do too many things at once, its employees end up getting very little done right. In the case of CFS (which some researchers are suggesting we rename chronic immune activation syndrome) after some initial disruption, the immune system has great difficulty returning to a calm, resting state; and in the throes of hyperactivity, one's own tissues may be targeted by immune cells, while many viruses are missed. For most but not all CFS patients, EBV is peculiarly active. With increasing frequency (now up to 25–30 percent of patients), HHV-6, another normally dormant virus (though suspected in some cases as a cause of the initial immune disruption), seems to be stirring to life. Cytomegalovirus is also rearing its head.

CYTOMEGALOVIRUS (CMV)

As a brother to EBV, cytomegalovirus usually presents itself in the same way. Diagnostically, specific antibody titers indicate its presence, and taking the titers at three-month intervals should be done to monitor progress against infection. Like EBV, CMV can cause a variety of neurological complications and has been implicated in some instances of learning disabilities. (Although not the cause, it can apparently amplify dyslexia.)

As for the rest of the herpes clan, they, like EBV and CMV, surround us. Ogden Nash once wrote, "God, in his wisdom, made the fly—and then forgot to tell us why." Herpes viruses don't seem to have any purpose on this Earth other than to remind us when we have put ourselves under too much stress.

HERPES ZOSTER (HHV-3)

Herpes zoster (varicella) produces the very contagious skin rash called chicken pox in children. The severity of the rash seems to correspond with the amount of stress the child is under at the time. Children who eat more real food (vegetables, grains, fruits, etc.), as opposed to a diet overly rich in candy, potato chips, and soft drinks, tend to have a lighter case of the rash. In its acute form, chicken pox can cause pneumonia, but this occurs more commonly in adults. After the pox have scabbed over and healed, the virus tends to migrate into the nerves, where it usually remains dormant for the rest of one's life, much as EBV can hibernate in B cells. In later life, a severe EBV bloom, emotional stress, chemotherapy, or other immune suppressants can cause the virus to reemerge as a painful attack of shingles.

The chicken pox virus has played quite a role in history. Old World peoples (Europeans, Asians, Africans) had adapted to the virus, and the virus to them, over many thousands of years. Polynesian and New World peoples had never been exposed to it. When it was introduced by European conquerors to Tahiti, Hawaii, and

North America, this seemingly harmless virus produced huge, painful sores all over the natives' bodies, often killing in days, and decimating more populations than did bullets and cannons.

HERPES SIMPLEX I (HSV-I)

Most people have their first bout of cold sores or fever blisters, caused by HSV-I, as young children. After the initial infection, the virus retreats into the facial nerves, reemerging as the typical blisters seen during times of stress and illness. HSV-I is considered relatively harmless, but can, in extreme cases, cause encephalitis (swelling of the brain). It can also cause damage to the cornea of the eye or to the nerves that surround it.

HERPES SIMPLEX II (HSV-II)

In the 1970s it became clear that a new breed of resistant venereal diseases had formed as a counterattack to the antibiotic revolution that at first had threatened to wipe them out. The antibiotics served as a natural selection filter, culling the most vulnerable strains and preserving the most resistant ones. One strain was known on college campuses as "super-syph" (it was actually gonorrhea, not syphilis, but super-syph sounded better than super-clap, hence the erroneous name). Not only was this bug resistant to penicillin, but it actually seemed to thrive on the stuff. This marked the beginning of the end for the sexual revolution. Super-syph sounded horrifying, but that was before we knew what else we were in for. A friend of ours, feeling a sting in his urine, once remarked that he hoped it was only ordinary syphilis or gonorrhea. Five years later, people could be heard saying, "Oh no! I hope it's only super-syph and not herpes." Super-syph was difficult to get rid of. Herpes was impossible. And then AIDS came along, and that *killed* you. There are more than a few who mourn for "the good old days" of herpes simplex II.

Herpes simplex II, like the other herpes-class viruses, is highly contagious and tends to recur during times of stress. It has been implicated as a promoter of cervical cancer, and an infant delivered through a vagina with active lesions may become infected, suffering blindness and brain damage as a result.

Diets high in the amino acid arginine tend to increase the frequency and severity of herpes simplex II attacks. Foods high in arginine include chocolate, peanuts and peanut butter, sugar (as it increases the need for the B vitamins), alcohol and coffee (as they deplete vitamin and mineral reserves), cashews, pecans, almonds, sesame seeds, and bleached white flour. Avoiding arginine, while adding 1,000 mg of lysine to the diet twice daily (along with the anti-EBV vitamins and remedies described elsewhere in this book) will, as a rule, cut the duration and severity of a herpes attack in half. Between attacks, decreasing the dosage of lysine (an amino acid) to 1,000 mg once per day will decrease the frequency and severity of the attacks. Preventing EBV blooms will also tend to lessen the activity of HSV-II. Of the two viruses, EBV is more easily knocked back into long-term (and possibly permanent) remission.

COXSACKIE VIRUS

The primary features of a Coxsackie bloom, commonly called myalgic encephalomyelitis (MEM), are fatigue, emotional lability, headache, muscle aches, and pains. (Sound familiar?) The first outbreak was described in 1934 in Los Angeles, where it appeared in the wake of a polio outbreak and was initially believed to be polio. It turned out to be a virus that now bears the name of a small upstate New York town, Coxsackie (no one really seems to know why). Along with Echo and polio virus, Coxsackie belongs to the family of *enteroviruses*. Though named for a New York town, most Coxsackie cases occur in the United Kingdom and Europe, where there is much interest in the syndrome. It is diagnosed in part by specific antibody titers. Since the virus causes abnormalities in muscle function, EMG (electromyograph—a test of the electromechanical energy of a muscle) testing is also a helpful diagnostic tool. Treatment is essentially the same as for CFS in which EBV, HHV-6, or CMV are active, with the addition of eight capsules of Efamol per day (four in the morning and four in the evening). A British double-blind study, in which neither the doctor nor the patient knew whether she was taking the therapeutic substance or a dummy placebo, revealed that 85 percent of ME patients improved on Efamol and only 18 percent improved on the placebo. Efamol is an essential fatty acid derived from the oil of the evening primrose flower, and one disorder common to ME patients involves metabolism of fatty acids. Unlike the herpes-class viruses, it can be completely kicked out of your system once your immune system counterattacks.

As research continues and we come to know more and more about the viruses already discovered, it is clear that CFS is a syndrome that can involve one or more viral diseases. Recently two more viruses have fallen under suspicion as causative agents, HHV-7 and the Spuma viruses. At this time there isn't very much known about them. We do know that HHV-7, like many other human herpes viruses, tends to attack the antibody producing B-cells. When reviewing the immunological function tests of people suffering from CFS we most commonly see dysfunction of the B-cells. However, in some patients there are unexplained abnormalities of the T-cells. Recently, researchers have taken a more in-depth look at some of the retroviruses, specifically the subfamily of Spuma viruses which are also known as foamy viruses because of the many vacuoles they induce in the cells that they infect. As the results of the research unfolds, the roles that these viruses play in the genesis of the chronic fatigue syndrome will become clearer. Stay tuned and look for the next edition of our book for further information.

HUMAN T LYMPHOTROPHIC VIRUSES (HTLV)

One of our newest insights into how the immune system fights cancer, and how certain viruses may actually cause cancer, comes from transplant research. A patient receiving a new kidney is always in danger of his own immune system attacking the foreign organ, a syndrome known as rejection. It is essentially an autoimmune response, much like the disordered hyperimmunity that produces the lesions in the nerve sheaths of a multiple sclerosis patient, or in the soft, connective tissue of an ankylosing sponylitis patient, or the pancreas of a young diabetic. In an attempt to prevent the rejection of transplanted organs, patients are usually given drugs that suppress the immune system. Doctors have learned two things from immunosuppressive drug therapy. First, such patients, not uncommonly, develop cancer while under treatment. Secondly, if the drugs are withdrawn and the immune system is allowed to recharge, the tumors often vanish.*

When connected, these two things point to a third thing no one knew before: the healthy immune system can destroy early tumors all by itself, and is probably doing so all the time. Keeping this lesson in mind, consider the activities of viruses—HHV-6, Coxsackie, HIV, and the herpes clan—that settle in our centers of immunity. One relative newcomer, the human T-lymphotrophic virus, is particularly target-specific. Whenever it bumps up against a T cell, the HTLV activates and finds a way in.

HTLV-1 is a rapidly emerging, cancerous cousin to HIV. But before we proceed any further, there is a point that cannot be repeated too often: HTLV-1, which is becoming more and more common in the blood of CFS patients, DOES NOT CAUSE AIDS. Nor do HHV-6, Coxsackie virus, Epstein-Barr virus, or any member of the herpes clan. A person whose blood contains antibodies to any or all of the above viruses cannot possibly proceed from chronic fatigue syndrome to acquired immune deficiency syndrome. The latter is caused only by the human immunodeficiency virus (HIV).

Like HIV, HTLV-1 is a retrovirus, lacking DNA of its own and using reverse transcriptase to pirate the DNA of T-lymphocytes. It was first isolated and identified in the blood of two leukemia patients in 1978 by the National Cancer Institute's Robert Gallo. From his subsequent work with Japanese researchers, we now know that the virus is responsible for a curious leukemia cluster known for a hundred years or more on the two southern-most islands of Japan.

Tracking backward, epidemiologists found clusters of the virus in Africa—where perhaps it emerged through the same simian to human path of infection now believed to be the source of the AIDS

---

*While this may be good news in so far as a developing cancer is concerned, it is bad news for the transplanted organ. Medicine does not have a solution for the resulting dilemma. Transplant technology has not come so far as most people would like to believe. We don't have all the science.

epidemic. Other clusters of the virus have turned up in the Caribbean, Venezuela, Portugal, and on the north shore of New Guinea. Again, the picture of spread begins to resemble a cascade of consequences arising from man's disruption of pristine environments, with a few other shameful human behaviors added.

The footprints of HTLV-1 lead out of Africa during the early sixteenth century when Portuguese traders bridged Africa and Japan, bringing pet monkeys with them. During the next century, one thriving route of slave trade carried the virus from Africa to the Caribbean and South America. The Japanese invasion of New Guinea probably carried the infection from Kyushu or Shikoku during World War II. Clusters of HTLV-1 are now being identified among Japanese descendants living in Hawaii and Alaska, and it is only a matter of time before modern transport blankets the world with the "new" cancer trigger.

Already a cluster of the rare, HTLV-1–related leukemia has turned up in New York's Bedford-Stuyvesant neighborhood. Once the T-cell leukemia develops, it progresses with terrifying rapidity. Within months of the New York cluster's discovery, all but one of the 17 known patients had died. Fortunately, only a small percentage of those exposed to HTLV-1 are likely to develop leukemia.* As an analogy for how viral assaults generally work, when a polio virus struck an African village whose people had never been vaccinated, within a month all of its one thousand inhabitants had become infected. Of that one thousand, twenty became ill. Of that twenty, ten recovered almost fully within a few weeks, seven developed permanent paralysis, and three died. None of the seven permanently disabled villagers experienced the same degree of paralysis in the same muscles. We are not robots. We do not all respond in the same way.

In Japan one million are said to be infected with HTLV-1. Of that million, approximately ten thousand are expected to become ill. HTLV-1 is nowhere near as violent as the AIDS virus; and

*The virus is also associated with what appears to be a form of multiple sclerosis especially common in Japan. Keeping the links between the immune system and the nervous system in mind, it is interesting to note that here again a virus that attacks immune cells also impacts nerve cells.

fortunately, like the AIDS virus, it does not pass through sneezes and handshakes from person to person. Intimate contact, including needle-exchanging, is required. In America, it has begun to circulate through the intravenous drug-using community, threatening to expand from there in every direction, to become yet another major health problem. In New York, in 1988, 12 percent of the intravenous drug addicts tested were producing antibodies to HTLV-1, evidence that they had been exposed to the virus. If the history of AIDS is any indication, the leukemia virus has probably spread more widely by now.

Chronic fatigue syndrome has spread more widely still. In North America alone, the number of people with CFS exceeds by at least four million the number of AIDS patients (approximately 150,000 in early 1991, with nearly an equal number already having died from the acquired immune deficiency syndrome). CFS patients often complain of being overlooked by medical researchers, arguing that their plight has been eclipsed by the enormous publicity attending the simultaneous onslaught of AIDS. This claim does not arise without supportive data. In 1991, $2 billion* were allocated for AIDS research, while a $1 million allowance from the federal government went to investigate CFS, and only a few tens of thousands of dollars went to ankylosing spondylitis (AS). This should not become a cause for despair among people living with CFS or such autoimmune diseases as ankylosing spondylitis. Many of the remedies now appearing on the horizon owe much to technological advances created directly by the AIDS crisis. As a case in point, such multisyllable miracles as transgenic rats (for studies of AS, an apparent trigger mechanism for CFS in one Charles Pellegrino), and the antibody titer monitoring techniques that allow diagnosis of CFS and tracking of subsequent treatment responses, actually arose from AIDS research.

AIDS is such a difficult syndrome to control that it is forcing us to learn a great deal about the human immune system and how it works far, far earlier than we ever would have otherwise. Newer

---

*To give you an idea what $2 billion means, if that amount were invested in government treasury bonds, it would yield $1 million in interest (the entire 1991 annual budget for CFS research) every two days.

and more viable treatments for AS, CFS, cancer, and many of the genetic misprints that cause paralysis, blindness, or early death will probably develop decades ahead of schedule.

Some have argued that such lessons will ultimately be worth the price of admission. Though one of us actually lives with a genetically-induced autoimmune disease, both of us disagree with that argument. If there is any truly valuable lesson to be drawn at all from the outbreak and explosive multiplication of the AIDS and HTLV-1 viruses, it is precisely the lesson most likely to be ignored. By far the most shocking and important fact now known about the AIDS menace is that, like the vanishing ozone shield and global warming, it has been brought on by man himself.

EXCERPT FROM THE DIARIES OF CHARLES R. PELLEGRINO FEBRUARY 12, 1988
EPSTEIN-BARR VIRAL CAPSID ANTIGEN TITER 5

I remember a time about three years ago, when I found the Strategic Defense Initiative (more popularly known as SDI or "Star Wars") at least mildly seductive. These days I am pushing for the Space Cooperation Initiative (SCI), which is aimed at decreasing the international tensions that might otherwise lead to war. This approach was always within me, but I believe the illness brought it very much to the fore. My concern these days is more and more for a five-year-old girl living a hundred years from now. We cannot escape the fact that the world will still exist in 2088. Though we will probably not be here, the Earth shall endure, and it will be what we make of it. Will that five-year-old girl be able to hold a leaf in the palm of her hand? Will she look up into the sky and know that people have gone out amidst the stars, and that they went there in peace? Or will she be starving in a radioactive wilderness?

Now more than ever before, I want to contribute what little I can to make 2088 a better world for the yet unborn. I have time—time that was taken away from me and then given back. I hope I'll use it well.

One other thing: I find myself spending more time than I used to with my family and friends. I guess in the long run this means I'll write a few less books over the next four or five decades. But what the hell? The world can survive with a few less Charlie Pellegrino books.

EXCERPT FROM CHARLES R. PELLEGRINO'S ADDRESS TO THE AMERICAN ASSOCIATION FOR THE ADVANCEMENT OF SCIENCE, BOSTON
FEBRUARY 12, 1988

We have been talking today about large-scale cooperative ventures in space, including international manned Mars expeditions and a U.S.-Soviet lunar base. Senator Matsunaga suggests that nations can develop new relationships in space. By working together on long-range peaceful goals, we can expect feedback to Earth, an easing of the international tensions that force-feed such things as the arms race. We can make a safer and richer world for tomorrow's child.

I am often told that working in space with the Soviets is sheer fantasy. Perhaps it is, but I prefer working for the fantasy to accepting the reality. The reality is that it is easier and likelier that we will destroy each other, that it is a thousand times easier to fund a "Star Wars" program than it is to fund a joint Mars mission (even though the former will cost a thousand times more than the latter), and that the hardware for our mutual destruction is already in place. These facts alone should force us to consider—to at least consider—new ways of dealing with our adversaries.

President Reagan has said that the one thing that could truly unite the world would be an invasion from space; otherwise, space itself is probably too big for us. Perhaps he is right. But there is a big disease with a little name that is every bit as dramatic as an invasion from space.

I once saw a sign on the back of a flatbed truck carrying a hydrogen bomb. It read: DO NOT DROP. That's exactly what the AIDS virus is telling us today. If there is any glimmer of light in the plague, it is that we should see immediately that here is the end of nuclear war.

Without a cure or a viable treatment, AIDS can potentially kill 70 percent of the world's population by 2020. This is challenge enough for existing and foreseeable medical technology. A post-war setting would leave the world utterly defenseless against a pestilence whose destructive potential far exceeds that of nuclear winter, fallout, and famine, and would in fact be enhanced by plutonium-weakened immune systems.

Even if we could make the Soviet Union vanish tomorrow, without any reprisals, without a trace of fallout coming our way, we would be destroying much-needed medical expertise, and vice versa. From every indication, AIDS is going to be a difficult bug to crack. By the time we do crack it, if that is possible, the virus should have taught us, along the way, how to deal with cancer cells and other aberrant bits of nucleic acid, including those in charge of genetic disorders. What AIDS will teach us about our immune systems alone could conceivably lead to methods for slowing down the aging process.

Mars, AIDS, and nuclear war. Three irrelevant oddities. At first glance, one would seem to have no connection at all with the other two. But they *are* connected. Because of AIDS, we DO NOT DROP. Because of AIDS, we must learn to cooperate, whether we like it or not, so we'd better learn to like it.

Every disease has lessons to teach.

If we are truly wise and pay attention, then when the Soviet Union and the United States, working together with other nations, have defeated this thing for the good of all humankind, we will barely remember the international tensions that divide us today. The foundation will already be set for the ascent of a common humanity in the solar system and beyond.

The stars are waiting. And ready or not, here we come.

EXCERPT FROM A UPI DISPATCH
OCTOBER 20, 1988

The United States and the Soviet Union yesterday signed a five-year agreement providing for joint research programs to fight AIDS, drug abuse, alcoholism, and polio.★

Valentin Pokrovsky, president of the Soviet Academy of Medical Sciences, expressed hope that the ceremony would mark the "beginning of a wonderful long road which we will travel together."

★Of particular interest is the condition known as myalgic encephalomyelitis (the European name for CFS), which seems to one degree or another (in Europe at least) to involve the polio virus's cousin, Coxsackie B.

Excerpt from the Diaries of Charles R. Pellegrino April 10, 1991

As I write, black rain is falling across Iran and India—courtesy of Saddam Hussein and the first known use of ecologic warfare.* The fires burning in Kuwait are nudging an already alarming accumulation of greenhouse gases upward ever so slightly, creating a ripple in the biosphere that shall be felt globally and for decades to come.

The unexpected easing of cold war tensions and the collapse of the Berlin Wall at least give the appearance that the threat of global nuclear war is diminishing. Now, new challenges to civilization, if not to the genus homo itself, are shifting to their rightful place at center stage. The Earth might have gone a lot easier on us if we had shifted our priorities ten or even twenty years earlier. But we were occupied. Civilization had entered adolescence with rockets and plutonium fists. We did not immediately see in our newly acquired powers the responsibilities of adulthood. Now at last I think I can detect signs of a healthy maturity—and none too soon. During our protracted adolescence and its attendant distractions, ozone holes began opening over our heads (with fully 5 percent of our protection now disappearing each decade), the residues of carbon-burning permeated our air, our water, and our tissues, and strange new diseases began breaking out of the wilderness.

There have been suggestions that at least one cause of CFS arises from an emerging and previously obscure virus, perhaps even the unidentified agent suspected of causing a cluster of the illness in the wilderness of New Zealand's South Island.† A

---

*To be sure, there was America's use of poisonous herbicides to defoliate the forests of Vietnam, and before that, Genghis Khan's destruction of Mesopotamia's irrigation systems, and in 146 B.C., Rome's destruction of the Carthaginians' fields by spreading salt on them. Nevertheless, the Iraqi tactic stands as the first use of eco-warfare, for in this case, the consequences (deliberately so) reach far beyond the boundaries of conflict. Nothing in the history of war can even furnish criteria for comparison to the Kuwait fires.

†Jesse Stoff comments: The New Zealand cluster of CFS was first described by physician Peter Snow following an outbreak of what he dubbed the "Tapanui Flu" during the early 1980s. Though an underlying autoimmune condition seems to have predisposed Charlie Pellegrino to CFS, it would not surprise me to learn that a viral agent layered on top of it acted as a backup trigger mechanism. What

pattern of subsequent clusters, ranging from Lake Tahoe to an entire symphony orchestra and several schools scattered across the United States, does suggest a new viral trigger mixed in or layered on top of all other possible CFS stressors. In several instances, whole families have been affected, yet in many such cases a mother and a child may become ill while a husband does not. The lessons of an African polio outbreak should not be forgotten. We do not all respond at once to a given irritant, or in the same manner.

I have come to view chronic fatigue syndrome more and more as an ecologic disease—not merely in the sense that, like AIDS and HTLV-1–related leukemia, at least one form of the syndrome may arise from human disruption of the environment—but in the sense that each of our bodies is a microcosm of the Earth, a small planet in its own right. The cells and organ systems of a person whose immune defenses are distracted by too many stresses will succumb more readily to even a relatively benign viral intrusion; much as, on a planet whose ozone shield is being steadily eroded, crops will diminish while skin cancers and other complications proliferate, and in the end, civilization itself may succumb to some hitherto unanticipated and otherwise survivable catastrophe—perhaps nothing more dramatic than an economic instability.

As above, so within.

As we threaten to exceed the Earth's boundaries of regeneration, so too has a person with CFS often exceeded his boundaries of stress. If CFS can be viewed as a breakdown of a person's own ecology, then illness is a signal to take pause, remove as many insults to the system as possible, make life-long changes (even sacrifices) where necessary, and hopefully tilt the scales toward a true healing of body and mind.

---

intrigues me is the knowledge that Charlie was conducting fossil digs on New Zealand's South Island at the time of the outbreak, and was even acquainted with Dr. Snow (they share an interest in meteorites). There has been much speculation in recent years, based upon the pattern of CFS cluster events (including the 1984 Lake Tahoe event), that a new viral trigger might have been carried out of New Zealand by as few as three or four people (or even one person) about 1982. Charlie left New Zealand in 1982. Was he patient zero? We may never know, but considering how both disaster and odd coincidence have a way of following Charlie, such a thing would come to no one who knows him as a surprise.

13

DON'T BLOW IT!

May you live in interesting times.

—An ancient Chinese curse
that on first hearing sounds
like a blessing

Let your heart not sink!
Wailing saves no man from the pit!
Make Holiday.
Do not weary of it.
Lo, none is allowed to take his goods with him.

—An inscription in the tomb of
Pharoah Intef, approximately
2,000 b.c.

There's more to life than increasing its speed.

—Ghandi

June 18, 1991. . . . Epstein-Barr Viral Capsid Antigen Titer 640 . . . Sometimes it comes back. Sometimes we begin to lose perspective, and sometimes we begin to move again toward the edge of the pit. Perhaps a look into the abyss is needed now and again, a healthy reminder to keep life's priorities in their proper order.

By early Spring 1991, I was working on five books and eight design projects simultaneously, and fighting two major battles. I did not quite fall out of remission from CFS, but I was getting perilously close to it. Some of the positive habits I'd picked up in 1985 (including nutritional common sense, aimed at keeping the whole body in as fine a working order as possible), probably forestalled a return to my 1985 condition. But the adrenals were becoming overworked nevertheless. Jesse was watching and ready for the stumble, and when it came, he was surprised only that signs of fatigue did not show up six months earlier. We are on top of it, now. Nipping it in the bud, so to speak (even before the first full-spectrum blood test, I was back on Echinacea*). We both suspected, sometime during the winter of 1990–91, that very soon my body would be trying to tell me something. Anyone with just a chapter's worth of background in psychoneuroimmunology could have seen it coming—*

People come to me who are sick and tired of feeling sick and tired. They bring medical records already one or two inches thick; yet after all the data are in, the hardest part of the treatment can be getting the patient to accept the diagnosis! Accepting the diagnosis means taking responsibility for the part one must play in staging his or her own recovery. This goes far beyond eating more sensibly, avoiding alcohol, taking vitamins and/or herbal remedies, going to sleep when the body needs it. To begin with, we must consider how we respond to stress—

The stressors of 1990–91 were very unusual indeed—to the extent that when police surrounded a restaurant last April because I was (unknowingly) dining in the company of a mass murderer (who, incidentally, got away), I merely crossed the incident off as just another unusual occurrence during the course of a year so spectacularly and disastrously unusual that an uninteresting dinner would have, on account of its not being unusual, been unusual for that very reason. Aside from a continued and often disturbing tendency to suddenly change my plans and book passage off planes that crash, * I got stuck in the middle of what will probably go down as one of*

---

*When a friend became hesitant about getting onto an elevator with me, the scientist and science fiction writer Arthur C. Clarke eased her fears by pointing out that I'm the one you want to be sitting next to when the plane loses all power (I was on the Air New Zealand DC-10 that miraculously regained power not far from a very hard landing in the mid-Pacific), "and if ever Charlie decides to get off an airplane, by all means follow him!"

archaeology's most disgraceful episodes of funding pilferage, blackmail, territorial passions, and guerilla warfare while exploring lost cities of the Middle East. A result of all this was that my 1990 research expedition was delayed (meaning that I was not where I was supposed to be on August 2, 1990: at an excavation in Southern Iraq, near the Kuwait border). Then, just when I thought my days could not possibly get any more interesting, I met my "number-one fan."—

Once having encountered CFS, if you want to regain and maintain your health, then by far the most important component is to nurture and savor your returning energy and not to expend it on old routines, as for example on old ways of dealing with stress—

Some stressors you cannot escape. Have you read Stephen King's Misery, or seen the movie? I lived it, more or less. My "number-one fan" was in some ways not quite as bad as Annie Wilkes, but in other ways a little bit worse. I still have both feet, for example, but there is one nasty possibility King did not consider when he created Annie Wilkes: she would have been a lot scarier with a solid background in law. Did you know, for a start, that if a death threat is phrased in a certain way, it is not, by the letter of the law, a threat, and that if repeated over the phone at specific times it is not, by the letter of the law, even harassment? Have you any idea how easy it is for someone to dig up the arrest record of a man with a name similar to yours and send it to the place where you teach? Nevermind that the middle initial is wrong, or that the ex-con with a similar name mismatches your birthdate by fifteen years and your social security numbers aren't even close, it will cause you trouble every time. People tend not to look at the details. And even if you do get a chance to present your case, to make them take a closer look, you may find yourself being told, as I was, that "you must have done something wrong, to get someone mad enough to expend all this energy. And besides, this person could be trouble—bad publicity, even. Who needs trouble?"

At least Charlie, during the horrors of 1990–91, found some unique ways of removing from his life the two or three things that were stressing him most, though it was not quite what I had in mind when I spoke to him about stress reduction. Suffice to say that his stressors, though still physically unharmed and walking the earth, no longer have enough time on their hands to be bothering him,★ as indicated, I suspect, by the growing chain reaction of indictments, claims, counter claims, and downright disintegration within certain foreign ministries. Suffice to say that one should never threaten a man who designs antimatter propulsion systems before breakfast—

Oh, yes—I did survive some close calls this year. And how well did psychoneuroimmunology come into play? How did I respond to stress? Quite honestly, not as well as I could have, but not as badly as I might have before CFS nearly took me apart in 1985. The special appreciation I'd acquired for life itself was still within me, and to one degree or another it kept me going. I continued to live by a policy of planning for every worst case scenario, while hoping for but not expecting anything better. The pessimistic approach to crisis was probably a source of stress in its own right, but let me tell you something: bad things have a way of getting a lot worse before they get better, and if you are relying on a certain game plan, and the plan should fail, and you do not have another plan, that will become the biggest stress of all. Yes, indeedy. (Though, as Jesse will soon point out, you can overdo the game plan.)

One other thing: very early in the game, Gloria and I laid down rule number 1: no matter how stressful life becomes, DO NOT TAKE THE STRESSES OUT ON EACH OTHER. And, if rule number 1 ever broke down, then the next, 100 percent unbreakable and mutually agreed to rule came into play: we can shout at each other all we wish, but if ever the fighting

---

★Charlie is probably one of the world's most powerful information-gathering machines, and he runs with people who are, well . . . in the business of learning almost everything about almost anything. I'll never know for certain why his "number-one fan" decided to stop bothering him, allowing him to relax a little and avoid a return to full-blown CFS, but I suspect it has to do with something he once told me about information-gathering. When you are pursued relentlessly by a monster, you automatically know two things: (1) Monsters tend to do a lot of nasty things that they don't want their enemies knowing about, and (2) they make lots of enemies. Once you know everything there is to know about a monster, including (most importantly) who its enemies are, then you let its enemies know everything you know. "It's senseless to waste time, energy, and money taking the monsters to court," Charlie once said. "Even if you win, you usually lose." It's cold logic. It's Charlie. And if Charlie were not by nature as gentle as a puppy, he'd scare the living hell out of me.

escalates beyond that point, the person who first throws something or invades the other with even a light, dare-you-to-touch-me-back touch, is the one undeniably at fault.* We managed to get through the bad times without internal, family conflagrations. To recognize that a growing urge to snap at loved ones had less to do with anything anyone on the home front had done than with external stressors was, for me, a billboard-sized signpost. I think it also helps to bear in mind, when you're living in an emotional pressure cooker (and if you live long enough, sooner or later you're bound to live through exceedingly interesting times), one common result of someone's aggression against you is for you and yours to end up doing and saying terrible things to each other, and if the aggressor could, through some sort of magic, peek in on the havoc he was creating, it would make him as happy as a clam at high tide. Never, never give a dragon that sort of power over your life.

I can't say how much of that particular signpost came from cold logic and how much came from my previous experience of CFS, when I'd peered into that black nothingness of a future and come back from nothing with more than I'd ever had before. I did understand, however, in walking through a "mean, nasty, ugly, horrible damned year" (1990–91), that my friends and family were of highest value, and that even being able to sit on a beach and listen to the night surf was a special gift. So Gloria and I managed to enjoy walking together, or going to a movie, and there was love and laughter even in the midst of crisis. And there were jokes with Jesse, too. And sand castles.

But there were also plans and backup plans to be drawn, contingencies to be foreseen and prepared for. And there was no easy escape. And the mind was in turmoil, and the body recoiled with a turmoil of its own.

What you feel has much to do with what you perceive and how you understand your perceptions. It has relatively little to do with reality. Reality is nothing more than a stimulus source. Yet, for those who boldly go through their tunnel, through their "dark night of the soul," there is light on the other side. Charlie and I have seen dozens of people on their healing journeys change jobs, rebuild or terminate poor relationships, rearrange their priorities, and abandon old habits (which may include simply eating too many

---

*My wife and I never fight, of course. We just have . . . loud disagreements.

of the most stressful foods) that overtaxed the system and led to illness in the first place.

Excessive stress is like putting the welcome mat out for the first evil germ (be it EBV, CMV, or Coxsackie virus) that feels like setting up camp.*

For many, health is an uncharted territory with new challenges and new responsibilities. In the team effort of doctor and patient, part of taking responsibility for your half of the healing process is to become consciously aware that you have control over the choices you make—

By March 1991, the fatigue was threatening to come back, the anemia had returned. And ankylosing spondylitis (which had been creeping back into my neck since a 1987 car wreck) began a furious assault. More ominously, the first murmurs of an unusual immune response to EBV could be read in my blood. My old nemesis was waiting in the wings, if I continued to travel on the course I was beginning to set. No doubt about

---

*Any stressful situation will drain energy and resources normally used to maintain mental and physical health. While depression may figure prominently in such immune-busting behaviors as overeating, diminished attention to proper hygiene and exercise, or increased use of alcohol and other liver stressors, recent studies (re: reports by Kiecolt Glaser, Ohio State University; Karl Goodikin, University of Miami; Stephen Manuck, University of Pittsburgh) suggest that stress has a far more important impact on immune function than depression. This conclusion is derived largely form observations that depressed people, as compared to stressed people, are likely to retain more of their normal immune functions. "Among psychologically healthy individuals with a compromised immune system, such as those infected with HIV," psychiatrist Karl Goodikin told *Science News* (as reported by Bruce Bower, April 6, 1991, vol. 139), "social support combines with two other psychological factors—stressful events and the person's style of coping with stress—to influence immune function. . . . Data on stressful occurrences during the previous year such as moving or undergoing a divorce, usually come from a patient's self-reports. Coping style in response to stress generally breaks down into two categories: passive coping, marked by resignation; and active coping, involving some sort of coordinated response to a threat. In a pilot study of 11 . . . men infected with HIV but showing no AIDS symptoms . . . the men with active coping styles and low levels of life stress possessed the most helper T cells. Active copers with high stress and passive copers under minimal stress displayed slightly lower numbers of helper T cells. Passive copers under high stress had the fewest such cells."

it: I had overstressed myself. First there was the danger of adrenal exhaustion, with predictable feedback on the liver and thyroid, which in turn threatened to feed back to the rest of the immune system, until once again, the cycle would try to kick in: AS (ankylosing spondylitis) feeding CFS, feeding AS, and in turn creating additional stress, additional adrenal output. The snake reared up, ready to eat its tail.

Repeat this: you have control over the choices you make. Every time you do something, you are choosing not to do several other things. If you choose to do house or office work in the evenings, then you are choosing not to spend time with your family, or to rest, or go to sleep early. If you choose to work sixty hours per week, then you are choosing to continue stressing what must already be an overburdened system. Becoming aware of what you do and why you do it is not a matter of asking you to feel guilty—which would serve only to further exhaust you and your immune system, and inevitably impede healing. Like Dorothy in the Land of Oz, the ability to "go home" and be true to yourself is a strength you've always possessed. Learn (even, if you must, with the aid of visualization, meditation, and/or prayer) to tune into your body and its needs. Learn how you've been shooting yourself in the foot. Charlie often points out that it is not mistakes that prevent us from being happy, it is the frequency with which we repeat these same mistakes. It's easy to fall back again into old patterns, sometimes with the all too familiar refrain: "Why again?"

"So, here we go again," I said. Jesse told me I was dwelling too much on the dragons, making too many backup plans for backup plans, for backup plans. It was the same obsessive determination through which a twelve-year-old boy who couldn't read books ended up writing them. But this time the old habit, the old stubborn nature, was turning against itself. I was at a point of drawing backup plans for events of ever-diminishing probability, and if I continued on that path, it might not be long before I'd be including preparations for such contingencies as getting struck by a meteorite.

"Let it go," Jesse said. "You've got to find a relief valve for your anger and your pain." Plotting a branching pattern of alternate outcomes, and preparing multiple plans for each one, had, at the start, provided the necessary valve, a means of active coping, but I was clearly carrying it too

far, getting lost in a maze of my own creation. Jesse was right. I had to change course, had to find a more constructive outlet.

A part of me felt like running angrily at full speed and taking history's most daring flying leap—which is what I did, sort of. I started writing "Oh, Miranda!" about a man forced over the solar system's highest ledge—ten miles straight down at one-one-hundredth Earth's gravity. And for an encore I killed off everyone who was bothering me, and then some: over a two month period I wrote Flying to Valhalla, *and with George Zebrowski I began* The Killing Star. *Between both novels I've managed to blow up my editor, my publisher, every other American publisher, America, the earth and most of the solar system.* I'm feeling much better now . . .*

Each of our lives is a microscopic evolutionary journey, a process of gradual (and sometimes sudden) change of mind and body. Health throughout life should be a parallel process, moving somewhat like a set of railroad tracks. If changes of body and conscious-

---

*Anger is a normal emotion. It is how we choose to deal with it that can cause harm. Expressing it physically at the expense of another is wrong. So, too, is swallowing it and growing an ulcer. Writing it out (but never in a letter that you mail), drawing or painting, or even taking a long hike (assuming you are not dealing with a severe case of CFS) are far, far more constructive. For further examples and advice, if anger is one of the major stressors in your life, we recommend a booklet written by Abigail Van Buren (known to most Americans as "Dear Abby") with Judd Marmor (past president of the American Psychiatric Association): *The Anger in All of Us and How to Deal with It,* which can be obtained by sending a business-size, self-addressed envelope, plus check or money order for $3.95 (postage is included in the purchase price) to Anger Booklet, "Dear Abby," c/o Newsday, 235 Pinelawn Road, Melville, NY 11747-4250. And while we're on the subject of anger, sometimes you will find that even when someone attacks you viciously and for no apparent reason, the damage they do shifts your life in unexpected and even beneficial directions. There is a certain Greek archaeologist, for example, who is to me as Bellock was to the fictional Indiana Jones. In 1988, he disrupted my plans on the Nile, causing me to switch booking, at the last minute, off a ship that subsequently went down, drowning half its passengers. Two years later, in a particularly relentless attack, again resulting in a change of my plans, he diverted me from being directly in the path of Saddam Hussein's tanks; and on yet another occasion he was the cause of my getting off a passenger ship that collided with a freighter, again with loss of life. If the poor man ever *really* wanted to bring calamity into my life, all he ever had to do was sit back and watch.

ness keep pace with each other, we grow old graciously and with wisdom. However, there are many opportunities for high-stress habits and obsessions to creep in and derail the mind, and then the body. There are also opportunities for viral infections, genetic tendencies or chance exposure to toxins, which may derail first one's physical health, leading to mental stress, which can in turn lead to further derailment of physical health. Again, the snake bites its tail.

I've seen many, many CFS patients who, upon realizing that they cannot control their universe and its natural laws, let alone their own bodies, turn to obsessive-compulsive thinking and behaviors as a means of creating a façade of security. If you want to get well and maintain a permanent remission accept the real universe and be very careful if you should find yourself blowing your much-needed energy on ritualistic underwear folding, washing your hands sixteen times a day, vacuuming and dusting the house three times a day, or making backup plans for backup plans *ad infinitum*. What you can take control of and responsibility for are the choices you make. So make them consciously and sensibly. And if you need a relief valve, find a constructive one. If blowing up the earth in a novel is not your way of coping, keeping a journal will do just as well. It is an easy, straightforward way of releasing your inner thoughts and feelings (even if only to jot thoughts and explosive doodles on pieces of paper and throw most of them in the garbage afterward). Be spontaneous and honest with your writing and/or drawing (yes, drawing your feelings is a legitimate part of journaling). Your journal can help you to be your own therapist. Through increased perspective, the first foundation of hope can be laid. *Hope* is a belief in a positive outcome.

The next major and fundamental principle for sustained healing from CFS is the notion of priorities. I've asked many patients to make a list of their current life priorities. The results are often difficult to believe. The president of the United States should be so ambitious. Time and again I've seen itemized agendas with everything neatly catalogued and listed . . . except the writer's health. Why are we living if there is no time for life? No time for fun? No time for developing a creative human potential? And why do I see among CFS patients a tendency to go from battle to battle, seemingly losing themselves among the dust, ruffled feathers and, of course, the "cause"—the cause usually being nothing more vital or constructive than winning at some aspect of office politics.

Are you a CFS patient? Does any of this sound familiar?

Some simple advice: choose your battles carefully. Reserve your energy for those instances when you see a real and present injustice, or for some truly unavoidable tragedy (a death in the family, or the collapse of the firm you work for), or for the day when one of those dragons that the world occasionally hatches (the ones who get some evil pleasure out of hurting people for no apparent reason) fixates on you and yours. Winning some relatively meaningless political battle at the office pales by comparison to losing the war and suffering a six week relapse.

Perspective. Don't forget what I'm telling you.

All battles, all stresses, are not escapable. But we do have a certain measure of choice over how we confront our stressors—

Quality of life is a concept beyond critical-linear thinking and can only be experienced intuitively, by the person on the healing journey—

Yes indeedy—

Quality of life is a personal decision that we can reach, based upon our inner and outer experiences of reality—what we want and the way we think things "should" be. I've known CFS patients who, after fifteen years of unrelenting illness, had most of their eighteen symptoms disappear, but described themselves as still being in a terrible condition. I also know a woman who came out of a car accident paralyzed from the neck down. She gets around in a motorized wheelchair (which she directs with her chin). She still teaches, and she usually describes her days as wonderful.

Perspective is the key. It can unlock the way to boosting your quality of life.

Blowing up the earth was a good start. Finding that particular relief valve for the anger and worry was a far better choice than excessive backup plans, or holding a self-pity party for one. And of course, you could get paid for writing novels. Endless worry produces nothing constructive, nothing of lasting value, not even pocket change.

Now that the bad emotions are vented, and some of the sewage unclogged from the base of my skull, from that core of Mesosaur brain that resides in us all, I can choose to better justify my existence. For all of us this should probably include helping others, simply by trying to shine a little light wherever we can, even if into the life of just one other human being. If you can do that, if you can make just one life a little happier, then somewhere in time, the earth is made a little bit better just by your having lived here—

Now, Charlie is a walking example of many odd things. Back in 1985, when his health was taking a swan dive into a pile of bricks and he was living koala bear hours,* his dreams for the future remained at center stage, sustaining him somehow. Continuing, with his colleagues at Brookhaven National Laboratory, to design antimatter rockets (actual starships) acted in some ways as an anaesthetic against physical pain. And he's still designing the damned things. His dreams are somewhat beyond most of us walking this earth today, and a little bit strange, and perhaps even a little frightening as well. Certainly they are nowhere near as immediate in their rewards as the dreams of a woman who continues to teach from a wheelchair, or the physician who seeks to heal. Charlie's perspectives may seem a little odd at times, but that is not to say that there are no lessons to be gleaned from them. He still deals daily with ankylosing spondylitis—for which there is no known cure (though attention to doing everything possible to maintain the best overall health, combined with two recently "rediscovered" Chinese remedies,† seems to be significantly slowing the progress of

---

*Koalas sleep twenty hours a day, coming out only to munch on eucalyptus and make more Koalas. What a life.

†Charles Pellegrino comments: My recent experience appears to bear out the results of double-blind studies (in which neither physician nor volunteer knew who was getting the test substance and who was getting the placebo) of ancient Chinese nutritional remedies, in particular a tradition of adding sea cucumber and shark fin soup to the diets of arthritis sufferers. Powdered extracts of Beeche de Mer (a mud-dwelling cousin to the starfish) can evidently slow the progress of autoimmune disease by up to 80 percent in some patients (myself included). The

the disease). His sheer lust for life is such that he has come to describe AS as an ever-present but relatively minor nuisance, "somewhat like background noise." Perspective. Strange, how he spends his time designing machines that are at least seventy or eighty years off in the future. He's right about one thing, though: the wild-eyed dreamers with the wandering minds are going to inherit the stars. On first hearing it seems sad that he'll never see it. At this point in history, human lifetimes just aren't long enough. He isn't meant to see his starships anymore than Moses was meant to cross over into Canaan with the children of Israel. But then I guess he doesn't need to see the Valkyries. It is enough for him to know that they are waiting out there, somewhere in the new millennium.

Ever since the dark days of July 1985 and the enormous shift that came with regained health and the sudden realization that a normal lifespan lay ahead of me, my perspective continues to change in odd, unexpected ways. There was a time when 80 percent of the design projects I either coordinated or participated in were for machines we hoped to one day launch into space. I have already described to you my belief that I came away from that first, rough encounter with CFS more of a planetary citizen than I'd ever been before. Allow me to add that on the heels of the 1985 awakening, I sailed with explorer Robert Ballard, who showed me that the flotsam and jetsam of human civilization were horribly apparent even in the mid-Pacific, thousands of miles from the nearest city. One direct result of the Ballard expedition was that more and more of my work began to encompass archaeology, and as I began to see how past civilizations fell, so too did I

---

mechanism of the slowing is not yet known. The typical daily dose (with your physician's guidance) is two capsules—one with breakfast, one with dinner. The induction period is slow, typically up to sixty days, and 60 to 80 percent of patients living with a variety of autoimmune diseases note improvements ranging from mild to profound. In my case, in addition to a greatly diminished frequency and duration of painful "flares," other symptoms of AS, including flaking of the skin and swelling of the eyes, have almost entirely disappeared. A second nutritional supplement, shark cartilage, is now marketed under the name Cartilade, and appears to disrupt the genetic commands that turn a body's immune system against its own connective tissue (dosage is weight dependent and should be supplemented with a stomach acid neutralizer under the direction of a physician).

find signposts pointing to the third millenium. I realize, now, that Valkyrie and all my other dreams of planetary and extrasolar exploration will never come to pass if we do not take pause and get down to some basics right here on Earth.*

Now, 80 percent of my work involves Earth-based projects, ranging from cheap, clean power production to a 3,000 mph Maglev train system (London to Sydney in six hours using three dollars' worth of electricity per passenger), an economically viable plan for converting America to solar power, and mile-high city towers that can be erected in the centers of rainforests, leaving the forests themselves untouched by urban sprawl—

Perspective can be recognized when we become aware of events and activities that feel like a push, and with this realization comes the opportunity to reframe your activities into something more positive and fulfilling.

But please be cautious. After a good dose of perspective comes the challenge of energy management. When you first embark on your healing journey, make a list of all the things you can do on your worst days, and during your first three months, at least, don't do more than that on your best days. Even after recovery, don't do anything to the point of exhaustion and always try to go to sleep at night with some energy left over. The energy to initiate activity can return before the stamina to complete it. If you spread yourself too thin you'll find that the façade of energy can evaporate and you will collapse like a house of cards. Slow and steady wins the race.

CFS is more than a virus, more than a dysfunctional immune system. It is a challenge to your whole way of life. Where did your particular stressors come from? Why did they accumulate to the

*Along the river worlds, from the Nile to the Tigris-Euphrates, there is an ominous and relevant pattern, dating back more than four thousand years, of new technologies permitting first beneficial exploitation and finally over-exploitation of local environments—something we now threaten to accomplish on a global scale. In the past, the consequences of exploitation to the limits of environmental stress have not manifested themselves as a science fiction–like wave of starvation and plagues, but as a more subtle pattern beginning with what is essentially an economic collapse followed by civil disorder, and ending with population crashes. Seen in this light, the history of civilization is simply this: the desire of every empire and every city, every hamlet and every individual, to live beyond its means.

breaking point? What are they? How can you prevent the circumstance that enabled them to occur from occurring again?

The journey inward is like a quest to the top of the mountain that rises above the chaos in your life and body. The trek is not by way of an escalator. It is a long, hard climb. The only way out of this mess is through it. Together we will walk the path, guided by signposts. The climb to the top, beyond illness, is worth the effort. When we have reached the summit you will have learned more about yourself and grown more than you ever dreamed was possible. There will be many hills and valleys along the way, and there may be times when you wonder, "Why bother?" Just remember this: when you are ascending the mountain you can look back down and know what was. But when you're deep in the valley you can't look up through the fog to see what will be. Trust. When you cross a small valley along your trek, the memory of what you have already seen and learned will sustain you.

If you stop along the way to really take in the signposts, then you are a special person indeed, for you are ready to put aside the fear of the unknown, of yourself, and really examine who and what you are. You are ready to love, accept, and appreciate yourself for who and what you are. You will learn to listen to yourself and to your body to fulfill its needs.

When you reach the summit, you can pause and reflect on what you have learned and re-create yourself. The power to do so is yours. And with your new strength you can now bring greater love to your family and friends. You will have gained a sense of maturity and perspective with which you can offer them a hand. This is what I will see when I look at you on the mountaintop: a person who can love, a person who can listen. An authentic human being.

When you look back, there will be no regret and remorse over lost time and opportunities. Instead, you will see that the greatest opportunity of your life is the illness now before you. Give me your hand and let us begin our journey.

EPILOGUE

As I walk through life I am impressed that much of our society functions on the basis of superficiality and immediacy. There is little understanding of the root causes of problems and even less commitment to lasting change or real solutions. Personal, business, and political decisions are often driven by greed, fear, or feelings of self-importance that have created a legacy of disharmony within our society and often within the individual. This has fostered an environment of global pollution previously unknown in the history of the earth and a consequent epidemic of new diseases almost faster than we can name them. Yet, there is hope. Each time a 4-H or Lions Club "adopts-a-highway," there is hope. Each time human beings like Ghandi or Martin Luther King take a public stand in the name of humanity, there is hope. Each time someone eats a carrot instead of smoking a cigarette, there is hope. As Norman Cousins pointed out:

> There is a healing biological response to hope. . . . Concern over "false hopes" tends to ignore the far more prevalent problem caused by "false fears." People tell me not to offer hope unless I know hope to be real, but I don't have the power not to respond to an outstretched hand. . . . I'm not sure anyone knows enough to deny hope. I have seen too many cases, these past ten years, when death predictions were delivered from high professional station only to be gloriously refuted by patients for reasons having less to do with tangible biology than the human spirit, admittedly a vague term but one that may well be the greatest force of all within the human arsenal.

Hope can free the ill from despair and help maintain a good quality of life and a reason for living. Hope, transformed by the will of the human spirit, can sustain life, even under the most difficult of circumstances. Life is the ultimate prize and it takes on ultimate value when we suddenly discover how tentative and fragile it can be. The essential art of healing and living is to respect and savor its preciousness from the smallest frog to the entire planet Earth.

—JESSE A. STOFF, M.D.

GLOSSARY

Acute illness—An illness having a rapid onset and a resolution of all symptoms within six weeks.

Adrenal gland—A small, triangular gland that sits on top of each kidney like a hat and synthesizes and releases a variety of hormones in response to various neurological or emotional states.

Anabolic metabolism—The metabolic processes that result in the building of substances.

Anemia—A nonspecific term used to describe the condition in which there is a reduced number of circulating red blood cells per volume of blood.

Anergy—A lack of response by the immune system to an antigen.

Antibody—A protein made by B lymphocytes or plasma cells in response to a perceived foreign or abnormal substance or organism.

Antigen—A foreign substance or organism that induces the formation of specific antibodies that react with it.

Arthralgia—Pain or tenderness of a joint.

Autism—A psychotic state of intense internal focus, to the exclusion of surrounding people and environment.

Autonomic nervous system—The part of the nervous system that controls the involuntary bodily functions.

Beta-carotene—A previtamin A substance derived from plant pigments, which may be converted to vitamin A as it is needed by the body.

Bile—A thick, bitter, greenish fluid secreted by the liver that is composed of many substances, including those resulting from the breakdown of old red blood cells; bile aids in the digestion of fats and helps stimulate the digestive system.

Calcium—An essential metal that is necessary in moderate amounts for the normal structure and functioning of the bones, teeth, skin, and nails.

Catabolic Metabolism—The metabolic processes that result in the breakdown of substances.

Chelation—A process whereby an amino acid is combined with a substance such as zinc or magnesium to increase its absorption and ease its assimilation into the body.

Chronic illness—An illness whose symptoms persist for longer than six weeks.

Circadian rhythm—A cyclic variation in physiologic processes, which may occur over a period of seconds or months; the menstrual cycle is one example.

Collagen—A gluelike protein found in the skin, bones, ligaments, and cartilage, which constitutes up to 30 percent of the body's protein.

Demyelination—The destruction of the myelin sheath, the soft, white, fatty substance surrounding certain nerves, which may or may not be reversible.

Depression—An exaggerated sense of sadness that results in abnormal and unfounded perceptions of hopelessness.

Encephalitis—An inflammation of the brain tissue that may be caused by a virus.

Endorphin—A narcotic-like substance produced and released in the brain during times of intense pain or stress.

Enzyme—A protein capable of catalyzing biochemical reactions.

Epstein-Barr virus (EBV)—A herpes-class virus that can cause acute, recurrent, or chronic disease depending upon the degree of immunosuppression or stress.

"Exceptional patients"—Those patients who are willing to work on issues of personal growth and development as a supplement to their medical care.

Gene—A group of nucleotides that together can convey a single message of heredity from the chromosome in the cell's nucleus to the production of a specific substance.

Glucagon—A hormone made and secreted by the pancreas that stimulates the breakdown of glycogen into sugar.

Glycogen—A complex carbohydrate, or starch, made from sugar molecules.

Glycogenesis—The building up of the glycogen molecule from glucose, a process that occurs primarily in the liver.

Glycogenolysis—The breakdown of glycogen into glucose when increased energy is required by the body.

Hepatitis—An inflammation of the liver tissue, which may be caused by a virus.

Histaminase—An enzyme responsible for breaking down histamine.

HTLV (Human T-Lymphocyte Virus)—A member of a family of viruses that attack T cells, including HTLV-III, which has been renamed HIV (human immunodeficiency virus) and is currently the prime suspect in the genesis of AIDS.

Hypoglycemia—Low blood sugar, which may occur as a result of a disturbance in the liver from an infection or metabolic imbalance.

Immune system—The whole group of special cells and organs that sense and destroy substances or organisms perceived as abnormal within the body.

I.U. (international units)—An agreed-upon measure of the potency of some vitamins.

Kupffer cells—Macrophage-like cells that are located in the liver.

Liver—The largest, warmest, and most metabolically active organ in the body, located just beneath the right lower ribs. It participates in and controls many aspects of fat, protein, sugar, and hormone metabolism as well as having many important immunologic functions.

Lymph nodes—Organs scattered around the body that range in size from a poppy seed to a grape, which filter foreign organisms from the lymph fluid, creating an opportunity for white blood cells to deal with them.

Macrophage—A special, highly mobile amoeboid cell of the immune system that has the ability to engulf and destroy foreign substances and/or organisms and then communicate with the other white blood cells.

Magnesium—An essential metal that is necessary in small amounts for the normal functioning of the liver.

Metabolism—The sum total of all the biochemical reactions in all the cells and systems of the body.

Multiple sclerosis—A chronic disease of the nervous system that is characterized by progressive damage to the nerve sheaths, with dysfunction and eventual death of the underlying nerve.

Myalgia—Pain or tenderness of a muscle.

Myositis—An inflammation of the muscle tissue that may be caused by a virus.

Neurotransmitters—Substances that are produced and released by nerves, which allow them to communicate with each other.

Oncogenesis—The development and production of a malignant tumor.

Parasympathetic nervous system—The part of the autonomic nervous system that is responsible for the "possum" response.

Placebo—A substance that is given to "please" a patient, with no expected physiologic effect.

Pneumonitis—An inflammation of the lung tissue.

Protocol—A methodical approach to treatment based upon the current understanding of the disease process.

Psychoneuroimmunology (PNI)—A branch of medical psychology that employs visualization exercises for specific immunologically therapeutic goals.

Reticulo endothelial system—The part of the immune system that is made up mainly of macrophage-like cells and is located primarily in the liver.

Shingles—A reactivation of the "chicken-pox" virus during times of stress, which can cause a painfully inflamed rash of small fluid-filled bubbles.

Streptococcus—A common bacteria that often blossoms into an acute infection of the throat during an acute or acute recurrent attack of Epstein-Barr virus. Some strains of strep can cause scarlet or rheumatic fever, which can be very dangerous and damaging.

Sympathetic nervous system—The part of the autonomic nervous system that is responsible for the "fight or flight" response.

Thymus gland—An organ about the size of two dried prunes that is located behind the upper part of the sternum (breast bone) and is essential in the maturation process of the T lymphocytes.

Thyroid gland—An organ about the size of two dried apricots that is located at the base of the neck and produces the hormones that largely control the speed of metabolism.

Titer—The highest dilution of antibodies that will still cause clumping with the antigen being tested.

Virus—A simple, minute, parasitic organism that depends entirely upon its host (victim) cell for its nutritional, metabolic, and reproductive needs.

Visualization—An elective state of intense internal focus wherein the imaginary images can be used to influence metabolic, immunologic, or physiologic processes.

Vitamin A—A fat-soluble vitamin that is essential for the normal growth and functioning of the eyes, teeth, bones, skin, liver, and immune system.

Vitamin B—A group of water-soluble vitamins that are essential for the normal functioning of the liver, digestive, and nervous systems.

Vitamin C—A water-soluble vitamin that is essential for the normal functioning of the connective tissue and the immune system.

Zinc—An essential metal that is necessary in trace amounts for the normal functioning of the immune system.

RECOMMENDED READING

Achterberg, Jeanne. *Imagery in Healing*. Boston: New Science Library, 1985.

Better Nutrition. For the latest, accessible information on nutrition, including useful leads into the technical literature, we recommend this magazine, published monthly by Communication Channels, Inc., 6255 Barfield Road, Atlanta, GA 30328 (404-256-9800).

Cousins, Norman. *Anatomy of an Illness*. New York: W.W. Norton, 1979.

———. *Head First: The Biology of Hope*. New York: E.P. Dutton, 1989.

Covey, Stephen R. *The 7 Habits of Highly Effective People*. New York: Simon & Schuster, 1989.

Culliton, Barbara J. "Emerging Viruses, Emerging Threat." *Science* 247: 279–280 (Jan. 19, 1990).

Frankl, Viktor E. *Man's Search for Meaning*. New York: Simon & Schuster, 1984.

Heschel, Abraham J. *Who Is Man?* Stanford, Calif.: Stanford University Press, 1965.

Hodgkinson, Neville, *Will to Be Well*. York Beach, Maine: Samuel Weiser, Inc., 1986.

Kaufman, Barry Neil. *Giant Steps*. New York: Ballantine Books, 1979.

———. *Happiness Is a Choice*. New York: Ballantine Books, 1991.

———. *To Love Is to Be Happy With*. New York: Ballantine Books, 1978.

Leviton, Richard. *Anthroposophic Medicine Today*. Hudson, New York: Anthroposophic Press, 1988.

Locke, Steven, and Douglas Colligan. *Healer Within*. New York: Signet Books, 1986.

McDermott, Robert A. *The Essential Steiner*. New York: Harper & Row, 1984.

Moss, Richard. *The Black Butterfly*. Berkeley, Calif.: Celestial Arts, 1986.

Nilsson, Lennart. *The Body Victorious*. New York: Delacorte Press, 1985.

Pellegrino, C. R. and J. A. Stoff. *Darwin's Universe: Origins and Crises in the History of Life,* 2nd ed. Blue Ridge Summit, PA: TAB Books, 1986.

Prudden, Bonnie. *Pain Erasure*. New York: Ballantine Books, 1980.

Siegel, Bernie S. *Love, Medicine & Miracles*. New York: Harper & Row, 1986.

Simonton, O. C., S. Matthews-Simonton, and J. L. Creighton. *Getting Well Again*. New York: Bantam Books, 1978.

Steiner, Rudolf. *Anthroposophical Approach to Medicine*. London: Anthroposophical Publishing, 1928.

Stortebecker, Patrick. *Mercury Poisoning from Dental Amalgam: A Hazard to Human Brain*. Stockholm, Sweden: Stortebecker Foundation for Research. Published in the United States by Bio-Probe Inc., P.O. Box 58010, Orlando, FL 1986.

Yiamouyiannis, J. *Flouride: The Aging Factor*. Ohio: Health Action Press, 1986.

BIBLIOGRAPHY

Achterberg, Jeanne, and G. Frank Lawlis. *Imagery of Disease*. Champaign, Ill.: Institute for Personality and Ability Testing, 1978.

Ader, Robert, ed. *Psychoneuroimmunology*. New York: Academic Press, 1981.

Akaboshi, I., J. Jamamoto, T. Katsuki, and I. Matsuda. "Unique pattern of Epstein-Barr virus specific antibodies in recurrent parotitis." *Lancet* 2:1049–51 (1983).

Alexander, Franz. *Psychosomatic Medicine*. New York: W. W. Norton, 1965.

Andiman, W. A. "The Epstein-Barr virus and EB virus infections in childhood." *J. Pediatr*. 95:171–82 (1979).

Annals of Internal Medicine. International Conference on Acquired Immunodeficiency Syndrome, November 1985, Vol. 103 #5.

Aoki, Tadao, et al. "Low Natural Killer Syndrome: Clinical and Immunologic Features," *Nat. Immun. Cell Growth Regul*. 6:116–128 (1987).

Askinazi, C., F. S. Cole, and J. L. Brusch. "Positive differential heterophile antibody test: persistence in a symptomatic patient." *JAMA* 236: 1492–93 (1976).

Atkins, Robert C. *Dr. Atkins Health Revolution*. New York: Bantam Books, 1990.

Behan, Peter O., and Wilhelmina M.H. Behan. "Essential fatty acids in the treatment of Postviral Fatigue Syndrome." *Pathophysiology and Roles in Clinical Medicine,* 20:275–282 (1990).

Behan, P. O., W. M. H. Behan, and D. Horrobin. "Effect of high doses of essential fatty acids on the postviral fatigue syndrome." *Acta Neurol Scand,* 82:209–216 (1990).

Bell, David S., M.D. Cheney, and Susan Dorman. "Interleukin-2 and the Chronic Fatigue Syndrome." *Annals of Internal Medicine,* 110:321 (Feb. 15, 1989).

Bender, C. E. "Recurrent mononucleosis." *JAMA* 182:954–56 (1962).

Bennet, Hal, and Mike Samuels. *The Well Body Book*. New York: Random House, 1973.

Bennett, John E., et al. *Principles and Practice of Infectious Diseases*. New York: Churchill Livingstone, 1990.

Benson, Herbert. *The Mind-Body Effect*. New York: Simon & Schuster, 1979.

Berkel, A. I., et al. "Epstein-Barr virus related antibody patterns in ataxia-telangiectasia." *Clin. Exp. Immunol*. 35:196–201 (1979).

Blaese, R. Michael, et al. "Characteristic T-Cell Dysfunction in Patients with Chronic Active Epstein-Barr Virus Infection (Chronic Infectious Mononucleosis)." *The Journal of Immunology*, 134:3082–3088 (May 1985).

Bresler, David E., and Richard Turbo. *Free Yourself from Pain*. New York: Simon & Schuster, 1979.

Breznitz, Shlomo, ed. *The Denial of Stress*. New York: International Universities Press, 1984.

Brody, Jane E., "Fibromyalgia: New light on an old syndrome marked by muscular pain and fatigue," *The New York Times*, Sept. 7, 1989.

Bry, Adelaide, and Marjorie Blair. *Directing the Movies of Your Mind*. New York: Harper & Row, 1978.

Buchwald, Dedra S., "Chronic Fatigue Syndrome," *Cortlandt Forum*, 125–136, March 1991.

Buchwald, D., et al. "Frequency of 'Chronic Active Epstein-Barr Virus Infection' in a General Medical Practice," *JAMA*, 257:2303–7 (1987).

Buscaglia, Leo. *Living, Loving & Learning*. Thorofare, NJ: Charles B. Slack, 1982.

———. *Love*. Thorofare, N.J.: Charles B. Slack, 1972. Rpt. New York: Fawcett Crest/Ballantine, 1982.

Cadie, M., F. J. Nye, and P. Storey. "Anxiety and depression after infectious mononucleosis." *Br. J. Psychiatry* 128:559–61 (1976).

Capra, Fritjof. *The Tao of Physics*. Boulder, Colo.: Shambhala, 1975. Rpt. New York: Bantam Books, 1977.

Carter, C., et al. "Cancer incidence following infectious mononucleosis." *Am. J. of Epidemiology*, 105:130–36 (1977).

Chang, R. S., J. P. Lewis, and C. F. Abildgaard. "Prevalence of oropharyngeal excreters of leukocyte-transforming agents among human populations." *N. Engl. J. Med*. 289:1325–29 (1973).

Chang, R. S., and R. Maddock. "Recurrence of infectious mononucleosis [Letter]." *Lancet* 1:704 (1980).

Chilton, M. D. "A vector for introducing new genes into plants," *Scientific American*, vol. 248, June 1983.

Chronic Fatigue Syndrome, prepared by Office of Communications, NIAID. National Institutes of Health, Bethesda, MD, Jan. 1989.

Cinque, Chris, "Fibromyalgia: Is exercise the cause or the cure?" *The Physician and Sportsmedicine,* 17:181–184 (Sept. 1989).

Cleary, M. L., et al. "Individual tumors of multifocal EB virus-induced malignant lymphomas in tamarins arise from different B-cell clones," *Science* 228:722–24 (1985).

Cooke, Robert. "Vaccine Blocks Diabetes in Mice." *Newsday,* April 1991.

Cousins, Norman. *Anatomy of an Illness as Perceived by the Patient.* New York: W. W. Norton, 1979. Rpt. New York: Bantam Books, 1981.

———. "Healing and Belief," *Human Options* New York: Berkley Books, 1983.

———. "A Nation of Hypochondriacs," *Time,* 18 June 1990.

Conference Journal. "Experimental Drug Held Effective for Chronic Fatigue Immune Dysfunction," vol. 12, no. 2, September 29–October 2, 1991.

Crowley, G., and Mary Hager. "A Clue to Chronic Fatigue," *Newsweek,* 66, 30 September 1991.

Crowley, Geoffrey, Mary Hager, and Nadine Joseph. "Chronic Fatigue Syndrome," *Newsweek,* 62–70, 12 November 1990.

Davenas, E., et al. "Human basophil degranulation triggered by very dilute antiserum against IgE," *Nature,* vol. 333, June 30, 1988, 816–18.

DeStefano, E., et al. "Acid labile human leukocyte interferon in homosexual men with Kaposi's sarcoma and lymphadenopathy." *J. Infect. Dis.* 146:451–59 (1982).

DiPalma, Joseph R., "Magnesium Replacement Therapy," *AFP Clinical Pharmacology,* 209:173–176 (July 1990).

Dowling, Colette. *The Cinderella Complex: Women's Hidden Fear of Independence.* New York: Summit Books, 1981. Rpt. New York: Pocket Books, 1981.

DuBois, R. E., et al. "Chronic mononucleosis syndrome." *South. Med. J.* 1984. (In press)

"Epidemic neuromyasthenia, 1934–1977: current approaches. Proceedings of a symposium held by the Council of the Royal Society of Medicine, April 7, 1978." *Postgraduate Medical Journal,* 54(637):705–74 (Nov. 1978).

Evans, Elida. *A Psychological Study of Cancer.* New York: Dodd, Mead, 1926.

Fackeldey-Larsen, Lynda. "About the Beam." *CFIDS Chronicle,* 19, 57 (Spring/Summer 1990).

Faggioni, A., et al. "Calcium Modulation Activates Epstein-Barr Virus Genome in Latently Infected Cells." *Science,* 232:1554–56 (1986).

Faraday, Ann. *Dream Power*. New York: Berkeley Books, 1973.

Fields, Bernard N., *Fundamental Virology*. New York: Raven Press, 1991.

Fischer, Thomas J. and Glenn J., Lawlor, Jr. *Manual of Allergy and Immunology*. Boston: Little Brown and Company, 1988.

Fleisher, G., and R. Bolognese. "Persistent Epstein-Barr virus infection and pregnancy." *J. Infect. Dis.* 147:982–86 (1983).

Fontenot, John M., and Stephen A. Levine. "Melatonin deficiency: Its role in oncogenesis and age-related pathology." *Journal of Orthomolecular Medicine*, 5:1 (1990).

Forslind, Kristina, Eva Fredriksson, and Ola Nived. "Does primary fibromyalgia exist?" *British Journal of Rheumatology*, 29:368–370 (1990).

Fosshage, James L., and Paul Olsen. *Healing: Implications for Psychotherapy*. New York: Human Sciences Press, 1978.

Fox, Emmet. *The Sermon on the Mount*. New York: Harper & Row, 1938.

Frankl, Viktor. *Man's Search for Meaning*. New York: Pocket Books, 1959, reissued 1980.

Friedman, Neil. *Experimental Therapy and Focusing*. New York: Half Court Press, 1982.

Fry, J. "Infectious mononucleosis: some new observations from a 15-year study." *J. Fam. Pract.* 10:1087–89 (1980).

Garfield, Charles, ed. *Psychosocial Care of the Dying Patient*. New York: McGraw-Hill, 1978.

Garfield, Patricia. *Creative Dreaming*. New York: Simon & Schuster, 1974.

Garrett, Laurie. "Rapid Growth of AIDS Virus." *Newsday*, April 1991.

Glassman, Judith. *The Cancer Survivors: And How They Did It*. New York: Doubleday, 1983.

Gould, S. J. "The ultimate parasite: What happens to bodies if genes act for themselves." *Natural History*, vol. 90, November 1981.

Graves, S., Jr. "Recurrent infectious mononucleosis." *J. Ky. Med. Assoc.* 1:790–93 (1970).

Green, Elmer, and Alyce Green. *Beyond Biofeedback*. New York: Delacorte Press, 1977.

Hall, R. P., et al. "IgA-containing immune complexes in dermatitis herpetiformis, Henoch-Schenlein purpura, systemic lupus erythematosus and other diseases." *Clin. Exp. Immunol.* 40:431–37 (1980).

Hanto, D. W., et al. "Epstein-Barr virus-induced B-cell lymphoma after renal transplantation: acyclovir therapy and transition from polyclonal to monoclonal B-cell proliferation." *N. Engl. J. Med.* 306:913–18 (1982).

————, et al. "Epstein-Barr Virus, Immunodeficiency, and B-cell Lymphoproliferation." *Transplantation*, 39:461–72 (1985).

Harris, Thomas A. *I'm OK—You're OK: A Practical Guide to Transactional Analysis.* New York: Harper & Row, 1969. Rpt. New York: Avon Books, 1982.

Henle, W., and G. Henle. "Epstein-Barr virus-specific serology in immunologically compromised individuals." *Cancer Res.* 41:4222–25 (1981).

———. "Immunology of Epstein-Barr Virus." In B. Roizman, ed., *The Herpes Viruses.* New York: Plenum Press, 1982, 209–52.

———. "The virus as the etiologic agent of infectious mononucleosis." In M. A. Epstein and B. G. Achong, eds., *The Epstein-Barr Virus.* New York: Springer-Verlag, 1979, 28–320.

Henle, W., et al. "Antibodies to Epstein-Barr virus in nasopharyngeal carcinoma, other head and neck neoplasms and control groups." *J. Natl. Cancer Inst.* 44:225–31 (1970).

Henle, W., et al. "Antibodies to Epstein-Barr virus-related antigens in nasopharyngeal carcinoma: comparison of active cases with long term survivors." *J. Natl. Cancer Inst.* 51:361–69 (1973).

Henle, W., G. Henle, and C. A. Horowitz. "Epstein-Barr virus-specific diagnostic tests in infectious mononucleosis." *Hum. Pathol.* 5:551–65 (1974).

Henle, G., et al. "Rheumatoid factor as a cause of positive reactions in tests for Epstein-Barr virus-specific IgM antibodies." *Clin. Exp. Immunol.* 36:415–22 (1979).

Hicks, M. J., et al. "Age-related changes in T- and B-lymphocyte subpopulations in the peripheral blood." *Arch. Pathol. Lab. Med.* 107: 518–23 (1983).

Hicks, M. J., et al. "Age-related changes in mitogen-induced lymphocyte function from birth to old age." *Am. J. Clin. Pathol.* 80:159–63 (1983).

Holmes, G., et al. "A cluster of patients with a chronic mononucleosis-like syndrome," *JAMA,* 257:2297–302 (1987).

Hooks, J. J., et al. "Multiple interferons in the circulation of patients with systemic lupus erythematosus and vasculitis." *Arthritis Rheum.* 25:396–400 (1982).

Horrobin, D. F., "Essential omega-6 and omega-3 fatty acids in medicine: A practical guide." *Journal of Advancement in Medicine,* 3 (Fall 1990).

Horrobin, David F., "Gamma linolenic acid: An intermediate in essential fatty acid metabolism with potential as an ethical pharmaceutical and as a food." *Review of Contemporary Pharmacotherapy,* 1:1–45 (1990).

Horwitz, C. A., et al. "Clinical evaluation of patients with infectious mononucleosis and development of antibodies to the R component of the Epstein-Barr virus-induced early antigen complex." *Am. J. Med.* 58:330–38 (1975).

Hutschnecker, Arnold. *The Will to Live.* New York: Cornerstone Library, 1951.

Isaacs, R. "Chronic infectious mononucleosis." *Blood* 3:8588–61 (1948).

"Immunology of Chronic Fatigue Syndrome." *Infectious Disease Alert,* 9:18 (June 15, 1990).

Jacobsen, H., et al. "Induction of ppp(A2'p)$_n$ A–dependent RNAse in murine JLS-V9r cells during growth inhibition." *Proc. Natl. Acad. Sci. USA.* 80:4954–58 (1983).

Jamal, G., et al. "Electrophysiological studies in the post-viral fatigue syndrome," *J. of Neurology,* 48:691–99 (1985).

James, Muriel, and Dorothy Jongeward. *Born to Win.* Boston: Addison-Wesley, 1971. Rpt. New York: New American Library, 1978.

Jampolsky, Gerald. *Love Is Letting Go of Fear.* Millbrae, Calif.: Celestial Arts, 1979.

———. *Teach Only Love: The Seven Principles of Attitudinal Healing.* New York: Bantam Books, 1983.

———. *There Is a Rainbow Behind Every Dark Cloud.* Berkeley, Calif.: Celestial Arts, 1978.

Johnson, F. N., and S. Johnson. "Gamma linolenic acid." *Review in Contemporary Pharmacotherapy,* 1:1, Carnforth, England: Marius Press, 1990.

Johnson, Robert A. *He: Understanding Masculine Psychology.* New York: Harper & Row, 1977.

———. *She: Understanding Feminine Psychology.* New York: Harper & Row, 1977.

Joncas, J., et al. "Unusual prevalence of antibodies to Epstein-Barr virus early antigen in ataxia telangiectasia [Letter]." *Lancet* 1:1160 (1977).

Jones, J. F., et al. "Serum interferon in Navajo children with severe combined immunodeficiency disease inhibits lymphoblastogenesis." *J. Clin. Immunol.* 3:14–21 (1983).

Jung, Carl G. *Man and His Symbols.* New York: Dell, 1968.

———. *Memories, Dreams, Reflections.* New York: Pantheon, 1963. Rpt. New York: Vintage, 1965.

———. *Modern Man in Search of a Soul.* New York: Harcourt Brace Jovanovich, 1955.

Kandil, Osma, et al. "Garlic and the immune system in humans: Its effect on natural killer cells." *Federation Proceedings,* vol. 46, no. 3, March 1, 1987.

Kasl, S. V., A. S. Evans, and J. C. Niederman. "Psychosocial risk factors in the development of infectious mononucleosis." *Psychosom Med*. 41:445–46 (1979).

Kaufman, Barry N. *To Love Is to Be Happy With*. Greenwich, Conn.: Fawcett, 1978.

Kaufman, R. E. "Recurrences in infectious mononucleosis." *Am. Pract*. 1:673–76 (1950).

Keleman, Stanley. *Living Your Dying*. New York: Random House, 1976.

Klein, E., and M. G. Masucci. "Cell mediated immunity against Epstein-Barr virus infected B lymphocytes." *Springer Semin. Immunopathol*. 5:63–73 (1982).

Kolata, Gina. "AIDS Overturns Theories on Two Medical Mysteries." *The New York Times*, October 27, 1987.

Koller, Alice. *An Unknown Woman: A Journey to Self-Discovery*. New York: Holt, Rinehart & Winston, 1982.

Kruger, Helen. *Other Healers, Other Cures*. Indianapolis: Bobbs-Merrill, 1974.

Kübler-Ross, Elisabeth. *On Death and Dying*. New York: Macmillan, 1969.

————. *Death: The Final Stage of Growth*. Englewood Cliffs, NJ: Prentice-Hall, 1975.

————. *To Live Until We Say Goodbye*. Englewood Cliffs, NJ: Prentice-Hall, 1978.

Kushner, Harold S. *When Bad Things Happen To Good People*. New York: Schocken, 1981. Rpt. New York: Avon Books, 1983.

Lair, Jess. *I Ain't Much Baby, But I'm All I've Got*. Greenwich, Conn.: Fawcett, 1978.

Lamy, M. E., et al. "Study of Epstein-Barr virus (EBV) antibodies: IgC and IgM VCA, IgC anti-EA, and IgG anti-EBNA obtained with an original microtiter technique: serologic criterions of primary and recurrent EBV infections and follow-up of infectious mononucleosis—seroepidemiology of EBV in Belgium based on 5178 sera from patients." *Acta Clin. Belg*. 37:281–98 (1982).

Landorf, Joyce. *Irregular People*. Waco, Tex.: Word Books, 1982.

Lane, William I., *Shark Cartilage Research Summary*, 1990.

Lang, B. J., et al. "Encephalitis in infectious mononucleosis: diagnostic considerations." *Pediatrics* 58:877–80 (1976).

Lange, B., et al. "Epstein-Barr virus related serology in marrow transplant recipients." *Int. J. Cancer*, 26:151–57 (1980).

Lapp, Frances Moore. *Diet for a Small Planet*. New York: Random House, 1971. Rpt. New York: Ballantine Books, 1975.

Lawley, R. J., et al. "Demonstration of circulating immune complexes in

Sj gren's syndrome." *J. Immunol.* 123:1382–87 (1979).

Leonard, Jonathan N., J. L. Hofer, and Nathan Pritikin. *Live Longer Now: The First One Hundred Years of Your Life*. New York: Grosset & Dunlap, 1974.

LeShan, Lawrence L. *You Can Fight for Your Life: Emotional Factors in the Causation of Cancer*. New York: Evans, 1977.

————. *How to Meditate*. Boston: Little, Brown, 1974. Rpt. New York: Bantam Books, 1975.

Levine, Arnold J. *Viruses*. New York: Scientific American Library, 1992.

Lewis, Howard, and Martha E. Lewis. *Psychosomatics: How Your Emotions Can Damage Your Health*. New York: Viking, 1972.

Leyvraz, S., et al. "Association of Epstein-Barr Virus with Thymic Carcinoma." *N. Engl. J. of Med.* 312:1296–99 (1985).

Lingerman, Hal. *The Healing Energies of Music*. Wheaton, Ill.: Theosophical Publishing House, 1983.

Livingston, Dennis, "Taking on Shirley MacLaine" (rev. of *The Ethical Implications of Creating Your Own Reality*). *Townsend Letter for Doctors*, February/March 1988.

Locke, Steven, and Mady Hornig-Rohan. *Mind and Immunity*. New York: Institute for the Advancement of Health, 1983.

Locke, S., et al. *Mind and Immunity: Behavioral Immunology*. New York: Praeger, Institute for the Advancement of Health, 1983.

"Magnesium May Play Role in Chronic Fatigue." *The New York Times*, April 30, 1991.

Mangi, R. J., et al. "Depression of cell-mediated immunity during acute infectious mononucleosis." *N. Engl. J. Med.* 291:1149–53 (1974).

Matarazzo, J. D., et al., eds. *Behavioral Health*. New York: John Wiley, 1984.

Mattson, K., et al. "Neurotoxicity of interferon [Letter]." *Cancer Treat. Rep.* 67:958–61 (1983).

McSherry, J. A. "Recurrent infectious mononucleosis [Letter]." *Can. Med. Assoc. J.* 126:899 (1982).

Miller, G., J. C. Niederman, and L. L. Andrews. "Prolonged oropharyngeal excretion of Epstein-Barr virus after infectious mononucleosis." *N. Engl. J. Med.* 288:229–32 (1973).

Monroe, Robert. *Journeys Out of the Body*. Garden City, NY: Anchor/Doubleday, 1971.

Moody, Raymond A., Jr. *Life After Life*. Covington, Ga.: Mockingbird Books, 1975. Rpt. New York: Bantam Books, 1976.

Morag, A., et al. "Elevated [2'–5']-oligo A synthetase activity in patients with prolonged illness associated with serological evidence of persistent EBV infection." *Lancet* 1:744–47 (1982).

Muller, Robert. *Most of All, They Taught Me Happiness*. New York: Doubleday, 1978.

"The Newest Human Herpesvirus Comes into Focus." *Lancet*, 335:325–326 (Feb. 10, 1990).

Newsweek, Special Issue. "Chronic Fatigue Syndrome," 12 November 1990.

Nouwen, Henri. *Out of Solitude*. Notre Dame, Ind.: Ave Maria Press, 1974.

———. *The Wounded Healer: Ministry in Contemporary Society*. New York: Doubleday, 1979.

———. *Genesee Diary: Report from a Trappist Monastery*. New York: Doubleday, 1981.

Ornstein, Robert E. *The Psychology of Consciousness*. San Francisco: W. H. Freeman, 1972. 2nd ed. New York: Harcourt Brace Jovanovich, 1977.

Ornstein, Robert and David Sobel. "The Healing Brain." *Psychology Today*, March 1987.

Oyle, Irving. *The Healing Mind*. New York: Pocket Books, 1975

———. *Time, Space & the Mind*. Berkeley, Calif.: Celestial Arts, 1976.

Palca, J. "AIDS Cooperation: U.S. and Soviet Science Deal to Be Renewed." *Nature*, 573, April 14, 1988.

Paterson, J. K., and J. L. Pinninger. "Recurrent infectious mononucleosis." *Br. Med. J.* 2:476 (1955).

Pearson, G. R. "The Humoral Response." In D. Schlossberg, ed., *Infectious Mononucleosis*. New York: Praeger Press, 1983, 141–58.

———, B. Johansson, and G. Klein. "Antibody-dependent cellular cytotoxicity against Epstein-Barr virus-associated antigens in African patients with nasopharyngeal carcinoma." *Int. J. Cancer* 22:120–25 (1978).

Peebles, C. L., et al. "A self-splicing RNA excises an intron lariat." *Cell*, vol. 44, 213 (1986).

Pelletier, Kenneth R. *Mind as Healer, Mind as Slayer*. New York: Delacorte Press, 1977. Rpt. New York: Delta, 1978.

———. *Toward a Science of Consciousness*. New York: Delacorte Press, 1978.

Peter, James B., *Use and Interpretation of Tests in Clinical Immunology*. Omaha, Nebraska: Interstate Press, 1990.

Preble, O. T., et al. "Systemic lupus erythematosus: presence in human serum of an unusual acid-labile leukocyte interferon." *Science* 216: 429–31 (1982).

————, et al. "Role of interferon in AIDS." *Ann. N.Y. Acad. Sci.* 1984. (In press)

Progoff, Ira, *The Well and the Cathedral.* 2nd ed. Dialogue House Library, 80 E. 11th St., New York, NY 10003, 1981.

————. *At a Journal Workshop: The Basic Text and Guide for Using the Intensive Journal.* Dialogue House Library, 80 E. 11th St., New York, NY 10003, 1981.

Purtilo, D. T., et al. "X-linked recessive progressive combined variable immunodeficiency (Duncan's disease)." *Lancet* 1:935–40 (1975).

————, et al. "Documentation of Epstein-Barr virus infection in immunodeficient patients with life threatening lymphoproliferative diseases by clinical, virological and immunopathological studies." *Cancer Res.* 41:4426–36 (1981).

————, et al. "Epstein-Barr virus infections in the X-linked recessive lymphoproliferative syndrome." *Lancet* 1:798–802 (1978).

Quality of Life and Cardiovascular Care, November/December, 1986.

Qualtierre, L. F., et al. "Identification of Epstein-Barr virus strain differences with monoclonal antibody to a membrane glycoprotein." *Proc. Natl. Acad. Sci. USA* 79:616–20 (1982).

Raiport, Gregory, "How to Get Motivated." *PRIVILEGEDinformation,* 1 February 1989.

Rapp, C. E., and J. F. Hewetson. "Infectious mononucleosis and the Epstein-Barr virus." *Am. J. Dis. Child.* 132:78–86 (1978).

Ray, C. G., et al. "Acute polyarthritis associated with active Epstein-Barr virus infections." *JAMA* 248:2990–93 (1982).

Reedman, B. M., and G. Klein. "Cellular localization of an Epstein-Barr virus (EBV)-associated complement-fixing antigen in producer and non-producer lymphoblastoid cell lines." *Int. J. Cancer,* 11:499–520 (1973).

Reinherz, E. L., et al. "Separation of functional subsets of human T cells by a monoclonal antibody." *Proc. Natl. Acad. Sci. USA* 76:4061–65 (1979).

Ritchie, George G., and Elizabeth Sherrill. *Return from Tomorrow.* Old Tappan, NJ: Fleming H. Revell, 1981.

Rocchi, G., et al. "Quantitative evaluation of Epstein-Barr-virus infected mononuclear peripheral blood leukocytes in infectious mononucleosis." *N. Engl. J. Med.* 296:132–34 (1977).

Roitt, I., J. Brustoff, and D. Male. *Immunology.* New York: C. V. Mosby Co., 1985.

Rush, Anne K. *Getting Clear.* New York: Random House, 1973.

Sakamoto, K., H. J. Freed, and D. T. Purtilo. "Antibody responses to

Epstein-Barr virus in families with the X-linked lymphoproliferative syndrome." *J. Immunol.* 125:921–25 (1980).

Salvaggio, John E., and Maria C. Soto-Aguilar. "Immunologic test in atopic and autoimmune disease." *Diagnosis,* 10:65–85 (Nov. 1988).

Samuels, Mike, and Nancy Samuels. *Seeing with the Mind's Eye.* New York: Random House, 1975.

Satir, Virginia M. *Peoplemaking.* Palo Alto, Calif.: Science 7 Behavior Books, 1972.

Schattner, A., et al. "Assay of an interferon-induced enzyme in white blood cells as a diagnostic aid in viral diseases." *Lancet* 2:497–99 (1981).

Schooley, R. T., et al. "Chronic Epstein-Barr Virus Infection Associated with Fever and Intestinal Pneumonitis," *Annals of Internal Medicine,* 104:636–43 (1986).

————, et al. "Association of herpes virus infections with T-lymphocyte subset alterations, glomerulopathy, and opportunistic infections after renal transplantation." *N. Engl. J. Med.,* 308:307–13 (1983).

Schucman, Helen. *A Course in Miracles.* Tiburon, Calif.: Foundation for Inner Peace, 1976.

Schultz, Will. *Profound Simplicity.* New York: Bantam Books, 1979.

Schwartz, Tony, "Making Waves," *New York Magazine,* 31–39, March 1991.

Scientific American (special issue). "The Molecules of Life," vol. 253, October 1985.

Selye, Hans. *The Stress of Life.* 2nd ed. New York: McGraw-Hill, 1978.

"Sharpening the focus on fibromyalgia." *Emergency Medicine,* 29–36 (Apr. 30, 1988).

Shealy, C. Norman. *The Pain Game.* Berkeley, Calif.: Celestial Arts, 1976.

Shearer, W., et al. "Epstein-Barr Virus-Associated B-cell proliferations of diverse clonal origins after bone marrow transplantation in a 12-year-old patient with severe combined immunodeficiency." *N. Engl. J. Med.,* 12:1151–59 (1985).

Siegal, Karen H., "The Alexander Technique: An innovative approach to reducing physical tension and stress." *Behavioral Medicine,* November/December 1981.

Simonton, O. Carl, Stephanie Matthews-Simonton, and James Creighton. *Getting Well Again.* Los Angeles: J. P. Tarcher, 1978. Rpt. New York: Bantam Books, 1980.

Sixbey, J. W., et al. "Epstein-Barr virus replication in oropharyngeal epithelial cells." *N. Engl. J. Med.,* 310:1225–30 (1984).

Smedley, H., et al. "Neurological effects of recombinant human interferon." *Br. Med. J.* 286:262–64 (1983).

Solzhenitsyn, Aleksandr. *Cancer Ward,* tr. Nicholas Bethell and David Burg. New York: Farrar, Straus & Giroux, 1969. Rpt. New York: Bantam Books, 1969.

Southern, P., et al., "Medical consequences of persistent viral infection." *New Engl. J. of Med.,* 314:359–67 (1986).

Straus, Stephen E., "The chronic mononucleosis syndrome." *The Journal of Infectious Diseases,* 157:405–412 (March 1988).

Su, T. P., et al. "Steroid binding at O receptors suggests a link between endocrine, nervous, and immune systems." *Science,* vol. 240, April 8, 1988.

Sumaya, C. V. "Endogenous reactivation of Epstein-Barr virus infection." *J. Infect. Dis.* 135:374–79 (1977).

———, et al. "Seroepidemiologic study of Epstein-Barr virus infections in a rural community." *J. Infect. Dis.* 131:403–08 (1975).

Svedmyr, E., et al. "EBV specific killer T cells and serologic responses after onset of infectious mononucleosis." *J. Clin. Lab. Immunol.* 1:325–32 (1978).

Sveinson, Kelly. *Learning to Live with Cancer.* New York: St. Martin's Press, 1977.

Tache, J., et al., eds. *Cancer, Stress and Death.* New York: Plenum Press, 1979.

Terasaki, P. I., ed. *Histocompatibility Testing,* 1980. Los Angeles: UCLA Tissue Typing Laboratory, 1980.

Theofilopoulos, A. N., C. B. Wilson, and F. J. Dixon. "The Raji cell radioimmune assay for detecting immune complexes in human sera." *J. Clin. Invest.* 57:169–82 (1976).

Time. "The New Age of Alternative Medicine," 4 November 1991.

Tobi, M., et al. "Prolonged atypical illness associated with serological evidence of persistent Epstein-Barr virus infection." *Lancet* 1:61–64 (1982).

Tosato, G., I. T. Magrath, and R. M. Blaese. "T cell-mediated immunoregulation of Epstein-Barr virus (EBV)-induced B cell activation in EBV-seropositive and EBV-seronegative individuals." *J. Immunol.* 128:575–79 (1982).

———, et al. "Abnormally elevated frequency of Epstein-Barr virus infected B cells in the blood of patients with rheumatoid arthritis." *J. Clin. Invest.* 1984. (In press)

Totman, Richard. *Social Causes of Illness.* New York: Pantheon, 1979.

Virelizier, J. L., G. Lenoir, and C. Griscelli. "Persistent Epstein-Barr virus infection in a child with hypergammaglobulinemia and immunoblastic proliferation associated with a selective defect in immune interferon secretion." *Lancet* 2:231–34 (1978).

Walker, Morton, "Non-Toxic Symptomatic Arthritis Relief Using Sea Cucumber (Beche de Mer), *Townsend Letter for Doctors,* Oct. 1990.

Ward, Milton. *The Brilliant Function of Pain.* New York: Optimus Books, and Lakemont, Ga.: CSA Press.

Weigle, K. A., C. U. Sumaya, and M. M. Montiel. "Changes in T-lymphocyte subsets during childhood Epstein-Barr virus infectious mononucleosis." *J. Clin. Immunol.* 3:151–55 (1983).

Weintraub, Michael and Richard Standish. "Ganciclovir: An antiviral agent for AIDS and other immunocompromised patients." *Hosp. Formul.,* 22:1011–1016 (Dec. 1987).

Yarchoan, R., et al. "Limiting dilution analyses of Epstein-Barr virus-induced immunoglobulin production by human B cell." *J. Exp. Med.* 157:1–14 (1983).

Zakim, D., and T. Boyer. *Hepatology.* Philadelphia: W. B. Saunders Co., 1982.

Zur Hausen, H., et al. "EBV DNA in biopsies of Burkitt's tumors and anaplastic carcinomas of the nasopharynx." *Nature* 228:1056–58 (1970).

INDEX

ABOUT THE AUTHORS

DR. JESSE A. STOFF is a graduate of New York Medical College and specializes in a holistic approach to treating people with severe and/or chronic diseases. He is the medical director of a very large multidisciplinary holistic health center in Tucson, Arizona. He also co-edits the *Journal of Anthroposophical Medicine*. He lectures internationally on anthroposophical and homeopathic medicine, a field in which he holds a specialty board licensure and has published in various national and international medical journals. In 1986 and 1989 he received a physician recognition award from the American Medical Association and was a guest on the AMA television program "Medical Rounds." He has written several articles and two previous books with Dr. Pellegrino on the subject of evolutionary biochemistry. Dr. Stoff is an avid gardener, collector of rocks and minerals, an an amateur photographer. He also enjoys playing the bagpipes. He can be contacted at 2661 N. Camino De Oeste, Tucson, AZ 84745, phone number (602) 323-2244.

DR. CHARLES R. PELLEGRINO wears many hats. He has been known to work simultaneously in crustaceology, paleobiology, preliminary design of advanced rocket systems, and marine archaeology. He is probably best summed up as an evolutionary biologist, although his real specialty appears to be the universe. Pellegrino writes for magazines and journals ranging from *Omni* and *Smithsonian* to *Evolutionary Theory* and *Crustaceana*. His work on ancient DNA in 95-million-year-old amber nuggets became the basis for the Michael Crichton novel, and Steven Spielberg movie, *Jurassic Park*. He is an award-winning painter and author of seven books, with five new books in the works. He currently lives on Long Island, where, at Brookhaven National Laboratory, he and physicist James Powell conduct brainstorming sessions on the next seventy years in space. In the late 1970s, Drs. Pellegrino and Stoff produced the original models that predicted the discovery of oceans inside the moons of Jupiter and Saturn. While looking at the requirements for robot exploration of those new oceans, Pellegrino sailed with Dr. Robert Ballard during the first scientific mission of the deep-sea robot *Argo,* which was used to locate and photograph the *Titanic.* He is a Fellow of the British Interplanetary Society, a founding member of the Challenger Center and, with the late Senator Matsunaga, framer of the 1992 International Space Year. In his spare time Pellegrino surfs, smashes atoms, and scares Stephen King.

Beating the Food Giants
Paul Stit

Empty Harvest mark Anderson
Bernard Jensen